The Essential Guide to

Selecting and Using
Core Reading Programs

Peter Dewitz, Susan B. Leahy, Jennifer Jones, Pamela Maslin Sullivan

INTERNATIONAL
Reading Associ
800 BARKSDALE ROAD, PO BOX
NEWARK, DE 19714-8139, USA
www.reading.org

D0813874

Executive Editor, Books   Corinne M. Mooney
Developmental Editor   Charlene M. Nichols
Developmental Editor   Tori Mello Bachman
Developmental Editor   Stacey L. Reid
Editorial Production Manager   Shannon T. Fortner
Design and Composition Manager   Anette Schuetz

Project Editors   Stacey L. Reid and Rebecca A. Stewart

Cover   Design, Adam Bohannon; Photographs (from left), Peter Dewitz, ©iStockphoto.com/Chris Schmidt, Peter Dewitz

Library of Congress Cataloging-in-Publication Data

The essential guide to selecting and using core reading programs / Peter Dewitz ... [et al.].
    p. cm.
 Includes bibliographical references and index.
 ISBN 978-0-87207-707-2
 1. Reading (Early childhood)--United States. 2. Language arts (Early childhood)--Social aspects--United States. 3. Language policy--United States. I. Dewitz, Peter, 1948- II. International Reading Association.
 LB1139.5.R43E75 2010
 372.4--dc22

                                   2010000944

7226003

CONTENTS

 **Peter Dewitz** splits his time between educational consulting, teaching, research, and writing. He has worked with school districts from Virginia, USA, to New South Wales, Australia, helping them improve their reading programs and reading achievement. Prior to working as a consultant, he was a professor at the University of Virginia in Charlottesville and the University of Toledo, Ohio. In Toledo he ran the university's reading clinic, which allowed him to learn from and assist struggling readers. At both schools, he focused on graduate education with a strong interest in reading comprehension, assessment, and intervention programs.

Peter completed his bachelor's degree at the University of California, Los Angeles, and taught at the elementary level for the Los Angeles City Schools. He also worked with learning-disabled students, which led him to question why intelligent children could have difficulty learning to read. His fascination with reading problems led him to an MA in educational psychology at the State University of California, Northridge, and a doctorate at Claremont Graduate University, also in California.

Peter's interest in core reading programs began when he worked as a consultant for Silver Burdett Ginn and then as an author for their core reading program, Literature Works. His consulting work with Reading First schools piqued his interest in the efficacy of these programs and their use. Peter has published in *The Reading Teacher*, *The Journal of Literacy Research*, *Reading Research Quarterly*, and other national publications. He has served on the editorial boards of *The Reading Teacher*, the *National Reading Conference Yearbook*, and *Reading Research Quarterly*. He is the recipient of the Elva Knight Research Grant from the International Reading Association and has served on the Board of Directors for the National Reading Conference. He is currently working on the fifth edition of *Teaching Reading in the 21st Century*. His research interests focus on the development of reading comprehension and design of instructional procedures most likely to improve students' understanding of text.

Susan B. Leahy is the Director of Reading in the Education Department in the School of Arts and Sciences at the University of Richmond in Virginia, USA. She teaches courses in reading methodology for undergraduate education students as well as postbaccalaureate students seeking their teaching credentials.

Susie began her teaching career in Massachusetts as a second-grade teacher. Eventually, she moved south to Richmond, Virginia, where she taught kindergarten and first grade. She also worked as a reading specialist for the Virginia Department of Education before moving to teaching at the university level. In addition to her current position at the University of Richmond, she has also taught at Radford University in Virginia.

Susie has presented to a wide variety of audiences across the United States. Her recent published work includes articles in *Science and Children* and *Reading Research Quarterly*.

Susie received her BA in English from Middlebury College in Vermont, her MEd in Elementary Education from Lesley College (now Lesley University) in Cambridge, Massachusetts, and her EdD in Curriculum and Instruction in Reading from the University of Virginia in Charlottesville.

Jennifer Jones is an Associate Professor of Literacy Education in the College of Education and Human Development's School of Teacher Education and Leadership at Radford University in Virginia, USA. She teaches teacher credential courses at the undergraduate level and graduate reading courses for the Literacy Education program.

Jennifer began her teaching career in her hometown of Tazewell, Virginia, where she worked as a teaching assistant in kindergarten and fourth-grade classrooms. She then moved on to teach grades 3 and 4 in Fluvanna County, Virginia. Jennifer has served as a reading consultant for grades K–12 in inner-city and rural school settings. She has presented her research across the United States as well as internationally. She likes to ground her research in practical settings and spends a great deal of her time in public schools.

Jennifer serves as vice president on the Board of Directors of the Virginia State Reading Association (VSRA) and has served as editor of *Reading in Virginia*, the peer-reviewed journal of the VSRA, for six years. She is also active in legislative advocacy for literacy issues. Jennifer has been the recipient of Radford

University's College of Education and Human Development's Outstanding Teaching Award and has twice received the college's Outstanding Scholarly Activity Award. She was also a recipient of Radford University's International Educator of the Year award.

Jennifer received her BA degree from Bluefield College in Virginia and her MEd and doctorate degrees from the University of Virginia in Charlottesville. Her work has been published in journals such as *The Reading Teacher*, *Reading Research Quarterly*, and *Science and Children*. Her research and teaching interests include comprehension, Response to Intervention, and professional development.

 **Pamela Maslin Sullivan** is an Assistant Professor in the Early, Elementary, and Reading Program in the College of Education at James Madison University in Harrisonburg, Virginia, USA. She teaches methods courses in literacy.

Pam began her teaching career as a special education teacher on Saipan, in the Commonwealth of the Northern Mariana Islands (CNMI). She was a school psychologist in the CNMI and in Portsmouth, Virginia. During her doctoral training, Pam was a coordinator for the Book Buddies program in Charlottesville, Virginia. Before joining the faculty at James Madison, she worked as the project manager for the professional development office of Reading First in Virginia.

Pam's research on reading programs began with a study at the University of South Florida, pilot testing the efficacy of a core reading program intended for special education students. In addition to core programs, her research focuses on early literacy and parents' reading aloud to children. She has published most recently in *Reading Improvement* and *Reading in Virginia*.

Pam earned her BA in Psychology from Bryn Mawr College in Pennsylvania, her MA and EdS in School Psychology from the University of South Florida, and her PhD in Curriculum and Instruction in Reading from the University of Virginia in Charlottesville.

ACKNOWLEDGMENTS

There are many who enlightened, stimulated, guided, and supported the development of this book. The concept really began in the public schools. As teachers and administrators struggled to find the best way to use core reading programs, our curiosity about these programs and how to use them deepened. Along with the teachers and administrators, we wondered if strict fidelity to the core was the right course or whether teacher prerogative and decision making should rule. From teachers and administrators across the United States, we received invaluable insights and information, which contributed much of the content of the book. Our gratitude goes out to each administrator, teacher, and student who enlightened our thinking about core reading programs.

Many thanks to each of our families for their enduring love, encouragement, and patience throughout the duration of this project. Thanks also go out to each of our universities, James Madison University, Radford University, and the University of Richmond, as well as our colleagues at each institution and beyond for their support. We would specifically like to thank Lili Claman and Jennifer Barnes, who contributed much to the analysis of new data that is reported in the book. Finally, we would like to thank Corinne Mooney and others at the International Reading Association who recognized the value in this work, especially Stacey Reid, who supported us through the revisions, and Rebecca Stewart, who supported us through the editing.

The exhibit hall of the 2008 International Reading Association (IRA) Annual Convention in Atlanta, Georgia, USA, covered 350,000 square feet, or 6.4 football fields, packed with reading materials. As you entered the hall, a guard carefully checked your badge, not to protect the security of the materials, but to ensure you had paid your IRA conference fees. The exhibit hall was laid out in 24 rows with six large center aisles running its length. Up and down these aisles were 1,082 exhibit booths rented by (among others) 340 educational publishers. These exhibitors sold books—little books, novels, nonfiction books, decodable books, leveled books, workbooks, and staff development books—as well as reading tests, manipulatives, reading cards, reading rods, reading rewards, and reading posters. Most exhibitors were small publishers renting just 100 or 200 square feet and spending US$1,500 to $3,000 for the five days of the conference.

Imagine being there. As you walk down these aisles browsing through books and materials, you occasionally glance up to where huge signs hang suspended from the ceiling—Pearson, Scholastic, McGraw-Hill, Harcourt, Sopris West. Approaching these signs, your feet notice the change first. The carpet is no longer commercial grade but plush, thick, and deep, costing at least $70 a square yard. Your feet wallow in the experience. Your pace slows, and you enter a new world. This is not a booth but an 11,000-square-foot educational environment costing about $150,000 just for the floor space.

There are luxurious displays of materials, benches on which to sit and peruse, street lamps to set the mood, treasure chests of information, a town full of literary encounters. The theme of each experience reflects the theme and title of the program. At a small stage, a sales representative gives a PowerPoint presentation or a video link takes you to a classroom hundreds of miles away to watch the program being used. A small sign lists the upcoming talks of the program authors. Computers everywhere allow you to try out the program's software. You may be invited to walk through a small labyrinth to tour the latest program, complete with a passport to track your journey. A sales representative will ask to assist you, give you sample materials, and take information about your needs and those of your school district. At the end of your journey, you will be offered pens, pencils, catalogs, leveled books, notepads, a candy bar on which the wrapper traces the reading skills in the program, and a tote bag complete with company logo, internal and external pockets, and a mesh holder for your water bottle. The bag is essential, because you must tote all those free goodies. Some of you will be invited to a company cocktail party, breakfast, or 5K run. A select few, those who are really in the market for a new core reading program, will be invited to an exclusive dinner at a restaurant way better than a family friendly, all-you-can-eat buffet. You have experienced the marketing of core reading programs, a multimillion-dollar industry.

You entered these little worlds because your district might be considering adopting a new core reading program or updating some component of its existing program. If you are a buyer, you have some difficult decisions to make. What core reading program should we adopt? How do we evaluate them? How different is the 2008 Harcourt program from the 2003 version? The program may have added navigation, but are the underlying engine and drivetrain still the same? If you are a buyer or part of an adoption committee, we wrote this book to guide you through the evaluation and selection process. Frankly, we believe there is better and more useful information in *Consumer Reports* for guiding your selection of a toaster than what currently exists for purchasing a core reading program. We are attempting to rectify that problem.

It's more likely that you are window shopping, seeing what the new styles for 2009 are like. If you are like most educators, your district has a core reading program, and in these recessionary times, it is unlikely your district will be spending the $75 to $125 per pupil to purchase a new program. If that is the case, this book can also help you make the best use of your existing program. We believe strongly in teacher prerogative and teacher decision making. We have spent considerable time examining core reading programs and the research behind them. The six years of Reading First have taught many lessons, but we seriously doubt that following a core reading program with strict fidelity will achieve the best results. Our research and that of others supports that view (Dewitz, Jones, & Leahy, 2009; Dewitz, Jones, Leahy, & Sullivan, 2008; McGill-Franzen, 2006), yet we still believe that core reading programs are essential. They are a rich toolbox of reading materials and instructional strategies. In the hands of skilled teachers, these tools can be chosen critically and used with precision. In the hands of a novice, the best core reading program will provide a structure so that first experiences in the classroom are organized, systematic, and successful. As the novice gains experience, he or she can innovate, adapt, and modify, using the tools in the box to craft a wonderful experience for students. Our book will help you pick the right program and use it effectively.

An Overview of This Book

In many ways, core reading programs define the content and methods of reading instruction in the United States. Formerly known as basal programs, core reading programs can be defined as the primary instructional tools used to teach children to read (Simmons & Kame'enui, 2003a). Core reading programs usually come in the form of a reading series, which consists of reading texts or anthologies for each grade level; additional texts for advanced, average, and struggling readers; workbooks; assessments; and instructional materials, such as word cards, letter tiles, and CDs, so students can listen to selections. These anthologies are organized around themes or units of study, with skills and strategies for reading taught within each anthology. All of this is tied together with a teacher's edition that can run over 2,500 pages for each grade level.

More than 80% of American children receive their reading instruction either in whole measure or in part from a core reading program (Education Market Research, 2007). While the influence of core reading programs on reading instruction in classrooms waxes and wanes, No Child Left Behind and Reading First legislation did much to solidify, at least for the time being, the stature of core reading programs, branding them as educational tools built on scientifically based reading research. Because of their importance and prominence, a thorough understanding of the programs is necessary for making the best possible decision when selecting and using one. In this book, we will help you understand core reading programs, with the ultimate goal of providing you with research-based information and a reference guide with which you can make informed decisions for reviewing, selecting, and using core reading programs in your school.

In Part I of the book, we explore the development of core reading programs, past and present. We begin by describing the evolution of these programs over time and illustrate how the instructional design principles of previous eras still influence instruction today. Reading programs are essentially conservative documents (Venezky, 1987). They follow the educational trends of an era; they do not lead. The importance of phonemic awareness instruction was a well-researched concept long before its instruction was a critical attribute of core reading programs. The work of Beck and her colleagues on vocabulary instruction dates back to the 1980s, yet it took the publication of the book *Bringing Words to Life* (Beck, McKeown, & Kucan, 2002) for their vocabulary ideas to make their way into core reading programs. In our short history, we want to establish one important point: Basals, or core reading programs, were always marketed as research-based programs.

Next, we enter into the world of core reading program publishing. Textbook publishing has been an entrepreneurial activity since the beginning of the nation. "Attacks on one's competition, coercion of adoption committees, and the alteration of reader content to appeal to special markets are enduring themes in the history of the American reading textbook" (Venezky, 1987, p. 248). As you learn how they are created, you will develop an understanding of the various influences that play upon the structure and content of core reading programs. Such knowledge allows you to use these programs more critically and successfully. In terms of questioning the author (Beck, McKeown, Sandora, Kucan, & Worthy, 1996), we want to challenge the authority of the text—the core reading programs themselves.

In Part II of our book, we undertake the task of guiding you in the evaluation of core reading programs, and help you critique the texts and the instruction in these programs. To do this, we examine core reading programs published from 2003 through 2009 by Houghton Mifflin, Harcourt, Scott Foresman, and the McGraw-Hill Companies, looking at instruction in kindergarten through fifth grade. We examine the texts that students read, and explore the breadth and depth of phonemic awareness, phonics, word recognition, vocabulary, and comprehension instruction within core reading programs. We also examine the assessments that come with these programs and the provisions they make to assist struggling readers. Publishers learn quickly, and in the era of Response to Intervention (RTI), core programs attempt to match their materials to the demands of Tier 1, 2, and 3 instruction. It is important to keep in mind that these evaluations are meant to highlight the critical issues in core reading programs and are not a complete evaluation of all the instruction in a given program. With this knowledge in hand, we discuss how to strategically and successfully select a core reading program using research to inform your decision-making process. We guide you through the process, from establishing a review committee to using an evaluation tool for each program you review. We base this advice on a series of case studies from school districts that have recently adopted core reading programs.

An important component of our book does not actually appear in the text. As a supplement, we created a guide for schools and school districts to use when evaluating core reading programs they are considering for adoption. We call this document a Reading Guide to Program Selection, or Reading GPS. This supplement is available online at www.reading.org/general/publications/books/bk707.aspx. You can download the Reading GPS from the webpage and use it to evaluate the texts, instruction, and assessments in core reading programs; the Reading GPS will take you through many of the procedures we used to create this book.

Finally, in Part III of the book, we discuss how to use your core reading program more effectively. We help improve and modify your instruction in phonemic awareness, phonics, fluency, vocabulary, and comprehension to meet the needs of all your students. In addition, we tackle issues like motivation and oral language development, which core reading programs tend to neglect. Core reading programs make assumptions about classroom organization and differentiation, and we will demonstrate how the programs can be modified to meet the needs and demands of your classroom by using portraits from both primary and intermediate settings. In the end, you will have the knowledge, tools, and power to choose a program, and the know-how to adjust the contents of your program to meet the needs of your students. We believe in teacher prerogative and hope that our book makes you feel more confident in your effectiveness.

In 2001, when Macintosh released a new operating system, it came without a manual. Shortly thereafter came the book *Mac OS X: The Missing Manual: The Book That Should Have Been in the Box* by David Pogue. Computer operating systems and core reading programs have much in common. Both have multiple parts, both have multiple tasks, and both, we contend, are poorly documented. We believe our book should have been in the basal reader box.

The Development of Core Reading Programs: Past and Present

In this part of *The Essential Guide to Selecting and Using Core Reading Programs*, we focus on the creation and development of such programs, taking first a historical perspective in Chapter 1, then providing a contemporary perspective in Chapter 2. By first taking a historical perspective, we want you to see the roots of the core reading program and understand that in every era the men and women who created these texts and instructional tools believed they were basing their work on the best scientific evidence of the day. Then, as now, there was competition among the ideas that shaped core reading programs. A historical look at these programs also highlights the political, economic, social, psychological, and educational forces that led to their creation. It is important to see educational materials as part of a slow evolution that responds to many research and market forces, and in order to do so, we need to see how core reading programs existed in the beginning and how they changed over time.

In Chapter 2, we explore how a contemporary core reading program is created. We think that if you understand this process and the forces that shape it, you will better understand the limits and the strengths of such programs. Like any complex system, core reading programs require the work of many individual authors, editors, market executives, and designers. Further, publishing is both an educational and a commercial enterprise. Unless the publishers make money, there will be no programs. Our goal is to give you a balanced view, neither to exalt the programs as pure examples of scientifically based reading research nor condemn them as crass commercial products. We hope you see them as a reasonable compromise between what the market requests and what the research suggests. As you come to understand how core reading programs are created, you will become less likely to be influenced by the claims of publishers' sales representatives and more confident to rely on your own knowledge and judgment.

The Development of Core Reading Programs: Past and Present

CHAPTER 1

A History of Core Reading Programs

We live in an era of education that is dominated by published core reading programs. In this chapter, we take a walk through time to explore the history of reading instruction programs in the United States. We have discovered a common thread across time: The people who wrote core reading programs many years ago are similar to the people who write our programs now. They have always thought they were writing scientifically based programs, and they marshaled evidence and expert opinion to support their claims. We begin this chapter by calling these programs *readers* because the term *basal reader* did not emerge until 1933 and is not found in a dictionary until 1963. The term *basal* may have been coined only to distinguish the text from the student. The term *core reading program* replaced *basal reader* at the beginning of the 21st century.

After reading this chapter, when you look at a core reading program, you will see its elements in light of the past. You will discover when graded texts were added, when skill instruction first emerged, and when the focus of reading instruction shifted from oral elocution to silent reading comprehension. "The past offers lessons that can guide actions and decision making in the present" (Moore, Monaghan, & Hartman, 1997, p. 98), but it requires knowing which lessons of the past can inform the present. For example, it is likely that the history of systematic skills instruction in the 1960s and 1970s has much to say about RTI, a special education initiative that focuses on explicit skill instruction and the regular assessment of students. Understanding that period of skills instruction and its consequences might help us implement RTI cautiously. History provides a context in which to view the present.

What You Will Learn

- The history of basal reading programs in America since the start of the nation, with a strong focus on programs since the 1960s

- The research base underlying reading programs since the middle of the 19th century

- The timing and implications of the semantic shift from *basal* to *core* reading programs

- The evolution of comprehension instruction in core reading programs since the 1970s

What You Will Be Able to Do

- Conduct a more thoughtful analysis of core reading programs

- Use knowledge of past instructional issues to guide your selection of new core reading programs

- Use knowledge of past instructional practices to make decisions about current practices in core reading programs

The 18th and 19th Centuries

Core reading programs are a staple of instruction in U.S. schools today, and just as these programs reflect the current political, social, and cultural climate, the materials used to first teach reading in our schools likewise reflected the political agenda of their day. Colonists seeking religious freedom viewed reading as an integral part of learning, memorizing, and reciting scripture; thus, the materials used to teach reading during the colonial period of U.S. history reflected overarching religious objectives within the context of learning how to read. The materials used to reach these goals employed letters, syllables, and Bible readings. The colonial school was, in many ways, a bleak place; there were few materials and the poorly trained teachers focused specifically on oral performance and rote memorization. The hallmark of good reading was strong oral performance with texts that were well known. Reading and interpreting a new or unknown text was not a goal for colonial school students.

The texts of the colonial era were designed to influence the moral compasses and religious beliefs of school-age students, yet most children received less than 90 days of schooling in their lifetime (Cubberley, 1934). Not yet programs, the earliest materials used in American schools consisted of hornbooks, psalters, and primers (Smith, 1986). A hornbook was a thin strip of wood 4 to 5 inches wide, to which was attached a sheet of paper (see Figure 1). On the paper, there

Figure 1. Sample of a Hornbook Used in Reading Instruction During the Colonial Period

Note. Courtesy of Indiana University–Purdue University Indianapolis. Retrieved February 18, 2010, from www.iupui.edu/~engwft/hornbook.html

were exercises for reciting the alphabet, syllables (such as *ba, be, bi, bo, bu*), a few religious sayings, or the Lord's Prayer.

The New-England Primer was the first widely used reader in America (Chall & Squire, 1991). Approximately 3.5 by 5 inches, 6 to 8 million copies of this small book were sold between 1680 and 1830. The *Primer* begins with the alphabet, vowels, syllables, word lists organized by the number of syllables, and alphabet rhymes (e.g., A—"In Adam's fall, We sinned all"). Later in the *Primer* are prayers and other religious tracts heavily influenced by the strict Calvinism of the day, such as the following:

> Now in the heat of youthful blood,
> Remember your Creator God.
> Behold the months come hastening on,
> When you shall say, "My joys are gone."
>
> Behold, the aged sinner goes,
> Laden with guilt and heavy woes,
> Down to the regions of the dead,
> With endless curses on his head. (n.p.)

Students learned to read by reciting the alphabet and syllables in the *Primer*, which was called the ABC method of instruction. Words were spelled before they were pronounced. After reciting the alphabet and the syllables, the students read the text. After the *Primer* the students moved on to psalters and the Bible.

Reading Programs in the New Country

In the late 18th century, in the newly founded United States, the focus of the reading curriculum shifted from religious objectives to those that promoted nationalism. George Washington urged educators to focus the content of their reading books on promoting identification with and allegiance to the United States. Drifting away from religious purpose, Noah Webster's *The American Spelling Book* (1788) came to dominate the market, replacing the *The New-England Primer*. Webster's spelling book, commonly referred to as the Blue-back Speller (it had a blue cover), was first published in 1783 and was in print through the mid-1830s. The book measured 3.5 by 6 inches, and the 1816 edition was 165 pages long. As in other contemporary readers of the time, it illuminated patriotic themes, emphasized the use of American English, and attempted to create a uniform American spelling and pronunciation (Smith, 1986). Webster himself wrote, "I have been attentive to the political interests in America" (cited in Smith, 1986, p. 49).

Webster's readers encompassed learning the alphabet, syllables, and word lists, along with modest amounts of connected text in the form of fables, stories, and dialogues (Smith, 1986). The book begins with a guide to pronunciation and work on letters and syllables, then provides lists of words organized by number of syllables followed by short fables and brief moral admonitions. Webster's careful attention to articulation and pronunciation, as seen in the following example, led students to read, write, and speak a common form of English (Monaghan, 1983).

> Lay not up for yourselves treasures on earth, where moth and rust do corrupt, and where thieves break through and steal; but lay up for yourselves treasures in heaven, where neither moths nor rust doth corrupt, and where thieves do not break through and steal: For where your treasure is, there will your heart be also. (Webster, 1788, n.p.)

Through the early decades of the 19th century children began to spend more time in school. In the Boston schools by 1826, students attended four grades or classes within the primary schools. The *New-England Primer* and

Webster's spelling books were not sufficient to meet the needs of teachers and students, so series of readers began to emerge. Webster himself modified the Blue-back Speller and added a Part 1, *The Little Reader's Assistant*, and Part 3, *An American Selection of Lessons in Reading and Speaking*, which Smith (1986) considers the first reading series.

Other reading series soon followed, with the most innovative being Samuel Worcester's readers. Worcester was perhaps the first to develop the concept of a lesson plan (Venezky, 1987). Before each selection were rules for reading the lesson, and after each selection teachers were directed to discuss common pronunciation errors, ask comprehension questions, and teach a list of spelling words. Worcester's readers were also important because they contained many of the elements found in the McGuffey Eclectic Readers. This was no coincidence. Worcester sued William McGuffey and his publisher for plagiarism. McGuffey, the future moral philosopher at the University of Virginia, paid an out-of-court settlement of $2,000 and then revised his series (Venezky, 1987).

Graded Readers and New Theories of Reading Instruction

The McGuffey Eclectic Readers were the most popular reading texts of this era, with over 122 million copies sold from 1836 to 1920 (Chall & Squire, 1991). The McGuffey series enjoyed a success not seen again until the Curriculum Foundations series ("Dick and Jane"), which was the dominant reading program from 1930 through the late 1960s. The McGuffey readers followed the nationalistic emphasis of the period and contained reading selections with some religious and moralistic material, often in the form of fables. However, the majority of the text was dedicated to inspiring patriotism among its readers (Smith, 1986).

The McGuffey graded series consisted of one book for each grade level. Each book began with instructions on articulation, listing words by their pronunciation elements—vocals, subvocals, and aspirates—and then lists of commonly mispronounced words (see Figure 2). The first reader introduced short-vowel words and used sentences about children and animals to demonstrate phonetic elements of words. McGuffey also employed repetition, which was new to reading instruction at the time. The texts in these early readers are what we would now call decodable. In the upper grades each lesson began with text, typically a poem, fable, or expository selection. After reading the selection the teacher reviewed definitions of words and engaged in exercises consisting of comprehension questions.

Figure 2. Pages From a McGuffey Reader

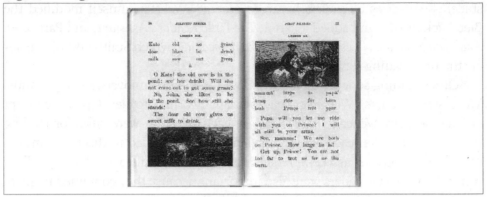

Note. From *McGuffey's First Eclectic Reader*, Revised Edition (1997), pp. 24–25. New York: American Book.

During the mid-19th century, Horace Mann, the secretary of the Massachusetts Board of Education, was a principal figure in the fight to reform the rote nature of American education. Mann was an influential leader who was himself heavily influenced by Prussian instructional practices, which in part embraced using the five senses and active learning rather than mere recitation in the classroom. Also an advocate of the whole-word method of teaching reading, he strongly objected to the ABC method and the teaching of phonics (Smith, 1986). He described letters as "skeleton-shaped, bloodless, ghostly apparitions.... It is no wonder that children look and feel so death-like when compelled to face them" (Balmuth, 1982, p. 190). In place of this "deathlike" experience, Mann advocated teaching whole words first. These lessons

> will be like an excursion to the fields of Elysium compared with the old method of plunging children, day by day, for months together, in the cold waters of oblivion, and compelling them to say falsely, that they love the chill and torpor of the immersion. (cited in Balmuth, 1982, pp. 190–191)

And you thought the current reading wars were vicious!

The whole-word method shifted the focus from first learning letters and sounds to first learning easy, whole words. The whole-word method was believed to be more thought provoking, as it focused more on meaning rather than phonetics. In the series of the day, vocabulary words were employed, with some remnants of phonetics remaining as well as some attention to meaning, including questions on content and definitions of keywords. Yet the whole-word method did not completely dominate reading instruction. Lewis Monroe's *The*

Chart-Primer, used in the late 19th century, included a phonics curriculum that, in fact, would likely hold up well against current core reading programs. Sounds were introduced aurally, blending was taught explicitly, and students moved through a series of short- and long-vowel patterns (Venezky, 1987).

By the late 1800s, the first professional books and articles on reading were published, marking the first scientific contributions to the reading field. Psychologists began to study the process of reading or, at least, word recognition. Like many cognitive psychologists today, these psychologists considered reading a convenient tool for studying the workings of the mind. James Cattell, working in Wilhelm Wundt's laboratory in Leipzig, Germany, demonstrated in 1886 that it took less time to recognize a word than it did to recognize a series of unconnected letters: "I find it takes twice as long to read...words which have no connexion as letters which make words, and letters which have no connexion as letters which make words" (cited in Willis, 2007, p. 52). This and other studies gave temporary support to the whole-word method, until subsequent research deepened our understanding of the complexity of word recognition. Much of this research that began at the end of the 19th century and continued into the early 20th century was summarized by Edmund Burke Huey (1908) in *The Psychology and Pedagogy of Reading*. This hugely influential work is still referenced today and addresses reading pedagogy, reading psychology, and the history of reading.

The Early 1900s: A More Scientific Approach Toward Reading Instruction

A more scientific approach to reading instruction began to emerge in the early 1900s, and materials used to teach reading began to follow the research trends of each pedagogical shift. Research pointed to the greater effectiveness of systematic approaches to instruction compared with less structured lessons and served as a catalyst toward heavy emphasis on the teacher's manual (Chall & Squire, 1991; Gray & Guthrie, 1984). According to Venezky (1987),

> One of the great ironies in the development of the modern basal is that as teachers received more and more preservice and in-service training in teaching reading, the authors of reading texts assumed that teachers knew less and less and expanded the teacher's manual and textbook instructions accordingly. (p. 252)

Webster's speller contained one paragraph of teacher directions, but when Worcester's *A Primer of the English Language* (c. 1826) was written, the teacher's edition had expanded to 13 pages of directions. The first true teacher's manuals may be *Pollard's Synthetic Method of Reading and Spelling* by Rebecca Smith Pollard (1889) and Edward G. Ward's *The Rational Method in Reading* (1894). Both authors' manuals gave directions for teaching the entire series, much longer than the 13 pages in Worcester's *Primer*, but they did not create a separate manual for each level of the program as publishers do today.

By 1900, the new science of psychology and measurement began to influence reading programs. Throughout the 20th century, Americans realized that education—the investment in human capital—was a key to economic well-being (Goldin & Katz, 2008). Social and economic changes made it essential that students understand what they read, so silent reading and comprehension increasingly became the focus of reading programs. The conceptual watershed may have been the publication in 1917 of "Reading as Reasoning: A Study of Mistakes in Paragraph Reading" (Thorndike, 1971). Research at this time explored silent reading (O'Brien, 1921, cited in Smith, 1986), as well as reading speed (Courtis, 1915; Gray, 1916, cited in Smith, 1986; Huey, 1908).

As school populations swelled with new immigrants, the schools needed cheap and efficient tools to measure educational attainment. First to emerge were Thorndike's (1910) handwriting scales and then the Kansas Silent Reading Tests (Kelly, 1916, cited in Pearson & Hamm, 2005). Combining the new emphasis on reading comprehension with the tools to measure it, reading programs began to change, but slowly. By the end of the 1920s, the goal of reading instruction was to translate printed words into ideas, yet, according to Venezky (1987), few innovative methods of teaching reading comprehension were incorporated into basal reading programs until the 1940s.

Since the mid-19th century, several basal reading programs included two components of comprehension instruction: the teaching of vocabulary and the asking of comprehension questions. Some developed vocabulary knowledge before reading the selection; others did so after. In the mid-1920s, with the publication of the *The 24th Yearbook of the National Society for the Study of Education* (Whipple, 1925), teaching reading comprehension skills became the next focus of instruction. Interestingly, these skills were first identified when classroom teachers were surveyed about their students' difficulty in comprehending content area materials. William S. Gray (1925), who conducted the survey, reported that teachers wanted students to determine the main idea, define the author's purpose, draw conclusions, distinguish fact from opinion, and compare and contrast what was read. This list should sound familiar because it still forms part of the comprehension scope and sequence in today's core reading programs.

The skills themselves first appear in the teacher's manual for The Children's Own Reader, Books Four, Five, and Six (Pennel & Cusack, 1929, cited in Smith, 1986). Pennel and Cusack stated,

> to assume that interpretation or thinking shall take place, there must be keen interest in the material to be read and a strong motive for reading. The following attitudes or habits are involved in such thinking: concentrating attention, associating meaning with symbols, anticipating the sequence of ideas, bringing past experience to bear on new material, selecting important meanings, and associating, organizing and evaluating meanings. (1929, cited in Smith 1986, p. 238)

Despite this emphasis, reading programs did little to formally develop comprehension skills or strategies. Little was known about the psychological process of comprehension, and behaviorism remained the dominant educational psychology. Educators did little more than promote the repetition of vocabulary words and exhort correct responses from students through the asking of comprehension questions.

1930 to 1965: Dick and Jane and Their Friends

Reading programs in the 1920s and 1930s dropped moralistic vignettes in favor of more realistic stories, adapting to the ever-changing social mores (Chall & Squire, 1991). In many ways, reading programs reflected the growing middle class values of the times. Fathers worked, mothers kept house, and the children played with the dog and the cat. The series that would grow to dominate pre– and post–World War II America was the Elson Readers (Elson et al., 1910–1936), later called the Basic Readers (Gray, Arbuthnot et al., 1940–1948), which finally became the Curriculum Foundation series. You know them better by the names of their main characters, Dick and Jane. Over 200 million Americans learned to read with Dick and Jane (Chall & Squire, 1991).

The lead author for almost the whole existence of Dick and Jane was William S. Gray, researcher, professor at the University of Chicago, and one of the dominant reading experts of his day. Gray and his contemporary Arthur Gates were at the beginning of a tradition that continues today, in which university-based academics served as authors for the major publishing houses. Today the names of P. David Pearson, Isabel Beck, Roger Farr, Scott Paris, and Connie Juel have taken the places held by Gray, Gates, and Monroe (Luke, 1988). Then, as now, the association of university professors with publishing companies allowed the publishers to keep abreast of the latest research and bask in the research aura of their authors. The authors used the basal as a vehicle to bring their research ideas into practice. All profited by the collaboration.

The Elson Readers and their competitors, The Work-Play Books (Gates & Huber, 1932–1939) and The Ginn Basic Readers (Russell & Ousley, 1948), exhibited some common attributes of teaching students to read. Research at the time pointed toward the "look-say" method of reading, which showcased semantically, lexically, and syntactically controlled texts to teach children to read (Luke, 1988; Smith, 1986). Repetition was the key, and the researchers of the era determined how often a child had to read a word before he could remember it. In a series of studies, Arthur Gates experimented with how many new words should be introduced per every 100 words of text. From this work, he guessed (his word) that the average word needed to be repeated 35 times in a beginning reading text (cited in Hiebert & Martin, 2009). This finding begat the style of writing and sentence structure that was prominent in the basal readers of the day.

In addition to word repetition, the Curriculum Foundation Series and its competitors embraced intrinsic or analytic phonics. Gray, Gates, and others believed that direct, explicit instruction in isolated letter sounds was unnecessary and detracted from the meaningfulness of reading. Teachers and students derived phonics principles best from real words. In addition, workbooks debuted on the reading scene during this era, providing systematic ways to practice skills (Chall & Squire, 1991). The workbooks that accompanied The Ginn Basic Readers and the Curriculum Foundations series had students match pictures to words and sentences, and as their skill developed, match one of three different sentences to a picture. The teacher directions in the back of the workbooks categorized these simple matching tasks as initial sound matching, vocabulary review, main idea, drawing conclusions, and story comprehension. Publishing companies had already begun to label and mention skills rather than teach them thoroughly.

From the 1930s through the 1950s, increased numbers of teacher's manuals were provided, and they grew in size (Smith, 1986). Within the manuals, skills charts were included, as well as scope and sequence charts. More detailed suggestions for grouping procedures were included, as well as assessments. Lesson suggestions within the manuals often included procedures for teacher-directed activities, independent work, and extension activities for integrating reading with other content areas (Smith, 1986). Researchers and professional organizations pushed for integration of reading instruction within the language arts. Reading series began to look more like our contemporary programs, offering more than just suggestions or scripts for instruction. Hence, "the scientifically designed and packaged reading series had come of age" (Luke, 1988, p. 72).

Reading the student anthology from any of the major programs of this period, one is struck by the fact that content predominantly takes a traditional white, middle class perspective and exhibits a lack of diversity. The first-grade books include stories about going to school, having a picnic, or visiting a farm, plus a number of selections about animals in the tradition of Peter Rabbit, yet no nonwhite individuals are pictured in the books. In the upper grades, the stories are a bit more diverse. Middle class life still predominates, but now exchange students from Denmark, Native Americans, and celebrants of Chinese New Year in San Francisco appear in some stories, yet the stories fall well short of an acceptable multicultural focus by today's standards. These programs, with their almost exclusively white, middle class, suburban focus, were last published in the mid-1960s, 10 years after *Brown v. Board of Education of Topeka*. In 1965, Curriculum Foundations added three African American characters, Mike and his younger twin sisters Pam and Penny (see Figure 3).

However, the look-say, sight word method used by basal readers since the 1930s had its critics. *Why Johnny Can't Read: And What You Can Do About It*, written

Figure 3. Page From the Curriculum Foundations Series

by Rudolf Flesch in 1955, addressed the shortfalls of the whole-word method in a grave and threatening way. He advocated a return to a phonics-based approach: "We have decided to forget that we write with letters, and [instead] learn to read English as if it were Chinese" ("Education: Why Johnny Can't Read," 1955, ¶ 2). This argument for a phonics-based approach to reading was followed by a wave of research in the reading community, culminating in "The Cooperative Research Program in First-Grade Reading Instruction" (Bond & Dykstra, 1967), or the First-Grade Studies. Although these 27 coordinated studies addressed a number of issues, such as what the best predictor of early reading acquisition is (hint: letter-name knowledge), they are best remembered for twin findings: (1) the phonics methods were found to be superior to the basal approach (remember the basals of that era did not stress phonics, but viewed it as support), and (2) there is considerable variation in effectiveness for any single approach to teaching beginning reading. In fact, an analysis of the First-Grade Studies (Pearson, 1997) arrived at the same time people were beginning to read Jeanne Chall's (1996) *Learning to Read: The Great Debate.* Chall undertook a critical review of past research and concluded that a phonics-first approach produced superior reading achievement compared with the whole-word approach. The "reading wars" that Horace Mann started in the 1840s were reignited.

1970s: Basal Reading Programs in the Skills-Based Era

At this point in our review, we are going to follow the evolution of core reading programs from the perspective of one publishing company. We do this for two reasons. First, we can document how instruction in core reading programs has changed over the last three decades, guided in some cases by the same program authors. Second, we can illustrate the contraction of the publishing industry through mergers and acquisitions.

Edwin Ginn and his brother Fred founded Ginn and Company in 1868. They were briefly joined by Daniel C. Heath, who left in 1885 to start his own publishing company. Ginn and Company existed as a privately owned company until 1968 when it was sold to Xerox. At that time there were 12 companies producing basal reading programs in the United States. In 1985, Xerox sold Ginn and Company to Gulf & Western, which later became Paramount and then Viacom. Paramount acquired Silver Burdett and merged it with Ginn, thus creating the Silver Burdett Ginn imprint under its Simon & Schuster division.

Finally, in 1998, Silver Burdett Ginn was sold to Pearson, a large British publishing company. In 2009, there are now five major core reading programs published by just three publishing companies. Harcourt recently purchased Houghton Mifflin and its new program, Journeys, was just introduced.

By the early 1970s, core reading programs more directly reflected the behaviorism of the preceding decades and not the "cognitive revolution" that was soon to begin. Add on the concept of mastery learning, and teachers and students were soon moving through complex and lengthy skill sequences. As **Venezky (1987) argued, basal reading programs consistently look backward** and not forward in the development of instructional ideas, yet surveys revealed that teachers believed the content of basal programs to be scientific (Barton & Wilder, 1964). We will turn to the cognitive revolution soon, but first let's consider the impact of behaviorism on reading education and basal readers.

Behaviorism, with its focus on measurable outcomes and little interest in inner cognitive activity, caused reading educators to slice and dice reading into myriad single skills. Phonics instruction reemerged as a prominent method for teaching students to read, following the research of Chall (1996) and Bond and Dykstra (1967). Phonics rules were emphasized, skills instruction was paramount, and worksheet practice and criterion-referenced tests served as the nuclei of the basal reading programs. Basal programs generally consisted of anthologies of stories for reading and discussing, as well as skills-management systems, which employed tests that identified isolated skills warranting mastery. Tests were accompanied by worksheets and reading exercises that were designed for practice until students attained adequate skill mastery (Pearson & Hamm, 2005). Multiple single-skill tests were available, sometimes testing up to 30 skills in a single unit of study (Pearson & Hamm, 2005).

In the 1970s, Ginn and Company produced two reading programs—Reading 360 and Reading 720—that shared this behavioral and skills-management approach. Reading 720 "is a carefully sequenced series of skills. The progression of this sequence is continuous and overlapping.... Students should work toward a high degree of mastery" (Clymer & Humphrey, 1973, p. 17). The skills-management system that accompanies Reading 360 was designed to identify explicitly what the students are to do, determine whether the intended learning has occurred, and provide appropriate supplementary instruction. We find it interesting that such single-skill assessments have recently resurfaced under a new label, *progress monitoring/curriculum-based measurements*, in an attempt to address RTI within the context of core reading programs.

Lessons found in basal reading programs from the 1970s illustrate the skills emphasis. Open the 1979 edition of Reading 720: Reading Rainbow, and you are introduced to the writers and consultants of the series, each with an array of impressive credentials, implicitly suggesting the text must be based on important reading research. The manual promises to offer customizable approaches to skill development, among other important dimensions of reading. Each lesson is divided into three parts: (1) teach the selection/guided reading, (2) develop the skill, and (3) adjust to individual needs. With each story, teachers are instructed to prepare students for reading by providing essential background information, introducing vocabulary, and setting purposes for reading. Teachers and students then read and discuss the selection. Following the reading, interrelated activities in language, literature, and creativity are offered, along with instructions for developing reading skills. This portion of the manual provides follow-up worksheets for skills practice.

We can get a good sense of instruction in this era by taking a close look at a main idea lesson from the Reading 720: Reading Rainbow teacher's manual (see Figure 4). This lesson is the first time fourth-grade students are introduced to finding the main idea. Reading 360 and Reading 720 lessons illustrate a behaviorist approach to reading instruction. Students received minimal direct instruction in the skill and then they practiced the skill until it was assessed. The lesson says little about how to determine the main idea and gives few hints about the mental process. A continuing concern of basals at the time was the lack of integration of the reading with teaching the skills. Like most programs, Reading 720 made no such integration.

The comprehension instruction in basal programs of this era was closely studied by Durkin (1981), following upon her influential classroom studies of reading comprehension instruction (Durkin, 1978). She examined programs to see how they helped a teacher "do or say something that ought to help children acquire the ability to understand, or work out, the meaning of connected text" (1981, p. 518). Overall Durkin found that only 5.3% of the content of program manuals was directed at instruction. The reviewed programs were remarkably similar, with none devoting more than 5.8% of the manual directions to instruction; basal reading programs had the students engage in practice while the teacher engaged in assessments. Durkin was surprised to discover the large discrepancy between instruction and practice. She was further concerned that when teachers engaged in direct instruction, they did so with assorted pieces of text, one or two sentences that would make it difficult for students to generalize

Figure 4. Main Idea Instruction in Reading 720 Reading Rainbow

---

Literal: The pupil will recognize a topic sentence in first or last position as the main idea of a paragraph. (Introductory Activity)

Discuss paragraph form with the students. Have them turn to page 23 in their books and read the first sentence. Ask them what they noticed about the way the sentence begins. (It is indented.) Explain that this is one way of showing where each new paragraph begins. Then have the other paragraphs in the story identified.

   Develop the understanding that paragraphs usually consist of several sentences all about the same main idea. Now ask the children to read the paragraph that you will write on the chalkboard. Write:

Lucy was ready for the rain. Lucy had boots
Lucy had an umbrella. Lucy had a raincoat

Ask the children which sentence in the paragraph tells the main idea of all the sentences. When the first sentence has been identified as the topic sentence, explain that the main idea sentence can also be the last sentence in a paragraph. Then rewrite the paragraph with the topic sentence in the final position. Finally, ask volunteers to underline the main idea sentence in each of the two paragraphs.

   To provide practice in recognizing topic sentences in the first or last position as main ideas of paragraphs, distribute activity page 7. Give help with the direction, word paragraph and the activity if necessary.

Note. From "A Lizard to Start With," Reading 720 Reading Rainbow, p. 121. Boston: Ginn and Company. © 1976–1980 by Ginn and Company. Reprinted by permission of Pearson Education, Inc. All rights reserved.

the instruction to complete stories. This is evident in our look at main idea instruction. Other than being told to look at the first or last sentence in a well-controlled paragraph, the students are given no specific strategy for finding the main idea or determining importance. Even in the upper grades when comprehension is supposed to receive a stronger focus, assessment, specifically in the form of questioning, predominates.

In 1982, Ginn and Company offered The Ginn Reading Program as the successor to Reading 720. We may view this program as a transition between the skills-based era and the soon to come literature-based programs. Basal programs during this time also offered a plethora of choices, sometimes consisting of up to 150–200 purchase options (Chall & Squire, 1991). Readers, teacher's manuals, workbooks, assessments, Big Books, and spelling and writing programs describe a few of the many options offered to schools when purchasing basal programs. It is during this era that basals began to be more explicit about reading skills instruction.

The Ginn Reading Program also displays a list of experts and contributing authors. The reading selections in the program resemble those of its predecessor. In the primary levels of the program, students read realistic stories, fantasy, poetry, and a small amount of nonfiction (Hoffman et al., 1994). Vocabulary was still well controlled, and a small number of words were repeated often. In the upper grades, the students read a mix of realistic fiction, historical fiction, nonfiction, poetry, and some fantasy. Many of the selections in the upper grades used revised excerpts from well-known children's literature. In a selection from *The One in the Middle Is the Green Kangaroo* (Blume, 1981) sentences are shortened, names are changed, and conflict is reduced. The overall power and interest of the story is compromised.

This basal program moves away from a strict skill management approach and begins to acknowledge Durkin's (1981) critique concerning the lack of explicit comprehension instruction in core reading programs. The teaching of main idea is more explicit, and the teacher's manual provides more insights into the underlying thinking (see Figure 5). The students practice the skills with the teacher before they are asked to do it on their own.

Figure 5. Main Idea Instruction in the Ginn Reading Program

Recognize: To help pupils see the difference between general and specific ideas, read the following list. Ask pupils to decide what one main category heading covers all things on the list. (All things are used to write or draw.)

pencil	paintbrush
crayon	marker
pen	

Tell pupils that the category heading is a general idea; it covers all the items in the list. Then explain that the main idea in a paragraph is like a category heading: it is a general idea that covers all the ideas in the paragraph.

Now put this paragraph on the chalkboard:

> My cat is very lazy. She won't chase mice and she takes ten naps a day. My cat won't walk if she can ride.

Point out that the first sentence is a general statement that tells what the whole paragraph is about. The other sentences give specific examples of the cat's laziness. Tell the pupils that when a paragraph has one sentence that states the main idea, it is often the first or last sentence in the paragraph.

Note. From Ginn and Company (1982). "Ride the Sunrise," *World of Reading*, pp. 30–31. Needham, MA: Author. Reprinted by permission of Pearson Education, Inc. All rights reserved.

As the lesson continues, the students and teacher read three paragraphs and practice identifying the main idea as either the first or the last sentence. In the third example, the manual makes clear that often writers do not state the main idea and the reader is obliged to infer it. This lesson reveals more of the thinking process behind finding the main idea but stops short of explaining a complete strategy. Text examples are still short and contrived. More practice follows the examples, and students complete several workbook pages that are indistinguishable from comprehension assessments. Like all basal programs, The Ginn Reading Program struggled with how to integrate the skills component of the lessons with the guided reading portion. A partial resolution to that question comes in the next generation of programs.

In the 1970s and 1980s, reading selections in the basal reading programs became more multicultural. Hispanic, Asian, and African American characters are featured in more of the selections; however, the programs made no attempt to feature authors from other ethnic groups. The content of the selections rarely revolves around cultural themes important to these ethnic groups, and problems and triumphs of disabled people are not mentioned. The programs of this era concentrated on strong skill instruction, and the literature took a back seat.

1980s to 1990s: Basal Reading Programs in the Literature-Based Era and Beyond

Two revolutions began to influence the content and methods of basal reading programs toward the end of the 1980s. First, the cognitive revolution and the work on psycholinguistics changed our conception of reading. Reading was no longer viewed as a sequence of skills, but rather a rich interactive language process. Readers sought to create meaning from text using prior knowledge and cognitive strategies. From this revolution, much of which took place at the Center for the Study of Reading at the University of Illinois, we gained story grammar instruction, question–answer relationships (QARs), graphic organizers, comprehension-strategy instruction, and reciprocal teaching.

The second revolution involved equality, civil rights, and increasing concern for the individual and the authentic in U.S. culture. By the mid- to late 1980s, schools were seeking more literary value in basal readers (Chall & Squire, 1991). Basal reader anthologies added quality children's literature, although text selections were usually abridged. More open, reflective teaching of comprehension was encouraged (Pearson & Hamm, 2005). This new "look" of basal readers was largely due to the influence of language-based strategies, reader-response theory (Rosenblatt, 1978), and the in vogue literacy philosophy of the time, whole language (Goodman, 1986). The California Reading Language Arts Framework written in the mid-1980s (California Department of Education, 1987) did much to codify these changes. Publishers who wanted to compete successfully in the 1989 California textbook adoption cycle had to adhere to the state's guidelines. With heavy emphasis on the teaching and measuring of single skills in the previous decade, it is easy to see how a more language-based, reader-oriented approach was welcomed during this new era of reading instruction.

Basal readers, however, continued to retain much of the skills approach developed in preceding generations of programs. The same skills could be easily traced through a year of instruction, but the criterion-referenced tests were toned down. Publishers were striving to embrace the current research on whole language and reader response, yet maintain the familiar skills of the traditional basal reading program. Mirroring the surveys of previous eras, a 1987 survey of teachers found that most believed the whole-language approach to be research based (Baumann, Hoffman, Moon, & Duffy-Hester, 1998).

The dominant program in the nation at the end of the decade was World of Reading from Silver Burdett Ginn (1989–1993). World of Reading captured over 50% of the market due to its quality literature, strong marketing campaign, and striking book covers (Ramirez, 1990). Text selections highlighted quality children's literature, including selections from award-winning authors Ezra Jack Keats, Langston Hughes, Robert Louis Stevenson, E.B. White, and Isaac Bashevis Singer. In what may be a first for basal readers, Silver Burdett Ginn employed focus groups of 2,000 students to evaluate the literature in the program, and the favorites were labeled Readers Choice.

The World of Reading teacher's manuals are more complete and directive than those we examined from the previous decade. Before reading the selection, the teacher developed background knowledge and set a purpose for reading. As students read the story, the teacher is instructed to conduct "guided reading," in which she or he is to ask two or three questions per page, while also addressing literary elements such as story language and character development. Questions are labeled according to the comprehension element being addressed, such as identifying details, cause and effect, or drawing conclusions. Skills were taught before reading the selection, and after reading a response to the literature was encouraged.

To teach main idea, the World of Reading teacher's manual offers a skill lesson that preceded the reading selection for students to apply as they read. The comprehension skills lessons are longer and more detailed than in any previous program, exhibiting the characteristics of direct explanation (Duffy, 2003). The lessons have a unique format. The left side of the page simply reminds the teacher to explain, model, or practice the skill while the right side provides a more detailed script. One side was for the expert, the other for the novice. This series may be the first time that the word *model* appeared in a basal reader.

The World of Reading lessons are divided into five parts. The "Warm Up" segment of the lesson has the teacher draw students' attention to the topic, the main idea, and the details that support it, such as,

> Explain that a main idea is a sentence that contains the topic—one or two words that tell what the writer is saying in most of the sentences. Explain that the supporting detail is a word, phrase, or sentence that goes with or tells something about the main idea. (Silver Burdett Ginn, 1989–1993, Grade 5 Teacher's Manual, p. 270)

In the next segment, "Teach," the teacher is directed to explain a procedure for finding the main idea and then model it. The teacher then models the process with paragraphs on a teaching chart. "Guided Practice" follows, with students articulating how to find the main idea during a whole-group lesson, then participating in written practice. "Wrap Up" reviews the concept and offers worksheets. "Application" encourages students to apply this skill when reading the text selection.

Despite the best attempts of authors and publishers, independent evaluations of the programs still identified problems. Researchers (e.g., Afflerbach & Walker, 1992; Miller & Blumenfeld, 1993) looked at main idea and cause-and-effect instruction in two basal programs, those of Silver Burdett Ginn and Houghton Mifflin. They found no evidence that the programs followed research-based recommendations on the frequency and pacing of guided practice. In short, the students (especially students of lower ability) did not get enough practice to ensure that they would learn the skills. Miller and Blumenfeld (1993) further found that the instruction in the basal lessons was not at a sufficiently high cognitive level to facilitate students' application of the skills. Schmitt and Hopkins (1993) examined comprehension skill and strategy instruction of basal reading programs, looking at programs with copyright dates in the early 1990s. They found that these programs taught important skills and strategies, but failed to do so with the explicitness suggested in the research. Franks, Mulhern, and Schillinger (1997), in an analysis of basal reading programs' teaching of making inferences, also found the instruction lacked the necessary explicitness suggested in the research.

The reading programs of the mid-1980s through the mid-1990s became considerably more multicultural during the decade. At the beginning of the 1980s, African American and Hispanic characters became more prominent in the reading selections, with some selections touching on specific ethnic themes, such as in John Steptoe's *Mufaro's Beautiful Daughters*, or on specific historical figures like Phyllis Wheatley. Early in the decade, the programs made no attempt to feature minority authors. By the end of the decade, many of the programs were highlighting the ethnic backgrounds of the authors, each receiving a photograph and short biography. The programs began to include some selections that featured children with a disability, but the theme of the stories was not about life with a disability. By the end of the decade, the teacher's edition of each program included many photographs of multiethnic students reading, writing, and playing in classrooms and schools. All of these changes continued and were expanded on in the next generation of programs, including an even stronger emphasis on Hispanic stories and authors.

Balanced Literacy and Beyond

Without historical hindsight it is impossible to know when an era begins or ends, much less apply a label to a set of educational trends. Several forces converged toward the end of the 20th century to shape the structure of core reading programs. First, Hoffman and his colleagues (1994, 1998) published two important studies raising questions about the texts used to teach reading in first grade. Second, a long series of studies on phonemic awareness and beginning reading instruction were starting to be influential, especially with the publication of *Beginning to Read* (Adams, 1990) and *Preventing Reading Difficulties* (Snow, Burns, & Griffin, 1998). Publishers responded to this research and began to add lessons on phonemic awareness and strengthen phonics instruction. This new focus existed alongside the literature-based selections and the reader-response activities: "Regardless of one's stance on the issues, what is clear is that we are entering a time of intense experimentation in the teaching of literacy" (Hoffman et al., 1994, p. 66). Third, educators were trying to find a middle ground between literature-based programs and the emerging emphasis on phonemic awareness and phonics.

We titled this section *balanced literacy*, using the most common term for this recent period as educators sought to combine—or balance—explicit phonics and comprehension instruction with authentic and extensive reading and writing. However, the term may have two close but different meanings. To educators like Pressley (2006) and Cunningham, Hall, and Defee (1998), the term *balanced* meant the integration of direct, explicit instruction in phonics, vocabulary, and comprehension with extensive reading and writing for real purposes. For the Guided Reading group (Fountas & Pinnell, 1996), balanced literacy meant giving children ample opportunities to read and write under the support and guidance of the teacher with a strong focus on meaning, but not insisting on the explicit teaching of phonics and comprehension strategies.

We turn once again to the *Reading/Language Arts Framework for California Public Schools* (California Department of Education, 1987), because this document guided the work of publishers as they created the next generation of basals. According to this document, the heart of a powerful reading program is "the relationship between explicit, systematic skills instruction and literature, language, and comprehension. While skills alone are insufficient to develop good readers, no reader can become proficient without these foundational skills" (n.p.). Honig (1996) similarly defines *balanced approach* as "one which combines the language and literature-rich activities associated with whole language with explicit teaching of the skills needed to decode words—for all children" (p. 13). Reading instruction should be about more than first grade and phonics.

In response to this call, Silver Burdett Ginn (1997–2000) produced a new basal reading program called Literature Works. (The first author of this book was on the author team of Literature Works.) In contrast to basal programs of the 1980s, unabridged, quality children's literature was included, as well as instruction in phonemic awareness, phonics, and comprehension skills and strategies (Hoffman et al., 1998). In other words, programs preserved quality children's literature in each anthology while adding more work on decoding through the addition of little decodable books for each main selection, provided at an additional cost. Compared with basals of the 1980s, basal texts in the mid-1990s had more diversity in regard to genre, format, and vocabulary (Hoffman et al., 1998). The most significant change was the addition of leveled and decodable text to supplement the literature-based anthology. All basal programs added these leveled texts, typically three per lesson, for strong, average, and struggling readers.

In regard to instructional design, the basal programs of the mid-1990s replaced directed reading with shared reading (Hoffman et al., 1994; Rasinski

& Hoffman, 2003). The tone of the teacher's manuals was less prescriptive, allowing more autonomy for the teacher to make instructional decisions. Even though skill instruction was still present, the new basals of the era focused on it to a lesser degree. Eliciting students' personal responses to literature was as important as skills instruction. Promoting a balanced approach to literacy, trade books were often suggested, or even provided, by basal publishers (Baumann, Hoffman, Moon, & Duffy-Hester, 1998).

Let's examine how comprehension instruction, specifically main idea instruction, looks in Literature Works. Each lesson provides resources for reading the selections, skills and strategies instruction, writing instruction, and relating the readings to other curriculum areas. Background building and purpose setting prepare students for the reading selection, and throughout each selection, teacher questions are suggested, identifying the skill each question intends to address. Strategies for reading, such as metacognition, purpose setting, and visualizing, are also offered for teachers to share with students. Discussion of the selection concludes the lesson, with instruction for eliciting students' responses, making cultural connections, and conducting comprehension practice, all accompanied by appropriate worksheet pages. Language, spelling, and speaking/listening are also addressed in the manuals, as well as cooperative learning suggestions. Trade book guides are also provided.

In Literature Works, the comprehension skills are taught after the students read and discuss the selection. This reverses the structure of the preceding program, World of Reading, and thus severs the connection between skill instruction and comprehending while reading. The lessons themselves are less explicit. Whereas World of Reading offers several reasons for learning to find the main idea, in Literature Works students are told "the main idea of a passage or paragraph helps the reader understand and remember what is read" (Literature Works, Level 5, p. T80). For instance, Table 1 compares procedures for determining the main idea in World of Reading and Literature Works. Where World of Reading has the teacher model the skill three times, in Literature Works only one opportunity for modeling is provided. Finally, the overall strategy in Literature Works is less explicit.

Jitendra, Chard, Hoppes, Renouf, and Gardill (2001) examined main idea instruction at grades 2, 4, and 6 in four commercial reading programs from the mid-1990s (Houghton Mifflin, Macmillan/McGraw-Hill, Scott Foresman, and Silver Burdett Ginn). They found that all of the programs contained explicit instruction of strategies for identifying the main ideas; however, the sequence of instruction

Table 1. Comparing Main Idea Instruction in World of Reading and Literature Works

World of Reading (1989–1993)	Literature Works (1997–2000)
Tell students that there is a strategy that they can use to help them find the main idea in a paragraph. First, read the paragraph. Next, decide what the writer is talking about in most of the sentences. Then look for a sentence that states the main idea or make one up. Tell students they can check themselves by rereading to see if the detail sentences support or go with the main idea. (From World of Reading, Grade 5, p. 234, © 1989 by Silver Burdett & Ginn)	Tell students that the main idea may be expressed at the beginning, the middle, or the end of a paragraph or passage. In some cases, however, the main idea is not stated, and the reader must infer or figure out the main idea from the supporting details. (From Literature Works, Grade 5, pp. T132–T133, © 1997 by Silver Burdett & Ginn)

was flawed. All programs started with the complex version of the skill, inferring the main idea, and moved to the simpler task of identifying the main idea. The authors believed that most programs provided insufficient amounts of practice to learn the strategies. Finally, all of the programs tended to teach and apply main idea strategies to texts that were above the students' reading level, thus complicating a difficult comprehension task with challenging print skills.

Creators of the core reading programs of the mid-to-late-1990s all believed they were responding to the current research on reading. They all incorporated authentic children's literature and stressed response to that literature. They included the new ideas on phonemic awareness, but without the thoroughness we would see in the next decade. They offered instruction in comprehension skills and strategies, but did try to distinguish between the two. All skills instruction— phonics, vocabulary, and comprehension—was less explicit in the late 1990s than some of what preceded it and much of what would follow it. The addition of leveled and decodable books enabled teachers to work with both good children's literature and text at the students' instructional levels. Basal readers continued to adjust to the research and to the marketplace.

The Current Era and Core Reading Programs

The significant event in the field of reading at the start of the 21st century was the publication of the *Report of the National Reading Panel* (NRP; National Institute of Child Health and Human Development [NICHD], 2000). The NRP report stressed five components of reading—phonemic awareness, phonics, fluency, vocabulary, and comprehension—and the research-based instructional strategies in each area. Just as important, the NRP report did not address oral language development, motivation, or effective classroom management processes and differentiation. Following on the heels of the NRP report, No Child Left Behind legislation and its Reading First initiative caused published reading programs to assume even more importance as the primary vehicles for classroom reading instruction. The charge of Reading First was to provide

> assistance to State Educational Agencies (SEAs) and Local Educational Agencies (LEAs) in establishing reading programs for students in kindergarten through grade 3 that are based on scientifically based reading research (SBRR) to ensure that every student can read at grade level or above no later than the end of grade 3. (No Child Left Behind Act of 2001, 2002, Title 1, Part B, § 1201)

Reading First also was to provide assistance to SEAs and LEAs in selecting or developing effective instructional materials, programs, learning systems, and strategies to implement methods that have been proven to prevent or remediate reading failure within a state. The new descriptive term *core reading programs* replaced *basals* and became synonymous with scientifically based reading instruction.

Since No Child Left Behind was introduced, what was once labeled a basal reading program is now titled a core reading program. With this shift comes a notable semantic change. The term *basal* means "forming a basis; fundamental; basic," and the term *core* means "the central, innermost, or most essential part of anything" (Dictionary.com). The shift in terms implies that what was once a basic, foundational piece of the reading curriculum, open to the use of trade books and other supplemental texts, is now embraced as the central, essential part of every reading program—no other texts needed.

Contemporary core reading programs stress their research base, but publishers throughout history have stressed that their reading programs were based on research. Horace Mann believed that the whole-word programs he inspired were based on the scientific thinking of Johann Pestalozzi. William S. Gray and Arthur Gates studied word repetitions and built their programs around this concept. The skills-management programs of the 1970s were based on the mastery learning work of John Carroll and Benjamin Bloom. The literature-based movement was built on the work of Louise Rosenblatt (1978) and Kenneth Goodman (1986). It would be appropriate to say that reading programs adapt to the times and adjust to consumers' wants, which are influenced by research. Whatever the case, publishers' well-crafted rationales based on the careful citations of reading research reports have created the belief that core reading programs are indeed based on scientific research, giving the impression that the programs themselves have been tested and proven effective. This is rarely, if ever, the case. More often, the "scientific, research-based" label indicates that research-based strategies and instructional approaches are employed within the program.

We end our history with the start of the 21st century, because Part II of the book will take a close look at contemporary core reading programs.

PUTTING IT ALL TOGETHER

As you look at core reading programs from the past 50 years, you are struck first by the consistency of these programs and then by the changes. The basic structure of core reading programs has remained relatively unchanged. Stories are introduced, knowledge and vocabulary are developed, stories are read and discussed, and students' responses to the text are made. Skills are taught sometimes before the story, sometimes afterward. Emphases in the types of texts have changed, largely due to shifts in American culture and the instructional pedagogy that is driving these materials. Core reading programs moved from controlled text to literature-based texts, and now use both. The influence of politics has also played a dominant role in the content and approaches adapted by core reading programs. Programs are now considered the *core* of reading instruction, rather than a simple base or foundational piece of the curriculum. Clearly, programs attempt to reflect the most relevant research available; yet, they often fall short. They do so because research is not the only factor that drives the development of a core reading program, and there is so much research that not all of it can find a home in a core reading program.

In the next chapter, we will explore how a core reading program is created and how reading research must compete with market research and the desires of the consumer. The history of reading instruction in America and the research behind it suggests that programs should be viewed as professional *tools*, used at the discretion of teachers who know their students and work to achieve important goals.

CHAPTER 2

How Core Reading Programs Are Created

In 1999, I (Dewitz, the first author of this book) was an author/consultant for core reading programs, but was asked by the publishing company to assist with a new elementary science program. My job was to design the reading lessons that accompanied the science content. What should the teacher do before the students read the text? How would he or she support students' comprehension while they read, and what should be the follow-up activities? I decided, with the approval of the editors, to begin each chapter with a graphic organizer. The teacher would present the bare elements of the graphic organizer, and through discussion and reading, the organizer would be fleshed out.

I designed several graphic organizers, and they were passed around the editorial table for discussion. Suggestions were made, and I executed a few revisions. Later that day, the publisher and I had a discussion, and he disagreed with the complexity of the graphic organizers. One in particular, at the sixth-grade level, depicted the three types of rocks—igneous, sedimentary, and metamorphic—organized around the rock cycle. The publisher wanted to eliminate the rock cycle, claiming that the graphic organizer was too complex and that teachers wanted simple graphic organizers. As we argued back and forth about the needs of teachers versus the accuracy of the graphic organizer, the publisher became exasperated. He finally declared, "Look, sales are more important than clarity and accuracy. We want the program to sell. Teachers can always change the graphic organizer on their own."

This story illuminates one—but certainly not the only—conflict that underlies the creation of educational materials. The process is more complex than simply translating research-based understanding about reading into sound instructional principles. In this chapter, we take you through the process of creating a core reading program, introduce you to the players who create these programs, and discuss the political, economic, and educational influences that shape such programs. The content of this chapter came from interviews with program authors, editors and managers at publishing companies, and executives at development houses. Most executives in development houses had previously served as editorial directors of reading and language arts for the major publishing houses. We interviewed people who were responsible for developing Harcourt's StoryTown (2008), Macmillan/McGraw-Hill's Treasures (2009), and Pearson Scott Foresman's Reading Street series (2008b). All were asked the same basic questions: How is a core reading program created, and what is your role in its creation? We wanted to be able to describe the process from multiple perspectives, because only a limited amount of research exists on how core reading programs are developed. We chose to interview authors and editors who had worked with core reading programs for at least 10 years; several had worked with programs for more than 20 years. These experienced professionals were asked to describe how the process of creating a core reading program had changed, because the latest generation of programs had to conform not only to the state guidelines but also to the influential NRP report (NICHD, 2000), all under the pressure of some very tight production guidelines.

All of the people interviewed requested that they remain anonymous. Like any employee (and at some level we are all employees), their personal views may not always reflect the stated policies of publishing company executives. As you will soon learn, the creation of a core reading program requires compromises. Sometimes an editor's, author's, or writer's views prevail, and at other times they do not.

What You Will Learn

- Who creates and writes a core reading program
- What influences the content and instruction in these programs
- What the process is of creating a core reading program
- How quality is controlled as core reading programs are created
- How the process of creating these programs influences the final product

What You Will Be Able to Do

- View your core program with less awe, liberating you to make changes to its use in order to better meet the needs of your students
- Explain to other educators and parents that a core reading program is a product of both experimental research and market research
- Weigh the research base of a core program against the needs of your students

This chapter serves a clear purpose: to show how the process of creating a core reading program will ultimately shape its content. Understanding how something is made gives the user greater appreciation for its strengths and limitations. We also believe that any school district that plans to pay tens of thousands of dollars for a new core reading program needs to have a clear appreciation of the decision-making process that was used to create the multiple components of that program. The creation process does not really start in the publishing company, but in the three large states that influence the content and methods in core reading programs—Texas, California, and Florida—and in many smaller states whose content standards for reading are studied and reviewed before lessons are designed and readings are selected. Before we look at the process of creating a core reading program, we review some early accounts of the publishing process.

Previous Research on the Creation of Core Reading Programs

Little has been written about how core reading programs are created, and what is known is dated, especially considering the changes in these programs over the past 20 years. The book *Report Card on Basal Readers* (Goodman, Shannon, Freeman, & Murphy, 1988) describes the process and emphasizes the shared roles of authors, editors, and marketing executives. Goodman et al. (1988) did little original research on the specific topic of how basal reading programs are created, but drew heavily on a series of interviews conducted earlier (Graham, 1978). Graham (cited in Goodman et al., 1988) emphasized the essential commercial nature of core reading program publishing and argued that programs are driven more by market forces than by the scholarly expertise of the program authors. In the 1970s, as one publisher was bringing out a new program that sought to emulate other successful programs, the publisher was reported to have said, "You can't be too advanced, or educators won't buy it. You can't be too late with innovations or your competition will have beaten you to it. You have to be exactly on target" (Graham, cited in Goodman et al., 1988, p. 53).

According to Goodman and his colleagues (1988), authors lent credibility to a core reading program and worked to promote the product, but for the most part they did not write the program. The shape of lesson plans, the reading selections, and the skill being taught were all determined by the marketplace. This view is somewhat at odds with what we learned from our interviews and suggests a much more uniform view of the author–publisher relationship than exists in all publishing companies. We believe that the role of the authors varied from one publisher to another and even from one author to another within one publishing house. Reading selections were either written in-house or selected from a corpus of children's literature. This selection process was driven by concerns for gender, ethnic, and racial balance and for the elimination of any reference to Communists, witches, or secular humanism. Most selections were heavily edited for readability and then edited again to make sure that there was a fit between the selection and the skill with which it was paired. Goodman et al. (1988) stressed that the goal of the publisher was to present a slick, attractive package with the aura of science surrounding it.

When Chall and Squire (1991) wrote about core reading programs a few years later, they stressed many of the same themes. Squire held a unique position and perspective on the publishing of core reading programs because he was both an acknowledged scholar in the area of language arts and a full-time employee of Ginn and Company. Chall was an influential scholar and analyst of reading instruction. In their discussion of the publishing process, they highlighted several trends that cause core reading program publishing to be a conservative endeavor. First, the costs of creating a program are high and the risks are even higher, so publishers cannot afford to be wrong. Chall and Squire pointed out that in the early 1990s, profit margins were small and barely exceeded what a company could earn by putting their money in a savings account. This led publishers to produce programs based on what the market demanded. Publishers rely on market research, especially focus groups attended by typical classroom teachers, to determine the appeal of their products. Programs must first pass the thumb, or flip, test, a quick cursory examination of the programs in which teachers look for a limited number of important elements. Art and graphic design are critical to the initial success of a program, because the graphic designer can make program elements pop.

Time and a complex market also limit the innovations in a core reading program. Chall and Squire (1991) documented that it took three to five years to produce a new program. That lengthy development period makes it difficult for publishers to respond to new research or educational trends. Publishing companies have to produce increasingly complex programs and include with each generation a greater number of components: student and teacher's editions, workbooks, assessments, and the like. Even if schools do not purchase all of the components, school districts expect to see them, just as it is nice to know that navigation is available on your new car even if you cannot afford it or don't need it. In order to keep pace with the competition, publishers must produce all of the components that their competitors produce, thus raising their costs. Finally, Chall and Squire argued that the rising costs to produce a core reading program comes from the number of groups that exert pressure on the content. They specifically addressed the influence of state and local curriculum standards on program development. These pressures on the publishing industry reinforced Venezky's (1987) argument that core reading programs are cautious, conservative documents, not on the leading edge of research.

The Cast of Characters: Who Creates the Programs?

A large cast of characters is responsible for creating a core reading program. Some of these people work for the publisher, some for universities, others for development houses that complete the outsourced work for the publisher, and some are freelance writers. At publishing houses, the cast typically includes the editors, senior editors, project managers, and marketing executives. Other editors, writers, and graphic designers work at the development houses or at independent companies to which much of the actual program writing is outsourced.

Publishers and Editors

The publisher, senior editors, program managers, and marketing executives decide on the scope and focus of the program. Their central role is to decide whether to produce a new core reading program and to weigh the development costs against the likely revenue. Creating a new core reading program is a high-risk financial enterprise, and the senior executives must get it right. In most cases, these senior executives are responsible for determining costs, revenues, and profit projections and providing them to corporate chief executive officers. They must create a program that is appealing to the market and balances costs against the likely revenue. A new core reading program costs anywhere from US$70 million to US$90 million to produce, plus at least half that again in marketing costs. So the senior management must weigh the philosophy and structure of the program against the demands of the market. They must create a program that will sell across the country and in all markets.

The marketing of a core reading program drives its development. At least three versions of each program are developed: one for California, one for Texas, and one for the rest of the nation. So the ultimate shape and scope of a core reading program is neither solely based on scientific research nor solely driven by the author team. The cost of each component must be weighed against the likely revenue. Core reading programs are a compromise shaped as much by market research as by scientific reading research.

Within the publishing companies, the programs are produced by senior editors, editors, program managers, and marketing executives. Core reading programs are complex, with numerous components. Each generation of core reading programs adds new components, but old components are rarely deleted. The current crop of programs includes the standard student and teacher's editions; sets of small leveled and decodable books; practice books for spelling, grammar, and writing; transparencies; word and picture cards; CDs that read all selections to the students; and so forth. For the 2008 and 2009 core reading programs, several publishers—Pearson Scott Foresman, Harcourt, and The McGraw-Hill Companies—added fluency builders; workbooks at multiple levels for advanced, on-level, and below-level readers; intervention kits that are integrated with the core reading program; and intervention kits that can stand alone.

It is the task of the editors and program managers to produce the prototypes for all these components and shepherd their development as writers and editors, both within and outside the company, create the text. These editors are typically fairly young (30 to 50 years old), often former schoolteachers, but not necessarily with any particular expertise in reading instruction. Those who have been with a company or in the publishing industry for a long time have developed their own knowledge of reading instruction, but their knowledge is not necessarily grounded in classroom applications. Editorial staffs change often. It is common for an editor to work for several publishers over the course of a career and for people to shift from one company to another while a program is being developed. This means there are few trade secrets, and a shared common vision about the nature of core reading programs exists. Publishers will closely study the competitive programs as they develop their own products.

Development Houses

Core reading programs are largely written and edited at development houses. Often, but not always, the student anthology or the teacher's edition is created at the publishing company. The rest of the writing and editing is outsourced. A development house is a small company that employs editors who write, assemble, review, edit, and coordinate the content of the core reading **program**.

The main function of a development house is to service publish**ers. Twenty** years ago, publishers employed their own editors. When a new **program** was being produced, the publisher would gear up and hire more writers or editors, only to let them go or shift them to something new after a project was completed. Now the finances of publishing have compelled publishers to outsource more of the writing to these small development houses. Development houses work for more than one publisher at a time. As one executive at a development house told me, "We are writing the third and fourth grades of Scott [Foresman] and the workbooks and assessments for Harcourt." The task of producing a core reading program is so large that no development house can undertake the project alone.

The writing of the core reading program is shared between editors in the development houses and freelance writers. One executive at a development house stated, "We rely on freelance writers for the most part to write the content of core programs, using the guidelines the publisher has given us." So in this model, the people outside the development house produce the content of the teacher's editions, the leveled books, the practice books, and the assessments, while employees at the development house do the editing. Some development houses use freelance writers and editors to create and edit the content, while the development house coordinates the process, seeing that specifications and timelines are met. In either case, it is a long supply chain from the original conception of a core reading program to the final writing and editing. For example, the leveled book your students read started with a set of guidelines from the publisher that may or may not have been reviewed by an author. These guidelines were given to a development house that delivered them to a freelance writer in Vermont. An editor at the development house in New York edited it, and a project manager in Illinois made sure it fit into the overall core reading program. Figure 6 is our view of how a core reading program is created based on the interviews we conducted. You can study this figure and return to it as you read through the chapter.

The Authors

The program authors are the public face of a core reading program and most likely the only names you will ever know. Their role in developing a program

Figure 6. The Process of Developing a Core Reading Program

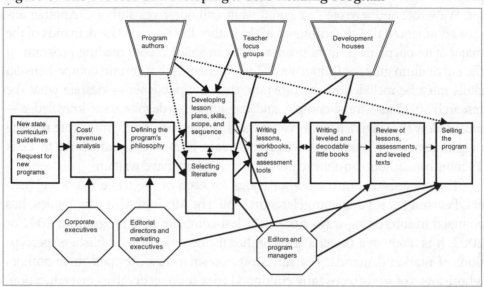

varies, depending on their area of expertise and the relationship between the authors and the publishing company. Some programs are very author driven, meaning the authors have considerable input about the design of the basic lessons and even participate in selecting the literature that goes into the student anthology. In other publishing companies, the authors' roles are much more proscribed—and more than one author told us that they had no idea how the literature was chosen and they were not involved in any of the decisions about workbooks, leveled readers, or assessments. As a consumer, you will not know which program is author driven and which program is not. Even within a publishing company, some authors take a more active role in creating a core reading program than others. It is important to understand that the concept of author in a core reading program has a very different meaning from its conventional usage. Ernest Hemingway wrote his novels, even though he had a wonderful editor, Maxwell Perkins. Core reading program authors do not write the programs. One very experienced author told us that the term *program author* was a euphemism.

The role of the author in a core reading program has changed significantly over the past 20 years. When programs were produced in the 1980s, authors had more influence on program content. One author stated, "We actually wrote the program. I got every page to read after it was formatted and developed by an editor. We wrote and rewrote. We could really call ourselves authors." Another author commented that the influence of the author has waned. The demands of the major state curricula limit how an author can shape a core reading program. If the curriculum guide of California or Texas demands that certain comprehension skills must be included in the program, then the publishers—despite what the research suggests—must comply, and the authors—despite their knowledge—must follow these guidelines. Because the timelines for developing a core reading program have been compressed in recent years, from 3 to 5 years down to 12 or 18 months, authors cannot even review what others have written.

The composition of the author teams for each of the three major publishers, Pearson Scott Foresman, Harcourt, and The McGraw-Hill Companies, has changed in interesting ways since their last complete new program in 2002 or 2003. It is likely that the changing author teams reflect the publishers' perceptions of market demands. Pearson Scott Foresman has dropped three authors whose areas of study were early childhood education, general special education, and cultural diversity and added very prominent names from the hot area of RTI, namely Sharon Vaughn, Deborah Simmons, and Edward Kame'enui.

At The McGraw-Hill Companies, prominent researchers James Flood and Steven Stahl have passed away, and researchers like Diane Lapp and James Hoffman were replaced with new authors whose expertise was in English-language learners (ELLs; Jana Echevarria) or multicultural education (Doris Walker-Dalhouse). Additionally, McGraw-Hill added Dolores Malcolm, a past president of IRA, and Adria Klein, a past president of the California Reading Association, perhaps to bolster their political clout.

At Harcourt, the author team replaced Nancy Roser, a generalist, and Hallie Yopp, an expert in phonemic awareness, with authors in the fields of multicultural education (Julie Washington and Robin Scarcells) and special education (Roxanne Hudson). At some publishing companies, the changes in the author teams suggest a move away from prominent researchers to teacher educators, and in all companies there is a need to establish bona fides with the current hot topics of the day: intervention and ELLs.

The Process of Creating a Core Reading Program

The creation of a new core reading program begins with an intense discussion around a complex set of factors that balance the philosophy of the new program against the market demands of the upcoming adoption states and the major trends in reading instruction. The current crop of new core reading programs had to encompass a new focus on differentiation and intervention, renewed interest in vocabulary instruction, and additional material for teaching ELLs. So the first step in core reading program development is an evaluation of the marketplace, determining which states and major cities are likely to purchase core reading programs in the next two years. Next, editorial and marketing executives study the reading standards or frameworks in key adoption states: California, Texas, Florida, and several others. One publisher reported that they study reading frameworks in 20 major states. The executives at a publishing company have to be sure that they can create a product that will sell in key markets and then gear their production timetables to when materials are due in those states. They have to balance program development and market costs against likely revenues. Only when they are reasonably sure that they can create a financially successful program will they proceed to develop a new core reading program. The thrust of a new program begins with the contents standards of the key adoption states. These states are important for several reasons. Each has a large multicultural population, the textbook selection process is largely centralized with considerable state-supported financing, and the textbook guidelines are very specific.

The Influence of California, Texas, and Florida

California issued its criteria for new reading programs, its revised content standards, and its timeline for the adoption process in April 2006. Publishers had until April 2008 to submit their materials for review. Although California's standards built on what had been adopted in 2002, several additional features had to be included in new core reading programs. California called for social studies and science content to be covered within the reading program in the primary grades. This meant more expository text. The new criteria also outlined a stronger focus on vocabulary and language development, an increased focus on oral reading fluency, and an improved assessment system including progress monitoring (California Department of Education, 2007). The *Reading Language Arts Framework for California Public Schools* (California Department of Education, 2007) also called for "30 minutes of extra support for struggling readers in kindergarten through grade eight" (p. 290). This meant that the publishers had to create an accompanying intervention program for California.

In September 2008, Texas issued its revised Texas Essential Knowledge and Skills and Proclamation, which were in effect the guidelines for new core reading programs that were to be submitted to the Texas Education Agency by April 2009. The Texas standards are quite specific and will cause the publishers to produce a product that is different from the one created for California, with the Texas program due just a year after the California program. In this next round of adoptions, Texas has mandated that 70 spelling–sound correspondences be taught in first grade and that all skills be included in both the teacher's edition of the program and the student edition. This means skill instruction must be written in simple language in the anthology. Texas also seeks to mandate the amount of practice a student receives for each essential knowledge and skill. Texas requires that instructional materials cover essential knowledge and skills five times in the student text in addition to the end-of-section review exercises, end-of-chapter activities, and unit tests. So while the publishers are working to create a California program that requires a coordination of science and social studies with the reading curriculum, they must also create a program for Texas that includes the skills three or five times in each student edition. The publishers must tailor the programs to the demands of each state and do so in less than a year. Almost all authors and editors told us that compressed timelines influence how a core reading program is developed. We think it may also influence the quality of the product.

The Florida Department of Education (2006) issued its guidelines for new core reading programs in 2006, and publishers had to submit their products for evaluation by May 1, 2007. Like Texas and California, Florida's guidelines were equally explicit, requiring an extensive series of benchmarks be met at each grade level, K through 5. In addition, Florida published a separate set of guidelines for special education students. Florida called for a core reading program that had explicit, systematic instruction in reading skills and rich literary text. The program had to contain assessment tools for progress monitoring and diagnosis aligned to the instructional materials. The guidelines called for a strong research base.

> Each publisher should carefully review the research basis for any program or strategy submitted for consideration. In particular, attention should be paid to the research that was conducted initially to develop the program as well as the research conducted *after* publication, such as program evaluations. (Florida Department of Education, 2006, p. 3)

Establishing a research base for a strategy demanded careful documentation using research studies that supported various instructional practices. However, program evaluation after publication is difficult because the Florida Department of Education allows, at the most, 18 months between the publication of the guidelines and the submission of the products.

In addition to these precise curriculum standards, Texas and California exert considerable control over the content of stories and nonfiction selections that students read. In California, the textbook publishers must conform to standards about the depiction of race, gender, nationality, and disability. Some outside interest groups have counted the number of boys and girls in a core reading program and pushed publishers to equally represent gender across a wide range of occupations. This led one publisher to change the sex of the train character in *The Little Engine That Could* to create more balance in the story. Some interest groups have gone so far as to prohibit stories that include references to birthday cakes and fast foods, because these are not healthy for students (Finn & Ravitch, 2004). A parallel set of problems faces publishers in Texas. There, traditionalists have objected to the inclusion of stories with witches and goblins, nontraditional gender roles, and skeptical views of religion. After a major legal suit in 1983, Holt, Rinehart & Winston revised its content, even though it won the suit filed by religious fundamentalists. These fundamentalists wanted to remove myths, goblins, and even some fairy tales from the core reading program. One group objected to *The Wizard of Oz*, because the Scarecrow, the Lion, and the Tin Man each achieved a personal goal—a ticking heart, a medal, and a diploma—without an appeal to God. Because the adoption process is centralized in 22 states, and 3 of those states carry considerable clout, outside interest groups have fewer targets for their lobbying and at times are effective.

Defining the Core Reading Program

Against the backdrop of these demands, the authors and editors of the core reading program pose this question, if you could have anything in a reading program, what would it be? A broad-ranging discussion of this question at one publishing company began with a focus on the texts that students read. The authors and editors wanted texts that mattered, were worthy of being read, renewed the emphasis on vocabulary instruction, and built students' knowledge from one selection to another. These authors and editors also wanted a more focused approach to comprehension skills and strategies, and responsible teaching of word study. Another author viewed these opening meetings as an attempt to position the product—would it be on the cutting edge or take a more conservative approach? For example, in 1992 Houghton Mifflin came out with a literature-based program, one that deemphasized skills and did very well. A few years later, Silver Burdett Ginn straddled the fence between literature and skills. They brought in Lee Galda to enhance the literature options in Literature Works, but the new publisher, who came from Open Court, pushed the program in a skills direction. In the end, the program tried to do too much, and sales were not robust.

Another author described these opening meetings as strong, positive brainstorming sessions. The participants are "enthusiastic, energetic, and nonevaluative." Ideas are offered and discussed, with authors suggesting program ideas that reflect those authors' areas of expertise. These meetings typically take place over several weeks or months. It then becomes the task of the editors to winnow down the ideas. Some are accepted and make their way into the program, while others are rejected. For example, one author might want students to focus on personal response after reading a text, while another is concerned with the follow-up comprehension questions. Ultimately, these ideas compete for space in the core reading program. As these academic ideas are offered and discussed, the in-house editorial staff gathers the ideas, endorsing some and dropping others. A core reading program cannot incorporate all research-based ideas. For instance, those advocating for the inclusion of QARs (Raphael, 1984) must compete with those arguing for reciprocal teaching (Palincsar & Brown, 1984).

The third area of input that drives the conceptualization of the program is the market. The senior sales representatives are the voices for the teachers. A new program has to contain the ideas that teachers are expecting. As one editor put it, teachers expect some "old friends" and will consider some new ideas. Gathering teacher input is accomplished through focus groups. Groups of teachers are brought into a room, often with a one-way glass, and are asked to review prototype lessons for the core reading program. The leader of the focus group (not an employee of the publishing company), following a script, asks the teachers questions about elements of the program. Teachers are asked to evaluate lesson plan layout, instructional language at point of use, and small program elements designed to support learning for ELLs or struggling readers. The opinions of these teachers influence which program elements make their way into a core reading program and which might be excluded.

One author described a very important step in the process as the process by which editors and senior management wrestle with what is included in a lesson and what is excluded, saying, "There are so many good ideas, how do you create a lesson that is clean and effective without being constraining?" This gets to the heart of the major issue in the development of a core reading program. The authors and editors have to juggle many wants and needs. There are many skills and strategies to teach, and many constituencies have needs that must be met. In one publishing company, a solution to the complexity of the lesson plan was to have each story read twice. In a first read, skills and strategies are used to establish general comprehension, and in a second read, issues of author's craft, purpose, literary style, and literary analysis are explored. Ultimately this idea, while attractive, was abandoned, as it was judged to be too radical for the traditional teacher population. The ultimate problem faced by the authors and editors is how to provide instructional guidance at the point of use. The questions, answers, and suggestions of modeling that run down the sides of the pages and across the bottom of the text are the point-of-use guidelines. What does the teacher say to the students before, during, and after reading? These decisions require professional judgments from authors and editors, not simply the transplanting of research ideas into a core reading program.

The other constraint on the development of a core reading program is money. Core reading programs evolve just like automobiles and word-processing programs, with each generation adding new features not seen in previous iterations. Each new feature costs money. So the inclusion of progress-monitoring assessments for oral reading fluency must be weighed against the cost of materials for ELLs. Management must judge the cost of these products against their likely revenue. One executive at a development house, who was a former editorial director at a major publisher, stated that publishers are "doing massive amounts of focus testing to make sure that their investment is going to be sound. It takes a lot of time until they feel they have gotten it right. You can't be wrong when you are spending $80 million."

Given this complex picture, it is almost simplistic to argue that core reading programs are built on scientifically based reading research. There is too much reading research for all of it to make it into a program. Comprehension strategy techniques like transactional strategy instruction (Brown, Pressley, Van Meter, & Schuder, 1996) must compete with research on book clubs (McMahon & Raphael, 1997). Therefore, research is only one of several considerations used to determine the content and structure of a core reading program. Equally important are the marketplace and teachers' wants and needs. If a program is too advanced, teachers will miss their old friends, and if a program is too conservative, it will not incorporate enough hot new ideas. Costs limit what publishers can put into a program. The aesthetics of graphic design and the need for some ideas to stand out limit what can be included in a lesson. Ultimately, the use of the phrase *scientifically based reading research* is a good marketing slogan, but it does not capture how core reading programs are designed.

Refining a Prototype Lesson

As the prototype for the lesson evolves, the author team is given various tasks to perform. They may write sample lessons, create lesson plan guidelines, and review developed prototypes. Ultimately, the editors, not the authors, produce a final lesson prototype for grades 1 and 4. The authors enter the development process again to critique the prototype lessons page by page and line by line. Many overnighted boxes appear on their doorsteps containing reading lessons that must be read and reviewed, often by the next day. One author described a six-hour telephone conference during which the prototype was examined line by line, feature by feature. The authors considered, are these the right callouts [embedded directions to the teacher], the right prompts that will get the kids to think more deeply about the text?

An author who has been involved with the development of core reading programs for 20 years believes that at this point in the development process, authors and editors should be beyond concern over what features are in a program, and instead should consider how well a feature works for the teacher. Authors should be asking themselves, what makes a good think-aloud? What makes a good postreading question? Once a prototype is approved, there is a final author meeting during which the prototype, the lesson, the language, and the details are given final approval. As one author put it, "We read every word, detail, and idea in the final lesson plan." The prototype lessons and the specifications for all the lessons then go to the development houses where the writing will take place. What is apparent at this stage of the development is the great seriousness of the authors and their commitment to solving difficult curriculum-design problems. Authors are not simply translating a research protocol into a set of directions in a teacher's edition. All that they know about reading research and reading instruction drive the decisions they make.

Selecting the Literature

At the same time, another critical component of the program, the literature, is being selected or written. An important concern in the development of a core reading program is the relationship between the skills and the literature—or more precisely, what leads. Most of the authors and editors we interviewed described a process in which the scope and sequence of the skills was laid down first, then literature was selected that facilitated the teaching of those skills. A few described a process in which stories were selected to fit within a theme and then the skills followed from the text. If a program has as its goal the development of knowledge from one selection to another, then organizing selections into themes is critical. However, if skill development is most important, then the literature is selected to fit the skills. Only by closely reading two or more programs will you be able to determine if the literature or the skills lead. From the multitude of literature selections, the choices are narrowed. What is clear is that publishers would prefer to use existing children's stories and information books rather than commission new works. They can then market the program on the basis of authentic literature and not contrived selections.

The leveled and decodable texts are written by freelance writers, and each selection carries their name. This is an enormous writing task because a new core reading program contains over 600 separate titles, most of them commissioned. The freelance writers and illustrators who create these books work from specifications developed by the editorial team. In some programs and at some grade levels, topic or unit theme dictates the content, while at other times genre leads. These freelance writers are not award-winning children's authors—although at one time, renowned authors Tomie dePaola and Maurice Sendak wrote for basal reading programs.

Some authors are involved in selecting the literature for a core reading program, and others are not. This varies from one publisher to another. At one publishing company, an author candidly revealed that he had no knowledge about how the literature was selected, whereas others in the same publishing company and at another house read every selection that was proposed for kindergarten through grade 3. Beyond fitting the literature to the skills, a cautious sense of audience and propriety drives the selection of the literature. It is unfair to call this self-censorship; rather, it is an attempt to put oneself in the place of the student who is reading this story in a public school classroom or a teacher who will be teaching this story. So stories about the death of a mother or persecution of African Americans are not included, in order to avoid painful emotional responses from the students and awkward teaching moments. Authors who are experts on multicultural issues and child development have a voice in the selection of the literature by excluding stories that might cause undue stress for students and teachers. However, in our opinion, some texts lose interest as the amount of conflict is minimized. (We explore this issue further in the next chapter.) Reading selections in the student anthology and in the leveled books are then organized into broad themes. The value of these themes is also considered in the next chapter.

Graphic Design

Another part of the development process is graphic design. The graphic design of a core reading program is important for two related reasons. First, the overall attractiveness of a program influences its sales. In 1989, when World of Reading (Silver Burdett Ginn, 1989–1993) was developed, many people argued that its shimmering metallic covers with a three-dimensional look were influential in selling the program (Ramirez, 1990). People may have judged a book by its cover. Beyond aesthetic appeal, a core reading program is complex, and the graphic design of the product helps the teacher navigate through it. The teacher must easily understand the hierarchy of elements in a lesson. The program must be easy to follow, and the content must fit comfortably on the page. Too much print will overwhelm the reader, and too much white space will give too little direction.

The graphic design of the core reading program is worked out at the same time the initial conceptions of the lessons are determined. "Design and editorial go hand in hand; they work together; it is a delicate balance between design and editorial," said one art director for a publishing company. The graphic design must reflect the philosophy that underlies the program. So several rounds of lesson templates are designed and reviewed by executives in editorial and marketing. The goal is an attractive and functional integration of text and graphic elements. Art directors may exert influence on writing by limiting the number of words on a page, and editors may direct graphic design by specifying the labels and headings that teachers expect. Graphic designers also select or produce all of the artwork in the program. They must meet the specific guidelines from the state frameworks that call for a certain percentage of African American, Hispanic, Asian, and Caucasian individuals in the photographs and illustrations. These guidelines also specify the number and types of people with disabilities that must be pictured. To complicate matters even more, the parameters change from one state to another. So a program that sells in the Midwest will have a smaller percentage of Hispanics than one designed for California or Texas.

Producing the Program

After the lesson plan prototype is finalized, and the components are determined, the production of a core reading program shifts to development houses. It is at the development house, or with freelancers they hire, that the actual writing takes place. The first step for the development house is to secure a contract from the publisher. First, the publisher asks development houses to respond to a Request for Information (RFI). The publisher wants to know who will work on the project and what it will cost. Once the publisher is satisfied with the skills and cost-consciousness of the development houses, they will ask for a second round of proposals in which the development houses compete for the work. One development house executive said,

> Everything has become much more focused on cost than ever before. It's really scary, from everybody's perspective. Basically, if a publisher wants some innovation, cost is going to have a bigger influence on what goes into a program than it might have 10 or 15 years ago.

Development houses write teacher's editions, leveled books, decodable books, workbooks, assessments—everything but the student edition. The publisher provides the development house with the prototype and a strict set of guidelines. From these documents, the editors or freelancers at the development house produce the content. A development house executive explained,

> If we at the development house were asked to produce the teacher's edition, we would get a set of guidelines with a thorough explanation of each part of the lesson plan. There would be some type of skill, so we could articulate the progression of skills within a grade level and across the grades.

In some cases, a series of teleconferences is arranged between the editors at the publishing house and the editors at the development house. The development house strives to understand what the publisher has intended and proceeds by writing a series of lessons and then conducting their own internal critique, making sure that they got it right. Sometimes this is done in consultation with the managers and editors at the publishing company and sometimes it is not.

Once the editors in the development house are sure they understand how to write the lessons, the actual writing begins. The editors at the development house will regularly submit their work to the program managers and grade-level editors at the publishing company. The writing is downloaded into the lesson templates provided by the publisher. After the work is reviewed at the publishing company the editors at the development house work to incorporate the changes.

One executive at a development house described clearly where the guidelines of the publisher end and the initiative of the development house begins. If the publisher's guidelines called for lessons on main idea, they would specify the focus of the lesson at each particular grade. What should the students know and be able to do? The publisher would determine the steps in the lesson—introduce, model, practice, apply—but "in terms of fleshing out those steps, it would be up to the writers." The publisher's guidelines would not specifically illustrate how to introduce and model a skill. The editors or writers in the development house craft the actual language. They would decide how a skill is modeled and how often. This is critical in the overall quality of the core reading program, because it is the language of instruction that guides the teacher. The development house would write the lessons, submit them to the publisher, and get feedback from project managers or grade-level editors. Then, the development house would incorporate the changes. It is not clear if this happens for every lesson or for just a sample of lessons. It is clear that the authors do not read individual lessons, as time does not permit it.

As we discuss further in Chapter 5, the actual language of a lesson makes the difference between a clear explanation and a muddled one. A clear explanation describes what skill will be taught, how the skill should be implemented, the process of instruction, why the skill is important, and when it should be used. Not all programs include all these elements; therefore, we believe that not all writers know to include them. Because core reading programs are produced in a relatively short time and by many different writers in more than one development house, authors do not have time to review much of what is actually written.

Note how we illustrated in Chapter 1 that the explicitness of comprehension lessons was stronger in the 1980s when editors at the publishing houses did more writing and authors reviewed more of their work. As the work shifted to development houses in the late 1990s and into the 21st century, the explicitness of instructional language declined. (You will see this decline more clearly when we examine specific elements of core reading programs in Chapters 3, 4, and 5.) Whether this decline in explicitness or clarity is a function of changing instructional philosophy, lack of quality control, or both is hard to say. Modeling a skill or strategy explicitly makes the difference between a lesson that is based on research guidelines and one that is not (Dewitz et al., 2009).

It is important to stress that the people writing the lessons at the development houses, and the freelance writers hired by them, are often former teachers. One executive at a development house stressed,

> These aren't people you just pick up off the street. These are people who are former teachers, many with master's degrees who have been in the business for a long time. You have a core stable of people who have taught kids to read or have been immersed in this kind of writing for a long time.

An author countered and said that many of the people who actually write the teacher's manuals have little or no experience in an elementary classroom. The process of creating a core reading program is a widely distributed effort. Another senior executive at a development house, who was formerly the director of reading for a major publisher, believes that outsourcing has diminished the quality of programs.

The one other factor that diminishes the quality of core reading programs is time. Almost all the authors and editors we interviewed said that 20 years ago, publishers took 30 to 36 months to produce a new core reading program. Now the timeline has been compressed to 18 months or less. This compressed timeline has led to more outsourcing. The task of producing all the components of a core reading program is too large for any one development house. More material is created by development houses, and despite their skill and intentions, authors and senior editors review less of that material. Some authors who had worked on core reading programs for more than 20 years stated that in the past, they had been able to review almost everything that had been written. Now the press of time makes that impossible. What complicated the time problem recently was the juxtaposition of the California and Texas textbook adoption cycles. (California adopted in 2008 and Texas in 2009.)

The other recent change in the development of a core reading program is the increasing authority given to the development houses to create components of a core reading program with minimal or no review from the editors in the publishing house. One senior executive in a development house said, "One thing that development houses are being asked to do much more of these days is what they call full-service work." In this case, the development houses do more than just the writing and editing; they also do the design, layout, and production of the components. For example, a development house would have almost complete control over the creation of the practice workbooks with only minimal review by the publisher. The closest parallel to the development of a core reading program is the automobile. Ford or Honda is responsible for the design, but the components—brakes, transmission, windshield wipers—are made all over the world.

New Programs and Revisions

A new core reading program is created approximately every seven to eight years, according to the adoption cycles in California, Texas, and Florida. In the interim, publishing companies produce revisions to update their copyrights. Some states can only purchase core reading programs with a recent copyright, so programs must be revised. The second factor that drives a revision is user feedback. Teachers may find it difficult to get through a particular part of the program, and this will drive a change in content or graphic design. Authors are typically not involved in these revisions, which are often mostly cosmetic changes. Because cost is always a factor, publishers will seek to change as little as possible but still conform to the legal requirements for a program to achieve a new copyright. Rewriting a student edition is costly because it also demands an equivalent rewrite in the more complex teacher's edition. Therefore, the 2001, 2003, and 2005 editions of the Macmillan/McGraw-Hill reading program, for example, have very similar literature selections.

A revision is much less extensive than a new core reading program. A revision involves changing 5% to 10% of the content. The reading selections and leveled books are rarely changed, but the teacher's edition may be updated. When Houghton Mifflin produced a new copyright in 2005, the major change in the program was a stronger emphasis on small-group instruction in the teacher's edition, but the scope and sequence of skills and the reading selections stayed virtually the same. At times, a revision will include a few changes to the student edition, but the changes are typically modest.

PUTTING IT ALL TOGETHER

We present this picture of how core reading programs are developed to illustrate a few important understandings. First, the creation of a core reading program is not an author-driven enterprise that merely translates research into practice. Authors have an important role to play, but their roles are not greater than those of marketing executives, editorial directors, art directors, and executives at development houses. When you examine a new core reading program, don't think that the author you just heard speak at a reading conference actually wrote the lessons you will be using. One author candidly stated that the creation of a core reading program has more to do with advertising than it does with reading research.

Second, core reading programs are driven by scientific reading research *and* market research. As the lesson plan is created, everyone at the table is competing for space on the page. For example, the university-based authors are trying to get their expertise in ELL instruction, comprehension instruction, and differentiation onto the page, but they must compete with teachers who are looking for familiar ideas and who are uncomfortable with some of the newest ideas. The wants of teachers and researchers must also conform to the curriculum frameworks of the major adoption states. All these ideas must fit within a graphic design that is pleasing to the teachers and the curriculum directors who spend only an hour or so with each product as they review new core reading programs for adoption.

Third, the quality of core reading programs is influenced by the manner in which they are produced. Compressed timelines, complex products, and outsourcing to development houses affect quality. Everyone we spoke to— authors, editors, and executives in development houses—talked about the pressures of producing a core reading program. Many spoke to the changes in the publishing industry, as large multinational companies bought out independent publishers and the financial experts gained more and more control. More work is outsourced, less work is reviewed within the publishing company, and still less is reviewed by the authors. Cost has had an increasing influence on production. From the perspective of several authors and editors, quality control has declined and the few remaining programs have become more homogenous. One executive in a development house, who has

(continued)

worked for all of the major publishers, believes core reading programs have lost their unique instructional elements. At one time, Ginn and Company (later Silver Burdett Ginn) was noted by the publishing field for their in-house expertise in reading, particularly under the guidance of James Squire and their other authors, and for the knowledge of their sales staff. From the perspective of several people we interviewed, the process now has more to do with marketing and less with producing a strong educational product. Yet, our interviews clearly suggest that the influence of authors varies from one company to another.

Perhaps the most distressing trend is the increased consolidation of the publishing companies. In 1991, Chall and Squire lamented that the number of basal publishers was down to 12 from a much larger group. Today only four companies produce core reading programs: Pearson Scott Foresman, The McGraw-Hill Companies, Houghton Mifflin Harcourt, and Zaner-Bloser. The formidable barriers of high production and marketing costs prevent small companies from entering the field. The larger companies maintain their dominance by carefully meeting state standards and lobbying state adoption committees (Sewall, 2005). Once their product is adopted by California, Texas, or Florida, the larger companies can control the field. Yet, in meeting the curriculum and content standards, the programs become increasingly homogenized (Watt, 2007).

Authors and editors behind a core reading program are serious profes-sionals working under multiple constraints to produce a product that will sell and provide support to classroom teachers who seek to create strong, inde-pendent readers. They try hard to ensure that research-based practices are included in core reading programs, but the broad label of "scientifically based reading research" may be a misnomer. Core reading programs are instruc-tional tools, and in the hands of skillful and thoughtful teachers, they help produce students who read well and like to read. One author summed up the process by saying, "I think the political reality is such that compromises are made so that the program is on the state approved list. Unless the program is on the list, we can't sell the book, and I can't influence practice."

PART II

How to Examine a Core Reading Program

C hoosing a core reading program is an important and complex decision. Core reading programs bring together a wide range of texts and materials that would be difficult for any teacher or school to assemble from scratch. They present a scope and sequence for teaching skills and strategies that also would be difficult to create, especially for the novice. Finally, core reading programs provide a structure for organizing time, skills, and texts. This structure will support new teachers until they are ready to make instructional decisions for themselves.

Selecting a core reading program must be done with care. A school or district must consider instructional needs and the district and state curriculum standards. Some may feel that beginning reading instruction needs considerable attention, and therefore, they will focus on the primary grades, closely examining word-recognition instruction. Others may feel that comprehension is their need, and therefore, a close study of texts, strategy instruction, and guided reading practices is required. All publishers will argue that their core reading programs correlate closely with the respective states' standards. We urge you to conduct your own study to verify this claim.

To evaluate a core reading program well, you need to read programs with care and in depth. You need to understand the components of a core reading program and how the components work together, to read and evaluate the texts provided in the programs, and to appraise and evaluate the instructional guidance that is offered in the teacher's manual. We believe that the decision to purchase a core reading program should be made after deliberation and study. We advocate an approach that is not a survey, but an in-depth examination of the most important instructional factors. Our method derives from Julia Child, the great American chef, teacher, and cookbook author. She advocated a simple method for evaluating a new cookbook prior to purchase: Find a few recipes in the cookbook that you know well and can cook well. Compare the recipes in the cookbook you are contemplating for purchase to how you prepare those same dishes. If the cookbook you are considering matches or improves on those recipes, then you will have some confidence in the rest of the book. Compare what you teach well to the lessons provided in a core reading program. Compare the texts you value to those provided in the program.

We proceed this way with our analysis of core reading programs. First, we describe some of the best practices for teaching reading and then compare those practices to what is suggested in core reading programs. If the core reading programs match or improve upon these basic practices, then we can have some confidence in the instruction within a core reading program. In short, we want to help you become a connoisseur of reading instruction, a person with informed and astute discrimination abilities (Eisner, 2004).

Our look at core reading programs is not exhaustive; we did not use a checklist and look at every possible element or feature of a core program. Rather, we believe some aspects of a core reading program are critical and others are not. A simple checklist will reveal that all core reading programs contain many of the same components—workbooks, Big Books, assessments, CDs, advice for ELLs and struggling readers, and so forth. The workbooks and other support materials, although they might make your teaching easier, are not critical to your success with your students. We will avoid the checklist approach to examining core reading programs.

Before we begin, a word about how we assembled our information about core reading programs. First, we closely read core reading programs with copyrights from 2003, 2005, 2007, 2008, and 2009. Included in our study were Trophies (Harcourt, 2003/2005), Macmillan/McGraw-Hill Reading (Macmillan/McGraw-Hill, 2003/2005), Houghton Mifflin Reading (Houghton Mifflin, 2003/2005), Scott Foresman Reading (Pearson Scott Foresman, 2004), Open Court Reading (SRA/McGraw-Hill, 2005), Treasures (Macmillan/McGraw-Hill, 2009), and StoryTown (Harcourt, 2008). We also examined some of the intervention programs that accompany these core reading programs. We want to stress that we are not providing an overall evaluation of each core reading program but citing certain instructional elements in these programs to illustrate how programs should be evaluated and how you should conduct your own evaluation. Some of this research, especially that which focuses on reading comprehension, has been previously published or presented at national reading research conferences (Dewitz et al., 2008, 2009). Some of the material on phonics instruction was also presented at a national reading conference (Dewitz et al., 2008). The new material—our analysis of texts, differentiated instruction, reading intervention programs, and assessments—was conducted by us or our assistants, and we worked until we reached a consensus in the evaluation. Finally, we sought to clearly distinguish between factual claims about core reading programs and our opinions on how they should be used.

The chapters that follow illustrate what you should look for and how you should examine a core reading program. We begin our study in Chapter 3 by examining the texts that students will be reading. In Chapter 4, we consider how print skills are taught in core reading programs, then take a close look at the teaching of comprehension in Chapter 5. In Chapter 6, we analyze the intervention programs for struggling readers and explore the assessments that are provided in core reading programs. Chapter 7 brings these elements together and details a process for critically evaluating core reading programs. To accompany this book, we created an instrument for evaluating core reading programs and for studying them as they are piloted in your schools. We call this the Reading Guide to Program Selection (Reading GPS); it can be found on the webpage for this book at www.reading.org/general/publications/books/bk707 .aspx. This instrument will help you evaluate and select a core reading program.

CHAPTER 3

What Students Read in Core Reading Programs

Enter any large bookstore, and your eye immediately sweeps the length and breadth of the store, scanning the terrain. You are trying to determine where in the 30,000 square feet of books you need to go first. You could be in the store for one of several reasons. Perhaps you need to pick up a book that you previously ordered. Perhaps you are there to search for a title recommended by a friend or a book you need for work. You may simply be browsing among the 100,000+ titles for something to take to the beach. Browsing has a pattern. Some people start with the bestsellers to see what is hot. Others go to the remainder tables looking for last year's books at inexpensive prices. Others move to their areas of interest—cooking, golf, fantasy, travel, or periodicals. What underlies all of these decisions is choice. Interest, taste, purpose, and knowledge drive our reading decisions.

Contrast this scene with students in an elementary classroom. At 8:45 a.m., the teacher tells them to take out their reading books and turn to page 114. Everyone in the room is reading or at least looking at the same story, and they may work with this story for a day or so. Later in the week, the better readers will read a more challenging leveled book linked to the theme of the anthology selection. The average and below-average readers will read similar leveled books that are matched to their reading levels. Once a week, the students will have the opportunity to visit the school's library and take out a few books. Occasionally, the students will have an opportunity to read from the classroom library. However, choice does not drive many of the reading decisions in many elementary classrooms. Therefore, we suggest that you find ways to expand choice in your classroom. Because choice in core reading programs is limited, it is imperative for teachers and administrators to understand the texts in the programs and how to select a core reading program critically.

Reading instruction begins with text. Although the contemporary core reading program has numerous components, including a teacher's edition, student workbooks, CDs, tests, and flashcards, the heart of a core reading program is its texts. Thus, we start our look at these programs by examining the texts that students read. We believe that this should be the starting point for your examination of core reading programs as well. School districts typically keep a core reading program for seven or more years. It will probably be easier to modify how you teach the skills and strategies than it will be to change the texts that you will be using. Our review looks at texts from Trophies (Harcourt, 2003/2005), StoryTown (Harcourt, 2008), Macmillan/McGraw-Hill Reading (Macmillan/McGraw-Hill, 2003/2005), Houghton Mifflin Reading (Houghton Mifflin, 2003/2005), and Open Court Reading (SRA/McGraw-Hill, 2005). Within these texts, we examine the student anthologies, leveled books, and decodable books that are part of each weekly lesson. We did not read every selection in every program, because in some cases the texts were not available, and in all cases there is too much text to read everything. In your study of core reading programs, you may face the same obstacles. The central question driving the study of first-grade texts is, what texts make it easier for young children to learn to read? Or as Hiebert (2009) presented the question, what texts should we use in beginning reading instruction for "students that depend on school to become literate" (p. 1)?

Although much has been written about texts for beginning reading instruction, much less is known about texts for students in the upper grades and, specifically, the texts that foster the development of reading comprehension. Although some writers have attempted to link the teaching of specific strategies with specific pieces of children's literature (Harvey & Goudvis, 2007), the overall characteristics of these texts have not been critically delineated. So we will add our questions to Hiebert's (2009) and also ask, what texts support and stimulate students' growth in comprehension? Are there text characteristics that facilitate engagement, curiosity, and thought? In this chapter, we start with a description of what students read in core reading programs.

Most of our discussion about texts for beginning readers is based on the extensive research of others. Beginning in the 1990s, many researches studied how texts have changed in first-grade reading instruction. That research has continued to the present. We summarize the research in the sections that follow to help you evaluate the texts in the core reading programs you are considering. After reviewing what is known about beginning reading texts, we discuss the texts that are used to develop students' comprehension skills in the upper grades. We end by considering how you should evaluate the texts in the new core reading program you are considering or in the one you are currently using.

What You Will Learn

- How the texts in core reading programs have changed over the past 20 years
- What constitutes decodable texts
- The characteristics of text that support and promote reading comprehension
- How text sets or sequences of texts may be important to the development of comprehension

What You Will Be Able to Do

- Evaluate texts for beginning reading instruction
- Evaluate the decodability of the texts in the core program you are considering
- Evaluate texts in the upper grades for interest and engagement
- Evaluate the quality of the text sets in a lesson or a unit that should build students' knowledge

The ideas in this chapter will help you complete an evaluation of the texts in core reading programs. Online at www.reading.org/general/publications/books/bk707.aspx, you can find our Reading GPS, an instrument that will guide you through the process of evaluating the texts in a core reading program. The Reading GPS and this chapter are meant to be used together.

Texts in Core Reading Programs: What Students Read

All contemporary core reading programs within our examination contain a student anthology, selections of small leveled books (sometimes called little books), decodable books, and Big Books. The small leveled books that accompany each anthology selection usually adhere to the theme or topic of the lesson, but offer additional reading for above-, on-, and below-level readers. Decodable books are usually little books that may be used to teach specific spelling or phonics patterns. Big Books are large in size, containing selections of children's literature. These texts allow the teacher to conduct group activities with the text in larger form so that all of the students can easily view it. In most programs, this array of texts is available for beginning readers.

In kindergarten, the typical core reading program provides in each lesson a Big Book, a library book or picture book read by the teacher, one or two decodable books, and three leveled readers. The Big Book and the library book are examples of authentic literature, because they most likely were published as trade books before being included in a core reading program. These books exist to develop vocabulary, expand students' knowledge, and model comprehension strategies. The decodable books and leveled readers provide practice with the pattern taught in the teacher-directed lessons and enable teachers to differentiate instruction.

In first grade, the newest core reading programs have an anthology with three reading selections for each week. A short selection introduces some of the new words and phonics patterns. This is followed by the main reading selection, then a poem or nonfiction selection closes out the readings. The weekly lesson also includes a decodable book and four leveled readers for below-, on-, and above-level students and for ELLs. The decodable books stress and repeat the phonics patterns for the week, whereas the little books, leveled using Lexiles (The Lexile Framework for Reading, 2009) or guided reading (Fountas & Pinnell, 1996), stress connections to science and social studies.

In the upper grades, the core reading programs also consist of a student anthology and a number of leveled books. The student anthologies in the newest core reading programs (published after 2007) differ from their predecessors in several ways. The student book is no longer just a collection of reading selections. Each lesson begins with a focus on the skill for the week. The skill is explained and is accompanied by a short paragraph and small graphic organizer that can be used for teacher or student modeling. Next, the new vocabulary is introduced via a word list and a short selection that highlights the use of the words in context. Before the main selection is read, the genre is explained and the skill is mentioned again. After reading the main selection, students are presented with comprehension questions, information about the author and the illustrator, a poem or nonfiction social studies or science connection, suggestions for vocabulary review, fluency practice, and finally lessons on writing in response to reading. What is striking about the new anthologies is the stronger emphasis on reading skills within the student anthology. The inclusion of skill instruction in the student anthology was a requirement of the 2008 Texas textbook guidelines, which we discussed in Chapter 2.

Another way to describe the texts that students read is to study the genres covered through the texts in these programs. Table 2 presents an analysis of the

Table 2. Percentages of Reading Selections in Each Genre in Selected Core Reading Programs

	Realistic Fiction	Historical Fiction	Fantasy	Folk Tales	Biography/ Autobiography	Exposition or Informational Text	Mixed Genre	Plays	Poetry
Trophies (Harcourt, 2003)									
Grades 1 & 2	34.6	0.0	26.9	7.7	0.0	23.0	0.0	0.0	7.7
Grades 3, 4, & 5	29.5	16.8	6.5	11.8	8.5	19.2	0.0	0.0	7.7
StoryTown (Harcourt, 2008)									
Grades 1 & 2	21.2	0.0	23.9	2.8	1.9	37.9	0.0	1.7	10.6
Grades 3, 4, & 5	11.6	6.2	2.7	9.8	10.7	36.6	0.0	11.6	10.7
Open Court (SRA/McGraw-Hill, 2005)									
Grades 1 & 2	37.1	0.0	19.7	16.7	2.8	14.7	0.0	4.5	4.5
Grades 3, 4, & 5	30.4	8.7	4.9	10.8	16.7	16.7	0.0	2.0	9.9
Treasures (Macmillan/McGraw-Hill, 2009)									
Grades 1 & 2	17.9	0.0	14.2	5.4	7.7	41.6	3.8	3.6	5.8
Grades 3, 4, & 5	15.8	8.4	6.9	7.3	6.5	45.7	0.0	2.5	6.9

genres that students read in the student anthology but not in the leveled books. We read all the selections and classified them into one of the following genres: realistic fiction, historical fiction, fantasy (making no distinction between science fiction and fantasy), folk tales, biography/autobiography, exposition or informational text, mixed genre (information within a narrative structure that fits more than one genre), plays, and poetry. When looking at the texts in core reading programs, we examined four programs: Trophies (2003), StoryTown (2008), Open Court Reading (2005), and Treasures (Macmillan/McGraw-Hill, 2009). The most dramatic change from 2003 to 2008 is the inclusion of more informational text and a decline in realistic fiction and historical fiction in the upper grades, as well as fewer fantasy selections. When Flood and Lapp (1986) looked at basals, expository text and biography accounted for a bit more than 15% of the pages in a core reading program. The increase in informational text since then may be seen as a response to research by Duke (2000) documenting the lack of informational text in primary classrooms and to new state guidelines calling for added emphasis on reading in the content areas.

Texts for Beginning Reading

There is no more controversial topic in reading instruction than the texts students use as they learn to read. Sixty years ago, core reading programs employed texts that stressed the repetition of high-frequency words both within and between stories. These were the "Dick and Jane" stories that embraced carefully crafted reading texts over "authentic literature" or natural sentence structures. The producers of these texts determined which words students needed to know and repeated them frequently. Gradually over time in some core reading programs, these first-grade texts changed. Some core reading programs, but not all, began to stress the use and repetition of words that repeated phonics elements (Juel & Roper/Schneider, 1985). Today we call these decodable texts.

With the adoption of new core reading programs in the early 1990s and the rising influence of both the whole-language movement and literature-based instruction, core reading programs abandoned controlled vocabulary and replaced it with more authentic literature. Selecting stories from well-known children's authors, the core reading programs were less concerned with the number of words in a story, the frequency of the words, or the repetition of words. It was believed that the natural language patterns of authentic literature coupled with the intrinsic appeal of these stories would motivate students to learn to read.

The texts in the student anthology are selected because they are authentic children's literature. By *authentic*, we mean that these texts were written to engage students and foster their interest in high-quality literature. These texts were not created for the purpose of teaching students to read. The stand-alone decodable books and leveled books, if they were part of the core reading program, existed to help students apply and practice phonics principles. By the late 1990s, most core reading programs had both a student anthology created from authentic literature and a series of leveled little books.

In the early 1990s, Jim Hoffman and his colleagues (Hoffman et al., 1994) compared first-grade texts found in basals from the late 1980s to those found in basals from the early 1990s. These texts were compared on a number of dimensions, including number of words students had to read, the number of unique words, readability, genre, decodability, and interest or engagement. Overall, in the six years between 1987 and 1993, the first-grade reading selections changed substantially. Table 3 reflects some of the changes he reported.

Between 1987 and 1993, basal reading programs changed in a number of important ways. First, the students read fewer total words during the first-grade year. In the late 1980s, students read more than 17,000 words, and six years later first graders were only reading about 12,000 to 14,000 words. These averages varied, and in some programs from the early 1990s, especially those

Table 3. Word and Sentence Analysis of Texts in Basal Readers

Criteria	1986/1987 Programs Mean (Range)	1993 Programs Without Trade Books Mean (Range)	1993 Programs With Trade Books Mean (Range)
Total number of words	17,319 (16,865–17,282)	12,265 (6,629–17,102)	14,272 (9,569–22,728)
Number of unique words	962 (847–1,051)	1,680 (1,171–2,238)	1,834 (1,536–2,458)
Readability	1.00 (1.00–1.00)	1.69 (1.28–2.14)	1.52 (1.22–1.96)
Syllables per word	1.117 (1.071–1.135)	1.200 (1.190–1.220)	1.195 (1.177–1.215)
Words per sentence	6.8 (6.5–6.9)	7.8 (7.2–8.4)	7.7 (7.2–8.2)

Note. From Hoffman, J.V., McCarthey, S.J., Abbott, J., Christian, C., Corman, L., Curry, C., et al. (1994). So what's new in the new basals? A focus on first grade. *Journal of Reading Behavior, 26*(1), 47–73. Reprinted with permission by the Literacy Research Association (formerly the National Reading Conference) and James V. Hoffman.

that included sets of trade books, the total number of words that students read equaled or exceeded what they read in the older programs. Students, however, had to learn more unique words, indicating that the vocabulary of these first-grade books was expanding. In the 1980s, students had to learn over 900 unique words in a school year; six years later, the basal reading programs had almost doubled the vocabulary load. It is not surprising that other things changed as well. The readability level of the stories, sentence length, and the number of words with more than one syllable all increased. In a number of ways, these new first-grade stories made greater demands on the students.

Hoffman and his colleagues (1994) reported other changes found in these basal reading programs. Because these new programs stressed literary characteristics over vocabulary control, the decodability of words declined while the literary characteristics of the programs increased. These programs had more two-syllable words, more words with complex vowel combinations, and fewer words with simple consonant and vowel patterns. Conversely, these new programs employed almost exclusively children's literature from original sources or minimally adapted literature. Hoffman and his colleagues judged these texts to be more engaging than their predecessors. These collections of texts were also more predictable than their predecessors, using greater amounts of rhyme and repeating text patterns. The selections contained more complex plots, exhibited greater character development, and required more interpretations on the part of the reader. The first-grade stories had changed considerably. The selections were more engaging to read, but word-recognition demands were increasing.

Rise of Decodable Text. In 1998, Texas issued a new proclamation for basal readers that were to be adopted in 2000. With this Texas proclamation, the reading wars (Pikulski, 1997; Strickland, 1995) swung away from an emphasis on the literary qualities of the texts back to a focus on skills. Texas called for decodable texts in the first grade. Publishers also began to incorporate more little leveled books into their lesson plans. At first these little books provided the decoding practice while the texts in the student anthology maintained a literary focus. Hoffman and his colleagues (Hoffman, Sailors, & Patterson, 2002) again analyzed the first-grade readers in these new programs and compared them to the previous analysis (Hoffman et al., 1994).

The 2000 basal reading programs that Hoffman and his colleagues studied revealed significant changes and a new set of questions (Hoffman et al., 2002). These new basal reading programs controlled vocabulary more tightly than did programs in 1993. The programs introduced fewer unique words than the 1993 basals, but still more unique words than the 1987 programs. The stories in the 2000 programs were not as predictable as the 1993 stories. That means that the stories contained fewer text patterns that supported the reader's word recognition attempts. In a predictable book, the students can anticipate the words and do not need to rely on decoding strategies. "Brown Bear, Brown Bear, What do you see? I see a red bird looking at me" (Martin, 1992, n.p.) is an example of a predictable book pattern, because the repetition of the lines and the pictures **helps the reader anticipate the words. Predictable texts also have their draw-**backs. Many words in the texts are what some have called *singletons*, meaning the words in the story or leveled book occur only once. Lacking any repetition in the text, these words are difficult for children to learn. One researcher found that after 10 readings of a book, less than 5% of the words were remembered (Johnston, 2000). Predictable text does not support independent word recognition (Cunningham, 2005).

Although the texts in the 2000 basals contained more decodable words and met the Texas guidelines, Hoffman and colleagues' (2002) research raised an important question about what the term *decodability* means. By Texas law, decodability meant that 80% of the words in the stories must contain phonic elements that had been previously taught in the lessons. But that definition does not speak to the number of repetitions of phonics elements in a story or repetition of those phonics patterns across adjacent stories. By Texas law, all of the new 2000 programs contained selections that were very decodable; the phonics patterns in each story had been previously taught. By the other measure of decodability, the frequency of decodable words, the programs were still more decodable than their 1993 counterparts, but the stories may not have been as decodable as struggling readers needed (Adams, 2009).

The findings of Hoffman and his colleagues (2002) are largely supported by the research of Foorman, Francis, Davidson, Harm, and Griffin (2004) with one important added understanding. Basal reading programs of the late 1990s and early 2000s varied considerably in terms of decodability. Foorman and her colleagues found that in one basal program, 46% of the unique words were decodable, whereas in another 94% were. They also reported that programs varied in the number of new words introduced. One program introduced 75 new words in the first six weeks with 50% of these words presented only once. Two other programs introduced 289 words (70.6% of words presented only once), and another introduced 992 words (71.1% presented only once) in the first six weeks of instruction. As Hiebert and Martin (2009) summarized, repetition of words and phonic patterns is important for beginning and struggling readers, but researchers are far from being able to set specific and optimal guidelines for the design of beginning reading texts.

Adams (2009) argued persuasively for decodable texts, especially in the first half of first grade. Decodable texts ensure that the process of learning to read makes sense to the students. When the same words that students have learned to decode and blend in isolation appear in the stories students are reading, the process of learning to read has a logical consistency. Decodable texts' second advantage is that "they engage children in attending carefully left to right, to the spellings and sounds of new words they read" (p. 32). Adams's argument suggests that there must be consistency between the letter–sound patterns taught in lessons and the words children encounter in the texts—the Texas definition. Moreover, these phonic patterns need to be repeated often so that students can practice their sequential blending skills.

Evaluating Beginning Text. All the research we presented in the preceding section has one particular problem: It was conducted by highly skilled investigators using computer programs designed to assess a broad number of factors about words in beginning reading texts. Using these programs, researchers could carefully quantify the number of unique words in first-grade texts, the total number of words, and the percentage of decodable words, whether they are linked to instruction or not. These analytic tools are not available to school district authorities, who must select from a few programs the one they believe will most likely assist their students, or as Hiebert (2009) stated, "students who depend upon school to become literate" (p. 1). These tools were not available to us, nor were we able to obtain all the texts a student might read in first grade. Therefore, we have devised a short analysis system that will give a committee studying beginning texts a modestly systematic means of evaluating these texts.

We began this evaluation system acknowledging the many limitations of the process. First, when you receive your samples from the publishing company, you will be given complete student editions for first through fifth grades. You will receive only one of six volumes of the teacher's edition in first grade, and you will have only a sample of the many decodable and leveled books available with the program. Second, you will not have access to a sophisticated computer-based evaluation system. Yet with these caveats in mind, we suggest the following procedures:

- Request from the publisher more examples of decodable and leveled books than your sample kit provides.

- Read the first book in first grade, which is typically divided into five or six lessons. Each of these lessons will have three reading selections with two focused on introducing sight words and phonics patterns. The third selection might be a poem or a nonfiction selection that does not stress the repetition of the vocabulary of the preceding stories.

- As you read, write down each unique word as it occurs in the story. This will tell you how many words are introduced in the first book or unit.

- Every time a word is repeated, place a check mark by the word. As you proceed through the book, you will gain a sense of how often words are repeated, and you can make comparisons across programs.

- You can apply some of the principles that were stressed in the research we reviewed. Specifically, you can compare programs and determine which ones introduce the greatest and least number of words. You can compare programs to determine which program provides more repetition on critical sight words and important phonics patterns.

Table 4 is a sample of this simple text analysis system, which we used on lessons in Macmillan/McGraw-Hill's Treasures (2009) and Harcourt's StoryTown (2008). In each program, the lesson consisted of two selections with a controlled vocabulary and one selection, either a poem or a nonfiction selection, in which vocabulary control was neglected in favor of literary qualities or information.

The analysis outlined in Table 4, albeit simple and incomplete, suggests several trends about the two programs. In one lesson, Harcourt introduces 44 words, of which 24 are repeated only once. Macmillan/McGraw-Hill introduces 33 words of which 25 are repeated only once. In Treasures, the students will encounter more words with fewer repetitions, whereas in StoryTown they will encounter fewer words with the same number repeated only once. Each program puts a different burden on the students and presents a different challenge to the teacher. Both programs introduce the short *a* pattern, but StoryTown seems to practice that vowel in more words with greater frequency. We suggest that a district adoption committee continue this analysis for several more lessons, trying to discern the number of words and phonics patterns taught and their frequency. The committee should also include the decodable texts in this analysis if the publisher is willing to provide them. An adoption committee will have to consider

Table 4. Analyzing Word and Word Pattern Repetitions in One Lesson of Beginning Reading Texts in Two Core Reading Programs

Treasures (Macmillan/McGraw-Hill, 2009)		StoryTown (Harcourt, 2008)	
can	✓✓✓✓✓✓	tag	✓✓✓✓✓✓
pat	✓✓	Sam	✓✓
jump	✓✓✓✓✓✓	tan	✓
up	✓✓✓	can	✓✓✓✓✓✓✓✓✓✓✓✓✓
down	✓✓	Dan	✓
not	✓✓✓	Pam	✓
look	✓✓	Pat	✓
Pam	✓✓✓✓✓✓	who	✓
and	✓✓	Dad	✓
Sam	✓✓✓✓✓✓✓✓	I	✓✓
like	✓✓	tap	✓✓✓✓✓✓✓✓✓
to	✓	you	✓✓✓✓
play	✓✓	help	✓✓
ran	✓✓	we	✓✓✓
go	✓	now	✓
with	✓	let's	✓
at	✓	puppies	✓
fly	✓	wag	✓
what	✓	bunnies	✓
day	✓✓	up	✓
is	✓✓	kittens	✓
the	✓	pounce	✓
best	✓✓	don't	✓
I	✓✓✓✓✓✓✓✓	stop	✓
Monday	✓	birds	✓
like	✓✓✓✓✓	flap	✓
ride	✓	bugs	✓
my	✓✓✓✓	crawl	✓
horse	✓	turtles	✓
and	✓	hide	✓
Tuesday	✓	do	✓
Wednesday	✓	it	✓
family	✓	all	✓
has	✓		
pizza	✓		
Thursday	✓		
help	✓		
mom	✓		
plant	✓		
my	✓		
friends	✓		
Friday	✓		
your	✓		
day	✓		
Total words 44		**Total words 33**	

these word issues against other criteria like genre, accessibility, and engagement before deciding if one or more core reading programs will meet its needs.

Texts for Comprehension: The Upper Grades

If it is relatively easy to locate criteria for evaluating texts used in beginning reading instruction, it is much more difficult to locate research or even opinion on what are the best kinds of texts that will develop the comprehension skills and strategies for older elementary students. We begin this exploration of upper grade texts by considering the characteristics of the texts we would use to help students build their comprehension skills. First, we would select texts that would hold the interests of our students and engage them while they read. Second, we would look for texts and text sets that build knowledge. Finally, we want some texts that present a challenge to the thinking and problem-solving skills of the students. Comprehension is thinking with text, and students need something substantive to think about.

Characteristics of Texts That Build Comprehension Skills. Comprehension is not a passive activity, because the reader needs to locate and construct meaning. Often this requires effort, and that effort will be rewarded if the text is interesting and engaging. More than 20 years ago, Bruce (1984) examined the stories in core reading programs, studying their engaging qualities and comparing them to quality children's literature. He studied three characteristics of stories that he felt would produce engagement and interest. He argued that interest and engagement are created by the degree of inside view, by the point of view of the narrator, and most of all, by conflict. The more the hero or heroine has to battle the environment, threats and challenges from others, and his or her own internal demons, the more interesting the narrative.

For example, *Click, Clack, Moo: Cows That Type* (Cronin, 2000), a story included in the second-grade Treasures (2009) program, offers the reader interpersonal conflict and implied environmental conflict—the cows are cold. They must examine their environment and use the tools necessary to solve the conflict. Hence, they go on strike against Farmer Brown, refusing to produce milk. They use their neutral colleagues, the ducks, to deliver their typewritten messages to the distraught farmer.

> Farmer Brown has a problem. His cows like to type. All day long he hears...
> Click, clack, MOO. Click, clack, MOO, Clickety, clack, MOO.

At first, he couldn't believe his ears. Cows that type? Impossible!

Click, clack, MOO. Click, clack, MOO, Clickety, clack, MOO.

Then he couldn't believe his eyes.

"Dear Farmer Brown,
The barn is very cold at night. We'd like some electric blankets.
Sincerely,
The Cows."

It was bad enough the cows had found the old typewriter in the barn, now they wanted electric blankets!

"No way," said Farmer Brown. "No electric blankets." So the cows went on strike. They left a note on the barn door.

"Sorry. We're closed. No milk today." (n.p. Reprinted with the permission of Simon & Schuster Books for Young Readers, an imprint of Simon & Schuster Children's Publishing Division, from *Click, Clack, Moo: Cows That Type* by Doreen Cronin. Text copyright © Doreen Cronin.)

When Bruce (1984) studied stories in core reading programs, he examined the amount of environmental, interpersonal, and internal conflict. He found that the amount of conflict and the amounts of different kinds of conflict in basal stories were lower than what he found in trade books. This was especially true for books at the primary level, but not the intermediate level. It is important to note, though, that Bruce conducted his research before well-known children's literature was included in basal readers (Hoffman et al., 1994).

Bruce (1984) also studied the amount of inside view employed by writers. Inside view allows the reader to enter into the thoughts, feelings, and beliefs of the character. We gain this insight from the inferences we make, the direct statements and actions of the characters, and what other characters say and do. The following example from a George and Martha story called "Split Pea Soup" (Marshall, 1974) reflects a high amount of inside view:

Martha was very fond of making split pea soup. Sometimes she made it all day long. Pots and pots of split pea soup.

If there was one thing that George was not fond of, it was split pea soup. As a matter of fact, George hated split pea soup more than anything else in the world. But it was so hard to tell Martha.

One day after George had eaten ten bowls of Martha's soup, he said to himself, "I just can't stand another bowl. Not even another spoonful."

So, while Martha was out in the kitchen, George carefully poured the rest of his soup into his loafers under the table. "Now she will think I have eaten it."

But Martha was watching from the kitchen. (pp. 10–14)

In this excerpt, we are privy to the thoughts of each character, providing us with an inside view of the characters and the surrounding situation. The amount of inside view can vary greatly, but Bruce found that trade books contained a greater amount of inside view than did basal stories. This trend was most pronounced in grades 1 though 3, with the differences between basal stories and trade books decreasing in the upper grades. He further found considerable variability among the three basal programs he studied. Finally, Bruce studied narration and found that trade books employed more first-person narration, in which the author is in the story, compared with basal stories that employed more third-person narration, in which the narrator is outside the story describing the action. Engaged narration pulls the reader into the story.

The second thing we know about the development of comprehension is the importance of prior knowledge. The more knowledge that the reader can bring to the page, the better he or she will understand the text. Knowledge helps the reader in several ways (Anderson & Pearson, 1984). First, prior knowledge is the building block of inferences. When the writer leaves something unstated, he or she counts on the reader to fill in the gaps. When the sentence reads, "Mary looked at her menu for the cheapest entrée, while John gazed lovingly in her eyes," we know that they are in a restaurant, Mary is concerned with price, and John is concerned with Mary. Prior knowledge is the building block of inferences; without prior knowledge, most text would not be comprehensible.

Prior knowledge provides a guide and a structure for determining what is important and for summarizing what we have read. When a student is reading about light during science, having some prior knowledge about reflection and refraction helps the student solidify understanding and sort important ideas from tangential digressions. The concepts of waves, particles, reflection, and refraction also help the reader formulate an organized summary of the passage. Finally, prior knowledge provides the foundation for deepening understanding. The more you know about a topic, the more you can build further understandings. Given the importance of prior knowledge, a core reading program should build students' knowledge before they read a selection, and each selection should provide knowledge that facilitates the understanding of the next selection. Walsh (2003) argued that the selections in core reading programs are loosely bound together, and these units do not systematically build the students' knowledge.

The third factor that affects comprehension is text difficulty. We don't mean readability, which is a measure of vocabulary and sentence complexity, but rather text coherence—how ideas hang together. In a coherent text, one clause or idea is closely linked to the next through the use of markers, pronouns (*he, she, it*), conjunctions (*and, but, nor, because*), adjectives (*few, more*), and adverbs (*next, last, eventually*). These words signal the relationship between ideas within and across sentences. The clearer these relationships are, the easier the comprehension.

Compare the opening lines of *Maniac Magee* (Spinelli, 1990) to those in *Because of Winn-Dixie* (DiCamillo, 2000):

> They say Maniac Magee was born in a dump. They say his stomach was a cereal box and his heart a sofa spring.
>
> They say he kept an eight-inch cockroach on a leash and that rats stood guard over him while he slept.
>
> They say if you knew he was coming and you sprinkled salt on the ground and he ran over it, within two or three blocks he would be as slow as everybody else.
>
> They say. (Spinelli, 1990, p. 1)

> My name is India Opal Buloni, and last summer my daddy, the preacher, sent me to the store for a box of macaroni-and-cheese, some white rice, and two tomatoes and I came back with a dog. This is what happened: I walked into the produce section of the Winn-Dixie grocery store to pick out my two tomatoes and I almost bumped right into the store manager. He was standing there all red-faced, screaming and waving his arms around. (DiCamillo, 2000, p. 7)

Maniac Magee demands more work on the part of the reader to establish coherence and build connections. The novel begins with a pronoun without a reference, and the reader must infer the antecedent. Just who does the indefinite pronoun *they* connect to? In contrast, the narration is clear and direct in *Because of Winn-Dixie*: Opal is the narrator and the main character, so this will be her story. Research on text coherence (Halliday & Hasan, 1976) has suggested that texts that are more coherent are easier to comprehend, but with one qualification. It appears that good readers, especially those with high amounts of prior knowledge, comprehend better and at higher levels when challenged by less coherent text (McNamara, Kintsch, Songer, & Kintsch, 1996). They must infer relationships that are not clearly stated. Unfortunately, we lack the ability within the scope of this book to present a system for evaluating the coherence of a text. However, we do suggest that as you read the texts in a core reading program, you should look for clear direct texts that will support the less proficient reader's comprehension and texts that are more challenging, having lower levels of coherence and inducing the good reader to more active and deeper levels of processing.

Evaluating Texts for Comprehension. Because each core reading program is filled with hundreds of reading selections, we decided to sample texts in each program, and we suggest you do the same when considering a new core program. We focused our analysis on grades 3 and 5, reading all the texts, main anthology selections, and leveled readers in two of the six units in each program. To evaluate texts for comprehension in core reading programs, we studied Trophies (2003/2005), Macmillan/McGraw-Hill Reading (2003/2005), and Houghton Mifflin Reading (2003/2005).

When we evaluated the leveled books, we wanted to know the length of each book and the consistency of the genre and content between the main anthology selection and the little leveled books. Genre consistency is necessary to develop an understanding of a genre. If the teacher's goal is to help the students understand the characteristics of a particular genre, then some repeated practice with the genre is needed within one week's lesson. Topic consistency is necessary to develop comprehension. When children cover the same topics by reading several texts within a lesson or across several lessons, their knowledge grows. When a unit jumps from one topic to another, comprehension is impaired by not building on prior knowledge. Two of us read each story and rated its interest level, type of conflict, and amount of inside view. The results of the two independent reviews were averaged to produce the following data.

Length. There is a relationship between how much students read and how much they grow as readers. Allington (1977, p. 57) pleaded with teachers and parents when he said, "If they don't read much, how are they ever gonna get good?" When Anderson, Wilson, and Fielding (1988) studied out-of-school reading, they found that growth in reading ability could be attributed to the amount of book reading children completed at home. Stanovich (1986) argued that the "poor get poorer" in reading skills in part because they read less. This prompted us to explore how much students read within a core reading program. Because all students read or listen to the main anthology selection, we examined how many words good, average, or weak readers would read in their leveled books in three of the core reading programs. Houghton Mifflin makes the analysis easy and prints the word count at the beginning of each book. For the other two series, we counted the number of words in all leveled books used

Table 5. Average Word Count for Above-, On-, and Below-Level Leveled Books in Two Units of Selected Core Reading Programs

	Macmillan/McGraw-Hill Reading (Macmillan/McGraw-Hill, 2005)			Trophies (Harcourt, 2005)			Houghton Mifflin Reading (Houghton Mifflin, 2005)		
	Above Level	On Level	Below Level	Above Level	On Level	Below Level	Above Level	On Level	Below Level
Grade 3	1,333	999	778	1,121	1,025	548	974	651	260
Grade 5	2,289	1,694	1,456	1,957	1,692	1,150	1,865	1,095	633

in two units of instruction. Table 5 presents the average word count for above-, on-, and below-level leveled books from the three programs.

The results are clear and easy to interpret. Fifth-grade students read more words per book than do third-grade students. The students who read the below-level readers will read half the number of words than the above-level students. The differences in the amount of reading are most pronounced in the Houghton Mifflin program. In both grade levels, the word count of the below-level book is a third or less of the word count in the above-level book. The savvy teacher will need to find other books and articles to supplement the reading diet of the struggling readers. A curriculum committee should ask publishers of core reading programs for the word counts of the leveled books in their program. Students who read more encounter more words, and students who practice more decoding build more vocabulary and are exposed to more ideas.

Text Interest. We examined the interest level of the reading selection by using a 1–5 rating scale developed by Hoffman et al. (1994). A high score of 5 reflected ideas that were personally, socially, and culturally important and concepts that stimulated thinking and feeling. Table 6 presents the results for the fifth-grade units, and Table 7 shows the results for the third-grade units.

We rated most of these stories as moderately interesting, which means the ideas were personally, socially, and culturally relevant. There was a development of ideas and themes, and the stories stimulated thinking and feeling (Hoffman et al., 1994). There did not appear to be much variation among the three reading programs in the interest rating of the reading selections, nor were there wide fluctuations in interest within a unit. The main anthology stories were consistently rated as more interesting than the leveled books that accompanied them, which is not surprising. A publisher has to commission approximately 100 or more leveled books for each grade level, whereas there are at most only 30 major anthology selections. Consistently producing many interesting and informative stories is a challenge.

Table 6. Mean Rating of Interest in Reading Selections of Two Units of Selected Core Reading Programs, Fifth Grade

	Macmillan/McGraw-Hill Reading (Macmillan/McGraw-Hill, 2003/2005)		Trophies (Harcourt, 2003/2005)		Houghton Mifflin Reading (Houghton Mifflin, 2003/2005)	
	Unit 1	Unit 3	Theme 1	Theme 3	Theme 1	Theme 3
Main anthology selection	4.00	3.33	3.10	3.70	3.87	3.75
Above-level reader	2.75	2.55	3.00	3.37	3.50	3.00
On-level reader	3.00	2.80	3.00	3.00	3.13	3.13
Below-level reader	3.00	3.15	3.00	2.75	3.00	3.38

Note. The range is 1–5, with 5 being the highest possible score.

Table 7. Mean Rating of Interest in Reading Selections of Two Units of Selected Core Reading Programs, Third Grade

	Macmillan/McGraw-Hill Reading (Macmillan/McGraw-Hill, 2005)		Trophies (Harcourt, 2005)		Houghton Mifflin Reading (Houghton Mifflin, 2005)	
	Unit 1	Unit 3	Theme 1	Theme 3	Theme 1	Theme 3
Main anthology selection	3.37	4.00	3.40	3.40	3.30	3.25
Above-level reader	3.75	3.75	2.66	2.80	3.65	2.87
On-level reader	2.75	3.25	3.00	2.80	3.00	2.87
Below-level reader	3.00	2.75	2.67	N/A	2.60	2.50

Note. The range is 1–5, with 5 being the highest possible score.

We were able to support our interest ratings by taking a closer look at just the narrative selections in the student anthologies. As Bruce (1984) did over 20 years ago, we examined the amount and type of conflict in the stories and the amount of inside view. Stories like *Officer Buckle and Gloria* (Rathmann, 1995), found in Houghton Mifflin Reading (2003/2005), and *Ramona Forever* (Cleary, 1984), found in Macmillan/McGraw-Hill Reading (2003/2005), had both conflict and high inside view. *Officer Buckle and Gloria* tells the story of a very dull and dry police officer who has to give safety speeches to elementary students. He is boring and routinely ignored until he brings along his dog, Gloria, who does stunts, poses, and mocks the officer's talks in numerous ways. There is physical conflict and slapstick, as people fall and collide, and an insider view, as we learn about the students' boredom, Officer Buckle's serious goals, and Gloria's mocking pratfall. In contrast, *A Very Important Day* (Herold, 1995), in Houghton Mifflin Reading, is a series of vignettes about 10 families in New York City preparing to go to a naturalization ceremony to become U.S. citizens. There is little insider view, the reader quickly learns that everyone is excited about an upcoming event, and there is no conflict except for a light snowfall. The program writers set no foundation for the concept of citizenship, and instead, they have students review what New York City is like. Those stories that we gave a high interest rating had significant conflict and the author took the reader inside the thoughts and feelings of the characters.

Knowledge Development. To explore how well the texts and the structure of the comprehension units develop students' knowledge, we explored three factors in the units. First, we wanted to understand how well the main anthology selection and the three leveled readers built knowledge in each lesson. Do these four texts all revolve around a similar topic, or do the texts cover different topics and themes? Second, we looked at topic consistency across the lessons within a theme. Does the knowledge the reader acquires from the first selection in an instructional unit help him or her understand the following selections in the unit? Third, we examined the consistency of the genres students read in a lesson. If the main anthology selection is fantasy, do the leveled readers continue with that genre or switch the focus to other genres? Genre knowledge likely promotes knowledge construction (Pappas & Pettegrew, 1998). It is likely that struggling readers would benefit from focusing on one consistent genre, mastering its structure and characteristics, before moving on.

When we examined the instructional units in core reading programs, we found great variability within and between programs in their cohesiveness.

Some units stick tightly to a unifying topic, building students' knowledge from one selection to another, while other units are little more than a loose collection under a vague title or theme. Unit 5 of the fourth-grade Open Court Reading (2005) anthology is tightly written and focuses all six of its informational reading selections on communication. Students read about animal communication, commercials, the invention of printing, communicating with great apes, and Louis Braille. Unit 5 in the fourth-grade Trophies (2003/2005) anthology contains five selections that have little relationship to each other. The unit begins with a nonfiction selection about firefighters, followed by a personal narrative about families achieving their U.S. citizenship. Next is a nonfiction piece about the saguaro cactus, followed by a realistic fiction story of a young girl living with her migrant family. Finally, the students read an autobiography about the celebrations of a Mexican family. These five selections are under the theme community ties. Although the desert life around a Saguaro cactus might be considered a community, that selection builds no knowledge that will be useful when the students next read about a young girl in a migrant family. In order to build knowledge, the selections in a unit must cohere.

A second level of knowledge building can occur within a lesson when students read the main anthology selection and then one or more of the leveled books. We studied the lessons for grades 3 and 5 in three core reading programs: Houghton Mifflin Reading (2003/2005), Trophies (2003/2005), and Macmillan/ McGraw-Hill Reading (2003/2005). For each grade level, we studied two units of instruction. We could not study the most recent programs from these publishers, because we were unable to locate complete sets of leveled texts.

We read each main anthology selection, determined its topic and theme, and then read each of the three leveled books. If the main anthology selection and the leveled book covered the same topic, we assigned the book a score of 2 out of 2. If the anthology selection and leveled book were related but the topics or themes were not perfectly aligned, then we assigned a score of 1. Finally, if the anthology selection and the leveled book were unrelated in any way, we assigned a score of 0. Because each lesson contains three leveled books, a tightly integrated lesson would receive a score of 6, or 2 points for each book. Table 8 indicates the average level of topic consistency in the weekly reading lessons.

We examined 12 themes in the same three core reading programs. There is considerable variation between and within programs in how tightly connected the content of the leveled books are to the main anthology selections. Houghton Mifflin has a number of tightly integrated lessons in Theme 3 for third grade.

Table 8. Average Level of Topic Consistency in Reading Lessons Between the Anthology Selection and the Leveled Books of Selected Core Reading Programs

	Macmillan/McGraw-Hill Reading (Macmillan/McGraw-Hill, 2005)		Trophies (Harcourt, 2005)		Houghton Mifflin Reading (Houghton Mifflin, 2005)	
	Unit 1	Unit 3	Theme 1	Theme 3	Theme 1	Theme 2
Grade 3	2.00	1.75	3.10	3.40	1.70	5.00
Grade 5	2.00	1.50	3.40	4.20	3.75	3.00

Note. The range is 0–6, with 6 being the highest possible score.

In the first lesson, the students read *The Keeping Quilt* (Polacco, 1988), a story about a Russian family and how it brought its old traditions to its new life in the United States. The three leveled books cover very similar themes. In one, a Jewish family shares its traditions around a Shabbat (Friday night dinner) table. Another leveled reader tells the story of grandpa, a musician, and his journey North playing the guitar. The final selection focuses on a baseball card and what a child learns about his grandfather's past from the card. In this lesson, after reading three different books, each child can bring to the table what they have learned about the telling of family stories and the importance of family history.

Just as some lessons and units are tightly structured, helping children build knowledge, others are not. One lesson from Macmillan/McGraw-Hill Reading for third grade illustrates a problem that teachers and students might face. The anthology selection is *Two Bad Ants*, a fantasy by Chris Van Allsburg (1988). That is followed by three leveled books: a nonfiction selection about what our world looks like under a microscope, a thinly disguised takeoff on "Jack and the Beanstalk," and an information book that introduces the concepts of big and small (e.g., large trees vs. bonsai, large plants vs. small plants). This lesson creates problems for the teacher. It is hard to determine what common concepts will assist the comprehension of the students reading these diverse stories. Similarly, after reading *Two Bad Ants*, the student has experienced some very good fantasy, but that does not help him or her understand a microscopic world or a common fairy tale.

The last aspect of knowledge development that we explored was the consistency of genre within a unit. We reasoned that if a student started a lesson reading a realistic fiction selection, then focusing on that same genre in the leveled books would support the student and help him or her learn that genre. Students would be looking for the same text structure and features. Conversely, if a lesson begins with a fantasy, like the story *Little Grunt and the Big Egg* (dePaola, 1990), a fantasy about a boy and a dinosaur, and then the accompanying leveled books are nonfiction informational selections, the students have poor preparation for the structure and the ideas in the nonfiction selection. We again examined two units from three different programs to look at the genre consistency within reading lessons. If the anthology selection began with realistic fiction and the leveled books were also fiction we judged that the lesson had some consistency and rated it a 2. If the lesson moved from realistic fiction to historical fiction, we judged that reader might have more difficulty, because the text features and structures are now somewhat different, and we assigned that lesson a 1. Finally, moving from fiction to nonfiction or nonfiction to fiction might be the most difficult leap, especially for students who struggle with comprehension. Thus, a tightly constructed lesson would have 6 possible points. Table 9 presents our ratings for the genre consistency of the lessons.

Students probably benefit from studying one genre during a weekly reading lesson—learning about the genre while reading and studying the anthology selection—and then applying what they have learned to their leveled text. The three core reading programs we studied showed considerable variation among and within programs in how consistently the genre in the anthology selection was repeated in the leveled books that followed. In three of the four units we examined from Houghton Mifflin, we found a great deal of consistency between the anthology selection and the leveled books, but in one unit, Theme 1 in

Table 9. Average Genre Consistency in Reading Lessons of Selected Core Reading Programs

	Macmillan/McGraw-Hill Reading (Macmillan/McGraw-Hill, 2003/2005)		Trophies (Harcourt, 2003/2005)		Houghton Mifflin Reading (Houghton Mifflin, 2003/2005)	
	Unit 1	Unit 3	Theme 1	Theme 3	Theme 1	Theme 2
Grade 3	2.00	1.75	2.80	4.60	1.30	4.00
Grade 5	1.00	1.50	3.40	4.40	5.50	5.50

Note. The range is 0–6, with 6 being the highest possible score.

grade 3, there was little. A strong lesson begins with a realistic fiction narrative about a sled dog, which is followed by three other realistic narratives dealing with incidents of survival in the wild. The selections from Macmillan/McGraw-Hill are loosely linked; sometimes the lesson begins with a folk tale, and the anthology selection and leveled books switch to informational text and realistic fiction. Yet, in the next story, all four selections might be informational around a common topic.

Text Complexity. We want to raise one final text factor that should be considered as you evaluate the texts in a new core reading program. To develop comprehension, the reader needs something to think about. The text needs some complexity, so the reader can grapple with the ideas. Isabel Beck and her colleagues (1996) said we must question the author, and others have found that especially for good readers, comprehension is developed when texts present some problems to be solved (McNamara et al., 1996). These problems can take many forms: a difficult-to-solve pronoun–noun relationship, a complex argument, or ideas introduced early in a text that must be linked to some new information. We all remember times when reading a novel that we must reconstruct familial relations, trying to remember how a character is related to one introduced earlier in the story. Therefore, we encourage you to look for texts that have some substance, some problems to solve. The trick is to think about these texts from the students' perspective. Following is a text from a fifth-grade leveled reader designed for students reading on grade level. This small passage presented tremendous problems for many of our students. The text is a biography of Bill Pickett, a famous rodeo star (Pitkin, 2004).

> One day young Bill saw a rancher using dogs to round up some stray cattle. The dogs were part bulldog, a breed that is known for biting and hanging on no matter what. The dogs used a special technique to subdue the cows. When they caught up with one, they leapt up and grabbed onto its upper lip with their teeth. Since this lip is very sensitive, the cow came to a shuddering stop and didn't move. The rancher could then take his time roping it. This method of catching is called bulldogging.
>
> While he was a ranch hand, Pickett developed all the skills a cowboy needed. He also experimented with new ways to handle livestock. One day, Pickett helped a group of cowboys brand some ornery calves. He told them he could quiet any calf. The cowboys laughed at him but agreed to let him try. He used the "bit-'em style" he had learned from the rancher's dogs. To the cowboys' amazement, Pickett managed to quiet the frisky calves. He later used this technique when he performed in rodeos and shows. (p. 6. From *Bill Pickett, Rodeo King* Copyright © 2004 by Houghton Mifflin Company. All rights reserved. Reproduced by permission of the publisher, Houghton Mifflin Harcourt Publishing Company.)

In this text, the reader is required to make several connections between ideas in the text. Many facts in the first paragraph must be connected to the main idea: a description of bulldogging or a way of subduing calves. This kind of thinking requires building coherence between nouns like *bulldog* and *breed* and then connecting this to the pronoun *they*. In the next paragraph, the students must link the "bit-'em style" mentioned in the second paragraph to the description developed in the first. The reader has to think strategically and monitor his comprehension. Texts of this difficulty require thinking. Duffy (2003) and his colleagues (Duffy et al., 1986) argued that we use strategies when there are comprehension problems to solve. Good texts have some problems to solve. Unfortunately, we cannot give you a checklist or rubric to follow when exploring the texts in core reading programs, but you should keep this important text attribute in mind. As you read the stories, think like an 8-, 9-, or 10-year-old. Adults who are proficient readers make connections easily and automatically, but elementary-grade students do not. To determine if a text will promote some thinking, you have to enter into the world of a child. If you find a text straightforward and bland, chances are a child will as well.

PUTTING IT ALL TOGETHER

In this chapter, we discussed the texts in core reading programs and presented some criteria for evaluating them. In the primary grades, we stress looking for texts that are decodable and regularly repeat words and phonics patterns. To evaluate beginning reading texts, we derived criteria from the extensive analysis of these texts that has been done over the past 15 years. We gave you a simple way to estimate the number of words that are introduced, the number of repetitions of these words, and the number of practice opportunities for phonics patterns. We also evaluated texts that teachers can read to students that will develop knowledge and vocabulary and that teachers can use to model comprehension strategies.

When we looked at texts in the upper grades, we had several criteria. First, we wanted a balance of genres so that students would develop skill in reading realistic fiction, fantasy, and nonfiction. We wanted texts that were engaging, and we gave you some guidelines for determining the power of a

(continued)

text to capture the interest of a child. We also looked at how text sets are assembled so that knowledge of topic and genre is developed within a lesson and across a unit or theme. Finally, we considered the elusive quality that the meaning of a text should not always be self-evident. Texts should demand some thinking on the part of the reader.

When you set out to examine a new core reading program, determining the quality of the texts requires more than a simple checklist. Therefore, we recommend some of the following:

- Read as many of the texts in the core reading program as you can.

- Ask the publishers for more copies of leveled and decodable books. The few samples they provide are not enough to evaluate their overall quality.

- Ask your students to read the new selections and ascertain their opinions of the interest of these selections.

- Read and count the number of words in the first-grade texts and look for the number of times each word is repeated across stories.

- Read all the selections within a lesson to see how knowledge of topic and genre is developed.

- Read all the selections within a unit or theme to see how knowledge of topic and genre is developed.

- Consider whether the texts you are purchasing will induce your students to think.

- The online Reading GPS will help you evaluate the texts in core reading programs. This free online supplement can be found on the webpage for this book at www.reading.org/general/publications/books/bk707 .aspx.

CHAPTER 4

How Print Skills Are Taught in Core Reading Programs

Ms. Mercy is halfway through her week of new-teacher orientation meetings, and finally she gets a chance to meet and plan with her other first-grade colleagues. She's been assigned to teach a first-grade class in a high-poverty inner city school. Her heterogeneous mix of 24 students includes an equal mix of Hispanic, African American, and Caucasian students. Two of the students are repeating first grade, and several of her students struggled in kindergarten.

With a heavy backpack, and excitement tempered with fear, Ms. Mercy joins the first-grade team. In front of her on the table are decodable books, authentic literature, letter tiles, workbooks, flashcards, and numerous phonics charts. "We've never been able to agree on the best approach," one first-grade teacher tells her, "so we are giving you everything we use to teach phonics." One teacher prefers the make-a-word method, with students creating words out of their individual letter tiles. Another likes direct instruction, with letters and patterns on flashcards to be learned individually. Both like decodable books for practice and literature for reading aloud. With so many tools in her possession, Ms. Mercy is certain that she'll be able to reach the students in her classroom.

Ms. Mercy's next stop, lugging her now bulging backpack, is with the reading specialist. "We are a Reading Recovery school," the specialist proudly announces. "I'll be working with two of your at-risk students." Ms. Mercy digs through her pile and brings out the letter tiles, flashcards, and one of the teacher's manuals from the core reading program. "Which of these methods do you use?" she asks, hoping for some guidance as to the correct approach. "Oh, none," says the reading specialist. "I teach phonics through an embedded approach, working with patterns in the little books we are reading as the students are ready to learn them."

Her head spinning, Ms. Mercy heads to her classroom to sort out the myriad approaches. How can teaching children to read be so complicated? she asks herself. Her eyes alight on the core reading program books on her desk and she thinks, Maybe these will help me sort it out. When she opens the books, Ms. Mercy is shocked to discover phonological awareness and phonics lessons, all laid out from day one to the final day of school, complete with materials and teaching instructions. She breathes a sigh of relief: I don't need to know those other techniques right now; I'll look through them when I have time.

Our goal in this chapter is to give you the skills to examine the phonemic awareness and phonics instruction in core reading programs. These programs have changed considerably in the past 15 years and continue to evolve. The pressure of No Child Left Behind, Reading First, and the curriculum frameworks in the major adoption states has pushed publishers to include more explicit and systematic instruction in phonemic awareness and phonics. In this chapter, we examine the major core programs from 2003–2005, looking at programs from Harcourt, The McGraw-Hill Companies, Pearson Scott Foresman, and Houghton Mifflin. We also study the instruction in the most recent Treasures (Macmillan/McGraw-Hill, 2009), Reading Street (Pearson Scott Foresman, 2008b), and StoryTown (Harcourt, 2008) programs. In our review, we highlight the critical elements of strong phonemic awareness and phonics instruction. If we help you develop a critical eye, you will be more astute when selecting a new core reading program or in using an existing one effectively. Later, in Chapter 10, we return to phonemic awareness and phonics instruction and help you put into action what you learned in this chapter. You will need to adapt the instruction in core reading programs to best meet the needs of your students.

What You Will Learn

- How the recognition and spelling of words develops

- The research-based concepts for teaching phonemic awareness

- The research-based concepts for teaching phonics

- How core reading programs teach phonemic awareness and phonics and how these programs differ

- What you should look for in phonemic awareness and phonics instruction

What You Will Be Able to Do

- Understand best practice as it applies to phonemic awareness and phonics

- Apply specific criteria about teaching phonemic awareness and phonics to the analysis of core reading programs

- Compare how phonemic awareness and phonics are taught in different core reading programs
- Select a program based on your school's or district's needs

The ideas in this chapter will help you complete an evaluation of the phonemic awareness and phonics instruction in core reading programs. Online at www.reading.org/general/publications/books/bk707.aspx, you can find our Reading GPS, an instrument that will guide you through the process of evaluating the texts in a core reading program. The Reading GPS and this chapter are meant to be used together.

How Children Learn to Read and Write Words

Our alphabetic writing system relies on 26 letters being arranged and rearranged to form words, then sentences, then entire concepts or thoughts. To use this system, readers need to make the link between spoken words and their written equivalents. Learning the alphabetic principle, that is, the idea that sounds heard as phonemes can be represented in print by letters, is no small task (McGill-Franzen, 2006). The spoken sounds are the phonemes, and the letters representing those sounds are the graphemes. Many children struggle to make this link, and indeed, many struggle with its component skill, hearing the sounds of language. The 2000 NRP (NICHD, 2000) report stated, "Being able to distinguish the separate phonemes in pronunciations of words so that they can be linked to graphemes is difficult" (p. 2-11).

Hearing these individual sounds (phonemic awareness), identifying the letters, and linking sounds to letters are some of the skills that students need to identify words. Phonics is a system taught to students so that they can use phoneme–grapheme correspondence to decode or spell words (NICHD, 2000). Students need a way to figure out unknown words they encounter in texts, a system that will be more efficient than memorization of individual words or guessing their identity from context. Learning to read is in large measure a self-teaching process, as students use phonics strategies to teach themselves many new words (Share, 1995). Using grapheme-to-phoneme relationships, a student will be able to sound out previously unknown words, expand his or her vocabulary, and learn to read.

Beginning reading is often discussed in terms of stages, and the model we draw on was developed by Ehri (1997). When students are starting to attend to words, they most often focus on the physical representation of the word in order to identify it (e.g., the shape of the stop sign for the word *stop*, the *oo* in the word *look*). Ehri called this the *visual stage* of reading. At this stage, students will tell you confidently that they know it is the word *stop* when they see the stop sign, even if it is actually another word within the sign. A student at this stage can recognize the word *McDonald's* when it is written in its distinctive red and yellow with the golden arches in the background. Gradually, as students acquire some awareness of letter sounds and some alphabet knowledge, they begin to focus on the letters to help them recognize a word. They are most likely to focus on the beginning or ending consonant. This is called the *partial alphabetic stage*. With additional knowledge of letters and sounds, students are able to use the entire string of letters to sound out the word. This is called the *alphabetic stage*. After initial recognition and continued exposure, each word eventually becomes a known or sight word requiring no additional decoding. Students are able to recognize most words automatically without a need for decoding. When decoding is required, novice readers look for and use known spelling or orthographic patterns within words. The word *Bangladesh* can be identified by using the following spelling patterns—*ang, la, esh*. The final stage of reading is called the *orthographic stage*. Readers are able to read patterns as whole units—for example, *-ing, -ence, -tion*—without having to isolate the individual sounds within these units (Ehri, 1991).

The same stages may be seen in development of students' spelling ability, with the addition of one stage. *Prephonemic stage* writers use pictures, shapes, and scribbles to represent meaning directly, without sounds or letters, although the broken scribbles of some young writers suggest a growing awareness of word boundaries. This early stage corresponds to the visual stage of reading. *Semiphonemic stage* writers realize that writing is different from pictures and will use letters to represent sounds, but they focus on a few salient sounds in each word (e.g., *DG* for *dog*), somewhat analogous to the partial alphabetic reader. In the third stage, *letter name*, students use what they know about letter names to help them spell. For example they might spell the word *drive* as *jriv* because the /dr/ blend sounds like the names of the letters *j* and *r*, and the /i/ and the /v/ sound like their names. There is no concept yet of the silent *e* patterns in long vowels. In the fourth stage, *within-word pattern*, students can spell simple, one-syllable words correctly (Bear & Templeton, 1998). In both the third and fourth stages, the student is working out the complex phonics patterns in the language just as the reader does in the alphabetic stage. Finally, in the last stage of spelling (in some systems it is two stages), the student is working out the *syllable juncture* of words and the spelling patterns that are used across multisyllable words.

This corresponds to the *orthographic stage* of reading in which the student uses spelling patterns to decode new words. It is important to stress that phonics instruction affects spelling, just as it does decoding skills. Table 10 shows the features of words that students use to decode and spell at these stages, contrasting the spelling stages with the reading stages.

Students grow in word knowledge through both direct instruction and self-teaching. Ehri (1997) stated that instruction is the key to moving students from the partial alphabetic stage to the full alphabetic stage. Through instruction, both direct modeling and guided practice, they learn to pronounce and blend all the sounds in a new word. Then, as readers gain more complete alphabet knowledge, they no longer have to process each letter and corresponding sound. They begin to process words in orthographic chunks or spelling patterns. As this occurs, the students are able to read more smoothly and quickly. Researchers agree that

> increased exposure to words appears to sensitize the reader to letter combinations that occur in particular positions in a number of different words. This sensitivity

Table 10. Developmental Decoding and Spelling Phonics Features Continuum

Partial Alphabetic Reading	Letter-Name Spelling	Full Alphabetic Reading	Within-Word Pattern Spelling	Orthographic Reading	Syllable Juncture Spelling
• Focus on letters to help recognize a word • Beginning and ending consonants	• Initial and final consonants • Initial consonant blends and digraphs • Short vowels • Affricates • Final consonant blends and digraphs	• Entire strings of letters used to decode words	• Long vowel VCe patterns • R-influenced vowel patterns • Other common long vowels • Complex consonant units • Abstract vowels: diphthongs, digraphs	• Known spelling patterns used to decode new words • Syllable breaks recognized in words	• Advanced spelling patterns • Syllable breaks identified in words • Rules for adding suffixes

Note. Adapted from Ganske, K. (1999). The developmental spelling analysis: A measure of orthographic knowledge. *Educational Assessment, 6*(1), 41–70, and Juel, C. (1991). Beginning reading. In R. Barr, M.L. Kamil, P. Mosenthal, & P.D. Pearson (Eds.), *Handbook of reading research* (Vol. 2, pp. 759–788). New York: Longman.

allows rapid processing of these versatile letter combinations and rapid mapping of letter strings to lexical entries. (Juel & Roper/Schneider, 1985, p. 136)

Growth in word recognition is also a product of self-teaching. The student learns from his or her exposure to the language. Therefore, a student who had learned the *sh* digraph in *ship*, the *u* vowel sound in *dug*, and the *bl* blend in *blue* would be able to put the same sounds together to say *blush* upon finding that word in a text selection. As individual sounds are learned and segmenting and blending skills are mastered, students begin to process orthographic cues more quickly and reliably. This leads to faster, more accurate reading of words not directly studied. The process of learning phonics and reading is reciprocal; that is, progress in skills in one area will lead to corresponding growth in the other. The more students read, the more opportunity they have to practice and refine their decoding skills.

The linchpins of word identification are letter identification and phonological awareness. It is obvious that an emergent reader has to be able to discriminate and recognize the letters of the alphabet. It is a bit less obvious that the young reader has to able to attend to, blend, and segment the sounds of language. In the act of reading, attaching sounds to letters and blending are critical. In the act of spelling, segmenting the word into sounds and attaching letters to sounds is equally critical. The awareness of and the ability to manipulate the sounds of language is called phonological awareness (NICHD, 2000). Students generally develop this ability in preschool through first grade and, as their skills become more highly developed, they are able to focus on and manipulate increasingly smaller units such as rhyming words, then syllables, then individual phonemes (Burgess, 2006). Research has shown consistently that phonemic awareness and letter knowledge are the best predictors of how well students will learn to read during the first two years of school (NICHD, 2000). Successful phonics instruction in later years depends on the development of phonemic awareness, which forms the basis of decoding and spelling strategies. There is very little debate, if any, that phonemic awareness instruction needs to be included in core reading programs. In fact basal programs can *potentially* be beneficial for novice teachers (Snow et al., 1998). Guidance provided in the core reading programs, for example, laying out the sequence of skills and instructional methods, can be very helpful for beginning teachers *if* that guidance aligns with research-validated practices. So we first look at what the research says about phonemic awareness development, then at instructional techniques and materials, and finally at what core reading programs provide.

Phonemic Awareness Development

Phonemic awareness is part of phonological awareness; the two terms are sometimes used interchangeably, but they are different. Phonological awareness refers to the overall awareness of the sounds of language. Phonemic awareness refers to the awareness of individual phonemes within a word and is the endpoint of phonological awareness. Children are developing language and phonological awareness skills from birth (Ezell & Justice, 2005). In their quest to communicate with those around them, children mimic sounds, speak words, and eventually begin to play with language. Part of this play is the discovery that words (previously considered self-contained entities) have parts. Children must become aware of words as separate units, sometimes referred to as *word awareness* or *concept of word*. They also need to become aware of rhymes, alliteration, syllables, onset–rime, and finally, individual phonemes. These discoveries, described here, are phonological awareness and are crucial for learning how to read.

Word awareness: Children begin to recognize words as separate entities around age 3 or 4, with awareness of spoken words as discrete units established by age 5. The concept of written words being separate follows by the end of kindergarten.

Syllables: The awareness that words have different numbers of syllables generally occurs around age 4.

Rhyme: Children will begin recognizing rhyme when they notice the sounds in a word. They will usually begin producing their own rhymes around age 3 or 4 years.

Alliteration: Children begin recognizing that words have the same beginning sound as early as 3 years of age.

Onset–rime awareness: Children can segment a one-syllable word into its onset and its rime. In *stop*, *st* is the onset and *op* is the rime. The full segmentation of the word follows this ability.

Phonemes: Phoneme awareness generally begins around age 4 or 5 and will continue to develop into more sophisticated forms through kindergarten and first grade. Children usually become aware of the first sound in a word, then the final sound, and then medial vowels. Being able to manipulate these sounds ("Say *cat*; say *cat* without the /c/") by segmenting, blending, or deleting is a higher level of skill than simple awareness ("How many sounds in *dog*: /d/, /o/, /g/"). Manipulation of individual phonemes starts with segmenting the initial consonant, the onset, from the vowel and final consonant, the rime (Ezell & Justice, 2005).

There is an accepted progression of skills, though these concepts overlap quite a bit. According to Burgess (2006), "Children generally master word-level skills before they master syllable-level skills, syllable-level skills before they master onset-rime level skills, and onset-rime level skills before they master phoneme-level skills" (p. 91).

In addition to phonological awareness, children need to learn the names and sounds of letters. Instruction in letter names helps students hear the phonemes in spoken words and also gives visual cues for generating phonemes. When a child says the names of *T, B, G,* and *J,* the sound associated with the letter is first found in the letter's name. In *M, N, R,* and *S,* the sound associated with that letter is contained somewhere in the letter name. Learning letter names is a clue to letter sounds. Learning letter sounds makes a child aware that words are made up of individual sounds and also helps develop concept of word by linking the known sounds to letters in individual words in print (Ehri & Roberts, 2006).

Researchers have shown that most children should be able to recognize 50–75% of upper- and lowercase letters, identify at least six phonemes, and match six to nine letters with their sounds by the end of preschool (McGee, 2005). By midkindergarten, children should be able to isolate the first sound in a simple word (i.e., /c/ from *cat*), and by the end of kindergarten, they should be able to match one-syllable words that rhyme, identify words with the same initial consonant sound, and segment and blend all the sounds in simple two or three phoneme words (i.e., /c/ /a/ /t/ from *cat*; McGill-Franzen, 2006; Phillips & Torgesen, 2006). By the end of kindergarten they should be able to recognize words that begin with the same phoneme, as well as name all the letters of the alphabet (Ehri & Roberts, 2006). By the end of first grade, they should be able to segment and blend more complicated words, such as *crush* and *trash* (Phillips & Torgesen, 2006).

Phoneme awareness and phonics are closely linked skills. One is not prerequisite to another (Stahl, 2001). Phoneme awareness instruction, specifically teaching students to blend and segment sounds, also benefits decoding instruction. Conversely, as a teacher helps a student decode a new word, the teacher is bringing that student's attention to the individual sounds in a word and the manipulation of those sounds. The letter–sound connection is the key to remembering words quickly. Students who do not learn the letter–sound cues early in their literacy development will remain struggling readers (Phillips & Torgesen, 2006).

Phonemic Awareness Instruction

Two issues present difficulties for students in developing phonological awareness. First, oral language is a continuous stream, with breaks at meaning chunks rather than individual words. This makes it difficult for students to achieve word awareness, much less focus on parts of language smaller than a word. Second, students are focused on meanings rather than the sounds of words, making it difficult to isolate and manipulate phonemes (Ehri & Roberts, 2006). For these reasons, the best instruction is described as "direct and explicit" (NICHD, 2000). This is a phrase that is used often in professional development and core reading programs with varying meanings; however, it is best defined as clearly stating the structure of oral language, stating what the reader must do, modeling the process, and providing corrective feedback (Santi, Menchetti, & Edwards, 2004).

Most students will begin formal instruction in phonological awareness in kindergarten and may begin anywhere along that continuum from word awareness to full phonemic awareness, depending on their prior experiences with language and print. Several aspects of instruction have been shown through research to have a positive impact on students' learning phonemic awareness. These include grade levels of instruction, grouping options, sequencing of instruction, instruction in segmenting and blending skills, and use of print or letters during instruction (Ehri & Roberts, 2006; McGee, 2005; NICHD, 2000; Santi et al., 2004). In Table 11, we outline some of the important factors to note when examining phonemic awareness instruction in core reading programs.

It is easy to forget, when talking about "direct, explicit instruction" and the importance of phonemic awareness skills for literacy development, that we are discussing instruction for students who are 4, 5, and 6 years old. It is imperative to consider that a planned and direct instructional method does not have to mean passive, worksheet-type activities. Indeed, the use of worksheets undermines the very auditory nature of the skill. The students need to be actively learning, making connections between the phonemic awareness lesson and the texts they are trying to read, and enjoying their discoveries about words (Ehri & Roberts, 2006; Sharp, Sinatra, & Reynolds, 2008). The activities listed previously provide direct, explicit instruction while keeping students engaged, motivated, and linked to stories or oral language.

Table 11. Criteria for Evaluating Phonemic Awareness Instruction in Core Reading Programs

Instructional Issues	What You Should Look For
Grade level	Instruction in phonological and phonemic awareness is most effective in kindergarten and lower. It is less effective in first grade and above, even with readers in those grades who are at a lower level developmentally.
Group size	The National Reading Panel (NICHD, 2000) found that it is most effective to teach phonemic awareness in small groups.
Sequence of instruction	It is important to sequence the instruction from easier (rhyme, syllable awareness) to harder (segmenting and blending phonemes) skills. Students make the most progress when they are taught segmenting and blending; however, they need to be proficient in the other skills first. The instruction should be direct, explicit, and focused on one or two skills at a time.
Teacher modeling and feedback	Each phonemic awareness activity requires teacher modeling and immediate student feedback. The typical format includes I do the activity (the teacher), we do the activity (teacher and students), you do the activity (students). In the we do and you do parts of the cycle, the teacher has to again model the right way to do the activity.
Placement and type of phonemes	It is easier for children to learn phonemes that occur at the beginning of the letter name (e.g., *dee*, *pee*) than those that happen at the end of the name (e.g., *en*). There can also be confusion when some graphemes represent more than one phoneme; for example, the letter *y* can have either the /y/ sound as in *yes* or the /ē/ sound as in *baby*. Conversely, some phonemes are represented by more than one grapheme; for example, the /s/ sound can be represented by either *s* as in *sat* or *c* as in *circle*. There are phonemes represented by more than one grapheme; for example, consonant and vowel digraphs such as *ai* or *sh* will have one sound with two letters (Ehri & Roberts, 2006).
Use of concrete markers	Instruction that included Elkonin (1963) boxes as a way to help children conceptualize the sounds they are hearing is more powerful than only teaching the sounds orally. ● ● ● ☐ ☐ ☐ Children move a marker into each box as they say the sounds in a word.

(continued)

Table 11. Criteria for Evaluating Phonemic Awareness Instruction in Core Reading Programs *(cont'd)*

Instructional Issues	What You Should Look For
Use of letters	Instruction that links the spoken phonemes to the written graphemes is more powerful than instruction using language alone. There is much evidence that phonemic awareness and decoding/spelling are reciprocal processes; that is, developing skill in one of these leads to skill increases in the other. When students engage in invented spelling or teacher-guided word sorts, they are learning about letter–sound relationships and becoming aware of sounds. Teaching phonemic awareness and decoding/spelling concurrently (as opposed to sequentially or separately) leads to bigger skill gains for the students. Also, being very explicit in applying the new awareness or skills to reading and writing has a bigger effect on students' learning.
Mouth movements	Asking children to attend to how their mouth moves when the say a letter sound helps build awareness of that sound. Try saying the sound /m/. Think to yourself, when I say the sound /m/, what is my tongue doing? What about my lips? Am I pushing out air?

Teaching Letter Names

Concurrent with phonological awareness, students should be learning the names and sounds of the letters. "Learning letters is difficult...there are 40 shapes, names, and sounds to be learned. All of this learning involves meaningless bits and arbitrary associations, so much practice and rehearsal are needed to achieve mastery" (Ehri & Roberts, 2006, p. 121). The names and sounds can and should be taught at the same time as opposed to sequentially. There is no research support for a given order of instruction for letter names and sounds, though it has been noted many times that the most salient letters appear to be those within the students' and their classmates' names (Burgess, 2006). Several researchers have suggested that focusing first on letters and sounds that are more easily discriminated will aid instruction (Carnine, Silbert, Kame'enui, & Tarver, 2003). In addition, teaching several commonly used consonants and vowels will allow students to start to make words. Activities for teaching letter names and sounds include alphabet books, handwriting lessons, finding letters in classmates' names, and matching letters with pictures of objects beginning with that letter (Ehri & Roberts, 2006; Ezell & Justice, 2005).

Conversely, effective instruction does not mean that students make random discoveries about words every day. There must be a developmentally appropriate plan for instruction across the entire year and a way of assessing progress with the ability to modify that plan if necessary (Snow et al., 1998). A truly effective phonological awareness instruction program will take both of these concerns into account.

Evaluation of Phonemic Awareness in Core Reading Programs

We focused our evaluation of phonemic awareness instruction in core reading programs on the factors that appear critical to student achievement. This evaluation is meant to highlight the issues you should consider when selecting a new core reading program. We did not conduct an analysis that evaluated every lesson in a reading program. In these core reading programs, we examined the grade levels in which phonemic awareness instruction occurs, grouping suggestions (whole- or small-group instruction), the sequence of instruction, direct explicit instruction, and the use of concrete markers or other manipulatives and letters to link phonemics to phonics (Ehri & Roberts, 2006; NICHD, 2000; Santi et al., 2004). We studied programs with 2003, 2005, 2007, 2008, and 2009 copyrights. Those programs published before 2007 were essentially responding to the state content standards that became more explicit about how phonemic awareness and phonics should be taught. We present carefully chosen examples from the reviewed programs as a demonstration of how teachers and administrators must evaluate the core reading programs they are using or planning to purchase.

Grade Level

All core reading programs provide phonemic awareness instruction in kindergarten and first grade. In Trophies (Harcourt, 2003/2005) phonemic awareness is introduced in the middle of kindergarten and continues through first grade. The second-grade level of the program has a phonemic awareness warm-up before new phonics patterns are presented, but the emphasis is clearly lighter than in the earlier grades. In Houghton Mifflin Reading (Houghton Mifflin, 2003/2005) phonemic awareness is taught in kindergarten and first grades. By second grade, phonemic awareness is included as the first step in a phonics lesson and only early in the week.

In the newer core reading programs, phonemic awareness instruction is included in all kindergarten and first-grade programs. StoryTown (2008) includes phonemic awareness in the kindergarten and first-grade levels of the program. By second grade, the program continues some emphasis on segmenting and blending sounds and distinguishing short- and long-vowel sounds. In Treasures (2009), phonemic awareness is taught in kindergarten, first grade, and into second grade. In second grade, the awareness of sounds is stressed as the prelude to the phonics lessons.

Group Size

In most core reading programs, phonemic awareness instruction is suggested for whole-group instruction, although the research stresses that its maximum benefit comes from small-group work. In core reading programs published before 2005, there was little or no stress on small-group instruction for any skill. In the more recent programs, specific plans are provided for small-group instruction, but phonemic awareness is not mentioned often as part of small-group instruction. StoryTown (Harcourt, 2008) focuses small-group work in first grade on reading the leveled books, and Treasures (2009) includes phonics lessons for each small group. Only the kindergarten levels of the program include suggestions for teaching phonemic awareness in small groups.

Treasures (2009) teaches phonemic awareness in kindergarten as a whole-class lesson with oral tasks:

> Listen to the sounds in the word "trap": /t/ /r/ /a/ /p/. I hear four sounds in "trap." Say the sounds in "trap" with me: /t/ /r/ /a/ /p/, /trrraaap/, "trap." How many sounds are in "trap"? What are the sounds? (p. 83K)

In first grade, lessons are aligned with the phonics instruction, meaning that the sounds presented in the phonemic awareness lesson are also the sounds of the features presented in the phonics lesson.

Treasures (2009) provides some instruction in small groups for students having difficulty during the whole-class lesson. These small-group lessons review or reteach skills for students who are struggling: more modeling of the skill as presented to the whole group, adding picture or letter cards for concrete examples, and additional practice with the same skills and words. Treasures includes very specific lessons in the Additional Resources section for teaching onset–rime, phoneme isolation, and phoneme deletion in first grade; however, these were one lesson for each skill, with no suggested follow-up if students continued to have difficulty. For example, the phoneme deletion lesson instructions were as follows:

I am going to say a word: "bat." Now I am going to take away the first sound /b/, the word "at" is left. Listen to this word: "bit." If I take away the first sound /b/, the word "it" is left. (p. T1)

The directions then specify guided practice with feedback for several practice words. There is no set of instructions in the teacher's manual for students who continue to have difficulty with phoneme deletion after this additional lesson.

Houghton Mifflin Reading (2003/2005) teaches phonemic awareness as part of the "Morning Message" in the kindergarten lessons for the whole group. It does align with phonics features; however, there are no options presented for below-level or advanced learners. This lesson contains two tasks for the students: beginning sounds, and words in oral sentences. For beginning sounds, the teacher says: "I am thinking of someone's name in this room. The name starts with /s/. Who has a name that starts with /s/?" The task continues until students name all the classmates whose names begin with the /s/ sound. For words in oral sentences, students are asked to clap once for each word they hear in a simple sentence, then tell how many words they heard. For confusion over what constitutes a word, the directions to the teacher read, "If children clap twice for yellow, explain that one word like yellow can have two parts. Give another example like Matthew or Caitlin" (p. T47). Although the tasks themselves are representative of good phonemic awareness instruction, note that there is no differentiation in either part of the lesson. All students complete the same tasks, work on the same skills, and use the same materials.

Sequence of Instruction

Core reading programs provide a written scope and sequence of their phonemic awareness instruction, typically found at the end of each teacher's edition. Aside from providing an easy way to check off the skills during a review, the scope and sequence chart provides very little information as to the actual sequence for teaching these skills. For example, one item on the Treasures (2009) list reads "Add, delete, and substitute phonemes," and is taught in both kindergarten and first grade. The item is so broad that you cannot know when the skills are taught or what instruction precedes and follows. So when you evaluate a core program you must ask, what is the true sequence of phonemic awareness instruction, and how does it conform to research recommendations?

To evaluate these programs carefully, you must read the individual lessons to determine what the sequence of phonemic awareness skills is. In Table 12, we present the scope and sequence of phonemic awareness instruction, in two core reading programs covering just the first six weeks of kindergarten. The differences between the two Harcourt programs are clear. The 2005 program covers three phonemic awareness skills each week, while the 2008 program generally sticks to the same skill for the whole week. The 2005 program appears to follow a spiral curriculum, whereas the 2008 version focuses on one level of phonological awareness before moving on to the next. Review is built into the 2008 program. The scope and sequence of the 2008 program is more consistent with research recommendations than is the 2005 program. When you set out to evaluate phonemic awareness instruction in core reading programs, we suggest you examine the actual lessons. This can be done relatively efficiently by reading the suggested lesson plan at the beginning of each week's lessons.

Table 12. Scope and Sequence of Phonemic Awareness Instruction in Two Core Reading Programs

Lesson	Trophies (Harcourt, 2003/2005)	StoryTown (Harcourt, 2008)
1	Segmenting sentences into words Rhyme recognition Syllable segmentation	Segmenting sentences into words
2	Segmenting sentences into words Rhyme recognition Syllable segmentation	Syllable blending
3	Rhyme recognition Phoneme Isolation Rhyme production	Syllable blending
4	Rhyme production Phoneme Isolation Onset–rime blending Phoneme matching	Segmenting and blending syllables
5	Word segmentation Phoneme isolation Rhyme production	Segmenting sentences into words Segmenting and blending syllables
6	Syllable segmentation Phoneme isolation Rhyme recognition	Alliteration

Direct, Explicit Instruction

Strong phonemic awareness instruction is direct and explicit. The teacher explains to the students what they are to do and why it is important. The students must be engaged. Next, the teacher models the process using several examples. Teacher language must be clear and understandable to all students in the classroom. Then, the students try out the skill or strategy while the teacher provides feedback (Carnine, Silbert, & Kame'enui, 1997). The corrective feedback needs to be explicit. Finally, the students engage in extended practice with decreasing amounts of teacher feedback. Often this practice takes the form of games or other interactive activities. In Table 13, we present three phonemic awareness lessons from three different core reading programs. For each lesson, we consider the explicitness of the instruction.

To evaluate core reading programs, it is necessary to look closely at how the individual phonemic awareness lessons are presented. In doing so, we recommend that you pick lessons from the same grade level and from the same point in the school year. It is difficult to match the exact skill from one program to another, because the programs differ considerably in what skills they teach and how they label the skills. Each program lists the skills according to research-based categories (i.e., identifying, segmenting, blending, substituting); however, the skills that are taught do not always live up to their label. Houghton Mifflin Reading (2003/2005) lists a task as a "same sound sort," leading you to believe that students would categorize items based on their beginning sound, only to follow up with directions for students to raise their hand if the words begin with the same letter—an identification task.

In the three lessons we reprinted in Table 13, we believe some common problems stand out. First, none of the lessons help students understand how the phonemic awareness task they are performing relates to the act of reading or spelling. Second, the lessons tend to have the teacher model the task only one time, then the students share in the responsibility. Third, none of these three lessons and others we examined give the teacher any clear guidelines on how to give the students feedback. Finally, the lessons lack direction on how to scaffold the task if the students encounter difficulty. Switching to easier words or providing more modeling is not suggested in these core reading programs. The knowledgeable teacher can still make these moment-to-moment decisions. The programs provide little directions for differentiation, so the teacher can delete the phonemic awareness portion of the lesson if the students do not need the instruction or expand it if they do.

Table 13. Phonemic Awareness Instruction in Three Core Reading Programs

StoryTown (Harcourt, 2008, Grade 1, p. 407)	Treasures (Macmillan/McGraw-Hill, 2009, Grade 1, p. 37B)		Houghton Mifflin Reading (Houghton Mifflin, 2003/2005, Grade 1, p. T21)
Phoneme Categorization: Initial	Identify Onset and Rime		Blending Phonemes
Explain that you are going to say three words; two will begin with the same sound and one will begin with a different sound. Model with the words *fit, fat, pet*. Have children repeat the words. Say "*fit, fat, pet. Fit* and *fat* begin with the same sound, /f/. *Pet* begins with a different sound, /p/." Have children repeat the following words and identify the word that has the different beginning sounds: *an, in, it, cup, pup, pop, last, lost, fist, add, man, map, sing, ring, rang, nest, rest, net, late, gate, lane, dock, doll, lock, back, tack, tock, man, ten, men.*	**Model** Read "Mary Pat." Use the Puppet to show children how to separate onset from rime. Repeat with cat. **Guided Practice** Have children practice identifying the onset and rime in words by segmenting. Guide practice, doing the first few together.	Happy [Puppet] will say a word. I will break the word into its beginning and ending parts. Pat. I am going to say Pat in two parts. The first part is /p/. The end part is /at/. I will say a word. You break the word into its beginning and ending parts. *mat, rat, pan, that, sat, did, fat, chat.*	Say "I'm gong to say a rhyme. Listen carefully to the last word of the rhyme! I will say the sounds in it. You blend the sounds together and say the word." Say "Mike is big. He drives a /r/ /i/ /g/. Blend the sounds. Raise your hand when you know the word." Continue with the following rhymes. Jack and Jill went up the /h/ /i/ /l/. Peculiar Pam eats lots of /h/ /a/ /m/. Do not stop. Let's reach the /t/ /o/ /p/. I can tap. I can /r/ /a/ /p/. Put the pin in that /b/ /i/ /n/.

Use of Concrete Markers and Letters

Phonemic awareness instruction is primarily based on verbal tasks; however, use of concrete objects can strengthen instruction. All programs that we reviewed provide teachers with concrete objects. In any of the programs, teachers will find Elkonin boxes, markers, printed rhymes or songs, picture cards, letter cards, objects grouped by letter sound, and puppets. Practice books or worksheets were used in one program as part of phonemic awareness and in all programs as part of phonics. The new programs, Treasures (2009) and StoryTown (2008), provide a wealth of materials.

Houghton Mifflin Reading (2003/2005) includes tasks in which the students move about the room, labeling an object with a sticky note when the object's name corresponds with the beginning sound they are learning, or sorting by consonant sounds based on the name of a picture they are holding. These activities appear to be age-appropriate and fun, but slightly limiting in terms of practice with the letter sounds for each student. Finally, we did not find that core reading programs incorporate instruction or feedback on mouth movements, which can improve the effectiveness of phoneme awareness instruction.

In evaluating the phonemic awareness instruction, teachers and administrators need to be aware of these potential issues. None of the core reading programs we reviewed taught phonemic awareness skills in small groups, and the sequence of skills as well as that of letter names and sounds did not appear to be based on a developmentally appropriate model. However, we did find that the individual lessons and activities were appropriate and engaging on their own. The concrete materials were very useful as well.

What Research Has to Say About Phonics Instruction

Good phonics instruction teaches students the alphabetic principle, or the insight that letters stand for sounds. Phonics then gives the student the tools to unlock the pronunciation of new words. "Research tells us that an early and systematic emphasis on teaching children to decode words leads to better achievement than a later or more haphazard approach" (Stahl, Duffy-Hester, & Stahl, 1998, p. 339). Research has shown that the most reliable method of teaching the alphabetic code is explicit, systematic phonics instruction with ample opportunities for applied practice (Foorman, Francis, Fletcher, Schatschneider, & Mehta, 1998). A strong phonics program includes developing phonological awareness, teaching letter recognition, and finally building letter–sound relationships. Because the sound structure of English is complex, students need to gradually learn the many spelling patterns of the language and a process or set of strategies for applying them. Sometimes it is useful to sound out a new word letter by letter (e.g., *clam*, *sink*), whereas other times it is useful to use known spelling patterns to decode a more complex word (e.g., *banter*, *reliable*). Finally, students need many opportunities to practice reading words in isolation, reading connected text, and spelling words. Ultimately, phonics instruction is only one part of an overall literacy program.

There are many different types of phonics instruction and the differences between these methods are small (NICHD, 2000; Stahl et al., 1998). Generally approaches that are direct and follow a well laid out system yield the best results. Table 14 lists the major types of phonics instruction.

Although there has been a great deal of debate concerning the best approach to teaching phonics, researchers including the NRP (NICHD, 2000) have found that all types of phonics instruction were more successful than no phonics instruction, and they have failed to find significant differences between

Table 14. Types of Phonics Instruction

Instructional Approach	Characteristics and Examples
Synthetic phonics	Letters are converted to phonemes and blended together to form a word. For example, students learn the letters *s*, *i* (the short vowel sound), and *p*, then they learn to blend those sounds together to form the word *sip*. Some examples of synthetic phonics programs are Orton-Gillingham and direct instruction.
Analytic phonics	A known word is analyzed into its component parts. Students learn the words *ball*, *bear*, and *beans* first, as whole words, then the instruction focuses on the first sound in each of these words. Examples of these types of programs include some basal program lessons.
Spelling-based	Students work with letters or features to analyze patterns and form words. They may be given the words *sip*, *tip*, *rip*, and *set*, *met*, *let* to sort into patterns with the headers *ip* and *et*. Examples of these types of programs include Word Study, Making Words, and Meta-phonics.
Decoding by analogy	Students learn to decode words using other words or word parts with which they are familiar. Students use their knowledge of the words *ship* and *out* to figure out the unknown word *shout*. An example of the analogy-based approach is the Benchmark Word Identification program.
Embedded phonics	These approaches teach orthographic features within the context of authentic reading and writing experiences. For example, a teacher might read aloud *The Cat in the Hat* and use that text to teach the *-at* family. One example of an embedded phonics approach is Reading Recovery.

Note. Adapted from Stahl et al. (1998). Everything you wanted to know about phonics (but were afraid to ask). *Reading Research Quarterly*, 33(3), 338–355.

approaches (Stahl et al., 1998). The crucial element seems to be "that they delineate a planned, sequential set of phonic elements and they teach those elements explicitly and systematically" (NICHD, 2000, p. 2-89). By examining the research, we believe that there are four factors that should be considered when evaluating phonics instruction: when phonics is taught, the group size for instruction (whole group vs. small group), the scope and sequence of teaching phonics principles, and finally the characteristics of the instruction itself—explanation, modeling, guided practice, and feedback.

Grade Level

The NRP (NICHD, 2000) found that phonics instruction is most effective in kindergarten and first grade, before students learned to read independently, but it was effective for students in grades 2–6 and struggling readers as well. Connor, Morrison, and Underwood (2007) found that when second-grade teachers spent more time on phonics or code-focused instruction, their students made more progress in word-learning skills. Surprisingly, these increased amounts of time were small, averaging just five minutes per day. Therefore, although phonics should be taught in all the primary grades, the most intense and focused phonics lessons should be for students who are at the initial phases of learning to read.

Group Size

The NRP (NICHD, 2000) found no differences in grouping for instructional delivery; that is, it was equally effective to teach phonics to students individually, in small groups, and as a whole class. Since the NRP's (NICHD, 2000) report was published, other research has emphasized the importance of small-group instruction. In a series of studies, Connor and her colleagues (Connor, Morrison, Fishman, Schatschneider, & Underwood, 2007; Connor, Morrison, & Underwood, 2007) demonstrated that when teachers differentiate instruction and provide weaker students with more direct instruction in word-learning skills growth improves. This is more likely to happen in small groups than for whole groups. However, it should be noted that the most effective phonics instruction is designed around student knowledge and rates of progress, so this should not be interpreted to mean that a one-size-fits-all phonics lesson delivered to the whole class will be equally effective for all students.

Scope and Sequence

There is little research on the sequence of teaching the phonics patterns. There is general agreement that some of the consonant sounds should be introduced first, because their letter–sound associations are more consistent than those of the vowels (Heilman, 2005). However, without vowel sounds, words cannot be decoded. So Beck (2006) argued that consonants and vowels should be taught together, but stick first to those vowel sounds that are consistent—short vowels.

Direct Instruction

Phonics instruction is usually discussed as a simple, concrete learning task. The features are explained to the student, the teacher models the task, then the student tries it out with positive or negative feedback from the teacher. There is more to phonics than just knowing the features; however, the reader has to apply them, and this requires a strategy or process. There is evidence that students are constructing knowledge of strategies as they learn phonics features and, for struggling readers, those strategies have to be explicitly modeled. That is, students learn not only the feature, but also how to spell or read words based on what has been modeled for them (Sharp et al., 2008; Stahl et al., 1998). A student who is instructed in decoding by analogy will apply that process to unknown words; a student who is instructed in synthetic phonics will sequentially blend the sounds to pronounce a new word. There is also a reciprocal relationship between strategy use and knowledge of decoding features in phonics. Instruction in one benefited the other and vice versa (Sharp et al., 2008). To evaluate instruction in the core reading programs, we needed a model of strong phonics instruction and turned to the recommendations of Beck (2006). We reproduce two suggested instructional sequences and then later apply these models to the core reading programs. Figure 7 presents a suggested lesson plan.

The last critical piece of phonics instruction is application. There is considerable evidence that students, especially the weakest readers, benefit from reading decodable text. We discussed the characteristics of decodable text in the previous chapters, but when they should be used is an important consideration. The consensus among researchers is that decodable text should be used for students in the partial alphabetic stage, usually the first half of first grade, but longer for struggling readers (Adams, 2009).

Figure 7. Suggested Lesson Plan to Teach Letter Sounds

Focus of Lesson Sequence	Procedure
1. Develop phonemic awareness of the target sound in the initial position.	"I know a story about a character called Mary Mouse who drank lots of milk. Who drank the milk? The words *Mary* and *Mouse* begin with the same sound: /m/. Watch my mouth: /m/. Now, you say /m/."
2. Connect the printed letter with the sound the letter represents.	Show children the large *m* card. "This is the letter *m*. The letter *m* stands for the /m/ sound in *Mary* and *Mouse*. You say /m/. Each time I touch the letter *m*, say /m/." [Touch *m* several times.]
3. Discriminate among words that begin with /m/ and those that do not.	At this point, students will need their own letter *m* card. "If the word I say begins with the /m/ sound, hold up your *m* card and say /m/. If it doesn't begin with the /m/ sound, shake your head no." Example words include *monkey, many, house, make, table,* and *money.*
4. Develop phonemic awareness of the target sound in the final position.	"I am used to sweep the floor. What am I?" After *broom* is said and repeated several times, explain that *broom* ends with the letter *m*, the letter that stands for the /m/ sound. Say some more words that end with the letter *m* and have students repeat them. Example words include *jam, room, drum,* and *farm.*
5. Discriminate among words that end with /m/ from those that do not.	This step is just like step 3, but the focus is on the final position.
6. Discriminate among words that have /m/ in the final position.	Students will need their word packets. "I'll say some words that begin with /m/ and some that end with /m/. When a word begins with /m/, put your letter *m* at the beginning of the word packet. When a word ends with /m/, put your letter *m* at the end of the word packet."

Note. Adapted from Beck, I.L. (2006). *Making sense of phonics: The hows and whys.* New York: Guilford.

Evaluation of Phonics Instruction in Core Reading Programs

We explored phonics instruction in selected core reading programs using the criteria we outlined above: grade level, group size, scope and sequence, and instructional approach. As you review and evaluate core reading programs you need to consider the same characteristics. Our review is not designed to be exhaustive, but to model the process that you need to follow.

Grade Level

Phonics is taught in all core reading programs with the strongest emphasis in kindergarten, first, and second grades. All programs provide phonics instruction in the upper grades, but it diminishes in emphasis and changes its focus. By examining older programs like Trophies (2003/2005), Scott Foresman Reading (Pearson Scott Foresman, 2004), and Houghton Mifflin Reading (2003/2005), you will discover that in the upper grades, a phonics lesson is provided each week that generally reviews basic phonics patterns, CVC or CVCe, and then may focus on one or two word families. The sequence for teaching these phonics skills generally repeats the sequences used in grades 1 and 2. The upper grade lessons do not incorporate decoding by analogy strategies, which can be very useful for older students. We believe that teachers will have difficulty using these lessons, because they may not match the needs of their students.

In the new core reading programs, a well-delineated phonics sequence is provided in kindergarten, first, and second grades. In the upper grades, phonics lessons continue to be provided and, in a typical week, Treasures (2009) provides work on long *a* words, decoding multisyllabic words, and playing with rhyming riddles or working with word families. StoryTown (2008) also provides some phonics lessons in the upper grades, typically one lesson a week, which may focus on a vowel pattern, word families, or structural analysis (e.g., prefixes, suffixes). A classroom teacher will need to decide if any of these lessons meets the needs of the students.

Grouping for Instruction

All of the reviewed core reading programs present phonics as a whole-class lesson. In the older core programs, those published before 2008, the suggested lesson plans do not include a small-group option. Leveled and decodable books are provided, and by implication these are to be read in small groups, but the teacher is not provided specific directions on how to differentiate phonics instruction. The newer core reading programs have small-group lesson plans, and some specifically provide direction for differentiating phonics instruction. Treasures (2009) provides a specific phonemic awareness and phonics lesson for below-level readers, decreases the focus on phonemic awareness for on-level students and for strong readers no phonics instruction is suggested. In StoryTown (2008), whole-class phonics lessons are thorough and well developed but not small-group lessons. The small-group lessons guide teachers in how to use the leveled and decodable books, but specific phonics lessons are not provided for students in small-group instruction or for students of differing needs.

Scope and Sequence

All of the core reading programs provide a scope and sequence chart, but these charts merely indicate which general phonics skills are taught and at what grade levels. To evaluate the true sequence of instruction, you must read and list the phonics skills taught in each lesson. This will be difficult to do, because most program sample kits provide only one of six teacher's editions per grade level. If you are truly interested in comparing scope and sequences between programs, ask your publisher's representative for a full set of teacher's editions. We have found that most programs follow a similar scope and sequence early in first grade—consonants, short vowels, and then CVCe words—but later in first grade, the programs diverge to some extent. All things being equal, you may want to pick a program with a scope and sequence that matches the goals and objectives of your district.

Direct Instruction

To capture the specifics of phonics instruction we decided to compare the same phonics lesson across three programs. We believe this tight focus on just one topic will give you a strong understanding of programs you are considering. We looked at Trophies (2003/2005), Treasures (2009), and StoryTown (2008). For each program, we examined the initial teaching of short *a*. Because these lessons are quite long, we decided not to reproduce each of the full lessons, but we provide a summary in Table 15.

These three lessons illustrate some important points about the explicitness of phonics instruction. Both of the current lessons, the ones in StoryTown (2008) and Treasures (2009), begin with phonemic awareness—the students' need to listen for the sounds—although in Trophies (2003/2005), the older program, phonemic awareness is not a component of the lesson. StoryTown (2008) requires the students to discriminate the words that contain short-vowel sounds, while the other two texts do not. Both of the recent lessons are very explicit

Table 15. Comparing Phonics Instruction in Three Core Reading Programs

StoryTown (Harcourt, 2008, Grade 1, pp. T36–T38)	Trophies (Harcourt, 2003, Grade 1, pp. 10I–10J)	Treasures (Macmillan/McGraw-Hill, 2009, Grade 1, p. 7C)
Short Vowel /a/	Short Vowel /a/	Introduce Short /a/
• Review the alphabet by pointing to letters at random. • Develop phonemic awareness of /a/ by asking children to say at, after, act and then say the initial sound. • Connect letter and sound. Display the Aa card, say the name and the sound. • Discriminate. Say a word (at, inch, add, own) and have children hold up A card when they hear the sound. Repeat with words that have /a/ in the middle of the word. • Word Blending. Using letter cards and pocket chart model blending words with short a. Repeat process with five additional words. • Word Building. Short a work continues in spelling lesson. Children make words with letter cards following teacher directions.	• Introduce short /a/ by displaying letter card and telling students that a can stand for the sound of /a/ in words like am, add, and act. • Blend and read words. Using a pocket chart model blending h a t. Then repeat for can, tap, and mad. • Use a pocket chart to model making words with letter cards. Students make the same words with their individual letter cards. Students will make seven more words. • Short a work continues in the spelling lesson where students sort short a words.	• Teach the sound–symbol short /a/. State name of the letter and sound of the letter with letter cards. • Teacher models the process; says mat and then says the short a while holding up the A Card. • Student practice holding up the A Card as teacher reads a series of words with and without short a. • Teacher puts m a t on a pocket chart and models the blending process. "This is the letter t. It stands for /t/. Listen as I blend all three sounds together." Students blend with her and this is repeated with several other words. • Guided Practice. Students practice blending ten additional words. • Building Fluency: Word Automaticity. Students practice reading additional short vowel words from a chart. • Additional practice and review is provided in small-group instruction.

about linking the letter to its name and sound, while the older lesson is a bit less so. All three of the lessons require the students to blend and make words. Finally, the Treasures (2009) lesson provides for more practice examples than does StoryTown (2008) or Trophies (2003/2005). Teachers are obviously free to add further practice. Overall, the StoryTown (2008) lesson conforms closely to Beck's (2006) model outlined previously, and Beck is, not coincidentally, one of the program authors for StoryTown. Treasures (2009), compared with the other programs, provides much more practice and application of the skill in small groups. All three of the programs, at least in this initial lesson, avoid a strict focus on word families. Students are asked to blend and make words with a variety of final letters. We cannot say that these differences will continue throughout all the phonics lessons in these core reading programs, but we believe that it is important for teachers to engage in this side-by-side comparison for at least a sample of the lessons to determine if the lessons they are considering will meet the needs of their students.

Core Reading Program Flexibility and Responsiveness

All core reading programs appeared to have difficulty including responsiveness or flexibility in their lessons. Each had options for small groups to follow the whole-class lesson; however, there was no option to work on skills different from the original lesson. For example, in StoryTown (2008), the teacher is directed to review or reteach the skill from the whole-class lesson, but no teaching directions are given for reviewing or reteaching features from previous weeks or units. In Treasures (2009), students in the approaching-level group (below-level readers) are asked to repeat the same task used with the whole-class lesson. The program suggests using additional letter cards to give visual clues for blending and Elkonin boxes for segmenting, but the same features and words are used. All of the newer programs provide for differentiation by providing separate workbooks for above-, on-, and below-level students. For example, the below-level students' review lesson was to supply the medial vowel (the feature being studied) in the blank between letters under a picture cue. For example, the student would see "r__t" and the picture of a rat; their task was to fill in an *a*. For students in the on-level group, the practice book task was to circle the word that names the picture from three options and write the word on a line under the picture. No further phonics instruction was suggested for students reading above grade level.

Decodable texts are included with each core reading program. One decodable book is aligned with each weekly whole-group phonics lesson. In Treasures (2009), they are used for the whole-group lesson on day 1 and again on day

5, and again with the below-level students in their small group. In StoryTown (2008), the decodable book is used during the whole-group lesson, then again for both the below-level and on-level small groups. The below-level group echo reads the book, and the on-level group partner reads the book.

The task of differentiating instruction has been a persistent problem for core reading programs and one that we can't judge too harshly. Core reading programs cannot make diagnostic decisions, only teachers can. The newest programs provide the structure for small-group instruction and, in some cases, a lesson plan to follow. The older programs do not. The program cannot anticipate the specific phonics patterns that below-level students need to learn. The best these programs can do is make sure the resources and lesson plans are available and easy to locate.

Sight-Word Instruction

Programs use high-frequency words and phonics words to practice automatic word recognition. These words usually make up the spelling lesson for the week, so there are 10 words that students are expected to know. The ratio of high-frequency to phonics words is different from program to program but generally ran 7 or 8 phonics words to 2 or 3 high-frequency words per week. In some programs, the high-frequency words are included in the word sorts with the expectation that they will be sorted into another column.

Phonics words are introduced with the phonemic awareness and phonics section of the lesson. High-frequency words were introduced separately. StoryTown (2008) covers high-frequency words in two parts of the lesson. As part of the morning message, the teacher reviews four or more words and then asks the students to read them as she or he points to them in a random order. Later in the lesson, new high-frequency words are introduced. The teacher points to and reads the word, then the students say the words. A sentence is read that contains the new high-frequency words, and the high-frequency words are spelled. Additional sentences are read with other high-frequency words. Review activities include sorting and writing the words.

In Treasures (2009) high-frequency words are introduced each week. Students are directed to read, spell, and write the words. The words are added to a word wall. The major difference in this lesson from StoryTown (2008) is the attention to phonics elements. The teacher draws the students' attention to phonics elements that have already been taught and are present in the sight words. The word wall is reviewed periodically during the week. In some review lessons, students are asked to reread all of the words on the wall. Students read sentences on the board that contain the high-frequency words ,and some students circle these words.

The high-frequency word lesson in the newer core reading programs differs little from the older versions of these programs. Houghton Mifflin Reading (2003/2005) and Trophies (2003/2005) have students read high-frequency words in isolation, in sentences, and in poems. Words are placed on a word wall. Students hold up word cards to signal recognition as the teacher reads them. The single innovation in the new programs is the stress on the phonics elements in the high-frequency word instruction, which is warranted considering the need for a student to attend to or fully analyze a word to remember it (Ehri, 1991).

PUTTING IT ALL TOGETHER

Both phonemic awareness and phonics instruction have been highly politicized and controversial over the years. In fact, arguments have been intense to the point of being referred to as the "reading wars." This has led to much uncertainty about what constitutes a good reading program and to very different core reading programs at different points in time (Maslin, 2003). However, we have a general consensus in research about guidelines for effective instruction. To understand the phonemic awareness and phonics instruction in a core reading program, it is important to examine several factors: grade level, grouping, scope and sequence, and the characteristics of the instruction (what the teachers and students say and do). Older and newer core reading programs do not differ when phonemic awareness and phonics are taught. The new programs provide more guidelines for small-group instruction, whereas in the older programs, that was limited to the use of decodable books. Scope and sequences are similar across programs and are difficult to evaluate, because publisher's samples do not include all manuals. Without all six grade-level manuals, it is impossible to track the sequence of skills development.

(continued)

PUTTING IT ALL TOGETHER *(cont'd)*

The explicitness of phonemic awareness and phonics instruction has improved over the last five to six years in core reading programs. Teachers are encouraged to be more declarative in identifying letter sounds and names and modeling blending. It also appears that the number and diversity of practice activities during direct instruction has improved. Ultimately, we believe that any district that wants to select a core reading program should adhere to our two major guidelines. First, consider your needs. If decoding in the primary grades is your major concern, then study that element of a core reading program closely. Second, read a sample of lessons closely, comparing the same skills and strategies across programs. Through this close study, you will determine which programs best meet your needs. The following questions are intended to start the process of evaluating a core reading program based on generally accepted research at this time:

- Are the concepts taught in a developmentally appropriate sequence of instruction?
- Does the program offer explicit instruction in word features and decoding strategies?
- Does the program use small groups for instruction that is flexible and responsive to differing levels of need?
- Does the program include concrete markers to help students grasp the concept of grapheme–phoneme relationships?
- Are students given assistance to apply decoding strategies while reading?
- Does the program teach letter names and sounds?
- Does the program provide active, engaging learning activities that include sorting, writing, and decoding words?
- Is the program teacher-led instead of being worksheet dependent?

CHAPTER 5

Comprehension Instruction in Core Reading Programs

Five third graders and their teacher are sitting around the kidney-shaped table reading and discussing *Ella and Her Mean Cousins* (Benjamin, 2003), one of the leveled books that accompanies their core reading program. This book, a take-off on "Cinderella," is intended for students reading below grade level. (Before reading the book, the teacher and the students refreshed their memories of the traditional "Cinderella" tale.) The students read the text on the first two pages:

> Once upon a time, a beautiful and kind young girl named Ella lived on a farm. When Ella was a baby, her mother died. For many years she and her father lived happily together. They delighted in each other's company. Ella took care of the house while her father took care of the farm.
>
> One spring day Ella's Aunt Letty and two cousins came to visit. Her older cousin, Betty, frowned all the time. Her younger cousin, Hetty, looked mean all the time. The wagon was piled high with all their trunks and suitcases.
>
> "I hope you don't mind a short visit from your favorite relatives," said Aunt Letty. (pp. 1–2)

The teacher begins the discussion:

Teacher: Can someone tell us what this story is about? What has the author told us?

Paula: Ella's cousins came to visit.

Teacher: Aliya, can you add to what Paula has told us?

Aliya: They have a lot of suitcases.

Teacher: Does anyone else want to add to the summary? George?

George: Ella lived with her dad.

Teacher: Can anyone put this all together; paraphrase the whole story so far? [*Teacher waits, but there is no complete response from the students, and the teacher then models for the students.*] Ella and her father have lived together on a farm since her mother died. One day her Aunt Letty and her two cousins Hetty and Betty came for a short visit. What can we figure out about Aunt Letty's plans that the author has not told us? [*Although the text is accompanied by a large illustration showing a woman, two young girls, and a large pile of luggage, there are no responses from the students.*] How long do you think Aunt Letty and cousins Hetty and Betty plan to stay? [*Again, no responses.*] If you were going for a short visit, would you pack a lot of clothes and take many suitcases?

Aliya: I would!

Teacher: Yes, and you are like my daughter, who needs a lot of clothes!

The students in this small group read the story with respectable oral reading fluency, yet they struggled to summarize the story and make an inference about Aunt Letty's intentions. The problems with summarizing, actually paraphrasing, may reflect their inability to construct an overall understanding of the story. In short, they did not link sentences and ideas together. The students' inferential problems stem either from lack of prior knowledge about traveling or their inability to use that knowledge to draw conclusions about the characters' intentions. These two problems in constructing an overall understanding of a text and making inferences go to the central problems of reading comprehension: strategies and knowledge. Both are essential elements for comprehension, and both must be addressed as part of reading comprehension instruction.

Over the past 30 years, educators and psychologists have worked to understand reading comprehension and the best methods for developing it. Some educators and psychologists have worked to understand the process of reading comprehension and just how we perform this complex and often enthralling act. Other educators have taken these theoretical insights and fashioned them into instructional procedures. Periodically, this research has been synthesized, most recently in the NRP report (NICHD, 2000) and by the RAND Reading Study Group (2002), and in a growing number of books on teaching reading comprehension. A growing consensus has emerged from this research about what works. Comprehension requires knowledge, thinking strategies, and motivation (Alexander, 2003).

As in the previous chapters, we divide our discussion into three parts. First, we explore what the research says about effective comprehension instruction. Second, we take a close look at how these research-based understandings have been developed in core reading programs. We describe the strengths and weaknesses of these programs based on some recent curriculum analyses. Finally, we give suggestions for evaluating your own core reading program. In Chapter 11, we look at how to use core reading programs effectively to develop comprehension. The ideas about comprehension instruction developed in this chapter should inform your thinking in Chapter 11.

What You Will Learn

- The importance of knowledge and strategies to becoming an effective reader
- The comprehension skills and strategies validated through research studies
- The characteristics of knowledge development lessons in core reading programs
- The characteristics and quality of comprehension skills and strategy instruction in core reading programs

What You Will Be Able to Do

- Analyze your core reading program to determine which comprehension skills and strategies are essential for your students
- Critique the lesson plan structure of comprehension skills and strategy instruction
- Change the guided reading portion of a lesson in a core reading program so that students more readily acquire the skills and begin to use them independently
- Identify and select core reading programs that have more robust comprehension instruction

The ideas in this chapter will help you complete an evaluation of the comprehension instruction in core reading programs. Online at www.reading.org/general/publications/books/bk707.aspx, you can find our Reading GPS, an instrument that will guide you through the process of evaluating the texts in a core reading program. The Reading GPS and this chapter are meant to be used together.

What Research Has to Say About Comprehension Instruction

Comprehension is an active, constructive process that demands knowledge, attention, purpose, thought, and evaluation. Unlike movies, in which images wash over you, and television, which tolerates or fosters inattention, reading requires focus and purpose. Good readers exhibit these characteristics:

- Have a goal that may be simply getting lost in the world of the author or an intense search for important ideas; continually evaluate whether they are meeting their goal
- Preview a text, noting its organization and length and determining how much they will be able to read in a sitting
- Predict, revise, and then predict again as they read
- Bring to the page knowledge of the world around them and their personal experiences
- Connect ideas from one sentence or paragraph to another, gradually building a cohesive understanding of the text
- Make connections or inferences, filling in the ideas that the author trusts the reader will supply
- Search for and retain important ideas
- Monitor their comprehension, stopping reading to summarize, confirm their understanding, or ask questions to seek clarification
- Have endurance, continuing to read even when the texts get difficult, realizing that often the goal is worth the effort
- Vary how they read depending on the demands of the text and their purpose—some texts demand a close read while in others the readers skim for surface features

Knowledge and Comprehension

For the last two decades, teaching comprehension strategies has been the primary means of increasing reading comprehension. It has been extensively argued that good comprehenders employ a set of comprehension strategies that keep them focused, enable them to follow the structure of ideas, assemble these ideas into a synthesis, make inferences, and monitor this process. But strategies are difficult to use when the reader has little or no prior knowledge. Consider the following passage. You can read all of the words, but comprehension is stopped by your lack of prior knowledge.

> The procedure is actually quite simple. First, you arrange the items into different groups. Of course, one pile may be sufficient depending on how much there is to do. If you have to go somewhere else due to lack of facilities that is the next step; otherwise, you are pretty well set. It is important not to overdo things. That is, it is better to do too few things at once than too many. In the short run this may not seem important, but complications can easily arise. A mistake can be expensive as well. At first, the whole procedure will seem complicated. Soon, however, it will become just another facet of life. It is difficult to foresee any end to the necessity for this task in the immediate future, but then, one never can tell. After the procedure is completed one arranges the material into different groups again. Then they can be put into their appropriate places. Eventually they will be used once more and the whole cycle will then have to be repeated. However, that is part of life. (Anderson & Pearson, 1984, p. 279)

Knowledge is essential for reading comprehension, and a number of studies suggest that knowledge and general verbal skill may be more important than strategies (Cain, Oakhill, & Bryant, 2004; Samuelstuen & Bråten, 2005; Willingham, 2006). The two most prominent views of the reading process—schema theory (Anderson & Pearson, 1984) and the construction-integration model (Kintsch, 1998)—have at their core the concept that understanding a text requires an integration of prior knowledge and text information. The excerpted paragraph would have made more sense if it carried the title "Laundry."

Understanding of the following sentence would be greatly impaired without prior knowledge and experiences: *Mary looked at her menu trying to find the cheapest entrée, while John gazed lovingly in her eyes.* Without knowledge of restaurants and courtship, this sentence is difficult to comprehend. Prior knowledge is the building block of inferences, what the reader brings to the text. Without knowledge, we would not be able to discern John's interest, Mary's motivation, or even where they are. A larger number of studies with students of varying ages supports the fact that when a reader has prior knowledge comprehension improves (e.g., Anderson, Reynolds, Schallert, & Goetz, 1977; Reynolds, Taylor, Steffensen, Shirey, & Anderson, 1982). In one study, when Jewish students read about a Catholic communion, they interpreted the text in light of their own experiences. The reverse was true when Catholic students read about a bar mitzvah (Lipson, 1983). The Catholic students understood and remembered less than did the Jewish children when the subject was a bar mitzvah. The more you know, the more you understand. So it makes sense that reading programs should build students' knowledge, and to do so, they would need to organize the reading selections and units of study so that students could build knowledge.

Having the necessary prior knowledge does not ensure that students will comprehend what they read. Obviously, students with weak word recognition skills will struggle, but there are fluent readers who fail to use the prior knowledge that they possess. In one study, 8-year-olds with similar word recognition ability were taught about an imaginary planet, Gan, and they all learned the information perfectly (Cain, Oakhill, Barnes, & Bryant, 2001). However, when the students read passages about Gan, not all achieved equal reading comprehension. Some students used the knowledge they gained to comprehend the passage better than others. In another study, researchers found that some students trusted their prior knowledge more than the text. When these students read about a pet lamb, their own ideas were so compelling that they ignored the causal statements in the text about why the lamb ran away (Nicholson & Imlach, 1981).

You may have noticed that many of the studies about the role of prior knowledge in comprehension are relatively old, dating from the 1980s. This is because prior knowledge was the central concern of researchers 25 years ago; now researchers and educators are more focused on comprehension strategies. Prior knowledge is necessary for comprehension but not sufficient. Comprehension strategies are thinking tools that guide the reader to pull ideas together, focus on what is important, and integrate what they know with what they are reading. Having background knowledge also makes strategies easier to use. When readers of varying ability are given a difficult passage to read, those with more prior knowledge of the passage exhibit greater use of strategies, especially those that help readers follow the organization of a text and monitor their developing comprehension (Samuelstuen & Bråten, 2005). So it is never an either–or situation: Good readers need strategies *and* knowledge.

Strategies and Comprehension: Which Strategies Should Be Taught?

Experts have reviewed research on comprehension instruction and reached conclusions about what are the most important strategies. In documents like the NRP report (NICHD, 2000) and *Reading for Understanding* (RAND Reading

Study Group, 2002) and in literature reviews from experts (Duke & Pearson, 2002; Pearson, Roehler, Dole, & Duffy, 1992), there has emerged a broad, but not absolute, consensus on the most important strategies that readers need. In addition, many of these strategies are included in the multiple-strategy routines like reciprocal teaching (Palincsar & Brown, 1984) and transactional strategy instruction (Brown et al., 1996).

This general consensus has honed the list down to seven comprehension strategies: *predicting, self-questioning, comprehension monitoring, summarizing, determining importance, making inferences*, and focusing on *text structure*. We can classify these strategies around three central comprehension processes: relating text ideas to one another, relating text ideas to prior knowledge, and monitoring the reader's developing understanding. Several strategies enable these three basic processes (Willingham, 2006):

- Relating sentence and text ideas to one another
  - Summarizing
  - Focusing on text structure
  - Determining importance
- Relating sentence and text ideas to prior knowledge
  - Predicting
  - Making inferences and connections
  - Determining importance
- Monitoring comprehension
  - Clarifying
  - Self-questioning
  - Predicting
  - Summarizing

Understanding text structure (story structure and informational structure) and summarizing help readers put ideas together to form a cohesive understanding of what they read. Making predictions, inferences, and connections helps the reader to relate text idea to prior knowledge. Clarifying, self-questioning, predicting, and summarizing induce readers to monitor what they read. What we think of as unique strategies may help the reader in more than one way. Summarizing what you read helps put ideas together, and generating a brief summary helps a reader check level of understanding. Some researchers endorse strategies like graphic organizers that are not true mental strategies but instructional tools used by teachers and students to guide and support strategy use and text understanding.

It should be obvious that some traditional skills, like determining the *author's purpose*, *cause and effect*, *sequence of events*, *drawing conclusions*, and *compare and contrast*, are not found in any of the consensus documents. As we discussed in Chapter 1, comprehension skills were included in core reading programs starting in the early 1930s, and now these traditional skills exist alongside comprehension strategies. Often core programs label skills as strategies and strategies as skills. The distinction between a skill and a strategy is not easy to make. Skills and strategies are both mental acts, thinking processes that facilitate text comprehension. Although a skill can be done automatically without conscious attention, a strategy is typically deliberate, purposeful, and within a reader's awareness (Afflerbach, Pearson, & Paris, 2008). With practice and growing expertise, a strategy becomes a skill. Skills can be turned into strategies through deliberate thinking. A skill like drawing conclusions, actually another name for making inferences, can be executed automatically without awareness, or invoked through conscious attention and purpose. Throughout this chapter, we discuss skills and strategies, because the core reading programs make little distinction between the two.

Teaching Comprehension Strategies

The basic lesson plan for strategy instruction has been established for some time as the gradual release of responsibility model (Pearson & Gallagher, 1983). The model has three stages. First, the teacher begins by explaining and modeling the strategy. At this stage, it is the teacher's responsibility to do the work. Explanation consists of identifying the strategy and explaining the mental steps a reader uses while engaging the strategy and the text clues that guide those steps. Explanation also involves describing why the strategy is valuable and when to use it. The teacher models the strategy, typically several times, and may return to modeling when the students do not understand how to use the strategy.

Second, the teacher helps the students gradually apply the strategy and incorporate it into their reading/thinking routine. Through guided practice or scaffolding, the students begin to use the strategy as the teacher guides the reading lessons. The students summarize, clarify, and predict. The teacher scaffolds the students, supporting and guiding their attempts to use the strategies. Verbal hints and prompts from the teacher guide the students' use of the strategy. Graphic organizers and sticky notes remind the students to use the strategy. Working in pairs, the students help each other use new strategies.

Eventually, in the third stage, the students assume full control of the strategy and are able to use it in student-led discussion groups or while reading on their own. The gradual release of responsibility model (Pearson & Gallagher, 1983) has been successfully applied to traditional skills such as finding the main idea, strategies such as self-questioning or comprehension monitoring, and multiple-strategy instruction.

There is no research that suggests a specific order or sequence for introducing comprehension skills and strategies. However, several researchers have considered the development of cognition, and these insights provide guidelines on when comprehension strategy instruction might begin (Paris & Jacobs, 1984; Smolkin & Donovan, 2002). Young students can use strategies with teacher guidance, but their memory and their ability to orchestrate mental actions is insufficiently developed to allow them to use strategies on their own. Therefore, some researchers argue that formal strategy instruction should not begin before the end of second grade (Willingham, 2006). Also, strategies that demand thinking at multiple levels, like summarizing and the generation of questions (see Raphael, 1984), may be beyond the capability of young students. But several researchers have demonstrated that second graders can learn about text structure, understand narrative and informational text (Williams, 2006), make predictive inferences (Hansen, 1981), link text ideas to their experiences (Tharp, 1982), ask questions, visualize, and retell stories. Other researchers, notably Brown et al. (1996), have successfully taught a wide range of cognitive and interpretative strategies through transactional strategy instruction to second graders. Finally, the texts that students can read in kindergarten and first grade provide little substance on which to build comprehension strategies.

The other important consideration is the amount of instruction and practice that students need before they can use a strategy independently. Note we are not talking about mastery of skills and strategies, because the concept of mastery cannot be logically applied to reading comprehension instruction. Despite an individual reader's skill with comprehension strategies, there will always be another piece of text so challenging, written in such a complex manner, that even the skilled reader is stopped in his or her tracks (e.g., *Gravity's Rainbow* by Thomas Pynchon). We can examine how much practice students require by looking at the research on massed and distributed practice and by examining how much practice researchers actually provided for students when they validated the comprehension strategies.

Massed practice is the practice students receive right after a skill or strategy is introduced; distributed practice occurs over an extended period of time in a variety of contexts. Researchers have demonstrated that distributed practice, over days and weeks, is more important than initial massed practice. When a skill or strategy is first introduced, students need frequent teacher-guided opportunities to practice that skill. After the skill or strategy is introduced, students need regular but more widely spaced practice opportunities to ensure that the strategy is internalized and that the student can transfer the strategy to different types of texts. An example of this process is the work of Fitzgerald and Spiegel (1983), who taught story structure to young children. The researchers employed two distinct phases to their story structure instruction. In the first intensive phase, the students were taught about story structure during six 30- to 45-minute sessions over two weeks. In the second phase of the instruction, the students studied story structure 10 times over five weeks. This argues for a reading curriculum in which strategies are cumulative. Once a strategy is introduced, it is employed regularly alongside other new and previously taught strategies.

To bring our discussion full circle, the most recent work on comprehension strategy instruction has strengthened the tie between reading strategies and knowledge. In Concept-Oriented Reading Instruction, Guthrie and his colleagues compared teaching comprehension strategies without embedding them in particular content to teaching comprehension strategies within a life science curriculum (Guthrie et al., 1998). These researchers found that comprehension improved more and strategy use was greater when students learned strategies within a science content. Guthrie et al. attributed this growth to the greater engagement, or self-focused motivated learning, of the students. Using comprehension strategies is demanding, and students need a strong incentive to do so. Given what we know of teaching and learning comprehension, we now examine how comprehension is developed in core reading programs.

Evaluating Comprehension Instruction in Core Reading Programs

Delores Durkin (1978) startled reading educators when she reported that teachers were spending precious little of their instructional time teaching students how to comprehend. Instead of teaching how, teachers mentioned skills to the students, provided time for them to practice skills, and interrogated them by asking comprehension questions. Durkin then turned her attention to core reading programs to see if the practices she observed in classrooms had their roots in the programs. She found that they did. Core reading programs directed teachers to mention skills, provide extensive independent practice (worksheets), and ask numerous comprehension questions (interrogation). Assessment exceeded instruction. Durkin also found that the programs' treatment of individual skills varied from thorough to cursory.

Roughly a decade later, Durkin (1990) repeated this analysis with a new generation of core reading programs by examining instruction for teaching story structure and determining the main idea. She found that the programs were not much different from their predecessors. The programs covered too many topics, with instruction provided quickly and often superficially. Others examined core reading programs and consistently found problems similar to those uncovered by Durkin: lack of direct instruction, limited focus on the mental process, limited practice on a skill, and too many skills covered in a short span of time (Franks et al., 1997; Miller & Blumenfeld, 1993; Schmitt & Hopkins, 1993).

A more recent look at core reading programs found that programs often used a flawed instructional sequence, introducing a complex version of a skill before a simpler one or using text that was above many students' instructional levels (Jitendra et al., 2001). Finally, McGill-Franzen, Zmach, Solic, and Zeig (2006) examined the predominant core reading programs in Florida and identified a relationship between program characteristics and student outcomes. In comparing two programs in a natural experiment, lower ability students who were taught with a program that included more questioning to develop interpretations performed better on the Florida state assessment than students using another program that stressed vocabulary instruction, fluency, and independent practice.

Since these curriculum studies appeared, core reading programs have assumed even greater importance in reading instruction, because state departments of education, research centers, and publishers have given them the label of scientifically based reading research. This claim caused us to take a close look at the comprehension skills and strategy instruction in the core reading programs that carried a 2005 copyright date (Dewitz et al., 2008, 2009). Before we help you improve instruction with your core reading programs, we needed to identify the following four problems you will be facing with your core reading program:

1. What skills and strategies are taught in the core reading program, and do these correspond to what researchers recommend?
2. How explicit is the comprehension strategy instruction in the core reading program?
3. Does the core reading program provide teachers with tools and directions to ensure that students internalize and apply comprehension strategies?
4. How well does the core reading program develop the knowledge and vocabulary students need to comprehend what they read?

We (Dewitz et al., 2009) examined the five most commonly used core reading programs in the country as of 2008: Trophies (Harcourt, 2003/2005), Scott Foresman Reading (Pearson Scott Foresman, 2004), Houghton Mifflin Reading (Houghton Mifflin, 2003/2005), Macmillan/McGraw-Hill Reading (Macmillan/McGraw-Hill, 2005), and Open Court Reading (SRA/McGraw-Hill, 2005). First, we determined which skills and strategies were taught in the program to see if they corresponded to recommendations of researchers. Second, we rated the instructional moves that the teacher was asked to make. A teacher might mention a skill, explain it, model it, provide guided practice, ask a question, engage students in a discussion, or provide independent practice. Because we read every lesson in every unit, we could track a skill or strategy across a unit or theme to see if the teacher moved the students from direct instruction to guided practice, and then to independent use of the strategies. Internalizing a strategy happens if students receive substantial practice with individual comprehension skills and strategies. Ultimately, we compared the amount of practice provided in the core reading program to the amount of practice researchers provided in instructional studies on the same skill or strategy in core reading programs.

In the other study, we examined knowledge development in core reading programs (Dewitz et al., 2008). First, we read the selections in the student anthology and looked to see what knowledge the program directed teachers to develop. Did this instruction help students understand what they were reading? We also considered the relationships among reading selections, trying to determine if what students learned in one selection helped them understand the next selection. We examine knowledge development first and then turn our attention to strategy instruction.

Knowledge Development in Core Reading Programs

Core reading programs provide several ways for teachers to develop students' knowledge. Before students read a selection, the teacher typically conducts a short read-aloud that is tied to the theme of the reading selections. New concepts and ideas are introduced. Next, all programs direct teachers to activate and develop students' prior knowledge that is specific to the reading selections for a lesson. Teachers are also directed to teach the meanings of specific vocabulary words that are necessary to comprehend the selection. Finally, each of the reading selections does not stand alone but is part of a thematic unit. It is presumed that what a student learns in one selection will carry over and enhance understanding of the next selections read. We (Dewitz et al., 2008) examined all the means of developing knowledge by closely reading themes in four core programs: Trophies (2003/2005), Scott Foresman Reading (2004), Houghton Mifflin Reading (2003/2005), and Open Court Reading (2005). We begin our analysis by looking at the way units of instruction are organized.

Unit Structure. All core reading programs in the upper grades are organized into six units or themes, and, within each unit, there are three to six major reading selections, a few shorter reading selections, and typically three leveled books for each major selection. These texts are tied together in a thematic structure, and the themes typically repeat across grade levels. Themes often, but not always, carry vague and insubstantial titles (Walsh, 2003). The first three themes in Trophies (2003/2005) are You Can Do It, Side by Side, and Make Yourself at Home. Open Court Reading's (2005) first three units are Risks and Consequences, Dollars and Sense, and From Mystery to Medicine, while in Scott Foresman Reading (2004) they are Focus on Family, A Wider View, and Keys to Success. We took a close look inside three themes to see how the reading selections were tied together. Table 16 presents an overview of one unit from each of the three programs. The Communication unit from Open Court Reading is actually the fifth one in the program.

These three units of instruction illustrate the difference between building knowledge and just having an overarching theme. The Scott Foresman Reading unit, Focus on Family, presents five selections all centered on the family, but each selection demands knowledge that is unique to that piece. So life on a cattle ranch in the West does little to prepare the reader for the plight of orphans moving to the Midwest in 1900. Nor does that selection help the reader understand the food and celebrations of Mexico. The selections reflect the overall theme, but

Table 16. The Content and Genres of Fourth-Grade Units in Three Core Reading Programs

| | Scott Foresman Reading (Pearson Scott Foresman, 2004) | | Trophies (Harcourt, 2003/2005) | | Open Court Reading (SRA/McGraw-Hill, 2005) | |
| Theme | Focus on Family | | You Can Do It | | Communication | |
Selection	Genre	Content	Genre	Content	Genre	Content
1	Realistic fiction	A boy visits his grandfather in the West and learns to ride horses, rope cows, and make biscuits.	Realistic fiction	A young girl helps her grandfather plant a city garden during the Depression.	Information	How whales and elephants communicate.
2	Historical fiction	Homeless orphan children in 1900 go West to find new homes.	Realistic fiction	A boy collects words that he keeps in a jar and must decide what to do with them.	Information	How commercials work and how they influence us.
3	Realistic fiction	A young Asian immigrant struggles to learn the violin and U.S. culture.	Realistic fiction	A young Latina girl works hard to get into the school play with her family's support.	Information	The invention of the printing press.
4	Personal narrative	Foods, celebrations, and cultural events in Mexico.	Biography	A short biography of Lou Gehrig.	Information	How a gorilla uses American Sign Language.
5	Historical fiction	A young girl copes with hardships while homesteading in the Dakotas in the 1880s.	Historical fiction	The meeting of Eleanor Roosevelt and Amelia Earhart.	Biography	How Louis Braille struggled to create an alphabet for the blind.
6					Fantasy	From *The Little Prince*, we do not always communicate what we think.

it is questionable if what is learned in one selection will help the reader understand the other selections in that particular unit. The Trophies theme, You Can Do It, describes instances of coping and problem solving. However, developing a city garden during the Great Depression has little to do with Lou Gehrig's fight against amyotrophic lateral sclerosis or an obscure meeting between Eleanor Roosevelt and Amelia Earhart. Only the Communication unit in Open Court Reading (2005) seems likely to develop knowledge from the first selection to the last. The unit begins with animal communication in whales and elephants, and that selection develops some basic concepts of communication that can be applied to other selections. Overall, we found that in most units within core reading programs, what students learn in one selection will not assist their comprehension in subsequent selections (Dewitz et al., 2008).

Developing Knowledge. A student's comprehension of each selection is dependent on the knowledge that the student brings with him or her. Core reading programs both assess knowledge before students read and provide teachers with suggestions for teaching the concepts students need to know. Our analysis of core reading programs indicates that they often do not develop the ideas that students need to comprehend each selection. We closely read two units from each of three major core reading programs and had teachers rate which ideas in each selection would most likely be unfamiliar to their students. In the core reading programs, we then read the three lesson segments that would develop that knowledge—background knowledge development lessons, the oral read-alouds, and the vocabulary lesson—to determine if the programs developed the knowledge that teachers believe students need. In the best of the lessons, 40% of the important but unfamiliar ideas were developed before students read the selection. In the worst of cases, as little as 10% or fewer ideas were discussed before students began to read. Overall, the programs developed less than a third of the ideas students would need in order to comprehend what they were reading. Lacking these ideas, students would be unable to make some critical inferences. For example, the comprehension of one Trophies (2003/2005) selection, *Centerfield Ballhawk* (Christopher, 1994), rests on the students' knowledge of baseball and the understanding that both the offensive skill of hitting and the defensive skill of fielding are essential to winning. Lacking this knowledge, readers will fail to understand the emotions of a young boy who is a talented fielder but only an adequate hitter.

In our analysis of core reading programs, each unit in each program varies in how well each of the three components supports the students. In some programs and units, such as Trophies (2003/2005) the read-aloud and the vocabulary instruction do more to support the students than does the background knowledge development portion of the lesson. In Houghton Mifflin Reading (2003/2005), the background knowledge development and vocabulary portions of the lesson carry the load, whereas the read-aloud is often irrelevant. Finally, in Open Court Reading (2005), all three components contribute to the students' knowledge development (Dewitz et al., 2008).

The Comprehension Curriculum

Core reading programs teach a mix of comprehension skills, strategies, genres, and text structure elements. Each program divides the comprehension curriculum into a different number of skills and strategies. Some programs make a clear distinction between a skill and a strategy, while others conflate the two and even consider concepts of genre and text structure as comprehension skills. Earlier in this chapter, we reviewed what experts and expert panels had identified as the most important comprehension strategies: *self-questioning, summarizing, making inferences, comprehension monitoring, determining importance,* and *text structure* for both narrative and informational texts. In comparison, core reading programs teach anywhere from 15 to 29 different comprehension skills and strategies. Table 17 lists the total count of assessed comprehension skills and strategies in each of the five major core programs (Dewitz et al., 2009).

It is important to note that Scott Foresman Reading (2004) and Trophies (2003/2005) list all parts of the comprehension curriculum as both skills and strategies and make no attempt to differentiate between the two. In Open Court Reading (2005), a clear distinction is made between skills and strategies. Strategies include predicting, clarifying, questioning, summarizing, and evaluating and are regularly repeated across lessons. Skills include finding the main idea, determining the author's purpose, and making inferences. Houghton Mifflin Reading (2003/2005) provides instruction in 17 comprehension skills and 6 comprehension strategies, with predicting taught as a skill in some lessons and a strategy in others. Macmillan/McGraw-Hill Reading (Macmillan/McGraw-Hill, 2003/2005) includes 15 comprehension skills and strategies, with everything labeled as both a skill and a strategy. All of the programs

Table 17. Number of Comprehension Skills and Strategies Taught in the Five Major Core Programs

Program	Comprehension Skills and Strategies	Comprehension Skills	Comprehension Strategies	Literary Elements and Craft
Scott Foresman Reading (Pearson Scott Foresman, 2004)	29	0	0	12
Trophies (Harcourt, 2003/2005)	17	0	0	15
Open Court Reading (SRA/McGraw-Hill, 2005)	0	10	7	0
Houghton Mifflin Reading (Houghton Mifflin, 2003/2005)	0	17	6	0
Macmillan/McGraw-Hill Reading (Macmillan/ McGraw-Hill, 2003/2005)	0	15	0	2

include considerably more skills and strategies than are found in the expert review documents.

Several patterns explain why there is so much for teachers to teach and for children to learn in these programs. First, some comprehension skills and strategies are taught under more than one label. All programs teach students to make inferences, and each of these programs also presents lessons on drawing conclusions and making generalizations. A careful reading of these fourth-grade lessons indicates that despite the label, the students are being taught the same mental process (Dewitz et al., 2009). Look at how Houghton Mifflin Reading (2003/2005) presents making inferences and drawing conclusions:

> Remind students that authors do not always put every bit of information about characters and events on the page. By leaving some information out, they let readers apply what they know from personal experience to the story they are reading. By looking at characters' actions, for example, readers often make inferences about those character's feelings and personalities. (Theme 4, p. 397)

A conclusion is a judgment that you infer or deduce from a story's facts and details. To draw conclusions you combine facts and details in the text with personal knowledge and experience.... When you draw conclusions you also use them to make generalizations that go beyond the story. A generalization always extends beyond the information provided by the story. (Theme 4, p. 127)

These two lessons demonstrate the close relationship between making inferences, drawing conclusions, and making generalizations. All demand information from the text, prior knowledge, and the use of that knowledge to complete what the author left out. Trophies (2003/2005) also presents making inferences and drawing conclusions in a very similar manner.

An inference is a connection that a reader makes between information that is given and what he or she already knows from experience. (Theme 2, p. 243B)

A conclusion is a judgment that you infer or deduce from a story's facts and details. To draw a conclusion you combine facts and details in the text with personal knowledge and experience.... When you draw conclusions you also use them to make generalizations that go beyond the story. A generalization always extends beyond the information provided by the story." (Theme 2, p. 138I)

These lessons describe a common underlying mental process. By using different labels for the same mental process, core reading programs appear to be teaching more skills and strategies than they actually are. How does the novice reader handle the problem of learning a new way of thinking with text when at different times during the year, the program and the teacher change the label? Ultimately, the curriculum must make sense to the students and the teachers. As teachers, we must be careful to recognize that drawing conclusions and making inferences are essentially the same.

A second pattern that increases the number of skills and strategies in core reading programs is the tendency to break one strategy or skill into components. In Houghton Mifflin Reading (2003/2005), noting details is taught as a separate skill from main idea, then taught again in conjunction with the main idea. Separating main idea from details breaks the relationship between these two structural or relational elements in a text, which is really just about determining importance. In effect, the details define or confine the main idea, and the main idea provides a categorization for the details. Macmillan/McGraw-Hill Reading (2003/2005) teaches main ideas, main ideas and details, and then important facts and unimportant facts. This adds a second label to an already difficult concept.

The teaching of narrative structure also presents undue complexity and accounts for some of the multiplicity of skills and strategies. In Scott Foresman Reading (2004), character, setting, plot, and theme are taught as separate skills but not in a unified manner. Providing additional emphasis on character development and setting makes sense but only if the overall structure of a narrative is developed first. Trophies (2003/2005) teaches narrative structure as a unitary skill, but also teaches separate lessons on sequencing, character development, and setting and not necessarily in that order. Houghton Mifflin Reading (2003/2005) teaches narrative structure as a unitary skill and then sequence of events as a separate skill without making clear the relationship between the two concepts. Finally, Macmillan/McGraw-Hill Reading (2003/2005) focuses on two tested skills, character and setting, but omits an overall focus on narrative structure. All the programs find a way to make the study of narrative structure complex by dividing it into parts. Additionally, the teaching of narrative structure varies little between second and fifth grade. Students are not exposed to an increasingly more sophisticated understanding of narratives. Core reading programs do not envision a developing reader who can handle greater sophistication or complexity of ideas at the end of the year than at the beginning of the year.

The third factor that accounts for program complexity is equating two different types of skills: one that focuses on meaning construction while reading and another that focuses on response after reading. While reading, we *predict*, *question*, *infer*, *clarify*, *question*, and *summarize*. After reading, or at least on taking a second look at a text, we *compare and contrast* elements, *classify* what we have learned, probe for the *author's purpose*, or *make judgments*. These latter skills are not considered in the lists of endorsed reading strategies, yet they are found in many state curricula and assessments, so core reading programs must include them to survive. Including these responses to text increases the total number of skills and strategies in the programs. The directions in core reading programs often fail to make a distinction between what readers do to construct meaning while they are reading and their thoughtful responses after they have read.

Finally, all of the core reading programs teach elements of genre and text structure and call them skills. When a core reading program teaches *fantasy versus reality*, they are actually teaching characteristics that help to define realistic fiction and fantasy. This is more properly thought of as knowledge rather than a thinking strategy like making an inference. But genre and concepts of text structure give the reader a strategic advantage. Knowing about romantic comedies, a moviegoer can anticipate the breakup and subsequent reconciliation of the boy and girl by the end of the movie. In a similar vein, knowing about the structure and characteristics of fables, mysteries, or personal narratives enables the reader to *predict, question, monitor,* and *summarize* with greater insight. Knowledge of text structure and genre may facilitate the use of strategies.

Teachers can simplify comprehension instruction if they understand why core reading programs teach more skills and strategies than researchers endorse. Core reading programs fail to instruct students and teachers in the process of comprehension. We offer suggestions on how to make your comprehension instruction more elegant and effective in Chapter 10.

Comprehension Skills and Strategies Instruction

Good comprehension skills and strategies instruction rests the following on three instructional principles:

- The clarity and explicitness of the teacher's explanation and modeling of comprehension strategies
- The support and scaffolding students receive while trying out comprehension skills and strategies
- The amount of practice that students receive, so they can learn the skills and strategies

Direct Explanation. We took as our model of strong comprehension instruction the work of Duffy and his colleagues (1986) on direct explanation. Originally working to improve the explanations of teachers, Duffy et al. developed a set of criteria that defined a good comprehension lesson. We applied these criteria to the directions in the teacher's manuals of core reading programs. Direct explanation means that the teacher will clearly identify and explain the skill or strategy, describing the mental process and the text features necessary to follow that process. To understand cause and effect, a reader should note signal words (e.g., *because, since, however*) and to determine the main idea, the reader should look at titles, headings, boldface print, and topic sentences, if they exist. Next, direct explanation means that the teacher can describe the sequence of the mental process necessary to implement the comprehension skill or strategy.

The manual should also direct the teacher to talk about why the strategy is useful and when it might be applied. The *why* provides motivation and purpose. Students need to understand that strategies have a purpose beyond their execution. Strategies must lead to deeper understanding of text, to learning new and interesting ideas, or to greater engagement and pleasure with a text. The *when* is also crucial. Strategies are used to solve text-processing problems. When reading is relatively effortless, we engage in little strategy use, or at least this use is not within our awareness—it is a well-learned skill. Good instruction alerts the reader to when a strategy should be employed. These explanations should be accompanied by explicit modeling with appropriate text examples.

We took Duffy and colleagues' (1986) criteria and applied them to the five major core reading programs we studied. The results are presented in Table 18. Each instructional characteristic was rated 2, 1, or 0. A 2 meant that the core reading program met the criteria for the element of direct explanation, a 1 meant that the criteria were partially met, and a 0 meant that the criteria were not met. The numbers in the table are the average rating for all the lessons we evaluated in each criteria. Therefore, a score of 1.8 means that most of the lessons for a specific criterion were rated a 2, and a few were rated a 1.

Table 18. Averages of Characteristics of Direct Explanation in the Five Major Core Reading Programs

Characteristic	Scott Foresman Reading (Pearson Scott Foresman, 2004)	Trophies (Harcourt, 2003/2005)	Open Court Reading (SRA/ McGraw-Hill, 2005)	Houghton Mifflin Reading (Houghton Mifflin, 2003/2005)	Macmillan/ McGraw-Hill Reading (Macmillan/ McGraw-Hill, 2003/2005)
Mental process	1.8	1.6	1.9	1.1	0.5
Text features	1.5	0.5	0.8	0.0	0.3
Sequence of mental process	0.1	0.0	0.0	0.0	0.1
Usefulness	0.4	1.1	0.8	0.0	0.3
When to use the strategy	0.0	0.0	0.1	0.0	0.3
Explicit modeling	1.3	1.8	1.1	1.2	2.0
Explicit feedback on the process	1.1	0.0	0.0	0.0	0.8

Note. From Dewitz et al. (2009). Comprehension strategy instruction in core reading programs. *Reading Research Quarterly, 44*(2), 102–126.

All of the core reading programs except Macmillan/McGraw-Hill Reading (2003/2005) scored relatively high on providing teachers with explicit direction about the mental process that underlies the strategy. The programs were, however, much less explicit in directing teachers to talk about important text cues. So some programs failed to mention signal words for teaching cause and effect or noting the sequence. Generally, the programs did not have teachers focus on a close examination of the text features that should guide strategy use. Additionally, the core reading programs failed to lay out for the teacher and then the students a sequence to the mental process. Granted, this is difficult to do.

In the area of metacognition, explaining why a strategy was important and when to use it, all core reading programs were equally weak. All failed to mention when a strategy should be used. In almost all lessons, the teacher triggers the use of a strategy when he or she asks a question. Students rarely initiate strategy use, and core reading program instructions do not direct students to choose among strategies. Students are not told to look for cues in the text or in themselves that prompt them to use a comprehension strategy. As Duffy and colleagues (1986) carefully pointed out, readers resort to strategies when they encounter difficulty. When we are not sure if we understand a passage, we might try to summarize it in our minds. When ideas don't cohere, drawing inferences brings things together. When a whole paragraph does not make sense, rereading is a good move.

The utility of comprehension strategies, why they are important, and when they should be used get some attention in Trophies (2003/2005); scant attention in Scott Foresman Reading (2004), Open Court Reading (2005), and Macmillan/McGraw-Hill Reading (2003/2005); and no attention in Houghton Mifflin Reading (2003/2005). Clueing children in to why strategies are important is vital. It moves reading comprehension instruction from assignment giving to purposeful inquiry. In the assignment approach to teaching, teachers direct students to engage in an activity because of the implicit assumption that those activities are good for them. Students are more likely to use strategies if they are part of a larger goal that they have personally embraced (Guthrie, Wigfield, & VonSecker, 2000).

Guided Practice. After teachers explain and model strategies, the next goal is to help students apply the strategies, eventually making them part of the students' mental toolbox. The most widely accepted means for moving the strategies from the teacher to the students is the gradual release of responsibility model that we discussed earlier. It is important to understand how a teacher following a core reading program's lesson plans will move students from direct explanation to independent practice of a strategy.

We took a close look at lesson plans in core reading programs, attempting to understand how they assisted students to internalize and use strategies. First, we counted the types of moves that a teacher was asked to make. We categorized teacher moves into 10 categories: (1) mentioning a skill or strategy, (2) asking a question, (3) asking a question followed immediately by teacher modeling of an answer, (4) explaining a skill or strategy, (5) providing information about the passage, (6) modeling a strategy, (7) providing guided practice and support in using the strategy, (8) engaging in direct explanation, (9) engaging in discussions, and (10) providing independent practice. Using these categories, we developed a picture of what the teacher did while students were reading to assist them in applying and internalizing the strategies. The results of this analysis are presented in Table 19.

Table 19. Percentage of Total Instructional Moves While Students Read a Selection

Instructional Move	Scott Foresman Reading (Pearson Scott Foresman, 2004)	Trophies (Harcourt, 2003/2005)	Open Court Reading (SRA/ McGraw-Hill, 2005)	Houghton Mifflin Reading (Houghton Mifflin, 2003/2005)	Macmillan/ McGraw-Hill Reading (Macmillan/ McGraw-Hill, 2003/2005)
Mentioning	0.0	0.5	3.2	0.9	0.9
Skill + explanation	0.3	1.2	22.1	0.5	2.1
Modeling	1.5	9.2	21.1	5.3	2.4
Information	0.0	3.7	2.9	0.0	0.9
Questioning	60.4	62.1	4.4	44.8	68.8
Questioning + modeling	2.1	9.4	0.0	0.7	9.5
Guided practice	6.3	3.2	30.6	23.0	12.3
Direct explanation	14.9	1.8	0.1	0.8	1.5
Independent practice	5.6	7.6	2.2	0.7	0.0
Discussion	8.8	0.9	13.2	23.3	1.6

Note. Adapted from Dewitz et al. (2009). Comprehension strategy instruction in core reading programs. *Reading Research Quarterly, 44*(2), 102–126.

In most core reading programs, teachers ask many questions: before students read, while they are reading, and after they read. In most programs, these questions are labeled by the skill or strategy they address, giving the impression that the teacher is focusing on strategies. We totaled the two categories that involved teacher questioning (labeled Questioning and Questioning + Modeling in Table 19). In Scott Foresman Reading (2004), 62.5% of the teacher moves while the students read involved asking questions. In Trophies (2003/2005), 71.5% of the teacher moves are questions. In Houghton Mifflin Reading (2003/2005) and Macmillan/McGraw-Hill Reading (2003/2005), the percentage of teacher moves that involve asking a question is 45.5% and 78.3%, respectively. Only in Open Court Reading (2005) is the teacher directed to spend most of his or her time modeling (21.1%) or engaging in guided practice (30.6%). The lesson design of Open Court Reading is in sharp contrast with the other four core reading programs. Asking questions could spark students to use strategies, yet research on the gradual release of responsibility model (Pearson & Gallagher, 1983) has suggested that other teacher moves are equally, if not more, important.

Core reading programs provide little guided practice, the scaffolding or assistance from a teacher that helps students engage in a strategy. Only 6.3% of teacher moves were coded as guided practice for Scott Foresman Reading (2004), 3.2% for Trophies (2003/2005), and 12.3% for Macmillan/McGraw-Hill Reading (2003/2005). As we pointed out earlier, Open Court Reading (2005), with 30.6%, provides the most guided practice of the five major core reading programs. During reading instruction in Open Court Reading, teachers are directed to model strategies, provide explanations for strategies, and guide students to use strategies.

Another way to look at how core reading programs help teachers help students is by tracking a strategy across a full unit of instruction. Typically, a core reading program will introduce a new comprehension skill or strategy early in a unit, then have the students employ that strategy in two or more reading selections. We tracked three comprehension strategies (making inferences, summarizing, and text structure) across complete units of instruction. We were trying to determine if the programs began with direct explanation and modeling of the strategy, then engaged in guided practice, leading eventually to independent practice. We present two lesson plan profiles, so you can understand the instructional design underlying two of the core reading programs. We drew our examples from programs that follow different patterns for teaching students to make inferences.

Making inferences is given a broad but not deep treatment in Scott Foresman Reading (2004). In the grade 4 version of the program, making inferences receives its most intense instruction in Unit 3, approximately 10 to 12 weeks into the school year. Figure 8 illustrates how the instruction is presented. In Unit 3, the formal instruction begins with Lesson 2 or Week 2. The teacher provides two direct explanation lessons on how to make inferences before the students read the selections (outside the text). The teacher reinforces these lessons with two additional lessons during the reading of the text, meaning the teacher can stop to model and explain making inferences again (inside the text). Next, the teacher is directed to ask more inferential questions, then the students engage in some independent practice, a worksheet. In the next lesson, the teacher asks more questions. The fourth lesson, Week 4, repeats the pattern of Week 2, direct explanation and teacher questioning, and that pattern is repeated again in Week 5. In Chapter 11, we explain how to resolve the four problems we have identified in these core reading programs.

Figure 8. Making Inferences in Scott Foresman Reading (Pearson Scott Foresman, 2004), Grade 4, Unit 3

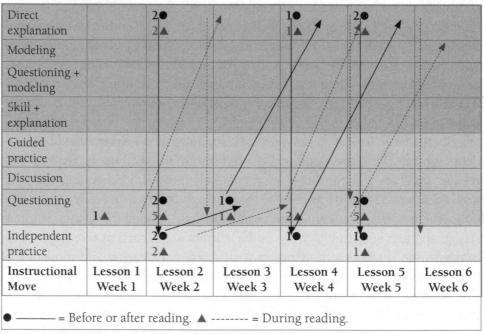

Instructional Move	Lesson 1 Week 1	Lesson 2 Week 2	Lesson 3 Week 3	Lesson 4 Week 4	Lesson 5 Week 5	Lesson 6 Week 6

● ——— = Before or after reading. ▲ ------- = During reading.

Note. Based on Dewitz et al. (2009). Comprehension strategy instruction in core reading programs. *Reading Research Quarterly, 44*(2), 102–126.

Three characteristics of these lessons stand out. First, over the course of the unit, the students receive eight lessons in making inferences. Some of these lessons occur before the students read the selections, and others while they are reading. Second, the teachers are directed to ask a number of inferential questions. These questions begin before the skill or strategy is formally taught. The teacher does all the questioning, so the inferences that the students make are not self-initiated but are responses to teacher prompts. Third, the students receive no guided practice to help them apply the skill while they are reading. Students are not led to generate inferences while they read, nor do they receive cues to help them draw inferences. While reading, the teacher provides little modeling, and the students are not asked to model the strategy.

In Open Court Reading (2005), students are provided instruction in making inferences in Units 2, 3, and 6, with the strongest emphasis in Unit 6. The treatment of this skill is graphed in Figure 9. In Unit 6, the students receive direct explanation of the skill in the second lesson, Week 2, and throughout

Figure 9. Making Inferences in Open Court Reading (SRA/McGraw-Hill, 2005), Grade 4, Unit 6

Instructional Move	Lesson 1 Week 1	Lesson 2 Week 2	Lesson 3 Week 3	Lesson 4 Week 4	Lesson 5 Week 5	Lesson 6 Week 6
Direct explanation		1●				
Modeling						
Questioning + modeling						
Skill + explanation						
Guided practice		4●				
Discussion						
Questioning	1▲	2▲			2▲	
Independent practice		1●			1●	

● ———— = Before or after reading. ▲ -------- = During reading.

Note. Based on Dewitz et al. (2009). Comprehension strategy instruction in core reading programs. *Reading Research Quarterly, 44*(2), 102–126.

the reading of the selection, the teacher provides guided practice in helping the students make inferences. Throughout the rest of the lessons in the unit, the students are asked inferential questions or engage in independent practice of the skill. Open Court Reading provides guided practice for one week of lessons, but the teacher support does not extend beyond that week.

These two lessons illustrate the problems with instructional design in most core reading programs. Skills and strategies are introduced, sometimes not well, then the programs move rapidly to teacher questioning and independent practice. The programs are weak on guided practice and on students' modeling and use of the strategies. These are key instructional moves necessary for students to internalize strategies.

PUTTING IT ALL TOGETHER

Our analysis of core reading programs reveals several critical flaws that may impair the development of students' comprehension (Dewitz et al., 2008, 2009). Core reading programs do a poor job of knowledge development (Dewitz et al., 2008). Often the programs fail to anticipate and provide the knowledge students need to comprehend the selections. Passages are not selected so that students' knowledge builds from one selection to another, although the main anthology selections are coordinated with the leveled books that follow. Teachers can remedy this problem, and we illustrate how in Chapter 11.

Core reading programs teach too many comprehension skills and strategies, often using two or more labels for the same mental process or breaking a unitary strategy into many components. They do this because of the pressure of state curriculum standards that insist all these skills be taught. Core reading programs are not as explicit as they should be, often avoiding the text cues that are critical to performing a strategy. These programs neglect to inform readers *why* a strategy is important and *when* it should be used. Most core reading programs do not follow a gradual release of responsibility model (Pearson & Gallagher, 1983); instead, they move quickly from the teacher's explanation to questioning the students on the skill. Core reading programs also fail to provide enough distributed practice so that students can learn the

(continued)

strategies well. None of the flaws are fatal. A teacher can and should make smart decisions when using a core reading program. In Chapter 11, we help you make these smart decisions.

The goal of this chapter is to help you understand the quality of the comprehension curriculum and instruction in core reading programs and give you some insights into how to evaluate the newer programs or use older ones. Our analysis, although timely, was done on older versions of several core reading programs. We hope you now have a greater understanding of how comprehension instruction is organized and presented in core reading programs. We presented this information so that you can understand your own core reading program better and teach more effectively. We expand on these ideas in Chapter 11 when we focus on teaching comprehension with core reading programs. We also wrote this chapter so that when you begin searching for a new core reading program, you will have a better set of criteria to guide your search. If comprehension is a major concern in your school or district, you will want to select a program with the strongest comprehension curriculum and instruction. On the webpage for this book, www.reading .org/general/publications/books/bk707.aspx, you will find our system for evaluating core reading programs, the Reading GPS. By using the Reading GPS, you will be able to evaluate the comprehension instruction in core reading programs. In doing so, you should consider the following questions:

- How well is knowledge developed within the core reading program?
- What vocabulary words are taught for each reading selection, and what is the quality of that instruction?
- What comprehension skills and strategies are taught in the core reading program? Which skills and strategies do your students need?
- Does the core reading program provide clear, direct explanations for comprehension skills and strategies? How can you make the instruction clearer and more explicit?
- Does the core reading program guide the students to apply the comprehension skills and strategies during actual reading? How can you as a teacher do this more effectively?

CHAPTER 6

Differentiation, Intervention, and Assessment in Core Reading Programs

Mrs. Williams is extremely concerned. As the principal of a large urban elementary school, the end of the year is filled with stressful tasks for her, but none is more unnerving than the annual release of the state test scores. The results are positive this year, yet the results are also negative. Although the school as a whole made adequate yearly progress (i.e., an average of 82% of the students passed the test in reading), the passing rate for special education students and for ELLs barely cracked 65%. Of the 67 special education students, 40 of them were unable to pass the reading assessment even with accommodations. The problems for the 94 ELLs at the school are a bit worse. That means that the school will not be fully accredited, and she and her staff will have to develop a school improvement plan that will be supervised by the state. This plan must provide more effective general classroom instruction plus improved intervention for special education and ELL students.

After the depressing news, Mrs. Williams calls a meeting of her school's literacy committee and presents the problem to them. At this meeting are two of the school's reading teachers, two special education teachers, four grade-level teachers, the English as a second language teacher, and the counselor. As the discussion begins, they first review what had been done last year to assist struggling readers—those identified as needing special education and those not—and ELLs. The school uses a core reading program, Houghton Mifflin Reading (Houghton Mifflin, 2003/2005) and has purchased a few stand-alone intervention programs. They have also fashioned their own reading intervention program based on a large set of decodable books plus some phonics instruction. It is clear that these efforts, although perhaps helpful, had not assisted all students, and many still struggled with the task of learning to read. It is mentioned that the district is about to start a search for a new core reading program, and although this new program is at least a year away, perhaps it will eventually provide more support for the students. Several teachers know that new core reading programs come with aligned intervention programs and feel that a new core reading program might, indeed, help solve their problems.

W hen core reading programs became large and comprehensive in the 1970s, they were expected to provide the text and the methods to teach most students to read. As Goodman et al. (1988) wrote, "The central premise of the basal reader is that a sequential, all-inclusive set of instructional materials can teach *all* [italics added] children to read regardless of teacher competence and regardless of learner differences" (p. 1). Whether it is *all* or *most*, it is difficult to put a number to the adjectives. McGill-Franzen et al. (2006) gave us a hint. They studied the impact of core reading programs on students' performance on the Florida Comprehensive Assessment Test. The results suggested that 30% of third graders using one of two core reading programs failed to meet a standard of proficiency sufficient to pass the state assessment. Taking another look at the problem, educators (Vaughn & Roberts, 2007) writing in the area of RTI, a schoolwide approach designed to help all students learn to read, argued that 20–30% of students will need additional intervention or assistance beyond what they get from the primary instructional program. If that primary instruction is built around a core reading program, then perhaps 20% of students will need something more.

This chapter focuses on struggling readers and what core reading programs offer teachers who work with these students. We also discuss the assessments available in core reading programs. The first step in assisting struggling readers is to provide strong differentiated instruction within the classroom. We considered some aspects of differentiation in Chapters 3 and 4, but we extend that discussion here. Next, we examine some of the specific instructional interventions that accompany core reading programs. We look at programs that were published before 2007, when the impact of the RTI model was not yet felt, and at programs that are more current. We also explore what core reading programs suggest for working with ELLs, a rapidly growing segment of many schools' populations. Finally, in the last section of this chapter, we describe assessments that are available in core reading programs. Assessments are essential, because they help teachers place students in instructional groups and in instructional-level reading texts. Different assessments provide feedback on the effectiveness of instruction, monitor student progress, and measure the overall effectiveness of an instructional program.

What You Will Learn

• Why children have difficulty learning to read

• What the characteristics of differentiated classroom instruction are

• What the characteristics of an effective early intervention program are

• What the characteristics of valid and reliable reading assessment tools are

What You Will Be Able to Do

• Evaluate the differentiated instruction options in core reading programs

• Evaluate reading intervention programs against a specific set of criteria

• Evaluate assessment tools in core reading programs

• Evaluate how core reading programs help teachers use and interpret assessments

The ideas in this chapter will help you complete an evaluation of the differentiation, intervention, and assessment in core reading programs. Online at www.reading.org, you can find our Reading GPS, an instrument that will guide you through the process of evaluating the texts in a core reading program. The Reading GPS and this chapter are meant to be used together.

What Research Says About Differentiating Instruction and Intervention

Students struggle to learn to read for a variety of reasons. Some students enter school lacking the cognitive wiring that is necessary to easily unlock the code of printed English (Shaywitz, Escobar, Shaywitz, Fletcher, & Makuch, 1992). Others come from home backgrounds with little focus on literacy (Delpit, 1995; Heath, 1983). Many of these students have limited oral language and vocabulary development stemming from a lack of exposure in the home to rich language experiences (Hart & Risley, 1995). Some students enter school speaking a language other than English and must traverse two languages while learning to read in one. Finally, students who may have one or more of these initial causes find that their reading difficulties have been complicated by a year or more of weak instruction. For all these students, regardless of the initial cause, the Matthew Effect (Stanovich, 1986) presents a further problem. Difficulty with reading promotes disinterest, dislike, and avoidance.

Differentiating Instruction and RTI

Despite the causes of reading problems, students who are reading below grade level at the end of first grade have an 88% chance of still reading below-level at the end of fourth grade (Juel, 1988). Reading problems develop and persist unless students receive both differentiated instruction within the general education classroom and intervention. The more enlightened the differentiation (Connor, Morrison, Fishman et al., 2007) and the earlier it's received, the more likely schools will be to prevent future reading problems (Snow et al., 1998). Many studies support the use of aggressive early interventions (Vaughn, Linan-Thompson, & Hickman, 2003; Vellutino et al., 1996). Vellutino et al.'s (1996) work, in particular, documented that 50% of the reading problems that would eventually result in a special education diagnosis can be prevented. Interventions can take many forms, from one-on-one tutoring to small-group instruction to volunteer programs (Wasik, 1998). For a review of these studies, we suggest you look at the work of Pikulski (1997), or for a more recent review, consider the work of Foorman (2007).

Differentiated instruction requires attention to and differentiation of texts, tasks, and time. Students should read texts at their *reading* level, not their *grade* level. O'Connor et al. (2002) demonstrated that students make more progress learning to read when they read texts at their instructional level not their frustration level, which is often their grade level. McGill-Franzen et al. (2006) produced a parallel finding. Looking at the research-based core reading programs sanctioned in Florida, they found that when students were instructed with materials geared to their grade level, 30% of the students in third grade failed to pass the state test.

In a series of studies, Connor and her colleagues (Connor, Morrison, Fishman et al., 2007; Connor, Morrison, & Underwood, 2007) demonstrated that successful instruction requires different tasks for different learners. They divided reading tasks into two categories. Some tasks focus on the code of the language—phonemic awareness, phonics, and decoding—and others on meaning—vocabulary, comprehension, and composition. These tasks may be directed by the teacher or conducted independently and directed by the students. Connor et al. (Connor, Morrison, Fishman et al., 2007; Connor, Morrison, & Underwood, 2007) found that weaker students benefit by spending more time in code-focused tasks directed by the teacher (e.g., intensive, small-group instruction) and less time in meaning-focused tasks directed by the students, such as on worksheets or with games at learning workstations. Good readers, conversely, make more progress when they work independently or with a partner on meaning-focused tasks (e.g., a book club discussion about a chapter book). Weaker readers require more small-group guided reading than do good readers (Connor, Jakobsons, Crowe, & Meadows, 2009).

Finally, a teacher can differentiate the use of time. Although the principal typically makes the school schedule and allocates time for a reading or language arts block, the teacher can differentiate how that time is used. Taylor, Pearson, Clark, and Walpole (2000) found that effective teachers spent more time in small-group instruction than did less effective teachers, with the most effective teachers in first and second grade spending 50 minutes or more in small-group instruction. Connor et al. (2009) found that adding five minutes a day of phonics instruction to the typical small-group time improved student achievement. Finally, Mathes and colleagues (2005) documented that it takes both differentiated instruction and intervention to reach some struggling readers.

Educators have recently formalized the processes of differentiation and intervention through RTI (Fuchs, Fuchs, & Vaughn, 2008). RTI is a procedure that provides early intervention in reading and identifies students for special education. Simply put, if a student has difficulty learning to read, the school provides increasing levels of support and intervention. If the student still has difficulty learning to read after a thorough intervention program, then he or she most likely has a disability and is a candidate for special education. RTI is a process that seeks to prevent reading problems and provide help when problems are identified. RTI begins with the universal screening of all students in a school to identify those needing additional help, which is provided in a range of intensity and duration.

Typically, RTI consists of three levels of help, but distinguishing between these levels is difficult. Tier 1 is basic classroom instruction, including both whole-group instruction and small-group differentiated instruction—what is typically outlined in recent core reading programs. As we progress up the tiers, the instruction becomes (a) more specific, explicit, and systematic, (b) more frequent, (c) of longer duration, (d) delivered to smaller, more homogeneous groups of students, and (e) reliant on instructors with greater degrees of expertise (Fuchs & Fuchs, 2006). Tier 2 intervention could be additional small-group instruction within the classroom delivered by either a reading specialist or special education teacher, or it might be an extra dose of small-group instruction delivered by the regular classroom teacher. The goal is to increase the time in small-group instruction, the precision of that instruction, or both. Tier 3 intervention includes all of the characteristics listed for the first two tiers as well as more instructional time in even smaller groups. The overlap among the tiers is not easy to sort out and depends on how time and human resources are available within a given school. Later we consider how the concept of RTI applies to core reading programs, because the application depends on the age of your program. Next, we turn to the concept of intervention.

Reading Intervention

The concept of a reading intervention first emerged when Reading Recovery, developed by Marie Clay (1993), was first brought to the United States in the 1980s from New Zealand. Reading Recovery is a one-on-one, daily tutoring program designed to aid first graders. During a Reading Recovery lesson, a student reads carefully selected leveled books to practice effective word-recognition strategies and build fluency. The teacher supports the students' strategies and coaches them on the use of effective word-recognition practices. The student also works on letter–sound knowledge through some embedded phonics instruction and writes letters, words, and sentences. Finally, the teacher takes a running record, an informal assessment, to determine which strategies should be the focus for subsequent lessons. Although research on the effectiveness of Reading Recovery has yielded mixed results (Shanahan & Barr, 1995) and is somewhat controversial (Hiebert, 1994), the intervention became a model for many other programs that followed. Thus, programs such as Early Intervention in Reading (Taylor, Short, Frye, & Shearer, 1992) and Book Buddies (Johnston, Invernizzi, & Juel, 1998) both have students read leveled text, work on phonemic segmentation, practice word-recognition skills, and engage in some guided writing.

Most reading intervention programs are a microcosm of classroom instruction and include many of the components that would be found in regular instruction. Students work on phonemic awareness and letter–sound knowledge, learn phonics patterns and word-recognition strategies, read books to apply these skills, engage in repeated readings to develop fluency, and experience some controlled writing practice. Only teacher read-alouds and a strong focus on vocabulary development are typically absent from reading intervention programs. These intervention programs differ in how much emphasis they place on word-recognition instruction in isolation—segmenting, blending, letter sounds, and decoding—and how much emphasis they place on reading connected text and applying strategies. Few studies exist that compare reading intervention programs.

Mathes and her colleagues (2005) examined two theoretically different intervention programs to explore their effects on struggling readers. One of the programs, Proactive Reading, stresses developing phonemic awareness, acquiring letter–sound knowledge, learning to sound out words, spelling words, and practicing reading these words in fully decodable text. As the students progress, the focus on decoding shifts to work on multisyllable words, oral reading fluency, and use of a few comprehension strategies, such as retelling, sequencing, and story grammar elements. The second intervention program, Responsive Reading, includes a focus on phonemic awareness and decoding, but the specific skills are dictated by the needs of the students, and the teacher does not follow an established scope and sequence. Teachers using Responsive Reading spent less time on word decoding than did the teachers in Proactive Reading. Each Responsive Reading lesson includes work on fluency, letter and word recognition, supported text reading, and supported writing. In Responsive Reading, the students read leveled text not decodable text. Students in Responsive Reading spend more time working on skills in context, whereas in Proactive Reading, more time is spent on skills in isolation. Finally, writing in Responsive Reading includes expressing thoughts in complete sentences, whereas in Proactive Reading, students spell only individual words.

Despite the contrasts in these two interventions, the results were quite similar (Mathes et al., 2005), and it is important to spend some time on them, as they will affect how you examine intervention treatments included within core reading programs. In these studies, some of the students received enhanced classroom instruction plus small-group intervention, while others received just one of the intervention programs. Classroom instruction was enhanced by giving teachers data on how their students performed throughout the year and providing expert advice on how to teach specific reading skills. Thus, as the teachers' knowledge grew, their classroom instruction became more effective. When enhanced classroom instruction was combined with either of the two intervention programs, most reading problems were prevented. At the end of the year, only 1–3% of the first graders in the study (Mathes et al., 2005) were experiencing reading difficulties. This study and others have suggested some important criteria for considering intervention programs that accompany core reading programs. We will get to these shortly, but first we consider how core reading programs differentiate instruction.

Differentiation in Core Reading Programs

The extensive research on reading intervention and RTI has had a significant influence on the structure and content of recent core reading programs. We use the copyright date of 2006 as a demarcation line. Those programs published before 2006 have less focus on differentiation than programs published more recently. Prior to 2006, the impact of research that stressed the importance of small-group instruction had not been felt (Taylor et al., 2000), the impact of RTI was increasing, and states like California and Texas had not yet published specific guidelines about the need for intervention.

Most core reading programs published before 2006 have a whole-group orientation. The five-day lesson plans in Trophies (2003/2005), Houghton Mifflin Reading (Houghton Mifflin, 2003/2005), Macmillan/McGraw-Hill Reading (Macmillan/McGraw-Hill, 2003/2005), and Scott Foresman Reading (Pearson Scott Foresman, 2004) do not specify a process in which the students are organized into instructional groups, although the lessons have repeated references to dealing with students who read above, on, and below grade level. All of these programs provide a leveled reader for each of these three types of readers, plus a leveled book for ELLs. Typically, the programs suggest that these books be used for independent reading. Each program has designated worksheets and workbook pages that are suitable for each type of reader.

Within the lessons themselves, the core reading program writers have included suggestions or tips for working with struggling readers. These suggestions are provided at point of use, when students encounter a difficult word or passage while reading the text under the teacher's guidance. We have listed three examples of this differentiation in Table 20. Macmillan/McGraw-Hill Reading (2003/2005) provides decoding support for students reading below level in the fourth grade under "Prevention/Intervention." Trophies (2003/2005) provides comprehension support for below-level readers, and Houghton Mifflin Reading (2003/2005) provides a recommendation for above-level readers, called Challenge. We believe that these teaching suggestions and tips are worthwhile, but they stop short of what we would consider a complete attempt to differentiate reading instruction. The decoding suggestion is a short, useful lesson, but it is not a differentiated curriculum or instruction for struggling readers. The suggestion in Trophies (2003/2005) is sound instructional advice for any type of reader, and the recommendation for advanced readers in Houghton Mifflin Reading (2003/2005) also could be applied to any student. Providing suggestions that teachers can follow while students read a selection may provide

Table 20. Differentiated Support in Three Core Reading Programs

Macmillan/McGraw-Hill Reading (Macmillan/McGraw-Hill, 2003/2005, Grade 4, Theme 1, p. 29)	Trophies (Harcourt, 2003/2005, Grade 5, Theme 3, p. 264)	Houghton Mifflin Reading (Houghton Mifflin, 2003/2005, Grade 3, Theme 1, p. 27)
Decoding	Below-Level	Challenge
Write sleep and beat on the chalkboard. Underline the phonograms -eep and -eat in the words as students pronounce them. Then circle the letters that stand for long e in each word. • What other words end with -eep or -eat? (Sample answers: *heat, meat, deep, peep*) Do all of them have the long /e/sound?	Help students summarize the main idea of the selection. (Summary is provided.) Review the sequence of events in the story and point out how it took eons for the Everglades to become perfect and how it has taken only a couple of hundred years for that perfection to be severely damaged.	Explain that suspense is a feeling of tension or uncertainty about a story's outcome. To create suspense, authors raise questions in readers' minds. For example, when Mona disappeared inside the bin, the boys wonder what has happened to her. Readers wonder what happened too. Have students list instances in the story where the author creates suspense. Also have them note the questions that were raised in their minds.

momentary support, but they do not help teachers construct a long-term program of differentiated instruction.

When we examined the most recent copyrights of the major core reading programs, we found significant changes in how they provide for differentiated instruction. In StoryTown (Harcourt, 2008), the basic five-day lesson plan has changed from Harcourt's previous core reading programs and now includes directions for each small group. The suggested lesson begins with whole-group time, followed by small-group time. During small-group time, each group works with its own leveled reader and completes follow-up activities in a leveled workbook. When students are not working with the teacher, the program provides suggestions for literacy workstations that focus on word study, reading, writing, fluency, and technology. These lessons clearly differentiate text, but the teacher's edition does not differentiate time. Equal amounts of time are spent with each group. The lessons do not noticeably differentiate tasks. All three groups engage in pre-, during-, and postreading activities, and if the below-level readers need more work with word recognition, those decisions will have to be made by the teacher.

Treasures (Macmillan/McGraw-Hill, 2009) lesson plans also include more suggestions for differentiation than appeared in previous versions of the publisher's core reading program. The teacher's edition includes a five-day plan that focuses on whole-group work, followed by a separate lesson plan for small-group differentiated instruction. In the differentiated lesson, the teacher is provided with detailed lessons to support word recognition and fluency for the below-level students, but the focus is vocabulary and comprehension strategies for students reading at or above level. Whether these task differences are appropriate is up to the judgment of the teacher, but they do align with suggestions of Connor and her colleagues (Connor, Morrison, & Underwood, 2007; Connor et al., 2009) that struggling readers need more code-focused instruction and strong readers need more meaning-focused instruction.

Scott Foresman Reading Street (Pearson Scott Foresman, 2008b) also differentiates its lessons at the small-group level, but because we were unable to obtain copies of their lessons, we did not include them in our analysis. Both programs we examined still leave time-allocation decisions up to the teacher. A teacher may work with the low group for a longer period of time than the high group and at times not see the high group at all. A teacher might also want to move through the leveled reader at a faster pace than the core reading programs suggest. All of these differentiated lessons still require teacher decisions about the pacing of the lesson and the use of texts.

Evaluating Intervention in Core Reading Programs

To evaluate intervention programs that accompany core reading programs, you need guidelines and criteria. The criteria in the section that follows were gleaned from successful intervention programs and from researchers, such as Wanzek and Vaughn (2007), who have reviewed multiple studies of reading intervention programs. To RTI experts, interventions come in two forms: the standard protocol model and the problem-solving model. The standard protocol model is a well-designed intervention with a preset lesson plan, scope, sequence of specific skills, and a specific instructional approach—in short, an intervention that comes in a box that you might purchase. In the problem-solving model, teachers design an intervention based on assessment data and teach the skills and strategies the students seem to lack. Because Wanzek and Vaughn could find no studies that evaluated the problem-solving model, we skip to the standard interventions. Wanzek and Vaughn's review of interventions looked at duration (how long the intervention lasted), the size of the group receiving the intervention, grade level, and the level of standardization (how well-defined the intervention plan and the daily lessons were). Considering the evidence from this evaluation study, we can develop some criteria for evaluating the interventions that accompany core reading programs.

Criteria of Successful Intervention Programs

Table 21 outlines the criteria for successful reading intervention programs. Almost all of these criteria are under the control of the school and the teachers. They can determine how much time to devote to intervention, the number of students within the intervention group, and the duration of the intervention.

According to the work of Wanzek and Vaughn (2007), early intervention programs that begin in kindergarten or first grade are more successful than

Table 21. Structural Characteristics of Reading Intervention Programs

Criteria of Successful Interventions	What the Research Reports
Grade level: Kindergarten or first grade	Interventions that begin in kindergarten or first grade are more successful than those used in grades 2 and 3, yet the students in the upper grades tend to have more severe problems.
Time: 30 to 45 minutes per day	The most successful interventions take place outside the regular classroom instruction, and students receive 30 to 45 minutes of extra classroom instruction three to five times a week.
Duration: Five months or longer	All successful interventions lasted at least five months, and some extended longer than an academic year.
Group size: Small group, three to five students	The most successful interventions were one-on-one, with small-group sizes yielding better results.
Instructors: Well trained	In the most successful interventions, the teachers delivering the interventions were well trained in the instructional approach.
Text: Decodable?	In some of the interventions, decodable texts were used, but they were not essential to the success of the intervention.
Intervention focus	Interventions that allocate a majority of the time to phonemic awareness and decoding skills and less time to reading connected text are as successful as interventions with the opposite emphasis, that is, greater time in reading of connected text.

those geared for the later grades. Programs that are successful work with students for more than five months and up to a year. There was little evidence that short intervention programs yielded strong results. Intervention is more effective when the size of the instructional group is smaller. One-on-one intervention is the most potent, but Wanzek and Vaughn did not locate enough small-group studies to make a meaningful comparison to one-on-one instruction. Finally, Wanzek and Vaughn compared interventions that were quite standardized to those more under the day-to-day control of the teacher and found that they have no important differences in their impact.

To look deeper into the characteristics of successful intervention programs, specifically the instruction, we decided to look at the following criteria (Coyne, Kame'enui, & Simmons, 2001). These are informed opinions; the authors did not statistically compare different types of interventions. Strong intervention programs exhibit the following characteristics:

- *Conspicuous instruction in strategies:* It is not enough for students to know letter sounds; they must have a strategy or process to use that knowledge. Teachers must make these strategies clear and model them explicitly.

- *Mediated scaffolding:* The student needs support when learning new skills or strategies. Sometimes the core reading program provides that support—easier letters and sounds are introduced before more difficult patterns—and sometimes the teacher provides it. Through coaching, hints, and modeling, the teacher helps the student try out the new strategy. (We provide a strong guide for scaffolding the decoding process in Chapter 10.)

- *Strategy integration:* Students should always understand that the separate skills of reading are not isolated. Phonemic awareness needs to be taught alongside decoding so that students understand that segmenting and blending sounds leads to ease in recognizing words. Phonemic awareness and decoding need to be taught along with reading of connected text. Through this integration, the whole process makes sense to the students.

- *Primed background knowledge:* Students with reading problems often have memory deficits, so previous knowledge and skills should be reviewed before new ideas are introduced. To spell, the student has to first segment the sounds in the word. Priming causes the student to think about segmenting before beginning to spell.

- *Judicious review:* Students with reading problems need considerable review. Coyne and colleagues (2001) reminded us that review needs to be distributed over time, cumulative, and varied. In a sense, we cannot simply assume mastery, drop a topic or skill, and move on.

- *Well-paced instruction:* In a good intervention, the teacher is organized, and several activities can be completed in a short amount of time. A well-paced lesson promotes students' interest and attention.

Intervention Programs Available With Core Reading Programs

Starting in 2000, publishers began to offer intervention programs alongside core reading programs. As far back as the 1980s, the Macmillan companies offered a second basal with the regular reading program. This alternative basal essentially presented the same skills and strategies, but the students' text was easier with readability levels half a year to a year below the main student anthology. Houghton Mifflin developed two intervention programs, Early Success (1999), designed for struggling first- and second-grade students, and Soar to Success (Cooper, 1999), essentially a comprehension program for students who have adequate decoding but weak reading comprehension. Soar to Success stresses both knowledge development and comprehension strategy instruction (predicting, self-questioning, clarifying, and summarizing) through reciprocal teaching (Palincsar & Brown, 1984). These two programs essentially stood apart from the main core reading programs.

The Trophies (2003/2005) program developed by Harcourt also contained an intervention program. The Intervention Reader includes the same key vocabulary, but the selections that the students read, although thematically compatible with the main anthology, were written at a lower readability level. The lesson plans offer some options, but typically the student listens to the teacher read the main story, and then the teacher and the students work with the Intervention Reader. During the week, they would work on decoding, increasing fluency, reading the Intervention Reader, and engaging in the same comprehension strategies that are featured in the main core reading program. The phonics skills follow a relatively traditional sequence and move at a brisk pace; short and long *a* words are taught in the same lesson. The program does not have a guide to gear the phonics instruction to the needs of the students.

The new core reading programs (those published after 2007) are all available with intervention programs. Some of these intervention programs are linked to the main core reading program, and others stand alone. The publishers are positioning these programs as either Tier 2 or Tier 3 programs using the language of RTI. Treasures (2009) has an accompanying intervention program that has its own student text and teacher's edition called Triumphs, but it also has a stand-alone intervention program. StoryTown (2008) has available two intervention programs. The Strategic Intervention Program (grades K–6) is designed for students needing some extra support and largely teaches the same comprehension and vocabulary skills taught in the core program. The Intervention Station is for students who have more difficulty learning to read. These interventions consist of decodable and leveled texts, a teacher's guide, worksheets, and manipulatives. The teacher's guide is a large set of detailed lessons, almost a menu, for teachers to use to bolster their instruction and students' achievement. The teacher can determine how long to focus on a specific skill.

Finally, Pearson Scott Foresman offers two intervention programs that accompany its Scott Foresman Reading Street (2008b) core reading program. The lowest level program, Early Intervention in Reading, is a tightly scripted program for kindergarten and first-grade students who are having difficulty with basic phonemic awareness, letter recognition, letter sounds, and word reading. My Sidewalks on Scott Foresman Reading Street (Pearson Scott Foresman, 2008a) continues the instruction from first grade up through sixth.

How to Examine Intervention Programs

Our next goal is not to review each of these intervention programs, but rather to give you the skills to reach your own judgments. We will, however, comment on the structure of these programs in light of what is known about effective reading intervention. There are outside resources that can help you evaluate an intervention program you are considering. The Florida Center for Reading Research has evaluated over 100 supplemental intervention programs, and those evaluations are available on their website (www.fcrr.org). The What Works Clearinghouse has also evaluated a number of early reading intervention programs. Its site (ies.ed.gov/ncee/wwc/) provides a measure of the clearinghouse's effectiveness along with an estimation of the extent and quality of the research that yielded those conclusions. Both websites are valuable, but they have not yet evaluated most of the new interventions that accompany the core reading programs.

To evaluate intervention programs, you need to employ two kinds of criteria. First, you need to examine the broad structural characteristics of intervention programs. These include the grade level the programs address, the length of an instructional lesson, the full duration of the program in weeks or months, the optimal group size of the instruction, and the training requirements of the instructor (Wanzek & Vaughn, 2007). The second set of criteria takes you deeper into the analysis and considers how the curriculum is organized and how the instruction is delivered. We concentrate on just a few of the intervention programs offered by the core reading program publishers to illustrate how the evaluation process should be conducted. We trust that these examples will help you critique core reading programs yourself. Our evaluation tool for looking at intervention programs (Reading GPS) can be found online at the website for this book at www.reading.org/general/publications/books/bk707.aspx.

My Sidewalks on Reading Street

My Sidewalks on Scott Foresman Reading Street (Pearson Scott Foresman, 2008a) is designed for students reading significantly below grade level. My Sidewalks is part of a three-tiered system with Scott Foresman Reading Street (Pearson Scott Foresman, 2008b), the basic core program, guiding Tier 1 instruction. Scott Foresman Early Reading Intervention (Simmons & Kame'enui, 2003b) and My Sidewalks provide Tier 2 and Tier 3 intervention. The Early Reading Intervention program is designed for struggling kindergarten and first-grade students. After that, Levels A to E of My Sidewalks are designed for first through fifth grades. The program is intended to help students accelerate to their grade level by the end of the school year. My Sidewalks can be used congruently with any core reading program. Each level includes 150 lessons that provide 30 to 45 minutes of instruction five days a week. The children are placed in small groups of two to five students. The program may be used in a classroom setting or as a pull-out intervention program. The group size, duration, and grade levels meet the criteria set out by Wanzek and Vaughn (2007). My Sidewalks was also designed to assist ELLs. We need to point out that Sharon Vaughn is both a researcher who studied the characteristics of effective intervention programs and one of the four listed authors for My Sidewalks.

Our study of My Sidewalks on Scott Foresman Reading Street is a demonstration, not a comprehensive review of the whole program. We examined one grade level, looking at three of its six units (see Table 22). The program requires a more comprehensive review before you consider adopting it. We know from independent reviews that the first part of this program, Early Reading Intervention (Simmons & Kame'enui, 2003b), received a favorable review from the Florida Center for Reading Research (see www.fcrr.org/FCRRReports/PDF/SFERI.pdf). Overall, our demonstration review of My Sidewalks suggests that it meets some,

Table 22. Evaluation of My Sidewalks on Scott Foresman Reading Street (Pearson Scott Foresman, 2008a)

Criteria	Instruction in Level D Teacher's Manual, Volume 1
Conspicuous strategy instruction	The program has defined strategies, but the process underlying the strategies is not well explained. For example, the fourth-grade level of the program introduces the multisyllabic word strategy, but does not explain how to determine the number of chunks in a word or how the vowel patterns can be used to do so. Summarizing is a prominent strategy for comprehension. The program directs teachers to model summarizing, and the language of a good summary is provided. The teacher is not directed to explain how that summary should be constructed.
Mediated scaffolding	The program and the program directions, despite the labels, do not appear to provide a great deal of scaffolding. For example, when sequencing is introduced as a strategy, teachers are directed to ask comprehension questions after the students finish reading, but the concept of sequencing and signal words is not reviewed in the discussion of the text. The same pattern occurs with other strategies. Word-recognition strategies are scaffolded when first presented, but the teachers are not given directions on how and when to correct students.
Strategy integration	The teacher directions give limited evidence of strategy integration. Some ongoing decoding strategies—the multisyllabic word strategy—are consistently related to the new vocabulary words, but vocabulary words are not related to text comprehension. The decoding patterns introduced each week are not related to the new vocabulary words.
Primed background knowledge	There is little evidence that knowledge is primed when new ideas or strategies are introduced. For example, when drawing conclusions is introduced the concept of a strategy is not discussed, nor is drawing conclusions related to other strategies the students are already using. When new phonics features are introduced, like *r*-controlled vowels, older vowel patterns do not serve as a springboard for these new patterns.
Judicious review	The amount of judicious review in the program is mixed. The phonics skills are practiced regularly during a week, but in the subsequent weeks, the program does not direct the teacher to review what was previously taught. Comprehension skills and strategies are regularly reviewed across the weeks. So drawing conclusions, which is introduced in the second week of the program, is regularly reviewed over the next 12 to 14 weeks.
Well-paced instruction	The lessons appear well paced. Each can be completed in 30 to 40 minutes, and the program provides the teachers with a time parameter for each segment of the lesson.

not all, of the criteria of a strong intervention program. Teachers can certainly use the program well, but they would need to provide more skill review, link new strategies to old strategies, and more carefully scaffold students' attempts to apply the strategies. In My Sidewalks, it appears that students spend more time working on skills and less time reading texts. This lack of balance my not be appropriate for some struggling readers who need to read more within core reading programs. It is not clear what kind of training is provided with My Sidewalks.

Strategic Intervention Resource Kit

The Strategic Intervention Resource Kit is part of the new StoryTown (2008) core reading program. It, too, is part of a three-tiered system. StoryTown provides classroom instruction at Tier 1. The Strategic Intervention Resource Kit provides the Tier 2 intervention, and the Intervention Station provides the Tier 3 intervention. The program provides 30 weeks of lessons that can be used in conjunction with the main core reading program or stand alone. We chose to review the Strategic Intervention Resource Kit as a stand-alone option, but at the end of this section, we comment on its use along with the core reading program. The program consists of a student book (the Interactive Reader), a practice book (worksheets), a teacher's guide, and some other resources like skill cards and vocabulary cards. The program is geared for small groups of four to six students, and each of the lessons can be completed in 30 minutes. The lesson each day consists of four segments: comprehension, vocabulary, spelling and decoding, and grammar and writing. Fluency practice is embedded throughout the program. The order of these segments changes from day to day. We now apply the criteria of Coyne et al. (2001) to the Strategic Intervention Resource Kit in Table 23.

The Strategic Intervention Resource Kit lacks some of the criteria outlined by Coyne et al. (2001). To use the program well, a teacher would need to provide more review of the skills and strategies and scaffold them more carefully. The teacher would also need to provide more explanation of how these strategies are linked together. While using the program, a teacher would discover if the four or five components recommended each day could be covered in the allocated 30 minutes. When the Strategic Intervention Resource Kit is used in conjunction with the core reading program, the sequence of instruction and review does not change, but the program provides more support for modeling and scaffolding the skills. The Coyne et al. criteria provide a very useful guide for examining intervention programs geared for Tier 2 and Tier 3 instruction. Our evaluation

Table 23. Evaluation of Strategic Intervention Kit in StoryTown (Harcourt, 2008)

Criteria	Instruction in Level D Teacher's Manual, Volume 1
Conspicuous strategy instruction	The program seems to lack explicit strategy instruction. We did not have the skills cards for instances where strategies are described, so we were not fully able to evaluate this portion of the program. Decoding skills are mentioned; there is a strong focus on the phonics features but not on strategies for decoding words. In terms of comprehension, the program lacks the language that the teacher would need to explain how to draw a conclusion or use text structure to understand cause and effect.
Mediated scaffolding	There is some evidence of scaffolding in the lesson, mostly in the fact that skills repeat over several lessons. However, the program generally lacks language that would guide a student through the use of a specific comprehension or decoding strategy.
Strategy integration	There is little evidence of strategy integration. The program does not help the teacher explain how decoding aids comprehension or how decoding and vocabulary knowledge can be linked together. Skills appear to be used in isolation from each other.
Primed background knowledge	The program regularly primes background knowledge of content and concepts but not of strategies. When new phonics or structural analysis features are introduced, they are not discussed in relationship to older features that have been previously taught. The students are reminded of what they should know about a comprehension strategy, but strategies are not related to each other.
Judicious review	The program does not appear to have as explicit a cycle of review as struggling readers might need. When a comprehension skill is introduced in a lesson, it will receive some review on subsequent days, but often the program shifts to new skills. Phonics patterns are studied for about a week, but there is little evidence that they are reviewed in the following weeks.
Well-paced instruction	The lessons are well paced. Each lesson segment appears with a small clock faces that suggests time limits. Typically, the program suggests that comprehension, decoding, vocabulary, and grammar and writing can be completed in 30 minutes.

was limited to one level of the program, and schools should ask for more components to conduct a more thorough evaluation on their own.

ELLs

The last component we examined is the resource manual for ELLs that accompanies Treasures (2009). Treasures also includes a complete intervention kit for struggling readers, Triumphs, which can be evaluated using the same criteria we have used. The ELL resource manual accompanies the main core reading program. There is a five-day plan for ELLs to go along with Treasures. The ELL resource manual provides support for teachers working with ELLs. The manual places more emphasis on oral language development than does the core reading program and has the teacher engage the students in some aspect of discussion every day. Over the five days of lessons, the Oral Language and Read and Respond segments are repeated every day. The third component shifts daily in the following order: Phonics, Vocabulary, Comprehension, Grammar, and a segment called Close that reviews the effective strategies for the week. The ELL resource manual also gives the teacher more explicit definitions of words, identifies important academic language, and points out potential conflicts between English and Spanish when teaching phonics and grammar.

The needs of ELLs are such that the criteria of Coyne et al. (2001) can be used to evaluate programs that support them. Instruction for ELLs and struggling native English-speaking students is in many respects the same, yet different in a few important ways (Lovett et al., 2008; Mathes, Pollard-Durodola, Cárdenas-Hagan, Linan-Thompson, & Vaughn, 2007). Both groups of students benefit from strong strategy instruction with careful teacher scaffolding. Strategy integration, the concept that reading skills should be integrated in the mind of the learner, is also necessary for both groups. The differences are the need for more explicit language instruction and the development of background knowledge for ELLs. ELLs are learning new oral language at the same time they are learning to read (Perogoy & Boyle, 2000).

We decided to examine the ELL resource book as a supplement to the regular teacher's guide from Treasures. These two guides must be used together, because the ELL resource manual expands upon the instruction in the Treasures manual. So this brief review actually looks at two components. We focus our analysis on the first three weeks of instruction in the third-grade manuals. The results of this analysis are presented in Table 24.

The ELL resource manual offers some instructional innovations over and above the main core reading program. The manual provides more support for students, the academic language is enhanced, some background knowledge is primed, and scaffolding is geared to the language skill level of the students. Vocabulary instruction is not particularly enhanced over that in the core reading program, nor is decoding instruction. This is clearly not a stand-alone pro-

Table 24. Evaluation of the English-Language Learner (ELL) Resources in Treasures (Macmillan/McGraw-Hill, 2009)

Criteria	ELL Resources (Grade 3)
Conspicuous strategy instruction	The strategy lessons for phonics and comprehension are explicit and carefully delineated. The ELL component of the lessons expands upon the academic language of the lesson. So concepts like vowels or the word *analyze*, as in analyze a story's structure, are more completely explained in the ELL resource manual.
Mediated scaffolding	The ELL resource manual offers scaffolding over that found in the core program. The program offers different amounts of support for text comprehension depending on the English skills of the students. The more skilled the students, the less their responses are structured by the teacher.
Strategy integration	Because the ELL resource manual offers more discussion of academic language, there is more focus on what strategies are and how they work. That, however, does not mean that strategies are related one to another. Vocabulary and phonics skills are not related to comprehension. However, at the end of the week, the core program encourages students to reflect on what helped them improve, an instructional move not part of the regular program.
Primed background knowledge	The lessons in the ELL resource prime background knowledge by helping the teacher with language transfer. Issues of phonics, grammar and Spanish cognates are addressed. For other skills the program does not augment what the core offers in priming background knowledge.
Judicious review	The amount of review is a direct reflection of the review process in the main core program. Phonics, which is more emphasized in the ELL guide is not well reviewed, since it is only directly taught one day a week, but it is taught more thoroughly in the main core program—*Treasures*.
Well-paced instruction	It is not appropriate to evaluate the pace of a lesson, since pace is not dictated by the ELL resource, but by the main core reading program.

gram, but one that functions with the regular program. The Coyne et al. (2001) criteria work well for analyzing this intervention program.

Effective criteria can be used to evaluate intervention programs that supplement core reading programs. When the programs stand alone, the criteria developed by Coyne et al. (2001) are a useful guide for examining the intervention programs. These criteria, when used carefully, can reveal if instruction is explicit, well scaffolded, and accompanied by sufficient review. The strongest example is

Scott Foresman Early Reading Intervention (Simmons & Kame'enui, 2003b). The singular focus on phonemic awareness, letter sounds, and word reading make extensive review, strong scaffolding, and quick pacing possible. Programs that are linked or integrated with the core reading programs are more difficult to evaluate, because the characteristics of their instruction are dependent on the quality of those programs. The success of any of these programs depends not only on their curriculum and instruction but also on the knowledge of the teachers (Piasta, Connor, Fishman, & Morrison, 2009).

What Research Has to Say About Assessments in Core Reading Programs

Over the past 25 years, schools have greatly expanded assessments, testing students more often and with more types of tests (Paris & Hoffman, 2004). The increase in testing is caused by federal and state accountability standards and the desire of schools to predict students' performance on high-stakes assessments and then provide remedial measures to ensure success. The second cause of increased testing is the evidence that if reading problems in young children are identified early, then proper instructional interventions can prevent future problems (Snow et al., 1998). This has resulted in more early literacy screening. The third cause is that the development of RTI and the increased use of curriculum-based measures push schools and teachers to monitor students' progress more frequently and more intently (Fuchs & Fuchs, 2008). Whether the new assessment culture leads to higher achievement is still an unanswered question (Pressley, 2006). Publishers of core reading programs have responded to expanding assessment demands by making more assessment tools available to users of core reading programs.

Many different assessments are in use in schools because different groups of stakeholders value different tools. Classroom teachers value informal assessments, sight-word fluency tests, spelling tests, running records, and quick oral and written comprehension checks. Classroom teachers must also assign grades, and they need tools to assess students' competence or mastery. Only 34% of teachers in a national survey of assessment practices used the core reading program assessments (Paris, Paris, & Carpenter, 2002). Administrators value standardized tests, especially those that emulate the state-administered high-stakes assessments. As a principal and central office administrator, it is important to gauge the likelihood that a given grade level or school will pass the reading test in May. Thus, administrators are attracted to any assessment that is likely to predict performance on state standards. Although publishers develop correlations between core reading programs and state standards, it is difficult to create assessments that mirror the various standards across the country. Finally, parents raise two assessment questions, and maybe children do as well: Is my child making progress in reading? How does my child's reading compare to other children of the same age or at the same grade level? Assessments need to provide answers to students, parents, administrators, and teachers.

Given the number of stakeholders in the assessment process, core reading programs have to provide a range of tools to satisfy their varying needs. Thus, all core reading programs have informal assessments for teachers, standardized assessments for administrators, and a means of assembling a portfolio so that parents can be apprised of their children's growth as readers. The problem facing the school and the teachers is selecting from among all these options, plus the other district and state required assessments, to develop a useful but parsimonious assessment system. The goal is to assess as little as possible yet make the right instructional decisions.

All core reading programs have as standard equipment a full range of reading assessments. These assessments are designed to place students at the right level and assess learning at the end of a week, the end of a unit (six weeks), or at the beginning, middle, and end of the year. Additionally, the programs have diagnostic tests, phonics surveys, phonemic awareness tests, and fluency assessments. Table 25 captures the assessments that are typically available in core reading programs, and often the program suggests when they be given. We decided to examine two newer core reading programs, Treasures (2009) and StoryTown (2008), and two older ones, Trophies (2003/2005) and Houghton Mifflin Reading (2003/2005). We were somewhat limited in our review, because the samples that publishers provide do not contain all of the assessment tools. Assessment tools are largely the same across programs and years. The one significant change is greater availability of fluency assessments, mostly sparked by the influence of DIBELS (Dynamic Indicators of Basic Early Literacy Skills; Good & Kaminski, 2003–2005) and other curriculum-based measures. Treasures comes with a large book of fluency assessments in addition to those available in the weekly assessments. StoryTown has a large number of passages available for assessing fluency. Running records, a form of informal reading inventory, was also added to most of the assessment inventories of core reading programs.

Table 25. Core Reading Program Assessment Tools and Their Suggested Frequency of Use

Assessment	Trophies (Harcourt, 2003/2005)	StoryTown (Harcourt, 2008)	Treasures (Macmillan/ McGraw-Hill, 2009)	Houghton Mifflin Reading (Houghton Mifflin, 2003/2005)
Screening tests	Beginning of year	Beginning of year	Beginning, middle, and end of year	Beginning of year
Placement test	Passage reading and comprehension	Passage reading and comprehension	Brief assessment of basic skills	Brief assessment of passage reading and comprehension
Benchmark tests	Middle and end of year Comprehension and vocabulary	Beginning, middle, and end of year Comprehension, vocabulary, word analysis, and fluency	Twice a year Comprehension, vocabulary, grammar, text features, study skills, and writing	Two to four times a year Comprehension, vocabulary, and grammar
Theme tests	Six times a year Comprehension, vocabulary, grammar, and writing	Six times a year Comprehension, vocabulary, grammar, spelling, writing, and fluency	Six times a year Comprehension, listening comprehension, literary elements, vocabulary, grammar, text features, study skills, and writing	Six times a year Comprehension, listening comprehension, literary elements, vocabulary, grammar, text features, study skills, and writing
Weekly lesson tests	Weekly Comprehension and vocabulary	Weekly Comprehension, phonics, vocabulary, grammar, and fluency	Weekly Vocabulary, comprehension (passage and skills), spelling, and grammar	Weekly Vocabulary, comprehension (passage), and grammar
Fluency assessment	At the teacher's discretion	At the teacher's discretion	At the teacher's discretion	Not available
Running records	Not available	At the teacher's discretion	Not available	Not available
Diagnostic tests	At the teacher's discretion Phonemic awareness and phonics	At the teacher's discretion Phonemic awareness and phonics	At the teacher's discretion Phonemic awareness, phonics, and informal reading inventory	At the teacher's discretion Phonics, decoding, and informal reading inventory

Evaluating Assessment Tools
in Core Reading Programs

Assessments are evaluated in terms of reliability, validity, and utility. Reliability refers to the precision of the assessment. Part of validity depends on the assessments and their utility. Whenever you measure anything, some error creeps into the measurement. A good test has high reliability. The reliability of tests in core reading programs is not reported. It may be available from the publisher, but it is not with the information provided in the samples. It will be necessary to question the publisher's representative about test reliability. Some researchers have argued that core reading program tests often lack reliability (Paris et al., 2002). StoryTown (2008) has a section in its assessment guide titled "Reliability and Validity." Although the senior author, Roger Farr, discusses validity, he does not discuss the reliability. Educators need to be very cautious making interpretations based on assessments that are not reliable or for which reliability data are not available.

A test is valid or has construct validity if it measures what theory tells us reading is. For a test to have construct validity, it has to have the right kinds of passages, not just sentences; ask the right kinds of questions, not just literal; and assess the right components of reading, not just oral reading fluency. A test that avoids assessing vocabulary might not be valid if vocabulary is an important part of reading. Construct validity is somewhat a matter of expert judgment. However, predictive validity and concurrent validity, two other types of validity, can be determined statistically. We want tests that accurately predict how well students are going to do. If the end-of-unit test predicts that your students will pass your state assessment and they don't, then the test has a validity problem. Concurrent validity means that the result of one test corresponds closely to the results of another test.

Most core reading programs do not report the validity of their tests. In StoryTown (2008), the senior author, Farr, describes how validity was determined and describes the pilot testing of the program's benchmark tests. We know that these tests were developed carefully, but he offers no data on their predictive validity. The sample materials from Treasures (2009) contain no information on the validity of the program's tests. We urge school districts to request this information for any core reading program. Ultimately, the validity of a test rests on the consequences of the tests (Messick, 1995). If giving the test and using its results improves the instructional program for students, and they make progress learning to read, we can infer that the test was valid. If, on the other hand, a school gives so many tests that instructional time is compromised, we can surmise that the consequences are weak and the testing lacks validity. Consequential validity can ultimately be determined by studying the impact of assessments within a school. We take a look at this issue in Chapter 8 when we describe how to craft an effective assessment program. If giving a test does not alter instruction in any way, the problem may be in the test or in teachers' interpretations of its results.

The core reading programs differ significantly in how much support they provide to teachers in the use and interpretation of these tests. Basically, core reading programs want to make many options available, but they do not want to usurp the decision-making authority of the teacher, the school, or the district. So the tests are there, and you can decide which ones to use. For example, StoryTown (2008) states,

> Using more than one kind of assessment will give you the clearest picture of your students' progress. Multiple measures are the key to a well-rounded view. First consider the assessments that are already mandated for you: Your district and your state will of course tell you which tests you must use and when. In addition to these, you should use curriculum-based assessments to monitor your students' progress in StoryTown. (Grade 1 Teacher's Manual, Theme 6, p. A1)

Treasures (2009) also urges teachers to use multiple measures: "To create instructional profiles for your children, look for patterns of results from any of the following assessments" (Grade 1 Teacher's Manual, Theme 1, p. 143M). Then, the program offers teachers the option of using a fluency assessment, a running record, or a benchmark assessment. All are quite different, and all might give teachers a different picture of the students' reading abilities. The Assessment Handbook for Treasures gives some guidelines on test interpretation and use, including some case studies. However, these documents are in a separate publication and not part of the regular teacher's guide. Teachers may not have the time to study this document along with all that has to be read in the teacher's guide.

All four of the reading programs we reviewed provide weekly, unit, and benchmark assessments. In most cases, the programs give little guidance regarding which of these assessment tools should be used. Treasures (2009) suggests that fluency be assessed every other week for struggling readers, every third week for on-level readers, and every six weeks for above-level readers. No guidance is provided for the other weekly or theme assessments. Houghton Mifflin

Reading (2003/2005) and StoryTown (2008) offer no particular guidance on how often to assess, but do explain the differences in the tests. Ultimately, testing frequency will be up to the judgment of the teachers and the administrators.

Interpreting tests is the bridge between the results and instruction. The core reading programs provide little guidance to the teachers. Typically, there is a page that directs teachers to additional instructional resources if the students perform poorly on one or more portions of the test. All of the programs urge the use of multiple assessments, as they should, but give little guidance on how to do so. For example, Houghton Mifflin Reading states, "Student progress is best evaluated through multiple measures, which can be collected in a portfolio. The portfolio provides a record of student progress over time and can be used in conferencing with the students, parents, or other educators" (Grade 3 Teacher's Manual, Theme 1, p. 123A).

Overall, core reading programs provide a wide range of assessment tools, and over the years, as assessment trends have changed, publishers have created more assessments. Core reading programs provide tools that align with the curriculum-based approach of RTI, and more authentic assessment can be used within a portfolio system. None of these assessment tools, however, are well researched. There is scant data on their reliability and validity. The use of these assessment tools will be up to the expert judgment of teachers and administrators. Over time, schools can determine if the assessments in core reading programs predict student performance and provide useful information to guide instruction.

PUTTING IT ALL TOGETHER

As core reading programs have evolved, they have tried to provide the tools necessary to teach all students to read. This requires differentiated instruction in the classroom, intervention curricula for students who struggle, and assessments to monitor the results of these efforts. In this chapter, we shared some criteria for evaluating intervention programs for struggling readers and ELL students. We did not survey all programs that are available, but we shared how we would go about evaluating these programs. To do so, we developed some specific criteria for evaluating intervention programs. We

(continued)

also described the assessments that are available in current and older core reading programs. We discussed the need to consider the reliability, validity, and utility of these assessments. As you begin your study of core reading programs, think about the following criteria:

Differentiated Instruction and Intervention Programs

- Does the core reading program provide specific guidelines for differentiating instruction for all students?

- Do the differentiation guidelines help the teacher vary texts, tasks, and time to meet the needs of all students?

- Is the intervention program structured for small-group, fast-paced, and engaging instruction?

- Does the core reading program provide a well-structured early intervention program?

- Does the intervention program teach strategies explicitly, provide scaffolding, and allow for sufficient review for students to acquire competence?

- Within the intervention program, is strategy instruction integrated and knowledge primed so that the act of learning to read makes sense to the students?

Assessments

- Do the assessments in the core reading program measure the components of reading deemed important in your district?

- Does the core reading program provide a range of standardized and informal assessments?

- Is there evidence that the assessments are valid, reliable, and useful?

- Is the core reading program helpful for interpreting test results and translating them into practice?

- Can assessment results be used to inform parents and students of progress or problems?

- Do any of the assessments predict student performance on high-stakes state assessments?

CHAPTER 7

Selecting a Core Reading Program

Ms. English, in one of her first tasks as the language arts curriculum coordinator, has been assigned the overwhelming job of directing her school system's adoption of a new reading program. Her school system is large with a wide range of literacy needs. Some schools serve predominantly middle to upper class neighborhoods with involved parents. Other schools are located in areas with high poverty. She also has to take into consideration the vast differences in teaching experience among her faculty. Some of her teachers have graduate degrees and many years of teaching, while others have just started their teaching careers. She needs a core reading program that not only provides structure and support for her novice teachers but also has the resources that experienced teachers need to make effective instructional decisions

In addition, Ms. English is trying to work her way through several new core reading programs and their many components. Core reading programs are complex, and it can be difficult to distinguish one program from another. She also is busily trying to organize a review committee. She has a wide variety of teachers, administrators, and parents to consider when constructing the review committee. And all of this work needs to be completed within eight months.

I n what follows, we guide you through the process of selecting a core reading program. In Chapters 3 through 6, we built the foundation as you learned how to evaluate a core reading program by examining their texts, tests, and instruction in word recognition, vocabulary, and comprehension. Now, we bring what you learned together in a process that can guide you through the task of selecting a core reading program.

What You Will Learn

- What the research has revealed about core reading program adoption practices
- How a variety of school systems have navigated the process of selection of a core reading program
- A process for adopting a core reading program in your district

What You Will Be Able to Do

- Develop district and school goals for reading instruction and use those to guide your search for a new core reading program

- Establish a systematic plan for adopting a reading series

- Evaluate a core reading program to make the best choice for your school system

- Design a pilot study of core reading programs and evaluate its results

- Evaluate all district data and opinions about core reading programs to reach a final decision

What We Know About the Textbook Adoption Process

For the majority of elementary schools in the United States, core reading programs are the main method of reading instruction and a substantial part of their materials budget. As Farr, Tulley, and Powell (1987) explained, "Considering the central role of basal readers in the classroom, the selection of a basal reader represents the selection of a reading curriculum in most American schools" (p. 267). Even in school districts that write their own curricula, a core reading program exerts a tremendous influence on teachers (Durkin, 1990). Based on the widespread use of core reading programs in schools today, decisions regarding which particular program to use should be of the utmost importance. Instead, research has suggested that the methods by which schools choose a core reading program are often haphazard due to the press of time (Chall & Squire, 1991; Farr et al., 1987; Finn & Ravitch, 2004).

The process of textbook adoption, although used widely, has been studied little. However, several publications (Chall & Squire, 1991; Farr et al., 1987; Whitman, 2004) have provided insight into how school systems and districts approach textbook adoption. Farr et al. (1987) provided an informative overview of the process. States are divided into two groups: adoption states or open (nonadoption) states. Adoption states, 22 in all, "maintain some form of centralized, state-level textbook evaluation and selection process" (Farr et al., p. 270), whereas open states choose textbooks with little or no state guidelines. The adoption states include the influential big three—California, Texas, and Florida—plus other states in the Southeast. This is a legacy of the Reconstruction

Era, when the post–Civil War southern state governments sought to control the content of textbooks to advance a particular point of view. Another contention is that state control is beneficial because centralized reviewing and adoptions lower costs. The open adoption states are found in the Northeast, the Midwest, and the far West.

Adoption states require state committees or commissions to review all submitted textbooks. From there, the committees create lists of state-approved textbooks for all subject areas. School systems must choose their textbooks from the lists. In more recent times, these lists have become easier to compile as the number of publishers has declined. In open states, school systems are free to adopt any textbook. The other issue cited by Farr et al. (1987) is the powerful influence that the larger adoption states have on textbook content. States like California and Texas provide major revenue for publishing companies. As a result, publishing companies focus textbook content and revision cycles on the needs of these larger, more lucrative states. In effect, the adoption process is really part of the textbook creation process. The major publishers do not create core reading programs until guidelines have been published in Texas and California, and these detailed guidelines exert significant influence on the content and methods in core reading programs.

Although selection processes vary widely between the open and adoption states, one of the most influential factors for both groups is the textbook adoption committee (Farr et al., 1987). The textbook adoption committee at the district level typically consists of teachers, administrators, and in some cases, parents. Their task is large, but research has suggested that many adoption procedures seem "to lack disciplined, systematic approaches" (Chall & Squire, 1991, p. 136). Indeed, Farr et al. (1987) found a number of concerns with textbook adoption committees as well as the overall process. The major issues include lack of in-depth analysis of the programs, lack of adequate time to review the materials, and an overall lack of training in textbook review processes. Although this research is old, many of you may experience similar problems. Our task is to guide you through the process to ensure a better outcome.

Oftentimes, textbook adoption committees use (or are provided with) worksheets or checklists with set criteria (Farr et al., 1987). Ironically, the adoption committees rarely have any input into the criteria used on the checklists. Furthermore, the checklists often contain so many items that it is exceedingly difficult for the adoption committees to give each item enough attention (Finn & Ravitch, 2004). According to Finn and Ravitch (2004), "Even the most ambitious reviewer who manages to read all the textbooks up for adoption in a given year is unlikely to provide coherent ratings, due to the plethora of criteria" (p. 25). Instead, committee members resort to checking for the presence of the criteria, the "flip test," rather than focusing on the quality of the activities and concepts within a core reading program (Farr et al., 1987). Equally as problematic is the fact that very few committee members consider what the research base associated with a program is, if any (Chall & Squire, 1991).

Stein, Stuen, Carnine, and Long (2001) also found that the adoption committees often abrogate their responsibility to the democratic vote of all teachers. A select and informed committee may study the core reading programs and reach a decision or at least rank the programs. Then, the final decision is turned over to the teachers for a vote, but teachers are less informed because they have spent less time studying the materials. In other districts, the textbook review committee is used to inform the curriculum directors or members of the board of education, who make the final decision. Before the textbook review and adoption process begins, the district must decide how the final decision will be made and whose vote will count.

It is little wonder that textbook adoption committee members opt for cursory reviews of the materials. In addition to the overwhelming checklists many systems use, the timeline for adoptions typically takes place within one school year. However, the committee members often review all of the materials in just two months (Farr et al., 1987). Review of the materials takes place in addition to regular teaching and administrative duties. It is not unusual to find teachers reviewing materials during their spare time on the weekends or late at night. The failure to provide release time to the curriculum review committee members undermines their efforts.

Despite the importance of choosing a well-suited program for a school system, it is unusual to find a textbook adoption committee that has received any kind of training on how to choose a textbook. Reviewers are often left to their own devices when it comes to making value judgments and decisions about the quality of the content of the core reading programs (Farr et al., 1987). In some instances, committee members have little understanding of the school system's reading approach or, even more disturbing, to the most current research on reading.

Ultimately, the review committee members will need to use some criteria to evaluate the textbooks, either by selecting an existing review document or designing their own. The creation of *A Consumer's Guide to Evaluating a Core Reading Program Grades K–3: A Critical Elements Analysis* (Simmons & Kame'enui, 2003a) was an attempt to improve the process of reviewing and evaluating core reading programs. This guide was developed to bring some scientific precision to the textbook evaluation process. It is in essence a checklist to be used by school systems to evaluate core reading programs. It gained popularity as a direct result of the federal government's Reading First initiative. The charge of Reading First was to "provide assistance to State educational agencies (SEAs) and local educational agencies (LEAs) in establishing reading programs for students in kindergarten through grade 3 that are based on scientifically based reading research" (No Child Left Behind Act of 2001, 2002, Title 1, Part B, §1201). Among the other goals of Reading First was helping school systems select or develop effective instructional materials to assist teachers in implementing the essential components of reading instruction. In fact, schools and states are under tremendous pressure to use a core reading program, particularly one that claims to be scientifically based, in order to receive federal funding under the Reading First grant.

As a result, almost all states defined a core reading program as materials and methods that could be purchased from a publishing company—in short, something that came in a box. Instructional approaches like reciprocal teaching (Palincsar & Brown, 1984), questioning the author (Beck et al., 1996), and transactional strategies instruction (Brown et al., 1996), although having a strong research base, were not listed as scientifically based reading research programs. Hence, published core reading programs became synonymous with scientifically based reading instruction.

Determining if a core reading program is built on scientifically based reading research is an almost impossible task. Core reading programs are not subjected to rigorous experimental research with students and teachers randomly assigned to treatment and control groups. At best, the label *scientifically based reading research* means that the authors, editors, and freelance writers created instructional lessons and incorporated skills and strategies that reflected their best understanding of the reading research. As we argued in Chapter 2, the process of creating a core reading program is a product of many forces, only some of which are founded in reading research.

The selection of a core reading program remains one of the most crucial decisions a school system can make. Yet many school systems approach the task of textbook adoption with little planning. Others seem to reinvent the wheel as they struggle to find a systematic process for textbook adoptions. Interestingly, one research study in particular (Farr et al., 1987) provided excellent guidelines for the adoption of core reading programs. In this chapter, we provide an additional tool for evaluating these programs.

Studying Four School Systems

We profiled the textbook adoption processes of four school systems in the United States to give you some insight about how others manage the process and to identify some of the factors that lead to a successful adoption, as well as some pitfalls. We focused on four school systems that were either in the midst of the textbook adoption process or had recently completed it. We selected these four districts because they represent small and large districts, rural and urban districts, and varying proportions of minority students. To gather useful information, various stakeholders in each school system were interviewed. The names and locations of these districts have been replaced with pseudonyms to ensure their anonymity.

Case Study 1: Piedmont Public Schools

This school system in the Southeast, with 38 elementary schools, is large and diverse with a mix of urban and suburban schools. The student body consists of equal proportions of African American, Caucasian, and Hispanic students. Because of its large size, the school system is divided into six regions. When Piedmont Public Schools began their search for a core reading program, they had in place a process that all textbook adoptions followed, so the procedures were replicated whenever a new textbook was needed. In fact, they have a manual that details how to proceed with a textbook adoption.

In the early fall, the elementary language arts specialist, who was in charge of the process, met with all the elementary school principals to give them an overview of the textbook adoption process and request recommendations for steering committee members. The steering committee consisted of a range of stakeholders, including two members of the elementary language arts department, one English as a second language teacher, one special education teacher, one gifted education teacher, one Title I teacher, six administrators (one from each region), six reading specialists (one from each region), six classroom teachers (one per grade level), and two parents. The purpose of the steering committee was to look at all the programs up for adoption and select a manageable number for consideration. By late October, the steering committee was in place.

The work of the steering committee began with a presentation from the elementary language arts specialist on best literacy practices. The purpose of the presentation was to review these practices and clarify the school system's philosophy on reading instruction, which was a balanced literacy approach. In doing so, the steering committee would be able to select reading materials that complemented the district's emphasis on balanced literacy. With a knowledge base in place, seven publishers presented their core reading programs to the steering committee. The steering committee met in mid-December to narrow the options to two. They had little trouble choosing just two, as the other five options did not fully complement the district's emphasis on balanced literacy.

In January, each principal was asked to identify one person from his or her school to serve on the selection committee. These individuals would oversee and organize the evaluations of the two programs at the school level. Additionally, they also attended a presentation by the elementary language arts specialist that detailed the county's philosophy on reading instruction. Again, balanced literacy was emphasized.

At a meeting in early February, the selection committee was briefed on the textbook adoption and evaluation process. Following this meeting, publishers' representatives for the two core reading programs gave a more in-depth review of their programs. This part of the meeting was open to all interested employees. Approximately one week after the presentation, sample textbooks from both programs were delivered to each elementary school for further review.

The selection committee at each school organized and cataloged all the materials from each core reading program. Materials were displayed for approximately two weeks where all of the teachers could readily access them. By late February, school-level discussions about the programs were held, and a comprehensive evaluation tool was used to consider the programs. Across the schools, teachers and administrators looked at how the various programs met the needs of a balanced literacy framework. The focus was on selecting material that both supported best practices and aligned with state standards. Following the discussions, all potential users of the core reading program were able to vote for their choices. The school system opted not to pilot the materials in classrooms.

Each school tallied the votes to determine the preferred core reading program at that school. From there, one member of each school committee was selected to serve as a delegate in the final divisionwide vote. Each school had one vote. In early March, the representatives from each school met for the final vote. The program with the most votes was chosen. This selection process illustrates an important contradiction. The selection committee devotes time to the process, learns the research base, and develops the expertise. The final decision then rests with the representatives' votes. This raises the question of whether buy-in from the teachers is more important than critical program analysis from trained reviewers.

However, the school system administrators did not stop with the core reading program adoption. At present, they are involved in educating their teachers not only on the new materials, but also in providing education on the philosophy behind balanced literacy. Their goal is to provide ongoing teacher training to develop reflective practitioners who can flexibly meet the needs of all of their students.

Case Study 2: Desert Sands Public School District

This case study provides an interesting contrast to the first one. It took place in a large, urban school system in the Southwest that was seeking a new core reading program for its 55 elementary schools. The school system population is 52% African American, 35% Hispanic, and 13% Caucasian. In this school system, there existed two distinct philosophical approaches to reading instruction. One group favored the use of traditional core reading programs, whereas the other group preferred the guided reading approach (Fountas & Pinnell, 1996). The philosophical differences centered on a basic belief about the nature of instruction and the role of teacher prerogative in instructional decisions. The core reading program group favored explicit instruction and clearly articulated skill sequences, with strict fidelity to the program. The guided reading group felt that skill instruction should be responsive to the needs of the students, but rejected a systematic approach and emphasized teacher prerogative. The conflict between the groups was evident throughout the adoption process. The leadership committee consisted of two science specialists, three reading specialists, two ELL specialists, and several curriculum directors. One member of the committee, the reading supervisor, felt the process was biased from the beginning, because the composition of the committee favored those who adhered to the guided reading philosophy. In his opinion, the more influential members of the committee were clearly in favor of the guided reading approach.

One obvious contrast between the two groups was how they considered the research base behind the various core reading programs. The group that favored a traditional core reading program recognized and valued the names of the author teams for each program and had faith in the scientific base of the programs. They relied on the NRP report (NICHD, 2000). Meanwhile, the guided reading group was more concerned with how the program conformed to their philosophy and the degree to which a core reading program could enable teacher decision making. They gave little credence to the authors of the programs and were somewhat dismissive of traditional notions of research and reluctant to embrace the NRP report and other such documents.

In an attempt to find some common ground, the leadership committee created a curriculum study group to guide the review of materials. The curriculum study group expanded the leadership committee by adding 6 classroom teachers, for a total of 15 members. The group began by studying current research on reading instruction. Although there was some disagreement about what research to study, the group opted to read works by one of the authors of the NRP report, Tim Shanahan, as well as *Schools That Work* (Allington & Cunningham, 2002) and *Classrooms That Work* (Cunningham & Allington, 2007).

Following the review of research on reading instruction, the curriculum study group wanted to examine all of the major core reading programs. However, some of the more vocal members of the leadership committee decided that it made more sense to limit their choices in the interest of time. Programs considered too rigid were not an option. It is unclear how they arrived at this decision, but Treasures (Macmillan/McGraw-Hill, 2009) was excluded from the search, and StoryTown (Harcourt, 2008), Scott Foresman Reading Street (Pearson Scott Foresman, 2008/2009), and Literacy by Design (Rigby/Houghton Mifflin Harcourt, 2007) were not. The committee also decided that representatives of the publishers should not be allowed to speak to the committee or any of the teachers. Later, this idea was modified to allow the representatives to confer with teachers during the piloting of their core reading programs. At any rate, the committee decided to pilot three different programs for a full year. Two programs were considered traditional core reading programs—StoryTown (2008) and Reading Street (2008)—while Literacy by Design (2007) was intended to support a guided reading or less traditional approach (Fountas & Pinnell, 1996).

Twenty teachers at each grade, Kindergarten through grade 5, each piloted one of the three core reading programs during 2007–2008. This pilot involved over 150 teachers and was fully funded by the three publishing companies. During the pilot study, teachers kept a log of how they used the assigned program's materials. Specifically, teachers described what was difficult to use in the programs and how they overcame the problems. They also kept track of how and when they supplemented instruction with resources outside the core reading program. In addition, teachers completed a survey at the end of the pilot study in which they shared their impressions of the assigned programs. All surveys were analyzed by the school system's research office.

As part of the pilot study, the district collected pre- and posttest data using the Stanford-10 (2006) reading test. All students in the pilot were assessed in September and May. The data were collected and analyzed by the research office. The initial data indicated that the core reading program that adhered to a guided reading approach, Literacy by Design (2007), provided stronger test results on the Stanford-10 in first grade, but in all other grades, there were no differences in achievement among the programs. However, the teacher log data showed that the teachers had to supplement the curriculum when using Literacy by Design (2007). In grades 2 through 5, there was no significant difference among the three programs in the posttest scores after controlling for pretest scores. But the teachers indicated in their logs that they did far less supplementing of the curriculum with the two more traditional reading programs—Reading Street (2008) and StoryTown (2008). The teachers were also quite clear that the more traditional programs were easier to follow and implement.

Following the analysis of the data, lengthy discussions took place among the leadership committee members. To some members of the committee, the results suggested that the guided reading approach does not work for all students. One member suggested that they adopt Literacy by Design (2007) anyway. Another member recommended adopting the program as well as an intervention program for those students who did not progress as expected. Still another member argued for purchasing the nontraditional program but also buying a supplemental phonics program.

Analysis of the teacher survey data also generated great discussion. Overall, the teachers responded negatively to the less traditional program, Literacy by Design (2007). However, the members of the committee that preferred the guided reading approach worried that a traditional core reading program would limit teachers' freedom. They expressed their reservations that a more traditional program would encourage teachers to rely solely on the core reading program and follow it lockstep. Others valued the fact that teachers had to modify a program, arguing that frequent supplements were good, reflecting active teacher decision making. Carrying this logic to the end, one administrator suggested that the school system not adopt any program but instead engage in extensive staff development. At this writing, no final decision has been made.

Unlike the school district in the first case study, this school district lacked an organized system or criteria for textbook adoption. This lack of clear criteria or consensus about the characteristics of effective reading instruction has plagued the adoption process. Although the district in the first case study knew they were looking for a program that fit its balanced literacy philosophy, this district had competing philosophies that could not be met in one program. Lacking clear goals, they could not coalesce around one program. The pilot study provided little useful information, as committee members argued about how to interpret the results. There did not seem to be anyone clearly in charge, nor did they have a specific timetable. Instead, the adoption process turned into a power struggle.

Case Study 3: Atlantic Public Schools

This small, urban school system in the Mid-Atlantic region has seven kindergarten through fourth grade elementary schools with a total school population of about 3,250 students. The district is approximately 50% African American, 40% Caucasian, and 10% Hispanic. As in the first case study, this school system followed a systematic and organized approach to the textbook adoption process.

The first step in the process was to form a textbook review committee consisting of the elementary curriculum director, two principals, some reading and special education teachers, and two teachers from each school. Teachers were selected so that each grade level had equal representation. The time required to serve on the committee was extensive, as members met one day per month for a year. In total, the committee spent about 45 to 60 hours considering the textbook materials; of that time, only two meetings were devoted to actually reading and evaluating the instructional materials.

The second step was to develop goals and expectations for the core reading program selection process. The committee began by identifying areas of need. They created a list of requirements for the program. They agreed on the following specific characteristics:

- The core reading program had to have an accompanying intervention program that complemented it.

- The anthology selections in the primary grades had to have a balance of decodable text and interesting, high-quality literature. This requirement pertained to the little books that accompanied the program as well.

- The program had to have a strong focus on phonemic awareness.

- The program needed to build in many opportunities for students to read.

Once the committee determined the most important characteristics of a core reading program, they began to study professional literature on reading research. It is interesting to note that the development of their list of requirements preceded their reading of the literature. Their reading material included research articles as well as the NRP report (NICHD, 2000). The next step was to order programs from Pearson Scott Foresman, Harcourt, and Macmillan/McGraw-Hill. They also considered continuing with their existing program from Houghton Mifflin. Representatives from each company presented their programs to the committee. The committee felt that they would not be unduly biased by the presentations of the publishing companies.

Following the presentations, the committee rated each of the core reading programs using *A Consumer's Guide to Evaluating a Core Reading Program Grades K–3* (Simmons & Kame'enui, 2003a). This rating process narrowed the search to three programs. They excluded the Houghton Mifflin Reading program, because it did not have an integrated intervention program. There was some sentiment among the committee at first to continue with the current program, because that would certainly simplify the staff development process, but others on the committee felt that they should examine only the new programs. After further discussion, the committee agreed to analyze the three new programs via pilot studies.

Each of the core reading programs was piloted for nine weeks, but each teacher in the pilot only worked with one program. The main purpose of the pilot study was to determine the ease of using the programs in real classrooms, but no achievement data was collected. At the end of the pilot, the participating teachers completed a survey and shared their impressions with the committee. The results of the pilot revealed that two of the programs were equally easy to implement. In addition, both programs had advantages over the third program; they had stronger phonemic awareness instruction that was implemented early in kindergarten. The third program also had no built-in intervention program, one of the school system's requirements.

After the completion of the pilot study, all of the teachers in the district were invited to listen to presentations from representatives of the two selected core reading programs. They were also able to review materials associated with each program. Approximately 150 of the 210 teachers in the district attended the after-school meeting. Teachers were able to cast one vote for their program choice. So teachers who had spent less than 30 minutes with each program were included in the vote to eliminate one from consideration. The final decision about which program to adopt rested on the quality of the texts within each program. The adopted program was judged by the review committee to have more engaging texts. Its collection of leveled books was extensive, with more engaging, colorful illustrations. It is interesting to note that at this late stage of the adoption process, a criterion that was not previously articulated—the engaging quality of the literature—helped guide the final decision.

Following the selection of the new core reading program, a press release was issued per the local school board policy. All of the soon-to-be adopted materials were displayed to allow the public to inspect them. All members of the public were able to rate the program with forms supplied by the school system. In doing so, all stakeholders, including administrators, teachers, parents and taxpayers, were able to voice their opinions on the selected reading program. Ultimately the curriculum director for the district overruled the teachers' preference, Scott Foresman Reading (Pearson Scott Foresman, 2004), and picked the other program, Trophies (Harcourt, 2003/2005). This decision raises important questions about the role of the review committee and the vote of the teachers. Although teacher participation promotes buy-in, teachers spent less than 30 minutes looking at materials, undermining the expertise and growing knowledge of the review committee. The final decision by the curriculum director further negated the work of the curriculum review committee.

Case Study 4: Rocky Hills Public Schools

Rocky Hills, a small school district, is located in the Rocky Mountains near a larger urban area. The student body is mostly Caucasian but has a growing Hispanic population, currently about 15%. After using a variety of materials for many years and experiencing some decline in reading test scores, the district decided to study reading instruction and consider adopting a core reading program. The district formed a curriculum study committee that consisted of reading specialists, classroom teachers from each of the five elementary schools, and two central office administrators.

Teachers and administrators were clamoring to pilot test some **new** material, but the district leadership felt that they first had to study their **own literacy** program. The district was using a program built around leveled little books from multiple publishers in kindergarten through second grade, supplemented with a spelling program, *Words Their Way* (Bear, Invernizzi, Templeton, & Johnston, 2006). The upper grades used Pegasus (Kendall/Hunt, 2000), a program that integrates reading instruction through novel study. The district leadership felt that there was no connection between these two approaches nor a consistent set of practices across the district.

This largely upper middle class school district was learning to deal with a growing population of Hispanic students. Examining data from school-mandated and state assessments proved daunting. The district's administrators found it difficult to use the data to locate the weaknesses in student performance and instructional programs. Most of the assessments reported on students' growth in word knowledge and fluency, but the perceived weaknesses in the district were in the upper grades and in comprehension. Ultimately, they wanted a reading program that would provide an overall structure to the curriculum yet allow teachers to be flexible in teaching diverse populations.

The curriculum committee first tried to develop a teacher survey about instructional practices and needs in the district. But they were unable to create a document short enough for teachers to complete easily but long enough to provide real insights. The leadership then decided that the next step was to visit schools that had similar demographics but were more successful than Rocky Hills was with its minority students. The committee wanted to learn which programs were being used, what the amount of instructional time was, and how intervention was delivered to students struggling to read. The committee visited approximately 20 different schools and observed regular classroom instruction and intervention delivered by reading specialists, noting instructional materials, assessments, and data reporting systems. Anywhere from 5 to 10 people visited each school and took notes on a common observation form.

When the committee finished their work, they conducted the same observational visits in their own schools, so they would have fresh notes and impressions to compare with what they learned in other schools. These observations were compiled, and programs and materials were identified that they wanted to implement in their own schools. The committee came to the conclusion that when schools study research, they are more likely to either dismiss the findings or assume that these instructional procedures already exist within their own classrooms. Observing successful schools made it harder to dismiss what they saw. As the curriculum director reported,

> We'd go into schools where the class size was a third more than what you would routinely see in our schools, and with far fewer resources, see them accomplish great things. You couldn't walk out of that without believing we can do the same thing.

The result of the school observations was a set of decisions that had to be made before materials could be ordered. The committee decided to recommend an increase in time for literacy instruction, mandating 120 minutes per day and a change in the role of the reading specialists. The reading specialists would spend less time pulling children out of class for intervention and would work more within the classroom. In addition, the reading specialists would assume responsibility for providing staff development to teachers and paraprofessionals, manage materials, and organize assessment data. Having developed an overall literacy plan for the school district, the committee was then ready to look at instructional materials.

The curriculum director's next concern was how to conduct a fair and thorough evaluation of reading programs. As the director explained,

> I've had the experience where you put the programs into the hands of the committee and they review a series of books, but it's not a comprehensive review. It's not really based on anything more than whether they like the pictures and the teacher's manual.

Rocky Hills agreed to use the Reading GPS evaluation process that accompanies this book. We divided the review process into three parts so that the reviewers could concentrate on either kindergarten materials, grades 1 and 2 materials, or grades 3 through 6 materials. The committee spent two full days reviewing program materials. About halfway through the process, the committee members reported that an in-depth evaluation revealed problems that were never apparent in the publishers' presentations or in the superficial inspection of the programs. Said one committee member, "When you really dig into these lessons, you question the favorable impression the publisher tried to create."

The committee members were reluctant to engage in a process of piloting core reading programs. In the past, they found that the teachers who piloted a particular program did so because they already liked the program and saw the pilot as a means of verifying their opinion. The district also was reluctant to engage in a pilot because they had not yet defined what they expected to learn from piloting a program. As we leave this case study, the review committee is still studying four core reading programs and is planning to pilot the programs early in the next school year. The goal of this pilot will be to evaluate the utility of the programs. The district administrators will use a systematic process of collecting information on how teachers actually use the programs. Teachers will note which parts of the lesson they use each day, what problems they encounter, and what changes or additions they make to the programs. We expand on the process they will use in the next section.

Guidelines for Textbook Adoption

The adoption process for a new core reading program is one that requires time, knowledge, and diligence. School personnel need to consider the composition of the adoption committee and the specific process and timeline for the adoption. We begin our discussion with an outline of the adoption process gleaned from our case studies and from others who have written about the textbook adoption process. We present this outline first, then we discuss the salient issues involved at each step of the process. Each district should have in place a textbook adoption process that covers the following points:

- Create a textbook adoption committee.
- Set goals.
  - Review board policies, state laws, and district guidelines for textbook adoptions.
  - Develop district-specific expectations or objectives for reading based on state guidelines, district grade-level objectives, and research.
  - Delineate the needs of your school or district.
- Learn about effective reading instruction.
  - Read and discuss the relevant research on reading instruction.
  - Visit schools in other districts that are achieving at high levels with similar demographics.
  - Invite guest speakers as needed to clarify knowledge of reading instruction.
- Select or develop a textbook evaluation instrument.
  - Review existing screening and evaluation tools.

- Field test screening criteria using existing core reading program materials.
- See the Reading GPS at the webpage for this book, www.reading.org/general/publications/books/bk707.aspx.
- Think through the process.
  - Who will make the final decision about program selection?
  - How will that person reach his or her decision?
- Order core reading programs and work with publishers.
  - Identify no fewer than two or more than five programs to review.
  - Arrange for publishers' presentations.
- Read and evaluate the core reading programs.
- Pilot core reading programs.
  - Decide on the purpose for piloting the programs and determine what data will be collected and analyzed.
  - Decide who will pilot which programs and the duration of the pilot.
  - Negotiate with the publishing companies for instructional materials.
- Negotiate with publishers on components to be purchased and their prices.
- Make final recommendations and plans.
  - Develop a communication plan to announce recommendations.
  - Prepare a school board presentation.
  - Develop individual school orders.
  - Develop a plan for staff development and program implementation.

Creating a Textbook Adoption Committee

The textbook adoption committee should consist primarily of reading specialists and classroom teachers. Reading specialists can provide input on current reading research, whereas both groups can speak to the specific needs of their students. The educators who know the most and will be using the materials should be the ones leading the selection and decision process. Curriculum directors and other administrators can help give a big picture overview of the district's budget and adoption procedures, but ultimately they should acknowledge either their limited knowledge, if that is the case, or limited experience in the current teaching of reading. This process is a bit like purchasing a gift for a loved one who is a skilled woodworker. The woodworker knows what tools he needs and the quality of those tools. The gift giver understands the limits of the budget.

The committee should reflect the racial, ethnic, and gender demographics of the district, and as Stein et al. (2001) have instructed, strong interpersonal skills are a must. The committee members must be able to listen, learn, reflect, and tolerate differing points of view. The committee in the second case study failed because they lacked the necessary expertise and simply could not tolerate and debate conflicting ideas. In a large school district, it might be useful to have several smaller committees that are trained by the district committee to review the reading programs and report their findings back to the district committee.

The district adoption committee also needs to lead a thorough screening of potential reading programs. Committees need to investigate with a critical eye the research base of each program. Has the publisher or an outside agency conducted a review or study of the educational materials? Ask the publishers' representatives for any data they might have about the efficacy of their programs. Some programs have been reviewed on the website for the Florida Center for Reading Research (www.fcrr.org) and others have been reviewed on the federal What Works Clearinghouse website (ies.ed.gov/ncee/wwc/). Much of the committee's work will be to verify the research base of the programs by conducting a rigorous review. Finally, the adoption committee should develop a timeline that is viable. Too often, school districts do not give committee members enough time to review materials, so it is crucial to provide enough time for a thoughtful examination.

Setting Goals

The adoption committee should begin the core reading program selection process by listing the concerns and needs of the district. This list should drive the review of programs, the pilot study, and the ultimate decision. There may not be a best core reading program, but there might be a program that is right for your school or district. For example, if the prime concern of the district is the number of students reading below grade level, then your first priority might be a strong intervention component. If the district's concern is the growing

ELL population, then a program that helps teachers learn about and meet the needs of ELL students is very useful. In some districts, the greater needs are in the primary grades in which students learn to decode and become fluent. Other districts may find that vocabulary and comprehension are their greatest concerns. Core reading programs can guide instruction and educate teachers. The Atlantic Public Schools in case study 3 did an excellent job of defining their needs and then searching for a program that meets those needs.

Learning About Effective Reading Instruction

The adoption process can be hindered by conflicting philosophies about reading instruction and a lack of awareness of the latest reading research. It is therefore desirable for the adoption committee members to increase their own expertise about reading instruction through study and trips to successful schools with similar demographics. A number of books and articles on reading instruction are produced each year, but despite the volume, ideas and practices in the field change slowly. We recommend the following books, which represent either a broad range of opinions or a balanced view of literacy. Our definition of balanced literacy comes from the work of Pressley (2006), who argued that students need both explicit instruction in reading skills and strategies plus the opportunity to read and write widely for real purposes and to real audiences.

In *Reading Instruction That Works*, Pressley (2006) gave a strong and balanced view about reading instruction. He addressed all of the vital topics: word recognition, fluency, vocabulary, comprehension, and motivation. The book smoothly integrates what has been learned from experimental research and from observations of exemplary schools and classrooms.

The NRP report (NICHD, 2000) is the definitive integration of research on phonemic awareness, phonics, fluency, vocabulary, and comprehension instruction. Although the report is flawed by what it omits—oral language development, motivation, differentiation of instruction, and interventions for struggling readers—it is essential to have a working knowledge of the research that it does cover in order to have a grounded discussion about reading instruction.

Farstrup and Samuels's (2002) *What Research Has to Say About Reading Instruction* presents concise reviews of topics ranging from basic reading theory to word recognition, early intervention, fluency, comprehension, and assessment. Two companion volumes, *Classrooms That Work* (Cunningham & Allington, 2007) and *Schools That Work* (Allington & Cunningham, 2002), provide a balanced look at successful reading instruction. The authors considered what builds successful readers from the perspective of the school and from the perspective of the classroom teacher. They presented a well-articulated, readable view of research.

Selecting or Developing an Evaluation Tool

The first key task for the adoption committee is to locate or develop a user-friendly evaluation tool for core reading programs. This tool must enable teachers and administrators to measure the components of the programs against the major components of reading identified by research—phonemic awareness, phonics, fluency, vocabulary, and comprehension—plus the equally important areas of assessment, differentiated instruction, small-group instruction and management, and oral language development. Second, the tool needs to be manageable in terms of time requirements. An evaluation tool that has too many components may encourage teachers to look for the presence of specific components without considering the quality of the components. Third, the evaluation tool must have some flexibility so that kindergarten teachers can evaluate their piece of the puzzle and fifth-grade teachers theirs.

A good current document is the *Review of Comprehensive Reading Programs*, developed by the Oregon Reading First Center (n.d.), a collection of professors, graduate students, researchers, district administrators, and one classroom teacher who convened to review, rate, and rank nine core reading programs. *A Consumer's Guide to Evaluating a Core Reading Program Grades K–3* (Simmons & Kame'enui, 2003a) was used by the panel to examine the nine reading programs at each of those grade levels, rating all five essential components: phonemic awareness, phonics, fluency, vocabulary, and comprehension. Within each component, there are priority items that must be found in strong reading instruction as well as discretionary items that were desirable but not essential. Within the priority items, the reviewers looked for how a critical skill is taught within a lesson, the scope and sequence of skills, and the progression of a skill over 10 consecutive lessons. Each of the elements was rated on a 3-point scale: element or item consistently meets or exceeds criterion (3), element partially meets or exceeds criterion (2), or element does not satisfy criterion (1).

For a core reading program to receive the imprimatur of a scientifically based reading research program, the endorsement of the Oregon Reading First Center (n.d.) has become almost essential. However, it is important to understand that its ratings, or any teacher's rating using the consumer's guide (Simmons & Kame'enui, 2003a), are based on expert judgment and impressions, not necessarily on a systematic and thorough review of the skills and strategies taught in the programs, the explicitness of instruction, or the instructional design principles that underlie the programs. For example, a teacher or administrator using the consumer's guide (Simmons & Kame'enui, 2003a) is asked to judge on a 3-point scale if a core reading program "continues skill and strategy instruction across several instructional sessions to illustrate the applicability and utility of the skill or strategy" (p. 47). The consumer's guide (Simmons & Kame'enui, 2003a) does not define *several* or *instructional sessions.* It cannot be known how many lessons or parts of lessons a teacher reviewing a program should examine, so it is impossible to know if a particular program develops a skill or strategy for days, weeks, or months. It further cannot be determined how much massed and distributed practice the programs provide (Dempster, 1987). On another item, the reviewer is asked to judge if the program "explicitly teaches comprehension strategies with the aid of carefully designed examples and practice" (Simmons & Kame'enui, 2003a, p. 48). The word *explicit* is not defined, and the criteria for explicit instruction—stressing declarative, procedural, and conditional knowledge when introducing a skill or strategy—are not mentioned (Duffy et al., 1986).

The strong endorsement of the Oregon Reading First Center (n.d.) using the consumer's guide (Simmons & Kame'enui, 2003a) has been seriously questioned by subsequent research. Five core reading programs that received strong endorsements for their comprehension instruction were found to be seriously lacking by other reviewers who conducted a more in-depth analysis (Dewitz et al., 2008, 2009). Other researchers (McGill-Franzen et al., 2006) questioned the efficacy of two core reading programs endorsed by the Oregon Reading First Center (n.d.) and specifically found that students were less likely to pass the state reading assessment when one of the two programs was used.

An important part of this book is the accompanying online curriculum review document, the Reading GPS, found at the webpage for this book, www .reading.org/general/publications/books/bk707.aspx. In this document, you will find a number of activities that will help you evaluate instruction in the core reading programs you are considering purchasing. *It is not a checklist.* Checklists cause you to look for specific components, such as phonemic awareness lessons, little books, activities for ELL learners, and progress-monitoring tools. Publishing companies are sophisticated and know what components you are seeking, so they make sure to include them. Only by looking deeply and examining critically will you be able to discern the quality of the instruction and the match between the program's instruction and your school's or district's curriculum goals. The Reading GPS has three components: one for kindergarten, one for grades 1 and 2, and one for grades 3 through 6. The Reading GPS has gone through several tryouts by school districts.

The Reading GPS will take you through a series of inquiries about reading instruction in a core reading program. You will be asked to look at a limited number of features, but your examination will require some time and thought. For example, you will need to read some of the program selections and rate the interest level and engagement of the text. You will need to read skill and strategy lessons to see how they measure up against specific criteria for explicit instruction. You will inspect the program as if you were about to teach from it, planning a lesson and considering how the instruction in the program will affect your students.

Many school districts require parents and other members of the community to review new textbook materials. These reviews add another set of eyes and standards to the process. Typically, parents can comment on the interest level of reading materials, the diversity of the stories with respect to social values, and the ability of the core reading programs to address the needs of all learners. We have developed the Reading GPS to help parents participate in the evaluation process.

Thinking Through the Process

We did not place the task of reaching a decision about a core reading program at the end of the process because we wanted you to think through the decision-making process before you have all the data in hand. Our four case studies taught us that at least two problems plague decisions. First, the committee can be overwhelmed with the data. At the end of the process, you will have information from your ratings of the programs. You will have teacher logs from your pilot, a wide array of subjective impressions of the programs, and you may have parent ratings as well. Before you reach the end of the process, you need to think through how all of this information will be integrated and weighted.

District politics is the second reason for thinking through the end of the process before you reach it. Power is not equally distributed within school districts. In one school we studied, and in others that we know of, the administrators overruled the work of teachers after a decision had been made and picked a program that did not have majority support. Although it is possible that the curriculum director made the right call, in so doing many hard feelings were engendered and months, if not years, of collaborative leadership were subverted.

For these reasons, it is valuable to discuss and agree on how the adoption decision will be made. It may be the case that the committee is charged to review and rank programs or that the committee's responsibility is to make a clear recommendation to the superintendent. We recommend that the committee develop a set of rules for reaching the final decision. These rules should in some way balance the needs of the district against the data from the core reading program evaluations and the pilots. For example, if one goal is to improve comprehension in the upper grades, then the final decision should give considerable weight to the comprehension evaluations of the programs and to the pilot teachers' evaluations in the upper grades.

Ordering Materials and Working With Publishers

At some point, almost all school districts invite publishers to present their core reading programs. The presentation is conducted by a consultant from the company with the sales representative and district manager coaching from the sidelines. Most consultants are women who have had some classroom teaching experience but are vague about the extent or freshness of that experience. At the presentation, you will be given lots of freebies, such as sample books, teacher's editions, pens, notepads, candy, and the famous book bag with the company logo. These gifts are not innocuous; they have the subtle goal of shifting the teachers' loyalties from the students to the publishing company. A similar shift has been documented in the pharmaceutical industry, which has used such selling techniques to substantially increase sales (Brownlee, 2007). When publishers present to a large school district, it is not uncommon to have one of the program authors give a short research talk to start off the presentation. These talks are often part of their contract with the company and add an air of scholarship to a sales presentation. When the author finishes, the consultant highlights how the new program exemplifies the best of this research.

The consultant typically has three goals. First, she wants the review committee to understand the overall structure and components of the program. In this presentation, typically involving slideshow software, interactive whiteboards, and Internet access, the audience learns about the program and hopefully is dazzled. What is not spelled out is the cost of each component. So you may be impressed with the website that allows students to read the stories at home, but you won't know if this is standard equipment or an upgrade. Second, the consultant makes sure that all of the current hot topics are addressed. Differentiation, ELL students, fluency, RTI, robust vocabulary instruction, and technology use in the program will be highlighted, but you will learn little about has-been topics like metacognition, response to literature, and letter recognition. Third, consultants understand the concerns teachers have about adopting and learning a new program. They are trained in the concerns-based adoption model (Loucks-Horsley, 1996), which posits that teachers' first concern is the difficulty of managing the new program. So the presentation will anticipate and try to assuage these needs. Consultants say things such as, "Do you ever have trouble finding the right text for a struggling reader? Well, we have this wonderful search tool on our website." "When I taught, it was difficult to find the right graphic organizer, so we have organized things so...." The underlying message is that this program will take care of you and your students. You should listen to consultants, but understand the nature of their message and don't be seduced by the free pen and tote bag.

Reading and Evaluating Core Reading Programs

Reading and rating core reading programs takes time. You should divide up the task according to the size of the committee. Have some people work on kindergarten and first-grade program components, another group work on second and third grades, and still another on fourth grade and up. Your committee members will bring different kinds of expertise to the review process. It is very useful if each individual can read and rate the two chosen programs. By contrasting the programs, differences emerge. This also helps avoid the checklist mentality.

In the process of reading and rating core reading programs, go for depth not breadth. It is more important to examine a few components carefully than to check off every component. As we illustrated in Chapter 5 on comprehension, study how the skills and strategies are taught, what vocabulary and knowledge is developed, and how a discussion is guided. Try to view these programs from the point of view of novice teachers. They need the support and guidance of a core reading program. With experience comes the knowledge to make sound instructional decisions and override the lessons in the programs. Read the texts carefully. You and your students will be reading them for years to come. A few districts have let students read and rate the selections in the new programs. Not only are their opinions valuable but also they are the ultimate consumers of the material, and this is a good way to build interest in reading.

We suggest that you use the Reading GPS for this process (found online at the webpage for this book, www.reading.org/general/publications/books/bk707 .aspx). The Reading GPS embodies our philosophy of depth versus breadth. Most programs have the same components, so a checklist is unnecessary.

Piloting Core Reading Programs

Many districts find it advantageous to pilot core reading programs before making their final selection. Publishers want you to do this, because as you become familiar with a program, your attitude toward it becomes more positive. Publishers believe that you are more likely to adopt their program if you pilot it. Three of the districts in our case studies conducted a pilot or are planning to do so. By working with these districts, we have gained some insights about piloting programs. The single most important part of the pilot process is to have a clear purpose in mind. Some districts pilot core reading programs but don't specifically know what information they are seeking and how that information will be used in the decision process.

Desert Sands Public School District conducted an extensive yearlong pilot involving over 150 teachers. They pre- and posttested all students, assuming that standardized assessments would reveal which program was more effective. Unfortunately, their data demonstrated no significant differences in any of the grades. We feel this result was predictable, because conducting a program evaluation is very difficult and demands that you employ random assignment of teachers and students to programs, something that is politically and logistically difficult to accomplish. Controlling for teacher and student variables is the only way to carefully study a program, and even then the results can be suspect. The most useful part of the pilot was the logs teachers maintained about their experiences using the program. Teachers wrote about difficulties with the program, such as understanding the various components and navigating through the teacher's edition, and how they had to modify and augment instruction to make it work for their students. This gave them firsthand evidence about the program's usefulness, extending and deepening the paper-and-pencil evaluation the committee had already completed. Figure 10 is a suggested form for teachers to use as they pilot core reading programs. They should complete the form every day.

Figure 10. Tracking Instructional Decisions While Piloting a Core Reading Program

Core Reading Program in Use _____ Unit/Theme _____		Date _____ Lesson _____
What parts of the lesson did you teach today? Check all that apply.	☐ Phonics/phonemic awareness ☐ Oral Read-Aloud ☐ Vocabulary ☐ Prior Knowledge ☐ Comprehension Skills ☐ Guided Reading ☐ Responding ☐ Spelling ☐ Writing	**Comments**
How effective were the lessons you taught in the core reading program today? ☐ Very effective ☐ Somewhat effective ☐ Needed modifications ☐ Ineffective	**What problems did you encounter?**	

(continued)

Figure 10. Tracking Instructional Decisions While Piloting a Core Reading Program *(cont'd)*

Describe any changes or additions that you made to the core reading program today.

How easy was it to find the materials, texts, and lessons today?	☐ It was very easy to find what I needed.
	☐ It was somewhat easy to find what I needed.
	☐ I had difficulty finding what I needed.
	☐ I found it very difficult to manage the program.

The following guidelines should help you design a successful pilot study.

- Narrow your choices to only a few core programs—two or three at most.

- Allow six to nine weeks for a pilot test. This is sufficient time to become familiar with how the programs work.

- If possible, teachers should pilot more than one program—six weeks with one program and six weeks with another. This allows the teachers to weigh the strengths and weaknesses of each.

• Teachers should keep a log of their impressions while they are using the program. These logs will be a valuable data source for understanding the strengths and weaknesses of the programs and the ways in which the programs had to be supplemented. Tally the results.

Using a process of qualitative data analysis, the program review committee can now look for and tally the numbers and types of problems the teachers encountered and the changes or additions they made to the programs they were using. The committee should also tally summative judgments on the effectiveness of the program components and the ease of using the materials. Finally, the committee will discover which components were used, which were ignored, and which required so much customization that the essence of the original program was lost.

Negotiating With Publishers

It is vital that school systems approach the task of purchasing a core reading program with a plan. The cost of a program, particularly when taking into account the various supplemental materials, can exceed US$100 per student. One school district was able to drastically reduce its costs by following a few simple guidelines. First, the school district insisted that the publishing company make the first offer. That offer had to specify which program components were included in the offer (student editions, teacher manuals, workbooks, picture cards, assessments, and so forth). The school district responded by simply saying that they could not afford the program at that price. The school district was careful to keep its actual budget and what it could afford to itself. The publishing company responded by lowering the price of the materials and even supplied all of the kindergarten materials for free. It is important to remember that districts can and should negotiate for their materials.

We also believe that you should not fall in love with a core reading program. Our research has indicated that there are more similarities than differences among these programs, so it might be useful to identify two programs that can meet your needs and try to negotiate the best price with each company. In your negotiations, make sure that the publisher puts together a staff development package that provides support for at least the first year of the program's implementation.

Making a Final Recommendation

Each district will have its own process for reaching a final recommendation. We suggest that the decision of the review committee should be the final word. The committee has spent the most time with the programs and knows the programs' strengths and weaknesses. The review committee is well suited to integrate data from the program review process (Reading GPS) and from the pilot study. The review committee should also represent the district as a whole and the needs of teachers across the grade levels. Once a decision has been made, the review committee typically makes a presentation to the school board and then hands off the rest of the tasks to the district administration. The administration must negotiate with the publishers, order the materials, and create a staff development plan that must be ongoing. As we have continually argued, it is the knowledge and skill of the teachers and not the programs themselves that drive excellent reading instruction.

PUTTING IT ALL TOGETHER

The textbook review and adoption process ends with a recommendation by the superintendent and the school board to purchase a new core reading program. That recommendation must be made to the board with the proper documentation from the textbook review process, the pilot, and reactions from the public. The process does not end with the purchase order. The teachers will need training about the program and how to make the best instructional decisions when using it. As we presented in earlier chapters, core reading programs are instructional tools—compilations of texts, lesson plans, and supporting materials. They all include more materials and activities than teachers can implement and all have flaws. To use a program well, a teacher needs to make sound instructional decisions. We help you make those decisions in the remaining chapters of this book.

PART III

Using Core Reading Programs Effectively

Despite the comprehensiveness of a core reading program, what comes in the box will not meet the needs of all students. Despite the many well-crafted lessons in the teacher's manual, teachers must make many decisions. Despite the attractiveness of the materials, developing a love of reading is a human endeavor, and to teach reading well, you will need to make some important instructional decisions about time, tasks, texts, teaching, and testing. Therefore, our goal in this part of the book is to help you use core reading programs effectively.

Core reading programs are complex instructional systems with many components. As a classroom teacher, you will need to make many instructional decisions about which components to use and which to ignore. If you are using an older program that emphasizes whole-group instruction, you will need to use its existing resources to provide small-group, differentiated instruction. If you are using a more contemporary program, you still need to decide which texts and tasks are suitable for each group. Do not feel bound by the program. You may need to augment the instruction provided in the program, and students should read beyond the core to explore the rich world of children's literature.

In Chapter 8, we discuss how to get started with using a core reading program and how a core program should be positioned within the school's total literacy program. We discuss how to allocate time both within the school and within the classroom, how to select texts and tasks, and how to use the testing resources in the core reading programs. In Chapter 9, we take you into a primary and an intermediate classroom and describe the best practices we have observed. In Chapter 10, we turn our attention to teaching word recognition effectively with core reading programs. You may decide to alter the scope and sequence of skills to meet your students' needs, provide more concrete practice than your core program suggests, and use books and resources beyond the core program. Finally, in Chapter 11, we offer suggestions on how to develop the vocabulary and comprehension skills of your students. You will need to make many instructional decisions, including selecting different words than the program suggests for instruction, teaching comprehension skills with greater explicitness, and guiding your students' comprehension with greater care and support. The core reading program should not be your complete reading program but simply an important tool in your classroom. The core program gives you structure on which you can base decisions and make elaborations. Ultimately, these decisions should be based on the needs of your students. These last four chapters will give you the knowledge to make those decisions wisely.

CHAPTER 8

Getting Started With a Core Reading Program

Bookville Elementary School is a suburban school district located on the fringe of a small city on the East Coast. The school district has a transient population and is composed of approximately 10,000 students. On the eastern side of the school district, poverty is evident, with housing projects and small, single-family homes in need of repair or refurbishing. To the north of the district, typical middle class, suburban homes mark the landscape. Housing developments are prevalent, and some are gated communities.

Bookville Elementary is a typical school. It is well run, the children are well mannered, and the environment is inviting and safe. The principal has made literacy the priority for the staff and the students. Five years ago, the district leaders made the decision that the core reading program would be the primary vehicle for teaching reading. They developed pacing guides to ensure that all the skills and strategies are covered before testing time in the spring. Each teacher across the school district is supposed to adhere to the pacing guide. Title I services are available for readers who struggle, as well as special education and speech-language services. Since the adoption of the core reading program, supplementary programs have been added. The primary grades have added stand-alone programs for developing phonemic awareness. A fluency program was purchased to improve the students' oral reading fluency, along with numerous Readers Theatre resources. Many comprehension workbooks abound to reteach and practice the skills measured by the state reading assessment. Lately the district has begun studying RTI and is reviewing the interventions they provide to struggling readers.

With all this as the backdrop, school and district administrators have concerns about state testing scores that have reached a plateau just as No Child Left Behind standards have accelerated. Upper-grade teachers blame the primary-grade teachers for promoting students who lack reading skills. Primary-grade teachers blame parents, and everyone except the principal has doubts about following the core reading program with fidelity. How should this school proceed?

As you can see, a problem is brewing at Bookville Elementary and possibly across the school district. Perhaps you have a similar situation in your school and are unsure about how or where to begin to handle the dilemma. We use this vignette, a composite of several schools we work with, to outline the problems that core reading programs cannot easily solve. We proceed in a whole-to-part fashion, first considering what it means to establish an effective reading program at the school level and to consider the role of a core reading program within the effective reading program. We want to be clear: An effective reading program and a core reading program are not synonymous. A core reading program is one tool used within an effective reading program. In Chapter 9, we describe effective programs within a primary and an intermediate classroom. We want you to understand how teachers make decisions with a core reading program and use programs effectively.

What You Will Learn

- What studies reveal about how teachers actually use core reading programs
- How a school needs to structure time and personnel to develop an effective reading program
- What a literate environment is, and why it is important for students' literacy growth
- The importance of motivating students and capturing their interests

What You Will Be Able to Do

- Set schoolwide goals and select assessments to evaluate them
- Create a reading/language arts schedule for your school and for individual classrooms
- Organize time, space, and texts to create a motivating, literate environment in your classroom
- Structure a motivating reading program in your classroom

How Core Reading Programs Are Actually Used

Until the advent of Reading First and the call to use core reading programs with fidelity, teachers rarely followed them in a tightly scripted fashion. Going back to the 1960s, teachers put their own instructional stamp even on core reading programs with a particular orientation. That is why at the end of the First-Grade Studies, which compared basal approaches, phonics approaches, and language experience, Bond and Dykstra (1967) concluded that there was considerable variation in student achievement within approaches to beginning reading instruction. When Durkin (1984) studied the use of basal reading programs, she found that teachers modified and omitted program suggestions. Some parts of a program, like the postreading questions, were followed closely, but teachers ignored many of the prereading suggestions like developing students' knowledge and setting a purpose for reading, something that many educators would view as a problem because comprehension requires knowledge building (Anderson & Pearson, 1984; Britton & Graesser, 1996). Almost all workbook pages were completed, but teachers consistently ignored the recommended instruction that accompanied these pages, so much of this student work was rote with little depth to it.

When Barr and Sadow (1989) studied teachers' use of two different basal programs from the mid-1980s, they found that "teachers do not mindlessly follow the suggestions in the guide; they actively select elements to enhance the reading experience" (p. 66). This is not to say that teachers are always active decision makers, but teachers develop routines for prereading and postreading activities that they implement in a regular fashion, sometimes tailoring these routines to the demands of the text or the needs of their students. Barr and Sadow also did not see teachers incorporating new ideas developed by researchers in their instruction. Their study concluded that teachers' use of basal readers was not mindless, yet it did not reflect active decision making either.

In the late 1990s, Hoffman et al. (1998) studied how teachers used the new literature-based basal readers. They studied how first-grade teachers taught reading for two years: the year before the introduction of a new literature-based basal and during its first year of use. The 16 teachers in the study embraced different approaches to instruction. Some leaned toward a trade book approach and deviated little from their established ways when they received the new basal program. Others held to a skills approach when using the old basal reader, but when the new program was introduced, they made a variety of changes. Some tried out the new program but kept vestiges of their old ways. Hoffman and his colleagues concluded, "We find no compelling support in our data for the argument that teachers were controlled by the basals" (p. 191). Rather, teachers, even those who embraced the new materials, did not change their beliefs or philosophy about teaching reading. Without this fundamental change in philosophy, it is likely that teachers will not change their practices, nor will new core reading programs significantly influence how teachers teach reading. A teacher committed to a skills approach to instruction was not likely to embrace a new literature-based basal.

While Hoffman et al.'s (1998) study was limited to case studies of 16 first-grade teachers, Baumann and Heubach (1996) looked at the same issue (teachers' use of core programs) by conducting a national survey of over 500 elementary teachers who were all members of the International Reading Association. Baumann and Heubach also found that "most teachers are discriminating consumers who view basal readers as just one instructional tool available to them as they plan literacy lessons" (p. 522). Teachers reported in the survey that they found basals to be an excellent source of ideas, and often the teacher's manual reminded them of old instructional practices that they had neglected. Fifty-five percent of the teachers reported that they supplemented the basal reading experience with trade books, and only 12% reported that they relied on the basal a great deal. Remember, these respondents were all "knowledgeable, experienced literacy educators" (p. 523). Knowledge—not just beliefs—may be critical in how teachers use core programs.

Consider the next study. Piasta et al. (2009) reported that students' growth in word reading ability was related to both the amount of explicit decoding instruction in a program and to teachers' knowledge of decoding instruction. It was not the scripted programs alone that accounted for students' growth but the use of these programs by knowledgeable and skillful teachers. As videotapes of the lessons showed, the knowledgeable teachers, during the act of reading, provided students with a large range of strategies to assist word recognition (e.g., word families, analogies, and syllables), whereas the less knowledgeable teachers stuck to simple letter–sound associations. Students who received scripted instruction from less knowledgeable teachers fared less well compared with knowledgeable teachers using a nonscripted program. This study and others (McCutchen, Abbott et al., 2002; McCutchen, Harry et al., 2002) have spotlighted the importance of teacher knowledge and should give any administrator pause when thinking that a scripted program will completely solve a school's literacy problems. Teachers have always made decisions about how to implement core reading programs, and the research of Piasta and his colleagues (2009) has pointed out that the quality of these decisions will be determined by the teachers' knowledge.

Against the backdrop of these studies, we now consider how core reading programs should be used in an era when publishers promote the research base of these programs and national reading initiatives call for such programs to be used with fidelity. We have watched principals conduct classroom walk-throughs with checklists to make sure that every item in the teacher's manual is being covered, and we have wondered what *fidelity* means exactly. The whole concept of fidelity is difficult to reconcile with what is known about core reading programs and the need for knowledgeable teachers. First, some components and instructional approaches are included in a program because of their research base (e.g., phonemic awareness, developing metacognition), whereas others are there to satisfy the demands of the market (e.g., workbooks). Second, all programs include more components and ideas than can be used in a 90- or 120-minute reading or language arts period. What should teachers be faithful to? No core reading program is fully pilot tested or studied before it is published, thus there is no standard implementation to which the concept of fidelity can be applied. So we take as good advice the recommendation of Barr and Sadow (1989):

> First, teachers need to learn more about judging which reading materials should be assigned and which omitted, and when supplementary materials are needed. Second, they need guidance in determining which basal guide suggestions should be omitted and which followed or modified for more effective instruction. Finally, they need to learn more about how to evaluate student responses to questions and how to generate more appropriate questions. (p. 69)

Planning Literacy Instruction at the School Level

Your core reading program provides an important set of tools within a comprehensive reading program. There are elements within the program that you must use. There are components that you may modify. There are texts and tasks that we hope you will use to augment what the program does not supply. How you use your core reading program depends on its age. As previously mentioned, programs published in the early 2000s or before tended to have a whole-group orientation with little support for small-group instruction. As the current decade progressed, core reading programs included more and more guidance for small-group instruction, and in the latest iterations of the programs, small-group instructional ideas and learning workstations are more fully explained. Therefore, those schools using older programs will need to make more changes than those using newer programs. However, all schools need to use programs thoughtfully and with discretion. Before we look specifically at the core reading program, we need to consider many important aspects of effective reading programs that have little to do with published core reading programs.

Establishing School Leadership

Decisions made by the whole school and by the classroom teacher determine literacy achievement, so let's begin by looking at the school and its leadership. The principal's first task is to make achievement the priority, not human relations. When human relations are the priority, the principal may strive to make sure teachers, administrators, and parents communicate well and get along and that feathers are not ruffled. However, in schools where achievement is the priority, the principal may sacrifice the feelings of a few to ensure success for the students. Teachers may have to take on tasks they do not relish and hear feedback they do not enjoy. In an achievement-oriented school, children excel (Levine & Lezotte, 1990).

First, the principal has to involve teachers in the process of setting goals. Goal setting should address some of the following questions:

- What are the expectations for reading across the grade levels? Are corresponding grade levels in agreement with these expectations?

- How will time be used most effectively?

- What programs and texts will be employed in the classroom? How will each of these texts be used to meet the literacy needs of the students?

- How are resource teachers (i.e., reading specialists, special educators, paraprofessionals, parent volunteers) used within the language arts block?

- How will intervention be provided for struggling readers?

- What assessments will be used to monitor progress toward these goals?

- How will progress be reported to teachers, administrators, parents, and students?

Instructional leaders are vital. Typically this leader is the principal, but a strong reading specialist, literacy coach, or assistant principal also can provide this instructional leadership. An instructional leader is more than the school manager; he or she directs the literacy program. The leader must know enough about reading instruction to support and supervise classroom teachers and lead them to the next level of competence. Leaders must know what information to gather, help teachers to understand the data, work to establish goals, and find the means to achieve them. Strong leadership must advocate for best practice and research-based strategies, such as the ones discussed in this book. Finally, the leader must understand which well-meaning but unproven literacy ideas and programs to exclude from a school. Instructional programs frequently and easily become clogged with overlapping texts and tasks, leaving teachers with more to do than there is time to accomplish. A clear school mission in regard to literacy must be established (Taylor, Pressley, & Pearson, 2002).

Grade-level expectations should be established through discussions among adjoining grade levels. Grade-level groups should arrive at the first meeting with expectations for students entering *and* exiting their grade level. For example, which texts should students be able to read when they enter third grade, and which texts when they leave? Goals should be set with consideration of phonemic awareness, phonics, word study, fluency, comprehension, and writing, as well as overall reading grade level. Some programs, such as Reading Recovery (Clay, 1993) and guided reading (Fountas & Pinnell, 1996), present useful way to assess reading levels. In addition, this process should include assessments that will be used to determine whether students have met the established goals. Schools may want to create goals that exceed merely passing the state assessment and include measures of the depth and breadth of students' reading. Grade levels should share and compare their lists and subsequently work together to establish common expectations. The chart in Figure 11 might be helpful for

Figure 11. Establishing Grade-Level Expectations

Expectation	Entry Expectations	End-of-Year Expectations	Assessments to Be Used
Functional reading level	*Instructional reading level:*	*Instructional reading level:*	
Phonemic awareness, phonics, and word study	*Mastery of the following:*	*Mastery of the following:*	
Fluency	*Accuracy:* *Words per minute:* *Prosody:*	*Accuracy:* *Words per minute:* *Prosody:*	
Writing	*Mastery of the following:*	*Mastery of the following:*	
Comprehension	*Mastery of the following:*	*Mastery of the following:*	

each grade level to complete before discussing expectations. After completing the chart, meet to find common ground and set grade-by-grade expectations that are realistic and acceptable to each adjoining grade level.

Although the teachers and administrators may establish expectations, many school districts have created pacing guides for reading. These guides ensure that the content is covered so that students will pass the state-designed assessments and meet No Child Left Behind guidelines. However, we find pacing guides for reading problematic. The question of pace really comes down to how much students should read each week and how long it will take for students to acquire skills and strategies. Our own and others' analyses of core reading programs (Dewitz et al., 2009; Miller & Blumenfeld, 1993) have shown that such programs do not provide enough practice for all students to acquire proficiency with skills or strategies. Similarly, teachers who teach a new reading strategy each week will find that many students never acquire proficiency with any skills. Teachers who dawdle through a program and spend a week or more on one story are not providing enough breadth of exposure to text to develop fluency or reading skills.

Using Time Wisely

Reading/language arts instruction should last approximately 120 minutes each day, especially in the primary grades. In the intermediate grades, the increasing demands of the content areas impose a limit on how much time can be devoted to reading instruction, but then again, children should be reading in their content subjects. In some schools, reading and language arts instruction approaches 180 minutes a day and encroaches on the time for teaching science and social studies. We find this trend disturbing, because literacy requires both knowledge and skill, and the content areas build knowledge. StoryTown (Harcourt, 2008) suggests 90 to 120 minutes for reading instruction in all grades, whereas Treasures (Macmillan/McGraw-Hill, 2009) avoids any mention of time. The reading/language arts time should include work with words (i.e., spelling, phonics, vocabulary), fluency development, comprehension, independent reading, and writing. In addition, some struggling students will need additional time for intervention, and intervention time should not take the place of the regularly scheduled reading/language arts time. It is the task of the principal to create this schedule with the input of the teachers. Core reading programs are largely silent on the allocation of time. The current programs suggest whole-group, small-group, and independent reading activities, whereas the older programs, those published before 2007, have much less guidance about small-group instruction and learning workstations. The older programs typically provide a vague chart titled "Universal Access" or "Reaching All Learners," which lists activities for below- and above-level students, often stressing the use of additional workbook pages. Some newer core reading programs provide a general guideline for how much time to spend in small-group instruction, but others do not (Taylor et al., 2000). The new programs do not spell out how long to spend in small-group instruction for different types of learners. This important decision is up to the teacher. Chapter 6 addresses some of these issues.

The principal's main contribution is often to create a schedule in which teachers and students will be disrupted as infrequently as possible. In the elementary school setting, the principal should also have policies and procedures that ensure the sanctity of all instructional time, not just reading. Opening activities, the Pledge of Allegiance, and announcements should be kept to a minimum and should end before instruction begins. The students and teachers should not be interrupted during teaching and learning by announcements from the office or telephone calls from parents about lost lunches or dentist appointments. It should be the policy of the principal not to interrupt instruction except for emergencies. The whole school works on moving students from their classrooms to specials or lunch as efficiently as possible. Once the principal has allocated time, it is the job of the teacher to organize this time to work with individuals, small groups, and the whole class. Research on effective teachers has indicated that the most effective teachers in the primary grades spend up to 60 minutes of their day in small-group instruction (20 minutes for each of three small groups) and the least effective teachers spend as little as 30 minutes a day in small-group instruction (Taylor et al., 2000).

However, within this framework, how do you use other trained professionals? During small-group instruction, consider how special educators, reading specialists, and paraprofessionals might best be used to maximize student instruction, differentiate instruction, and provide scaffolding for students who are struggling. For example, after small-reading group work with the classroom teacher, students might rotate to the special educator or reading specialist for additional small-group or one-on-one instruction while other students complete spelling or fluency-oriented activities with a paraprofessional. Another alternative is that during workstation time, small groups of children might rotate in and out of reading instruction with these trained professionals to supplement whole-group instruction that has taken place within the core reading program earlier in the day. To facilitate this type of support across the entire school, Allington and Cunningham (2002) have suggested forming professional "teams" of reading professionals who rotate from classroom to classroom throughout the school day to increase the amount of small-group time teachers have with struggling readers. Despite this additional small-group instruction, a 30-minute intervention may still be necessary for students with severe reading disabilities.

During the school day, the sound management of transition routines helps move students quickly from one activity to another with little time lost as students try to determine what to do next. Each day the teacher should post the calendar or schedule and review it with the students. Once routines are learned, students will follow them with little direction from the teachers. *Guided Reading* (Fountas & Pinnell, 1996) offers excellent suggestions for establishing classroom routines, managing small groups, and moving students easily from one activity to another.

Planning Instruction With a Core Reading Program

Core reading programs are typically organized into six units or themes, with each theme having four to six lessons. A lesson contains directions for developing vocabulary and prior knowledge, teaching a comprehension skill and strategy, and then reading and discussing the main anthology selection. After the teacher and the students finish with the main anthology selection, they can move on to a shorter supplemental selection, the leveled books, and additional comprehension, fluency, vocabulary, and decoding lessons. Almost all programs also provide instruction in spelling, grammar, writing, speaking, and listening. The developers of StoryTown (2008), for example, estimated that all this will take between 135 and 180 minutes per day, but some lesson segments may take longer than program developers expect.

Schools must first decide which segments of a core reading program they will use and which they will ignore. For instance, a school may already have in place a well-organized developmental spelling program or writing program, in which case lessons on spelling and writing in the core reading program are redundant. Within the reading lessons themselves, the teachers will need to decide which elements to use and which to ignore. The lessons used to introduce and develop prior knowledge and vocabulary before reading the main selection are most likely essential, as are the skill lessons for phonics, phonemic awareness, vocabulary, and comprehension. After reading the selection, core reading programs provide additional lessons for comprehension, fluency, vocabulary, grammar, and oral language development. There is a buffet of suggestions, and schools and teachers must decide how to sharpen the focus of the instruction so that reading has a clear set of goals and a limited number of procedures for reaching those goals. Finally, there are the workbooks. In the new core programs, there are separate workbooks for above-, on-, and below-level readers, plus additional workbooks for spelling, grammar, and ELL students. It will be important to closely review the program to decide which lessons the teachers will use, which components are essential, and what they should ignore.

In planning with a core reading program, schools must consider, at each grade level, how they expect students to change during the course of the academic year. Core reading programs make few assumptions about student change (Chambliss & Calfee, 1998). In kindergarten and first and second grades, the texts obviously become more difficult over the course of the year as decoding skills become more advanced. In the upper grades, too, the texts get more difficult, but the reading experiences are largely the same from the first week in September to the last week in May. Students learn skills, develop knowledge, read short selections, and then discuss them. Core programs do not posit that students will and should be more independent as readers, more self-directed as the year progresses, given larger projects, involved in reading longer books, and engaged in thinking at a deeper level. For example, in the first unit of Scott Foresman Reading (Pearson Scott Foresman, 2004) Grade 4, students learn about setting, sequence, compare and contrast, author's purpose, and characters. In the sixth and last unit, the students study visualizing, steps in a process, fact and opinion, main idea, and again, author's purpose. None of these lessons suggest that the skills or strategies have been taught or studied before. No developing expertise is assumed or expected.

Teachers and schools need to decide what their students' goals are, what types of texts they expect students to be reading, and what kinds of thinking they expect of students by the middle or end of the year. If fourth graders start in the core reading program, when should they be ready to move into longer and more demanding texts? When do chapter books, nonfiction trade books, and novels begin to replace or accompany the leveled books that are part of each lesson? It is reasonable for schools to assume that students will be able to read and understand longer and more complex texts by the end of the year. Students should be able to read fiction for its messages about the human condition and develop the skills to study character and plot development over 100 pages or more. Nonfiction reading demands studying and learning complex ideas, often integrating ideas from multiple texts. The core reading program can be used for teaching the skills and strategies necessary to meet these goals. But once students have developed some expertise and skill, they are ready to move to these more complex texts. Teachers in each grade level should consider which novels and nonfiction trade books their students will be reading, and when in the course of the year the core reading program will move to the background and the other texts and tasks move to the foreground. The best readers in the class may start reading novels and nonfiction trade books by October or November, with even the average and struggling reader getting there by the middle of the year.

Planning in this way requires a close look at the scope and sequence of skill and strategy instruction, and some adjustments may need to be made. Some comprehension skills and strategies should be taught early and well, so students have these tools to draw on throughout the course of the year. Learning to be a strategic reader who sets a purpose, questions, predicts, monitors, and summarizes are early and important goals. Similarly, in the area of vocabulary, the earlier students learn to use the dictionary and context cues to determine word meanings, the sooner they can become independent learners. Other comprehension skills and strategies may be necessary when students explore a particular genre. Nonfiction reading will require a close look at its text structure, and requires that students know how to determine what is important and how to summarize. Reading fiction demands a close study of its genres, text structures, and conventions. Teaching and reading in this way will require teachers to alter the order of reading selections in a core program, so they can focus for a time on one genre in order to build the strategic expertise that students need.

Texts Within and Outside the Core Reading Program

The major resource for teaching reading will be your core reading program, but all students should read outside the core program for a variety of reasons, as discussed in the previous section and in previous chapters. Some students will need additional work with decodable texts, which the core reading program may not provide, whereas others will require more leveled texts. Finally, as students grow as readers, they may have reading interests and challenges that are beyond the scope of a core reading program. All teachers should ask, what do my students need to read to become good readers? As we explained in Chapter 3, not every text in a core reading program is optimal or even interesting. Arthur Gates said it well in 1964:

> I have always believed that if one accepts the theory that the basal reading program must be used it should be adjusted to individual needs and that each child should be encouraged to move on into wider and more advanced material as rapidly as possible. (cited in Smith, 1986, p. 224)

A central space within the school should be created for teachers to use and share reading materials, often called a book room. Text sets could be created to supplement skills and strategies, as well as to further develop what is addressed within the core reading program. Text sets are multiple copies of books on various reading levels that are centered on common themes, topics, or genres (Giorgis & Johnson, 2002). Themed text sets might be arranged to address learning standards in the content areas at each grade level or to extend the themes or selections within the core reading program. For example, the third unit in Houghton Mifflin Reading's (Houghton Mifflin, 2003/2005) third-grade program has the theme of Animal Habitats, which consists of a nonfiction selection about puffins and two realistic fiction stories involving animals and people. A text set for this theme might include additional nonfiction titles on birds, seals, or wild animals living in suburban habitats. We elaborate on the use of text sets in Chapter 11 when we discuss comprehension instruction.

A primary text set room and an intermediate text set room located somewhere in the school building is ideal. In some schools, the library is a logical choice for housing these text sets. In addition to text sets, book rooms might include manipulatives for word study and phonics instruction, puppets for phonemic awareness instruction, charts and materials for comprehension and writing instruction, and a space for teachers to share successful plans and ideas centered on core reading programs accompanied by the corresponding texts. A simple check-out system should be established so that materials in the text room may be shared among teachers throughout the school. Parent organizations and community groups are often willing to contribute funds or materials for text rooms.

An Assessment System

A data-driven instruction system is ideal, but data-driven instruction can easily become overwhelming. As we discuss in Chapter 6, core reading programs come with a full complement of assessments, but most schools have assessment tools that are dictated by state demands or required by one of many federal (e.g., Reading First) or state (e.g., Comprehensive School Improvement) grant programs. In addition, most schools and districts have adopted standardized and informal assessments to measure the progress their students are making toward mastering the assessment standards. Over time, these assessment tools accumulate, so before adding any of the tools from the core reading program, an audit is necessary. Just as a school must plan the use of time wisely, schools must plan the use of assessments.

A simple audit of reading assessments starts with the list of assessments currently begin given, the components of reading assessed by each, and their purposes. Figure 12 is an example of such an audit from a school in Virginia. The state of Virginia essentially mandates two assessments, the Standards of Learning, a summative assessment of reading and language arts given in third through eighth grades, and the Phonological Awareness Literacy Screening (PALS-K and PALS 1–3, 2007), a screening and diagnostic tool of basic early literacy concepts given in kindergarten through third grade. In the left column, we have listed the assessment tools currently being employed in the school. The other columns mark the components of reading being assessed and the purpose of the assessments. An inspection of this audit reveals concerns and opens the discussion for the place of core reading program assessments in the total assessment system.

The audit indicates that many components of reading are assessed in multiple ways. Many functions, like progress monitoring, repeat more often than may be necessary. The components of word identification, like phonemic awareness, letter sounds, and decoding, are assessed multiple times through the use of both placement tests (e.g., PALS), progress monitoring (e.g., DIBELS), and district-constructed assessments (e.g., benchmarks). Similarly, comprehension is assessed with the end-of-selection and theme skills tests from the core reading program. Attitudes and motivation are not assessed in any systematic way, but can be (McKenna, Kear, & Ellsworth, 1995).

This school is using Houghton Mifflin Reading (2003/2005) as a core reading program. It comes with placement tests that report students' ability to read leveled passages using individually administered and group tests, some of which include measures of phonics. The program also monitors students' progress with weekly end-of-selection tests, end-of-theme assessments, and quarterly benchmark progress tests. These assess either individual skills or passage comprehension from a

Figure 12. Sample Audit of Assessment Tools and Their Functions

Assessment Tool	Grade Level	Letter Recognition	Letter Sounds	Concept of Word	Phonemic Awareness	Decoding and Phonics	Sight Words	Spelling	Oral Reading Fluency	Vocabulary	Reading Comprehension	Interest and Motivation
Phonological Awareness Literacy Screening	K–3	D PM	D PM	D PM			D PM	D PL PM	D PM			
Developmental Reading Assessment	K–3					D PL PM			D PL PM		D PL PM	
Qualitative Reading Inventory	1–5					D PL	D PL		D PL		D PL	
Developmental spelling inventory	1–5				D PL			D PL				
Segment tests	1–5	PM	PM			PM				PM	PM	
Benchmark assessments	K–5	PM	PM			PM	PM			PM	PM	
DIBELS WRF, ORF	K–3	PM	PM		PM	PM			PM	PM		
Teacher-designed CBM	K–5	PM	PM	PM	PM	PM	PM					
End-of-selection tests	K–5									PM	PM	
Theme skills tests	K–5									PM	PM	
Standards of Learning	3–5										S	

Note. D = diagnostic; PL= placement; PM = progress monitoring; S = summative.

holistic view of reading. This older core reading program lacks extensive resources for monitoring oral reading fluency, which newer programs have in abundance, and newer programs also have weekly assessments that monitor comprehension skill attainment, not just knowledge of the passage content.

Against the backdrop of the assessments mandated by the state and those developed by the district, each school must develop an assessment system that provides the knowledge teachers and administrators need to make instructional decisions and have some assurance that students are learning to read. Core reading programs do not assess students' attitudes toward reading or their actual reading behavior. Therefore, we offer the following suggestions to guide the development of your assessment system:

- Assess students as infrequently as possible.
- Monitor students' progress on a few key components (e.g., decoding, oral reading fluency, comprehension); research has suggested that this should be done less frequently but with greater depth (Jenkins, Graff, & Miglioretti, 2009).
- Given the importance of high-stakes state assessments, you need to assess student progress on these standards three times a year. Assessments in core reading programs do not align well with most state assessments.
- End-of-selection tests are not very useful, because it takes more than a week for a student to use a new skill or strategy with any sense of competence.
- Do not overlook the importance of informal assessments and observations in the classroom. Keep your eyes and ears open during small-group instruction. By listening carefully, you can gain useful information about students' progress. Keep notes (Reutzel, Jones, Fawson, & Smith, 2008).

Now that a schoolwide framework has been established, we can turn our attention to the use of core reading programs at the classroom level. The schoolwide framework guides the use of time for whole-group and small-group instruction; maximizes the use of teacher, paraprofessional, and volunteer resources; sets goals and expectations for each grade level; and establishes an efficient assessment system.

Planning Literacy Instruction for Your Classroom

The teaching of reading involves more than implementing the core reading program. Although it is a valuable tool, especially if you are a new teacher, there are instructional decisions that underlie and enhance a core reading program. We are more specific about the use of core reading programs in Chapter 9. Teachers must construct a learning environment that makes reading and writing engaging, informative, and exciting. Teachers do this through the arrangement of space, time, tasks, and text. Educators are frequently more concerned with what students bring to the learning environment and less concerned with how teachers can shape that environment to influence students' learning (Neuman & Roskos, 1993). Elementary school classrooms need to have spaces for whole-group work, small-group work (either teacher or student led), and individual work. Physical design decisions are never permanent; many teachers spend considerable amounts of time redesigning their classrooms to suit their needs. The physical design and the print in your room must change as the activities and topics of study change. A well-organized physical space promotes the interactions that stimulate language growth and minimizes transitions from one activity to another. A pace that is quick but not hurried characterizes good teaching. Organization promotes this pace, because disorganization causes teachers and students to spend valuable time looking for materials rather than using them.

Creating Physical Spaces in the Classroom

Before school starts, think about the learning environment you want to create. The decisions you make at this time will have an influence on how language is used and developed in the classroom. Your classroom is not just a physical arrangement of furniture and graphics, but a dynamic environment that influences your students' developing literacy, and in turn, their literacy activities will reshape how that environment grows. Literacy takes place in a social environment, and how literacy is used in that environment influences the developing skills of the students in your classroom. Core reading programs offer the content and methods of instruction, but they do not fashion the emotional and intellectual environment in the room.

The way in which we construct and arrange a physical environment influences the behavior of the people in it. This has proven true in an array of environmental settings, from grocery stores to museums. For instance, why do department stores periodically rearrange their merchandise? Why do supermarkets put the sale items at the ends of aisles? Why does your trip through a supermarket frequently start with the produce section? Why have large bookstores added comfortable seating with chairs and couches? These decisions always have a purpose behind them. Just as the commercial environment influences your behavior as a consumer, the classroom environment will influence students' literary behaviors.

Start with a few simple questions about literacy activities and purposes in your classroom, and these will lead to decisions about classroom design. Keep in mind that form follows function. Ask yourself the following questions:

- Do you plan to have small-group instruction? Where will it take place?

- Will your students read independently? Where?

- What literacy-related activities will your students complete independently? Will these activities consist of group work? Where?

- How will your students transition from whole-group to small-group work? What classroom space will you need to do this?

- How will your students know what to do in your classroom? How will you provide direction to the students?

As you answer these questions, the design of your classroom will gradually emerge. Obviously each student will need a desk, a space to work and keep his or her possessions. Not only is a desk important for productive work but also it is central to one of the important lessons you will teach your students: organization. Where do they keep their materials, and how should they be organized? Teaching students to use folders, three-ring binders, dividers, and agendas helps them manage their classroom lives and prepare them for their adult lives, which will require the same type of organizational skills. In teaching organization, we are also teaching the functional use of language. When children use agendas or you use your personal digital assistant, you are all using language to manage your lives.

You will need a round or kidney-shaped table for teacher-directed small-group instruction. The table should be large enough to hold five to eight students and your materials. Although intermediate teachers tend to stick to the traditional arrangement of desks in rows, the lack of a table for small-group instruction is both a message about the value of that instruction and a barrier to establishing it. You will need tables or spaces for students to congregate for small-group work. These spaces are both centers for individual and group projects and places to enliven interest in science, social studies, art, music, mathematics, and writing. Reading is a social event. Use the tables in your classroom to make this happen.

A Print-Rich Environment

Beyond the arrangement of tables, chairs, rugs, and pillows, a classroom contains print. What you hang on the wall will influence how you teach and how well your students achieve. A print-rich environment will have some or all of the following kinds of texts: a student anthology, leveled and decodable books, fiction and nonfiction trade books, reference materials, magazines and newspapers, computers and electronic texts, teacher-created process charts, a word wall, alphabet charts, spelling demons, organizational and management charts, games, puzzles, manipulatives, published student work, and social, personal, or inspirational text displays.

Core reading programs do not directly address how to create a print-rich environment. Although they provide some of the literacy tools necessary in a rich environment, they—almost by definition—cannot provide all of the tools. The first component of a rich literary environment is texts for students to read. Core reading programs provide a student anthology, leveled and decodable texts, and optional trade books. However, a full range of trade books, magazines, newspapers, and online resources is beyond the scope of a core reading program. The core program provides some materials and activities to begin learning workstations, including management charts, but most teachers will find that they have to create or purchase additional materials. Finally, the core reading program cannot provide the local texts that are authored by the teacher and the students. Some research has suggested that these local texts (e.g., language experience charts or charts that illustrate comprehension strategies, track content learned, and document students' work) are a strong predictor of students' comprehension growth (Hoffman, Sailors, Duffy, & Beretvas, 2004). These locally produced texts may be more important than the commercial charts that come with your core reading program or that you purchase at a teacher supply store. If you take the time to craft a chart to explain how to find the main idea or construct an essay, you have validated the importance of the strategy by providing a careful visual illustration. These charts also exist as a reminder to the students of how to select or execute a strategy.

Instructional Texts and Classroom Libraries

Literate behavior is chosen not imposed. To encourage choice, students need books and the time and space to exercise that choice. Core reading programs provide the texts for instruction but not for independent reading. All core programs include suggestions for additional reading; they provide a bibliography of children's books related to each theme. Independent reading is not stressed in these programs despite the fact that there is a relationship between how much students read and their growth in reading ability (Anderson et al., 1988). Perhaps independent reading is downplayed in core reading programs because of the implicit assumption that the comprehensiveness of these programs will teach all children to read (Goodman et al., 1988). Teachers need to encourage accountable independent reading (Reutzel et al., 2008), and the classroom library will be important in meeting that goal.

To learn about classroom libraries, we suggest that you take a trip to your local large retail bookstore. There you will see several merchandising techniques that should be incorporated into your classroom library. First, books you want to "sell" are displayed with their covers facing outward; the spine of a book does not grab attention. Second, comfortable seating allows your students to feel free to browse among the books. Organize your books so that students can find them by genres, authors, topics, and reading levels. In intermediate classrooms, you might even establish a classroom library routine in which your students help you organize and maintain the structure of your library. By including your students in the organizational process, you create ownership, and they learn about the books and the authors.

In creating your classroom library, researchers have identified some crucial features that must be included (Fractor, Woodruff, Martinez, & Teale, 1993):

- A semiprivate focal area that is attractive and communicates the importance of the library in the classroom
- Comfortable seating
- Room for five or six children
- At least five or six books per child in your classroom
- Books with a variety of genres, topics, and reading levels; magazines, newspapers, manuals, and electronic text are also options
- Shelving that holds books for displaying either the cover or the spine
- Literature-oriented displays and props, such as posters, puppets, bulletin boards about the latest books, and book jackets

To further student ownership of the classroom library, students might enjoy taking responsibility for bulletin boards to recommend specific books to classmates.

As you build your classroom library, use your resources. The school librarian can provide books to rotate in and out of your classroom library, and the book room is also a nice resource. Additionally, there are many resources to help you acquire books inexpensively. The Scholastic Book Club is an excellent source. As your students purchase books, you earn points that are redeemable for additional books. Finally, think about garage sales as an excellent source of books to add to your classroom library.

Your classroom library should change regularly. Hold some books back and feature new ones weekly as you focus on different authors and genres. This will keep your students interested and awaken their curiosity. Include books that you have read aloud to the class. Although classroom libraries are less common in the upper grades, they are just as important and should be an integral component of the classroom environment. Time pressures are greater in the intermediate grades, but independent reading is still necessary to build reading skills.

It is often asked why the classroom library is so important if the school has a central library for all to use. In most schools, students visit the school library once a week, and the number of books they can check out is limited, yet they read every day. So, it is imperative that students have ready access to a large collection of books that will whet their appetites and provide endless practice. The school library enables students to do research, learn about new authors and books, and check out books for independent reading. The classroom library provides books and reading daily.

To highlight the titles and print materials available in the classroom library, teachers should conduct weekly "book looks." Each Monday or at a designated time each week, the teacher provides a short book talk about selections that can be found in the classroom library. Such book looks are a tool commonly used by public librarians to entice young people into reading. Book talks should be brief, engaging, and enticing. To conduct a book talk, you might use any of the following techniques to hook students into reading books found in your classroom library:

- Read a snippet from the text that will entice students to read more. Be dramatic with your reading. Stop at a cliffhanger.

- Give some obscure or unusual information about the author of a particular text.

- Point out vivid illustrations in picture books. Encourage students to make predictions using the pictures.

- Relate the text to personal situations in the students' lives or connect it to a unit of study or piece of literature found in the core reading program.

- Don't forget that you can talk up articles in magazines.

- Point out texts that have been used as read-alouds in the classroom. Note that these texts are available for reading in the classroom library.

Independent Activities and Literacy-Based Learning Workstations

An important part of the total literacy program is independent work in which students can read on their own, respond to what they have read, and apply the skills they are learning. Until recently, core reading programs relied on workbooks for independent practice. Teacher's manuals also continued suggestions for students to apply the ideas and themes that they were studying to science, social studies, or art. Most programs also provided an application involving the Internet. The research on workbook activities has suggested that good readers complete the work easily and poor readers are often inaccurate and inattentive, questioning the value of the work itself (Anderson, Brubaker, Alleman-Brooks, & Duffy, 1985). Others have found that most workbook activities require little application of previously learned skills to real reading tasks and that workbooks do not provide for cumulative review (Osborn, 1984).

The newest core reading programs have solved one of the major dilemmas of workbooks by providing separate practice books for students reading below, on, or above grade level. We were unable to analyze these materials to see if they were well differentiated, but we urge you to do so. The newest programs also provide more detailed suggestions for literacy-based learning workstations and the procedures necessary to manage them. Macmillan/McGraw-Hill's Treasures (2009) includes workstation activities for reading, word work, writing, and social studies/science. The activities are provided in stand-up flipcharts that must be made or assembled by the teacher. StoryTown (2008) provides activities for five types of workstations: word study, reading, writing, technology, and fluency. The activities are explained on cards that the teacher can place in the workstation. There are two points of caution. First, we don't know if these workstation resources are part of the basic core reading program package or extras that require additional costs. Second, many of these activities, such as making a word web, writing a journal response, and performing a timed repeated reading, are typically in the repertoire of a knowledgeable teacher.

Literacy-based learning workstations and independent work are essential when implementing small-group instruction. As a teacher works with a small group, the rest of the class must be engaged in useful literacy activities. Rather than relying solely on worksheets as a means to keep students working independently, students can rotate from one workstation to the next. An important study by Connor and her colleagues (2009) stressed that strong readers grow

Table 26. Desired Literacy Workstations

Workstation	Targeted Literacy Skills
Listening: Students listen to a book on tape while following along with a copy of the text. Require a written or oral response so that students' work is purpose driven.	Comprehension Fluency
Word study and phonics games: Students play various games to sort, make, and pronounce words that reinforce previously studied phonics concepts and spelling patterns.	Phonics, word study, and spelling
Computer games: Students work on the computer independently or with one partner using software or websites predetermined by the teacher.	Fluency Phonics, word study, and spelling Vocabulary Writing
Independent reading: Students read self-selected stories, frequently with a partner. They may complete a reading log or other accountability activities like oral sharing of the book.	Fluency Phonics, word study, and spelling Vocabulary
Comprehension activities: Students read books, write about them, relate one text to another, compare characters and settings, complete graphic organizers, prepare questions, and locate new, interesting words.	Comprehension

in reading ability when they engage in meaning-oriented comprehension and writing activities. Pressley (2006) reminded us that in effective schools, independent work is long (lasting a day or more), interesting, and challenging. For many readers, meaningful projects are more important than quick activities. In Table 26, we present our suggestions for types of workstations needed in most classrooms. Workstation activities must be connected to the needs of the students and the ongoing curriculum.

A Motivating Environment: The Three Cs

Consider the three Cs of literacy motivation as you conceptualize your classroom environment: choice, collaboration, and challenge. Choice is very important (Gambrell & Morrow, 1996; Turner, 1995). We all have a better attitude when we know we have options and when we have at least some control of those options. How can you incorporate choice into your reading/language arts block? You might provide choice of tasks or activities during workstations, choice of texts to be used during small-group reading instruction, or choice of texts in the classroom library.

Collaboration is another component of motivation (Guthrie et al., 2000). We all tend to feel more secure and work better when we have the option to collaborate with others. Through collaboration, we have opportunities to view models of the task at hand, perhaps reading or writing, and we have opportunities to discuss. Reading is a social activity. Collaboration provides the fuel. Do you provide your students with opportunities for collaboration during the school day and during the reading/language arts block?

Challenge is the third component of a motivating classroom environment (Wigfield & Guthrie, 1997). Let's take a moment to consider video games. When you begin playing a video game, you start at the easiest level, a level at which you are usually successful. This immediate taste of success entices you to continue playing the game. As you play, the challenge or difficulty increases ever so slightly. Note that the challenge is subtle: It requires some work, yet success is attainable with a little effort. Most young people, and adults for that matter, are willing to spend hours playing video games for this very reason. This is the instructional level at which challenge in the reading classroom should take place. Consider what would happen if video games did not gradually increase the challenge and instead jumped to the most difficult level. Without doubt, the video game industry would not be the billion-dollar success it is today if it employed this method. Likewise, students in your classroom will not be motivated to read if they are consistently asked to read material that is frustrating in nature, too difficult to attain success. Do you know your students' functional reading levels? Are you matching your students' reading levels to the texts you are using with them in class? Is the challenge placed at an appropriate level to facilitate success?

Also consider how rewards are used within your classroom or perhaps at the school level. Many types of rewards are prevalent in schools and classrooms, such as treasure boxes, visits to the school store, and food prizes, and many systems for earning rewards are in place as well. In some reward systems, students cash in reading points for prizes; some schools offer collective prizes to grade levels or classrooms that attain reading goals, or students may work for prizes within classroom-level systems that are unique to individual teachers. Naturally, schools and teachers use prize systems in a well-meaning effort to encourage students to read. We encourage you to consider the behavior that you are trying to encourage through these prizes—reading. Perhaps the reward systems we use should reflect the value of the task we are trying to promote. When instituting reward systems, why not try reward students with prizes that encourage reading and reflect the value of reading, such as books, bookmarks, or special uninterrupted time to read with the teacher or principal? Are you allowing students to *choose* to participate in such programs? Is *collaboration* involved?

PUTTING IT ALL TOGETHER

Years ago, one of us attended a back-to-school night for a then-third-grade son. On every desk was the daily schedule of activities. The morning started with announcements followed by mathematics. Third on the list was Macmillan. Feigning naivete, I asked the teacher, "What is Macmillan?" "Reading," she responded. I thought to myself, you are not teaching Macmillan, you are teaching reading or literacy. A core reading program is not your literacy program. Your core reading program is an important tool in your total literacy program. The school has to organize time and people so that students can receive the instruction they need. A parsimonious assessment system needs to be developed so that all the stakeholders have information about students' progress, and this includes the students. The effective teacher has to organize time, space, and texts to create a literate environment. A teacher has to motivate his or her students to read. In Chapter 9, we take you into a first-grade classroom and a fourth-grade classroom to describe how a core reading program is used within an effective literacy program. The decisions that teachers make, stemming from their knowledge and beliefs, will ultimately determine the quality and effectiveness of their instruction.

CHAPTER 9

Core Reading Programs in Action

City Elementary School is a large school located in a small, urban district. The students come from a diverse set of backgrounds, since the school borders a larger military base. Forty-five percent of the students are African American, 30% are Caucasian, and 25% are Hispanic. Seventy percent of the students receive free or reduced-cost lunch. The school is currently in its fifth year as a Reading First school, which affects grades kindergarten through third.

City Elementary School uses the Trophies (Harcourt, 2003/2005) core reading program. The program was adopted four years ago, and by now the teachers are well versed in the program and have put their own brand on it. This core program includes four leveled books for each main basal selection, some decodable books in first grade, and an intervention program that parallels the main core materials. The intervention program covers the same skills and vocabulary, but with reading selections that are at a lower readability level. Over the last four years, the district has purchased a number of supplements. The number of little books was expanded when the district purchased extensive sets of leveled books focused on sight words and phonics patterns. Novel sets have been slowly added to the school's collection, and all these books are stored in the school's book room. Other supplemental materials include a computer-based program for developing phonemic awareness and phonics skills and *Road to the Code* (Blachman, Ball, Black, & Tangel, 2000), another phonemic awareness program.

In Chapter 8, we discussed some of the general principles of using a core reading program well and how to get started with using one. In this chapter, we use sample classroom experiences to specifically illustrate what a core reading program looks like in action, and we share how decisions need to be made at the classroom level. We take you into two classrooms: the first-grade classroom of Mrs. Farrington, who is in her fifth year of teaching but her first year in first grade, and then into the fourth-grade classroom of Ms. Hernandez, who is in her tenth year of teaching. The names of the school and the teachers are pseudonyms based on an actual school we have worked with.

What You Will Learn

- The components of a basic lesson plan in a core reading program
- How the structure of a core reading program imposes instructional routines that may or may not benefit your students
- The aspects of strong literacy instruction that go beyond a core reading program
- That you, as a teacher, have the prerogative to modify the lesson plan of a core reading program to meet the needs of your students

What You Will Be Able to Do

- Make instructional decisions about the use of core reading programs to meet the needs of your students
- Modify a core reading program lesson plan for teaching in the primary grades
- Modify a core reading program lesson plan for teaching in the intermediate grades
- Know what additional materials should be incorporated into your teaching and when to use them
- Differentiate instruction for your students

Understanding Core Reading Program Lesson Structure

Core reading programs have more components and activities than can be completed within the time allocated for instruction. Following core programs with fidelity is a topic open to discussion, because core programs do not specify which components must be used and which are optional. So let's examine the basic lesson plan in a core program and the decisions teachers will have to face. We concentrate on Trophies (2003/2005) but also discuss more recent versions of all core programs. All lessons in Trophies (and other programs) begin by identifying the text and resources that teachers and students may use during the week. This is followed by a five-day lesson plan that is divided into four major sections each day: oral language (sharing literature), skills and strategies (comprehension and vocabulary), reading (guided comprehension, independent reading, cross-curriculum connections), and language arts (writing, grammar, and spelling). Other programs vary this structure a bit. During the week, the teachers move from prereading to during reading activities, and then to postreading activities. The five-day plan suggests when to use each component. For example, Trophies suggests that the leveled readers can be read any day of the week for independent reading, whereas the Scott Foresman Reading (Pearson Scott Foresman, 2004) program suggests that the leveled readers be used on days 3, 4, and 5. Kindergarten and first-grade five-day plans are more specific than those in the upper grades.

According to the analysis of Chambliss and Calfee (1998), four themes underlie the structure of a core reading program. First, the programs foster the use of repetitive routines and emphasize planning and management. What teachers do the first week of school is largely identical to what they do the last week of school. Second, core reading programs are largely about the development of skills and strategies for decoding, fluency, and comprehension, and not about the development of concepts. Core reading programs do not build students' knowledge of the world or knowledge of text. Third, core reading programs are more about learning to read narratives than they are about reading informational texts, and this is especially true in the primary grades (Duke, 2000). Fourth, management in core reading programs is a major goal. With the plethora of activities, workbooks, workstations, and texts, the teacher's job is to keep all the children busy and all the plates in the air. Planning often focuses more on activities than on goals.

Strive for a few clear objectives each week and have a clear focus for each lesson. You will not have time to use all of the components in a core reading program, and as the year goes by and your students grow as readers and writers, your lessons and goals must change. Consider the following objectives:

- Your students need to gain some content knowledge—to learn something about the world around them and expand their vocabulary.

- Your students need to learn about genres and the structures of and purposes for the texts they read.

- Your students need to learn new strategies for decoding or comprehension and refine their ability to use old strategies.

- Your students need to read widely and deeply and complete as few worksheets as possible.

- Your students need to be motivated and excited by books and the process of becoming literate.

In Figure 13, we list the major components of a core reading program and the kinds of decisions you need to make.

Figure 13. The Structure of a Weekly Lesson in a Core Reading Program and the Decisions Teachers Might Make

Lesson Component	Reflections and Teacher Decisions
Lesson Organizer	
Five-day lesson planner	It is useful to review this plan, but you may want to ignore some ideas, add some ideas, and move some activities to other days. For example, you might use the leveled books for guided reading on specific days and not for independent reading as suggested.
Cross-curriculum stations	Most programs have suggestions for learning workstations, especially the post-2007 copyright programs. Consider what the program suggests and what fits into the time available. Add your own ideas as well.
Oral Language	
Question of the day	Ask a question that causes students to think about the theme or content of the reading selections. We address other ideas in Chapter 11.
Read-aloud	All programs include read-alouds, but frequently they are short and do not allow you to develop concepts and vocabulary or model comprehension strategies. Consider substituting a children's literature selection for the read-aloud provided.
Skills and Strategies	
Comprehension skills and strategies	In many programs, you will want to modify which skills and strategies are taught and how they are taught. We explore these ideas more fully in Chapter 11.
Building background	Depending on your students, you may have to build more genre and content knowledge than is suggested in the program.
Vocabulary	Teacher decisions are needed about which words to teach. Words may be taught that are critical to the story but neglected in the program's lesson plan. Other words in the lesson plan may be taught with less emphasis. Know your students' needs.
Reading	
Prereading strategies	Programs tend to repeat the same purpose-setting directions from one lesson to another. You may want to vary the lesson depending on the selection, the competence of the students, and your overall goals for the week.
Guided comprehension	Each two-page spread in the teacher's manual provides directions on the sides of the pages and at the bottom. The directions on the sides of the pages focus on comprehension questions and modeling of strategies. We explore these suggestions more fully in Chapter 11. The directions at the bottom of the pages discuss options for supporting below- and above-level readers and ELL students, and for linking the selection to other

(continued)

Figure 13. The Structure of a Weekly Lesson in a Core Reading Program and the Decisions Teachers Might Make (*cont'd*)

Reading (cont'd)	
Guided comprehension (*continued*)	curricular areas. Below-level, advanced, and ELL students need a more comprehensive program than can be encapsulated in a small box. The focus on other curricular areas may be a source of good postreading or workstation activities. Be selective.
Making connections	All programs recommend postreading questions. You may want to modify the suggested questions in the program depending on your purpose for reading the selection. You might want to use the postreading questions to make connections to other stories or the read-aloud or reinforce how the strategy assisted the students' understanding.
Skill and strategy instruction and review	Most programs review comprehension skills and strategies after reading the selection and sometimes introduce new skills and strategies. Keep your lesson focus clean. Do not introduce or review too many skills and strategies. If the whole class does not need to review a phonics principle, reserve this for the small group that does need it.
Language Arts	
Writer's craft	Core reading programs provide reasonably complete suggestions for teaching writing, including a five-day plan. Some of these five-day plans focus on learning to write a specific genre, while others focus on a craft skill, such as word choice or sentence structure. Use these plans with the overall writing program in your school or district.
Grammar	Most core programs include a five-day lesson plan for teaching grammar. We recommend following these lesson plans only if your students are having difficulty with grammatical principles in writing and speaking. Think diagnostically.
Spelling	The spelling program in a core reading program is linked to the phonics program. Many schools have their own independent spelling programs. The use of the core program's spelling lessons should be a school or district decision.
Guided reading options: Leveled books	Guided reading with leveled books is not stressed as thoroughly in core programs published before 2007 as it is in newer programs. The more recent programs have more articulated lessons. The lessons developed in the core programs may have to be modified based on the needs of your students. See our suggestions in Chapter 11.
Listening and speaking	Read the listening and speaking lessons. You may want to incorporate some of these ideas during the week.

A Literacy Model for a Primary Classroom

Primary-grade teachers will need to make several types of decisions as they use the tools in their core reading programs. These decisions will vary with the age of the program and the resources it provides. Teachers using core reading programs created before 2007 will need to design their own small-group instruction, and teachers using programs of any vintage will need to think about how to differentiate instruction, incorporate more children's literature, and adapt the programs to the growing reading skills of their students. All teachers will need to think about the literary environment they construct in their classroom.

In our sample first-grade classroom, even though this is the beginning of the year, Mrs. Farrington must plan for a diverse group of students. She has 4 students already reading at a second-grade level or better, and the first-grade core reading program lacks the texts that will engage these students. For the 12 students just starting to read but with normally developing skills, the core program provides many resources. For the few who have not yet learned letter names or sounds and have weak phonological awareness skills, Mrs. Farrington must locate resources to assist them. The core program will be an important tool in her classroom, but not for all students.

The Learning Space and Environment

Mrs. Farrington finds herself teaching first grade after spending the past nine years teaching fifth grade. Although she is excited for the opportunity to teach younger students, she is a little overwhelmed at the differences in materials and physical space between a first-grade classroom and a fifth-grade classroom. She needs to think carefully about how to set up her classroom to accommodate the learning styles of 6-year-olds. Rather than having rows of desks, she puts the desks into groups of four. By clustering the desks into groups, she frees up more space in the classroom for learning workstations, a cozy reading nook, and a corner of the room prepped for her small reading groups. The reading group corner has a kidney-shaped table, a dry-erase board behind the table, and several shelves to store the various materials needed for leading a small reading group.

Mrs. Farrington has also created a classroom that is filled with books. A frequent yard sale shopper, she has built a large classroom library of quality children's literature. She also checks out books from the local library that pertain to current events or units of study. The overall feeling in the classroom is a combination of organization with plenty of action. Around the classroom, signs of an active learning environment are everywhere. A quick scan reveals a math workstation with many well-used math manipulatives in tubs and a science workstation where small plants grow in plastic cups. The classroom pet, a lazy, well-fed bunny, rests nearby in his crate. Grizzly, as he is known around the school, has been the subject of many journal entries over the years.

Near the entrance of the classroom, just past the jacket hooks and lunchbox cubbies, there is a large carpeted area, which the children usually refer to as the "calendar area." The area is bordered by a bulletin board where math skills are reviewed daily via the calendar exercises. Children assemble on the rug each morning to review the day's schedule. Mrs. Farrington typically sits in the rocking chair during calendar time.

In the center of the room are the students' desks, a place to store their materials even though learning takes place at the desks and in nearly every nook and cranny of the room in an organized but free-flowing manner. The print-rich environment is also reflected on the walls of the room, and what dominates these walls are words, charts, and materials that are almost exclusively teacher and student made. There is the ubiquitous alphabet strip and a number line, but virtually everything else is created by one of the creative inhabitants of Mrs. Farrington's classroom. We will walk you through a typical day in her classroom.

Daily and Weekly Schedules

At the beginning of the school year, the school district provided Mrs. Farrington with a schedule for her instructional time. On most days, she has at least 100 minutes of time allocated to reading instruction and an additional 30 to 45 minutes for language arts. She also has 30 minutes for intervention and enrichment. Her core reading program makes no specific provision for small-group instruction, but it is a requirement of the school district. Mrs. Farrington does not follow the time suggestions of the core program; instead, she makes decisions that she feels will benefit her students. She organizes her instruction into 40 minutes of whole-group time—when she focuses on phonemic awareness and phonics instruction, vocabulary development and comprehension skills, and strategy instruction—followed by 60 minutes of small-group and workstation time.

Mrs. Farrington spends considerable time planning her workstation and small-group times. She knows how vital it is for students to remain engaged throughout the academic day. Too much teaching time is often lost during transitions (Allington & Cunningham, 2002). Mrs. Farrington's students typically begin the reading block time by looking at the "Workstation Chart." The newest core programs from Pearson Scott Foresman, Harcourt, and McGraw-Hill provide management charts, but they might lack the complexity or explicitness all teachers need. Mrs. Farrington's chart provides a daily plan for each student's independent work time at literacy-based learning workstations. The class is grouped heterogeneously into four different groups. A pocket chart with index cards guides the students to their learning workstations. For instance, group A (a heterogeneous group of above-, at-, and below-level readers) looks at the pocket chart to see the following order: listening workstation, word study games, computers, independent reading. The members of group A understand that they will spend approximately 15 minutes at the listening workstation. Mrs. Farrington will provide a signal (usually a bell) when the first literacy-based learning workstation rotation is complete. At that time, the students know it is their job to put away any materials from their workstation. From there, they quietly proceed to their next workstation, word study games. Meanwhile, the other three heterogeneous groups (B, C, and D) follow their own respective rotations. Obviously, Mrs. Farrington has structured the rotations so that only one group is at a workstation at a time.

Whole-Group Reading Instruction. Mrs. Farrington opens each day with a whole-group time, during which she and the students develop a morning message and work on some basic phonemic awareness and phonics concepts, then she reads to them to develop vocabulary knowledge and model comprehension strategies. The morning message is typically a time when teachers review basic math facts, concepts of time, the calendar, the schedule for the day, and reading skills, such as letter–sound relationships, phonological awareness, and phonics. The morning message routine is prescribed in the core program and is essentially the same lesson from the first day of school to the last, but Mrs. Farrington realizes that her students' abilities grow and her routines must change. At the beginning of the year, she follows the routine in the core program using the sentences suggested and having the students help her complete the cloze blanks.

By the middle of the year, the morning message has morphed into an interactive writing activity. Mrs. Farrington suggests various topics, usually tied into what the students are studying in science or social studies or the theme of the core reading program. She then lets the students take the lead in composing a story and uses the developing story to review concepts of print, text structure, basic grammar, punctuation, and spelling. Students are asked to spell words, and if they need help, she guides them to segment the words into phonemes. The completed stories are typed, copied, and taken home for students to practice their reading. By the end of the year, the morning message may actually serve as a time to study a topic or genre in depth—in May the students are reading and writing about reptiles and amphibians—and during the morning message, the students share what they have learned the previous day.

Following the morning message and calendar time, Mrs. Farrington spends 10 to 15 minutes on phonological awareness and phonics activities. She generally follows the activities outlined in the core reading program, but she also uses phonemic awareness ideas from other sources. The lesson in the core reading program is presented to the whole class, but additional phonics and phonemic awareness lessons are presented in the small-group lessons. This allows her to differentiate instruction, teaching and reviewing the skills that each group of students needs. Because Mrs. Farrington has several ELLs in her room, she also uses the time to talk about word meanings and focus on their use in context. So when new words are used as examples in phonemic awareness lessons, their meanings are discussed before the words are segmented or blended. Thus, through anchored instruction (Juel, Biancarosa, Coker, & Deffes, 2003), the teacher builds word knowledge along with basic reading skills.

The third whole-group activity is an oral read-aloud. The core reading program provides one each day. A Big Book is read on Mondays, and each day for the rest of the week, the teacher's manual offers a short poem that is linked to the theme of the lesson. Mrs. Farrington uses good children's literature, fiction, and nonfiction for her read-alouds instead of the read-aloud suggested by the core program. She wants to expose her students to good children's literature and the themes they portray. If the main selection in the core program is about seasons, she might use a book like *The Mitten* by Jan Brett (1990) for her read-aloud. She chooses to focus on four to six critical vocabulary words from each book, briefly defining them as she reads and then expanding their meaning after she reads. Mrs. Farrington is essentially following the procedures in Text Talk (Beck et al., 2002). On the second day, she reads the book again and models the use of comprehension strategies. On the third day, they again review the vocabulary from the story. This process builds her students' awareness of comprehension skills, using books that have the complexity, interest, and sophistication that leveled texts do not (Smolkin & Donovan, 2002).

Mrs. Farrington has to spend a fair amount of time choosing appropriate reading materials for each group. It is vital that she places her students in books that are on their instructional level, not simply their grade level. Students who are reading above grade level may read from the core reading program or from trade books. The on-level students may read from the core reading program or from the decodable books that come with the program. The below-level readers, however, often find the selections in the core reading program too difficult. Even the leveled readers designated for the below-level students may be too difficult for them. Mrs. Farrington frequently chooses other books, such as the decodable readers or books like the Ready Readers (Modern Curriculum Press/ Pearson Learning, 1996–2004), for her struggling readers. By carefully choosing appropriate reading material for the different needs of her students, she effectively differentiates her literacy instruction.

Small-Group Reading Instruction. Next, Mrs. Farrington shifts to small-group work. Small-group instruction allows her to differentiate the instruction and provide the time for students to apply what they are learning. Students are either reading in small groups with her or rotating to literacy-based reading workstations. Based on assessments, Mrs. Farrington has grouped her class into three different small reading groups but four workstation groups. Although the reading groups are homogeneous, the workstation groups are heterogeneous. She groups together students reading at the same level. Typically, she has one group that reads above grade level, one group that reads on grade level, and another group that reads below grade level. As the children rotate through workstations, Mrs. Farrington meets with small reading groups. She calls different students from their literacy-based workstations to the reading corner. Although the students may be busy at a workstation, they know that they will have time another day to continue with the activity. Mrs. Farrington pays close attention to the reading progress of all of her students. It is expected that students will move to different reading groups over the course of the year as their skills improve.

Mrs. Farrington uses the texts in the core reading program for some of her small-group lessons. The program she is using, Trophies (2003/2005), comes with a main anthology selection each week, plus a decodable book and four leveled books. This structure is typical of most core programs, even the most recent publications. She makes decisions regarding which groups are capable of reading each of the selections and supplements with other materials as needed.

Mrs. Farrington also has to make decisions as to which of the many activities provided in the core reading program she will use. Her above-level readers, for instance, may be able to read the main anthology selection independently. They will not require the scaffolded instruction detailed in the teacher's manual. The on-level group may read the main anthology selection with a partner or with teacher support, but will require more discussion with the teacher. The below-level students may simply listen to the story being read and focus most of their energies on the leveled and decodable books. By the end of the year, Mrs. Farrington expects that most of her students will be reading books outside the core reading program, delving into short chapter books and nonfiction trade books. Figure 14 shows the types of texts her students will read and how they will read them. Her goal is to have the students read many different books during the week.

The teacher's manual in core reading programs offers little guidance for how these texts should be read. The Trophies program suggests that the below-level

Figure 14. Texts and How First-Grade Students Might Read Them by the End of the School Year

Reading Level	Day 1	Day 2	Day 3	Day 4	Day 5
Above-level	*Anthology selection* Independent silent reading	*Leveled reader* Independent or partner reading during guided reading	*Leveled reader* Independent or partner reading during guided reading	*Additional selection or chapter book* Independent silent reading and guided reading	*Additional selection or chapter book* Independent silent reading and guided reading
On-level	*Anthology selection* Echo and partner reading	*Decodable text* Echo, partner, or individual reading	*Leveled reader* Echo, partner, or individual reading	*Leveled reader* Echo, partner, or individual reading	*Additional text* Echo, partner, or individual reading
Below-level	*Anthology selection* Listening	*Decodable text* Echo, partner, or individual reading	*Decodable text* Partner or individual reading	*Decodable text* Individual reading	*Additional text* Partner or individual reading

students take turns reading each page aloud, with the teacher providing word-recognition support. On-level and advanced students should be supported with guided reading questions or simply read the selection independently. Trophies is not the only program to neglect clear direction on how selections should be read, and the omission continues in the two most current core reading programs: Treasures (Macmillan/McGraw-Hill, 2009) and StoryTown (Harcourt, 2008). Teachers have many options, ranging from the common round robin reading to choral, echo, partner, or individual reading. We suggest that primary students read as much of the texts as possible by themselves. This means avoiding round robin reading and stressing partner reading and independent reading, sometimes called whisper reading. The negative views on round robin reading stem from the fact that students are engaged with the text only during their turn. Mrs. Farrington solves that problem by having one student read a page, then the rest of the group echoes the student not the teacher (Opitz & Rasinski, 1998). If students have to read a relatively difficulty text, then Mrs. Farrington provides support through an extensive picture walk or by engaging in echo reading of a text they select on their own. Fountas and Pinnell (1996) have counseled that teachers should vary the support students need, depending on the difficulty of the text.

One reading of each of these little books is rarely sufficient. Students should be encouraged to reread the text or portions of it to work on accuracy and fluency. These texts may be read with a partner later in the day. One successful lesson plan moved from whole-text reading to reading sentence strips from the story, to finally reading words from the story written on flashcards (Johnston, 2000). The little books can be retyped and sent home for the students to read. This removes picture support and forces the students to focus on the words. In one variation of this procedure, called autograph stories, the student seeks a signature from each person who listens to him or her read the story, and family pets are not excluded even though they are graphically challenged.

A Sample Small-Group Reading Lesson. Many teachers consider the teacher's manual a guide or framework for their lesson planning. It is nearly impossible to complete all of the activities with all of the students. Figure 15 provides a plan for adapting the core reading program to the various needs of a kindergarten or first-grade classroom, especially if you have a core program that lacks an explicit small-group plan. We based this plan on some of the recent work on differentiated instruction (Connor, Morrison, Fishman et al., 2007; Connor,

Figure 15. Small-Group Guided Reading Lessons for the Primary Grades

Advanced Readers	On-Level Readers	Below-Level Readers
Phonics and vocabulary (5 minutes) • Review main phonics pattern from whole-group lesson. • Apply decoding strategies to new words. • Engage students in one decoding activity. *Read leveled book or story from core reading program.* (10 minutes) • Introduce new book and develop prior knowledge. • Introduce essential vocabulary. • Read the story (possible options: partner read or Directed-Reading Thinking Activity). • Reread portions of the text to work on expression. • Use white board to review and model decoding strategies for difficult words. • Have students retell the story; ask comprehension questions.	*Phonics* (10 minutes) • Introduce and review phonics patterns based on students' needs. • Model decoding strategies. • Engage students in one decoding activity. *Read leveled book or story from core reading program.* (10 minutes) • Introduce new book and develop prior knowledge. • Introduce essential vocabulary. • Echo or choral read the text. • Have students partner read the text and coach those who have difficulty. • Reread portions of the text to work on expression. • Use white board to review and model decoding strategies for difficult words. • Have students retell the story; ask comprehension questions.	*Phonics and phonological awareness* (15 minutes) • Segment and blend sounds. • Introduce or review phonics patterns based on students' needs. • Engage in one or two decoding activities. *Read leveled book.* (10 minutes) • Introduce new book with picture walk or shared reading by the teacher (both are not necessary). • Echo or choral read, depending on the students' needs. • Have students partner read the text and coach those who have difficulty. • Use white board to review and model decoding strategies for difficult words. • Reread the story. • Have students retell the story; ask comprehension questions.

Morrison, & Underwood, 2007). A teacher can differentiate texts, time, and tasks when working with homogeneous groups. The lesson plan in Figure 15 begins by differentiating time in two ways. The below-level readers spend more total time with the teacher (25 minutes per day) than do the on-level and advanced readers. The advanced readers might not work with the teacher in a small group each day, and if they do, it is only for a short amount of time.

The below-level readers spend more time in phonics and phonological awareness each day than do the on-level and advanced readers. When they work with the teacher, the above-level readers focus their energies on vocabulary. Connor, Morrison, and Underwood (2007) found that second-grade teachers who added five minutes of phonics instruction to their small groups, versus those who did not, had significantly greater reading achievement. Connor et al. also found that the best readers benefited the most from the independent stretches of time in which they could work with interesting texts and on meaningful projects.

This lesson plan also provides for differentiated tasks during small-group instruction. The below-level readers work on the phonics skills that they lack rather than review the phonics skills taught in whole groups. The teacher determines which phonics patterns the students need to learn and selects the appropriate activities and texts. The on-level students review the phonics from the whole-group instruction, and the above-level readers work on vocabulary or apply a decoding strategy like structural analysis that might be beyond what the rest of the class needs. Working in a small group with an engaged and supportive teacher can be the highlight of the day for many children. Students thrive not only on reading appropriate level materials but also on taking part in lively discussions about books in a positive atmosphere.

As small-group work is planned, it is useful for each group to read about the same topic or theme or read the same genre. This allows the group to share in a common discussion at the end of the week. If each group is reading about growing plants, then at the end of the week, the teacher and students can consolidate what they have learned into a chart or other graphic organizer. This allows everyone to be part of larger projects and develops in students a sense of community and commitment. So in many classrooms, the small-group time is followed by a second but shorter whole-group time in which students share what they have read, what they have written, and what they have learned. It is during this second whole-group time that students and teachers reflect on the goals and the objective and consider what they have accomplished and what they need to do the next day.

A Literacy Model for an Intermediate Classroom

Ms. Hernandez also teaches at City Elementary, but because she works with fourth graders, the rules and regulations of Reading First touch her more lightly.

She is still committed to following the yearly reading schedule laid out in the core reading program. However, the structure and content of her reading/language arts program is more clearly bound by the dictates of the high-stakes state assessments that her students must take and her personal goal to provide an enriching and thoughtful literacy experience. In this grade, her students will take tests in reading, writing, mathematics, and American history. The state standards for reading are clear and precise, and the district has developed a pacing guide to ensure that the teachers cover these standards. Progress toward meeting these standards is assessed through district-constructed benchmark tests administered in November, January, and April. The benchmark tests and the quarterly writing prompts are taken quite seriously, and gradually these formative assessments have assumed the emotional pressure of a summative test.

Working within this structured pressure, Ms. Hernandez feels committed to instilling in her students a love of reading and exposing them to a wide breadth of literature and informational texts. In addition to enjoying reading, she wants her students to view reading as a way to learn about the world and to embrace texts, both written and electronic, as stimulus for inquiry and as a means for learning and solving problems. So Ms. Hernandez conducts a balancing act. She covers the skills and strategies from the core reading program, often deviating from the selections in the student anthology to substitute fiction and nonfiction trade books.

Ms. Hernandez faces other challenges in her room, because not all of her students read well. Despite the impact of Reading First, 5 of her 24 students are still reading a year or more below grade level, and they too must pass the state reading assessment. So she must differentiate instruction and help her students acquire the word-recognition skills that they still lack. Unfortunately, the core reading program she is using provides little guidance and support. But one of the reading teachers spends 30 minutes a day in Ms. Hernandez's room working with the students in the lower groups. Together, Ms. Hernandez and the reading teacher have crafted an instructional program that is helping all students achieve. Let's take a look at this program and see how the core program and the supplemental materials work together.

The Learning Space and Environment

Ms. Hernandez has created a classroom environment that stimulates learning and reflects what the students are learning. She does this by effectively arranging her room and the print in it. At the front of the room is a large dry-erase board and overhead projector. Moving clockwise around the room, you first encounter a small table where the teacher works with students in reading groups. Behind the table are shelves holding trade books and the leveled books that come with the school's core reading program. Moving around the room to the right, you find additional bookshelves, a small anteroom that serves as the teacher's office, a large rectangular table that holds science experiments and projects, and another table that the reading teacher uses.

On the back wall of the classroom are tables for computers, more leveled books, and a reading fluency workstation. The students use the computers to complete accelerated reader assessments, conduct Internet searches, and publish writing assignments. The fluency workstation, designed by one of the school's reading specialists, has a large number of grade-level passages and stopwatches so that students can read passages, time one another, and then record the reading rates. The rest of the back wall contains metal shelving that serves as a writing workstation. The shelves hold various kinds of writing paper, card stock, and construction paper for making books, along with highlighters, scissors, and writing implements.

On the far right wall, Ms. Hernandez displays students' work and records what has been learned in content area study. At this point in the year, one large part of the wall is covered with the plans and directions for creating a class newspaper. The bulletin board lists the parts of the newspaper, the organization or structure of a typical news article, and the articles, stories, and features that the students are planning to write. The bulletin board is used to plan and organize the students' writing assignments. Because the students have discussed the newspaper, this bulletin board is the product of their thinking. It is also a public record of what they have accomplished.

In the last corner of the room, close to the front, is a comprehension workstation on a small mobile cart with racks for books written by well-known children's authors and small horizontal shelves that hold graphic organizers. The cart is on rollers, and students move it as they need to. The students use the cart during their reading/language arts time. A standing assignment in the room is to read at least one picture book a week and then complete a graphic organizer about the book. The graphic organizers for fiction might focus on plot or character development, or tone and mood. Each week the teacher introduces one new graphic organizer and guides the students through its use with the story of the week. During subsequent weeks, the students are to use that or other graphic organizers to respond to the ever-changing books on the comprehension cart.

On the periphery of the classroom, but playing a central role, is the "wonderful word wall." Ms. Hernandez was searching for an ongoing activity that would involve all of the students, thus was born the word wall. The word wall is actually a series of colored index cards organized into a chain that snakes around the room. The students select which words to place on the wall, with words coming from any piece of reading or any content text that engages them. If the word is a noun, it is written on a blue card. Verbs are written on yellow cards, and so forth for other parts of speech. Words that have more than one usage are listed twice. Attached to the cards are small strips of paper that indicate the names of the students who found the word, the names of the students who have used the word, and the definition or usage of the word supplied by one or more students. At the end of the school year, there were 425 unique words on the wall, and the chain had circumnavigated the classroom twice. The word wall became the vocabulary workstation of the room and involved all students. They read the words, added words to the wall, discussed words, and used words in their writing and in their oral presentations. Ms. Hernandez's room is not large enough to have a well-defined reading area, but books are everywhere. In addition to the rolling comprehension cart, there are boxes of leveled books from the core reading program, wire racks that hold trade books, and a display of featured trade books on the ledge under the dry-erase board in front of the room. Although there is no real cozy space to read, this does not appear to prevent the children from reading.

Daily and Weekly Schedules

The reading/language arts schedule developed by the principal allocates 90 minutes each day for reading, 45 minutes for writing, and a 30-minute extension and enrichment time during which the struggling readers work with a reading specialist while the rest of the class engages in enrichment activities. The day begins at 8:30 at City Elementary School. At this time, teachers are expected to be in their classrooms, and students may enter the building. Because City is a Title I school with 70% of its students receiving free- or reduced-cost lunch, many of the students head right for the cafeteria to eat breakfast. The rest, as they trickle in, go to their classrooms. So the formal part of the school day truly begins at 8:45 with the end of the Pledge of Allegiance and morning announcements. But from 8:30 to 8:50, many students are actively engaged in reading/language arts activities.

Whole-Group Reading Instruction. After the informal reading time that begins each day, Ms. Hernandez starts her whole-group time. She views this as a time to build common goals for the whole class and set clear purposes for the week. So on Monday the goals for the week might be to study biographies, learn more about animal survival, and introduce comprehension monitoring as an important strategy. A never-changing goal is vocabulary and the learning of new words. These common goals reduce the stigma that grouping within a classroom might impart. Even though the struggling readers may spend more time working on decoding in small groups, they still contribute to the whole-class goals of reading biographies and adding to the word wall. Ms. Hernandez's goals come from the core program, but with some modifications. She uses the goals suggested by the core reading program, but often narrows them so that they are more manageable. For example, the first theme in Trophies (2003/2005) is titled "You Can Do It" and is a collection of readings, fiction and biography, about people overcoming obstacles and pursuing their own interests. Ms. Hernandez might narrow the topic to focus on personal obstacles and select a read-aloud accordingly. In this case, she chooses *The Voyage of the* Frog by Gary Paulsen (1990), the story of a young boy's survival at sea.

Three activities dominate the whole-group time: the development of prior knowledge, the introduction or reviewing of comprehension strategies, and the development of vocabulary. Ms. Hernandez draws on children's literature for much of the comprehension and vocabulary work. On Mondays, especially if a new strategy is introduced, she explains and models the strategy, often using a piece of fiction or nonfiction that ties in with what the students are studying. If it is a new strategy, she spends more time in direct instruction, whereas older strategies require modest amounts of review. The read-aloud selections, the use of video, and the development of graphic organizers help the students learn and organize new ideas. Throughout the week, she develops and organizes what students are learning. We expand on this idea when we discuss comprehension in Chapter 11.

Twice a week, the children walk along the word wall in pairs. Each pair walks along the wall and stops to discuss the words. The students point to words and ask their partners to define them. If a student is stuck, the other would ask questions or help by using the word in a sentence. If neither of the partners could define the word, then the students would turn to the dictionary. They like to challenge each other, look up words, and see how many of the words they know. When the word wall is not being used, the teacher focuses on the spelling lists for the week, and the students practice their spelling using worksheets from the reading program, sorting words, or engaging in making words (Cunningham, 2005).

Small-Group Reading Instruction. Ms. Hernandez has organized her 24 students into three groups. Eight students are reading above grade level according to the informal reading inventory administered early in the school year. The middle group consists of 10 students reading at grade level, and the last group contains 6 students reading between a low second- and low third-grade level. The big questions that Ms. Hernandez faces in her planning is how to meet the needs of her students given the tools offered in the core reading program. Trophies (2003/2005) provides an anthology selection, plus three leveled books that are tied to the theme of the main selection. She knows that what the core program provides is not enough text for her students. Let's examine how she plans her small-group and independent work. Ms. Hernandez has some learning workstations, and the students alternate between these workstations and independent work. She also works with one of the reading teachers, who spends 30 minutes each day in her classroom. During this time, the reading teacher works with the below-level readers, and then Ms. Hernandez sees them again. Figure 16 outlines how the small-group work is differentiated.

Several principles underlie what Ms. Hernandez does during her guided reading time. These allow her to differentiate time, tasks, and texts. First, she does not see all groups for the same amount of time. The students reading below grade level are seen for approximately 30 minutes per day and then spend another 20 minutes with the reading specialists. The students reading on grade level work in small groups for 20 or more minutes per day, and the above-level readers are seen for 20 minutes or less each day. On some days, the above- and on-level students might work independently in a literature circle or in pairs. Should the reading specialist be unavailable, Ms. Hernandez would still see her struggling readers for a longer amount of time.

Second, she differentiates the texts that students read to supplement the core reading program extensively. She believes that her core program does not provide enough texts for students to become proficient readers (Brenner & Hiebert, 2010). Each week the students are expected to read at least three texts or their

Figure 16. Small-Group Guided Reading Lessons for the Upper Grades

Above-Level Readers: Vocabulary and Comprehension	On-Level Readers: Vocabulary and Comprehension	Below-Level Readers: Decoding, Fluency, and Comprehension
Vocabulary (5 minutes) • Introduce or review new vocabulary. • Apply decoding strategies to new vocabulary words as needed. *Read text selection for comprehension.* (15 minutes) • Introduce new book or chapter and develop prior knowledge. • Review reading comprehension strategies. • Read text silently and apply comprehension strategies at each stopping point. • After reading, engage in application and discussion of postreading strategies (e.g., author's purpose, main idea, compare and contrast). • Continue or begin graphic organizer to apply main comprehension skill.	*Decoding and vocabulary* (7 minutes) • Introduce or review new vocabulary. • Apply decoding strategies to new vocabulary from texts using decoding by analogy. *Read text selection for fluency and comprehension.* (15 minutes) • Introduce new book and develop prior knowledge. • Review reading comprehension strategies. • Read text with a partner or silent read. • Reread portions of the text to work on reading rate and prosody (expression). • After reading each text segment, have students summarize, engage in comprehension monitoring, and apply main SOL comprehension skills. • Begin graphic organizer to apply main comprehension skill, to be completed at a workstation, or assign writing task.	*Decoding* (15 minutes) • Introduce or review new word family patterns. • Model decoding by analogy. • Engage students in one or two decoding activities. • Apply decoding by analogy to new vocabulary words and review meanings. *Read leveled and decodable book for fluency.* (15 minutes) • Introduce new book with a preview and develop prior knowledge. • Echo, partner, or individual read depending on students' needs. • Read with one or more students to coach on word identification strategies. • Use dry-erase board to review and model decoding strategies for difficult words. • Reread text segments to work on oral reading fluency. • Have students retell the story; ask comprehension questions. • After reading, apply postreading strategies (e.g., author's purpose, main idea, compare and contrast).

equivalent. The above-level readers are expected to read the anthology selection, their leveled reader from the core program, and at least one other selection during the week. Sometimes Ms. Hernandez decides that a novel or nonfiction selection will provide greater interest or challenge, and she will substitute it for all the material in the core program. Reading and discussing this selection may span two weeks or more. The students reading at grade level will typically read the anthology selection, the appropriate leveled book, and at least one other selection that is tied in to the theme of the week. As with the above-level readers, Ms. Hernandez will occasionally substitute a novel or nonfiction book for all the texts in the core program. Finally, the below-level students will read the below-level reader and at least two other little books that pair well with the topic or theme of the week. The students will be exposed to the main anthology selection as they read it with the teacher or listen to it on a CD.

The core reading program is not very directive on how these selections should be read. The directions in the core program call for the above-level students to read the selection independently, the on-level students to read with a partner, and for the below-level students, teachers should "Preview the selection with students. Discuss the meanings of these words [words will vary from one selection to another]. Guide students in setting a purpose for reading through page [page number is given]" (Harcourt, 2003/2005, Grade 4, Theme 1, p. 22). The strong readers in Ms. Hernandez's room read most texts silently, but they read orally to share a favorite passage, justify an answer, or dramatic rendition for texts like plays or poetry. She works with the on-level readers in much the same way, except she might have them engage in some oral reading as a diagnostic check on their fluency or decoding accuracy. The below-level readers might engage in echo and partner reading to build fluency. Also, Ms. Hernandez will have the students read orally at times to check on their developing decoding skills. Her goal during the year is to move the students from oral to silent reading and increase their endurance by reading larger and larger chunks of text. As you can see, she has a lot of moment-to-moment decisions to make to improve the decoding and fluency of her students (Opitz & Rasinski, 1998).

Third, Ms. Hernandez will differentiate the tasks that her students will perform. For those reading at or above grade level, the focus will remain fixed on comprehension strategies and vocabulary development. During small-group discussions, the students will be guided to apply the comprehension strategies and discuss vocabulary words. Independent work will focus on either discussion preparation or projects that extend what the students have been reading.

For example, before the students meet with the teacher, they will read the text, generate questions, and search for vocabulary words that bear discussing. Because they have been working on QARs (Raphael, 1984) the students are versed in generating "right there," "think and search," "author and me," and "on my own" questions. Postreading follow-up typically explores some aspect of the selection. Ms. Hernandez looks through the core reading program for its suggested activities. For example, the first selection in fourth grade and the accompanying leveled readers are about growing plants, and the core program suggests an engaging independent activity. Ms. Hernandez collects lots of books about plants from the library and then develops some research activities for the students to complete. They have to research the different conditions necessary for growing radishes in paper cups. This activity will eventually tie in with the students' work in science. At the end of the week, the students will be given time to report on what they have learned.

The challenge Ms. Hernandez faces when working with her below-level students is maintaining an engaging focus on meaning, but still developing the word recognition and fluency skills that the students lack. She is helped by the services of the reading specialists, but let's pretend for a moment that these services are lacking; how would she proceed on her own? Remember that she allocates more of her time to the struggling readers, so she can provide work on both decoding and comprehension, because the evidence indicates that struggling readers need a strong focus not just on words and fluency but also on comprehension (Anderson, Wilkinson, & Mason, 1991).

To develop her students' decoding abilities, Ms. Hernandez has chosen to use a decoding by analogy approach (Gaskins, Gaskins, & Gaskins, 1991; White, 2005). Unfortunately, Trophies provides no guidance for decoding instruction in its core reading program. The new version of Harcourt's program, StoryTown (2008), provides some options for decoding instruction in the upper grades, and its competitors—Scott Foresman Reading Street (Pearson Scott Foresman, 2008b) and Treasures (2009)—provide even more. The trick is to match any type of decoding instruction to the developmental needs of the students. Decoding by analogy is particularly well suited to older elementary students, because mastering the analogy process gives them quick access to longer and harder words and also focuses on the metacognitive control that many lack (Lovett et al., 2000). In decoding by analogy, students use known words such as *can* and *her* to decode unknown words such as *banter*: "If I know *can*, then that is *ban*, and if I know *her*, then that is *ter*. The word is *banter.*"

Each week Ms. Hernandez introduces three to five word-family patterns using "key words." *Place* is the key word for the pattern *ace*, and *bike* is the key word for the pattern *ike*. These key words are arranged by vowel sounds on a large piece of chart paper and used to decode new words. Each day Ms. Hernandez models the decoding by analogy process with difficult words from the students' reading in science, social studies, math, and reading. The students practice using the key words to decode and spell more new and difficult words. These activities take many forms, including word sorts, writing sorts, making words, and other word-making games. The decoding by analogy approach is then applied when students are reading in context. The teacher reminds students to use the words they know to figure out the unknown words.

Next, she meets with her average and above-average readers. How long and how often she sees these groups depends on what they are reading and the projects that engage them. Typically she sees her average readers daily, but the better readers require less attention. The small-group time allows the teacher to develop prior knowledge, review vocabulary, apply comprehension strategies, and promote her students' independent use of the strategies. When students are not meeting with the teacher, they might be preparing for their guided reading period, writing in response to their reading, working in literature circles, completing graphic organizers, or working on their reading fluency. Ms. Hernandez also finds time to confer with individual students and help them select books that match their interests and ability. There is always one common assignment that students must complete each week. This assignment ties together what each group has learned about the objective for the week. So if the class is studying character development, each group discusses an intriguing character from their reading and methods the author used to develop that character.

After the small-group time, Ms. Hernandez reads to the students. Typically she reads from novels, which allows the students to study the works of several authors during the school year. This is also an opportunity to build language skills, increase vocabulary, and foster an interest in reading. This oral reading time is also a springboard for writing.

Students in Ms. Hernandez's class write all of the time, especially during social studies and science, but 30 to 40 minutes every day involve a concentrated focus on writing. The district quarterly writing prompts guide many of the writing assignments; the students have to learn to write narratives, informational reports, persuasions, and extended text-based responses. The district writing prompts are a direct parallel to the expectations of the state assessments. To this list of genres, Ms. Hernandez adds work on poetry, writing a classroom newspaper, critiques from their reading, journal responses, and informational reports from science and social studies.

Monitoring Student Progress and Monitoring Instruction

City Elementary School has worked hard to create an informative but refined assessment system. The assessment tools that the school uses provide both diagnostic information when it is needed and progress-monitoring data so that all the stakeholders—teachers, students, parents, and administrators—appreciate the progress that students are making. In all grade levels, students performing below the 25th percentile on the district's standardized test are given an informal reading inventory. This diagnostic information is used to guide small-group instruction. Students' progress is monitored using oral reading fluency measures from the core reading program, theme skills tests in the primary grades, and the district-designed benchmark tests in the intermediate grades. Students, teachers, and parents all know how much progress is being made. In addition, students keep portfolios of their class work and projects and meet with their teacher quarterly to review their progress.

Monitoring students is important, and so is monitoring instruction. First, it is important for instructional leaders to be aware of the daily routines and instruction occurring within the classroom. Using information we have shared in previous chapters as a guide, it might be helpful for instructional leaders to view lesson plans on a weekly basis. Plans should reflect effective use of direct instruction, modeling, and guided practice, as well as articulate how differentiation will take place to meet the needs of all students in the classroom. Frequent classroom visits will further highlight how time is being used at the classroom level, in addition to the way texts are being used and the way resource teachers are active within the classroom setting. An observation checklist may be used as a guideline when conducting classroom observations. We have included such a checklist in our Reading GPS online on the webpage for this book at www.reading.org/general/publications/books/bk707.aspx. Review of lesson plans and observations also provides helpful information about areas of literacy in which professional development is most needed.

PUTTING IT ALL TOGETHER

The two classroom teachers described in this chapter use their core reading program extensively, with both teachers exercising their prerogative to make instructional decisions that will benefit their students. Both teachers have found a way to differentiate time, texts, and tasks in their classrooms. Throughout the descriptions of these two classrooms, we have cited the research from which these decisions stem. While some have called for following scientifically based core reading programs with fidelity, our two teachers are making instructional decisions based on research evidence. These two classrooms offer evidence that core reading programs do not lead to the deskilling of teachers (Baumann & Heubach, 1996). Let's review those decisions and the evidence that supports them.

- Students read core reading program texts and supplemental texts that are at their instructional level (O'Connor et al., 2002).

- Students read core reading program texts and supplemental texts that engage them in learning about a common topic or theme, thus building motivation and strategy use (Guthrie et al., 1998).

- Students and teachers work to build genre and content knowledge while reading strategically. Knowledge is good (Landis, Reitman, & Simmons, 1978; Willingham, 2006).

- Comprehension strategies are modeled in whole-group instruction and applied through a gradual release of responsibility model in small-group instruction (NICHD, 2000; Pressley, 2000).

- Time is differentiated so that below-level readers have more time with the teacher on word-focused instruction and above-level readers spend more time working independently on meaning-focused activities (Connor et al., 2009).

- Vocabulary learning stresses direct instruction in word meanings, rich language experiences, read-alouds, and fostering a sense of word consciousness (Baumann, Ware, & Edwards, 2007; Graves, 2006).

- Oral reading fluency is developed through wide reading, partner reading, and teacher-assisted reading (Kuhn & Stahl, 2003).

(continued)

PUTTING IT ALL TOGETHER *(cont'd)*

- Decoding strategies are developed by using a decoding by analogy approach with the struggling readers (Gaskins et al., 1991; Lovett et al., 2000; White, 2005).

- Student motivation is built by wrapping reading instruction in a rich, meaningful context, promoting peer collaboration, and providing students with a picture of how they are improving as readers (Guthrie et al., 2000; Wigfield & Guthrie, 1997).

CHAPTER 10

Developing Print Skills
With Core Reading Programs

It is mid-January, and Donna Mercy, Helen Kitty, Joan Byrd, Ed Horowitz, and Maria Gonzales (pseudonyms) are reviewing the data on their first-grade students. They teach at Smithfield Elementary School, a high-poverty, rural school with approximately equal numbers of Caucasian, Hispanic, and African American students. The school uses the Houghton Mifflin Reading (Houghton Mifflin, 2003/2005) core reading program, and these teachers have been closely following the sequence of instruction prescribed in the program. This particular core program stresses whole-group instruction, but the teachers—following the guidelines of the school district—have organized their students into three or four small groups. They each meet with their small groups for 15 to 20 minutes every day. Some of the teachers who have been around a while incorporate some of the phonics approaches they have learned from previous programs that the district has tried and abandoned, specifically blending activities and word sorts.

The focus of the discussion today is on the first graders who are not making adequate progress. In early January, all students at the primary grades are given an informal reading inventory, and it would be desirable if most students were reading at a primer level or higher at that time. The school data indicate that some significant problems exist in every classroom. Table 27 indicates the reading levels of the students in each first-grade classroom. (Please note that the data are real; only the names are pseudonyms.)

In each classroom, about a third of the students are reading below the district goal for January of the first grade—being able to read a word list and a passage at the primer level. Each of the teachers has been following the instructional sequence for phonemic awareness and phonics in the core program and has adapted the use of the core program with three guided reading groups. The goal of their meeting is to discuss and decide on some instructional approaches that can be incorporated into the core reading program to accelerate the students' progress. Various suggestions are offered. Some believe that the

Table 27. Number of Students in Each First-Grade Class at Each Reading Level in a Sample School

Level	Ms. Mercy	Ms. Kitty	Ms. Byrd	Mr. Horowitz	Ms. Gonzales
Below preprimer	3	2	2	2	1
Preprimer	6	5	4	7	5
Primer	6	5	7	5	8
First grade	4	3	3	5	3
Second grade	2	5	3	2	3

students need to read more decodable books. Others think that they need to go back to review the teaching of short vowels before moving on to long vowels. Still others think that several of these children should be referred for special education evaluations.

Given these suggestions, we use this chapter to consider what can be done to improve decoding instruction even with the new and enhanced core reading programs. In Chapter 4, we reviewed what research has to say about teaching phonemic awareness and phonics and then looked at how these components are presented in core reading programs. We found that the majority of the programs taught phonemic awareness and phonics in a fixed sequence within a whole-group format. The programs supplied a plethora of materials for teachers to use and also included some very good instructional directions. In Chapters 8 and 9, we presented some ideas on how to make effective decisions with a core reading program, organize a classroom, manage time, and differentiate instruction using small groups. This is especially important if you are using an older core program (one published before 2007) that does not provide the lesson structure for working with flexible small groups in your classroom. In this chapter, we make our suggestions more explicit and focus particularly on how to improve phonemic awareness and phonics instruction. We also discuss how to develop students' oral reading fluency. Although we began the chapter with a vignette about first-grade readers, we also consider how to assist the students in grades 3, 4, and 5 who still struggle with decoding.

In this chapter, we demonstrate how to adapt and augment a core reading program to make its prescribed phonemic awareness and phonics instruction better align with the needs of your students and with best practice. Based on our review of the research and our study of core reading programs, we crafted four specific suggestions. First, we advise delivering much of the phonics and phonemic awareness instruction to small groups, adding more teacher modeling, and giving students more opportunities to practice the phonics patterns through writing and spelling words. Second, we believe that teachers need to sharpen their coaching skills so that they can assist students in applying word identification strategies while students read. Core programs provide little direction for this crucial task, but coaching is an issue of moment-to-moment teacher support, something that cannot be scripted (Piasta et al., 2009; Taylor et al., 2000). Third, we believe that students can benefit from more activities at workstations, where pairs of students engage in reading and spelling words, often using game formats. One additional change we recommend for phonics is the addition of more decodable text. Finally, we believe that teachers need to add some fluency building routines into their classroom practices. Fluency is addressed in core programs but often lacks thorough attention, especially in the older programs. We begin by considering how to improve decoding instruction in the primary classrooms and then look at the upper grades.

What You Will Learn
- Characteristics of effective phonemic awareness and phonics instruction
- Strengths and weaknesses of phonemic awareness and phonics instruction in core reading programs
- The differences between a synthetic phonics program and decoding by analogy
- What is required to meet the needs of older students who still have decoding problems

What You Will Be Able to Do
- Apply knowledge of effective instruction to plan phonemic awareness and phonics lessons
- Adapt core reading program lessons so that phonemic awareness and phonics are taught more explicitly and efficiently
- Differentiate decoding instruction for readers with a range of abilities
- Assist older students who struggle with decoding
- Gather ideas and resources for independent activities that improve decoding and fluency

Phonemic Awareness in Core Reading Programs

Researchers have pinpointed many of the critical attributes of strong phonemic awareness instruction. First and foremost, instruction should be "direct and explicit" (NICHD, 2000). Phonemic awareness programs become explicit when they address three components (Murray, 2006):

1. Focus on individual phonemes during instruction.

2. Make the phoneme memorable by connecting it to gestures, concrete objects, or letters.

3. Teach the students to find the phoneme in the spoken word.

In addition, instruction is most effective when it takes place in kindergarten, is taught in small groups, focuses on one or two skills at a time, includes concrete markers, and links to print or letters. Instruction needs to be student-centered, active, and enjoyable, with a developmentally appropriate sequence.

Kindergarten and first-grade classroom teachers can make a number of changes to improve the phonemic awareness instruction provided in the core reading program. While keeping the whole-class lessons that the core program provides, a teacher can add additional phonemic awareness practice in small groups, especially when using an older program. Second, the teacher can alter the scope and sequence of the core program. If students still lack initial consonant awareness, the teacher can work on that skill in small groups while the whole class is blending onsets and rimes. Third, the teacher can strive to become more direct and explicit in his or her instruction. Finally, he or she can locate and develop an engaging set of practice activities that can be used at workstations.

Grouping for Instruction

Phonemic awareness is best taught in small groups, because they allow for more precise corrective feedback and facilitate student interaction, so students will hear the modeling of the teacher and the other students (Connor, Morrison, Fishman et al., 2007). You should begin by using informal assessment data to group the students by needs (e.g., phonemic awareness) or by reading level. We believe either method will be effective. Plan to spend about 10 minutes of your 20-minute small-group time working on phonics and phonemic awareness, because both are more powerful when they are taught concurrently (NICHD, 2000).

There should be three to six students in each group, with each group focusing on their particular needs. So let's examine one of the first-grade classrooms and its small groups. The 21 students in Ms. Mercy's class (see Table 27) are spread across five reading levels. It is unrealistic to have five reading groups, unless a reading or special education teacher can push in for extra support. There is a trade-off between the number of groups and the amount of time you can spend with each group. We recommend a maximum of four small groups per classroom. The lowest group would be made up of the students below pre primer level and some of the preprimer students (guided reading levels B and C). The next group would be students at the preprimer level and perhaps the lower level primer readers (guided reading levels C, D, and E). The rest of the students would comprise a group reading on grade level and another group reading above grade level. Planning for small groups takes more time and necessitates more materials than does a whole-group lesson, so effective management becomes an issue. Ms. Mercy will also have to design workstation activities where students can continue to practice their phonemic awareness skills.

Scope and Sequence

The scope and sequence of phonemic awareness skills varies from one core reading program to another. For example, Houghton Mifflin Reading (2003/2005) begins in first grade with sound awareness, review of all letter sounds, and then a review of rhyming. Next, students blend phonemes, which continues over the next three weeks. Should students lack skill in phoneme segmentation, the teacher will have to design the lesson and create the materials. In StoryTown (Harcourt, 2008), the program begins with word segmentation and sound awareness, but the second lesson switches to blending syllables, segmenting syllables, blending onsets and rimes, and segmenting onsets and rimes. In short, many skills are combined in this one lesson. The recommended sequence for phonemic awareness is rhyming, segmenting sentences, segmenting words into syllables, developing initial and final sound awareness, segmenting and blending at the onset–rime level, and segmenting and blending phonemes (Adams, Foorman, Lundberg, & Beeler, 1998). We recommend that kindergarten and first-grade teachers determine the students' current levels of skill and start instruction at that point. Several diagnostic instruments are available, including the Phonological Awareness Test (2008), and an informal assessment of phonemic awareness is available in *Phonemic Awareness for Young Children* (Adams et al., 1998). These assessments are necessary only for the students in the lowest groups. At times, teachers need to ignore the sequence of instruction in the core program to meet the needs of their students.

Direct Instruction and Modeling

Many core reading programs offer two phonemic awareness lessons each day in kindergarten and first grade. The first lesson is part of the daily warm-up and may be an extension of the morning message. The second lesson is typically longer and more complete and is part of the phonics lesson. For example, in StoryTown (2008), the first lesson, part of the warm-up, asks students to segment sentences into words, and the lesson that is part of phonics instruction asks students to blend letters into words. Both of these lessons tend to be directed to the whole class. We suggest anchoring these skills in the larger purpose of reading and writing so that phonemic awareness is more than an abstract task. We also suggest incorporating more modeling into both of these lessons. Modeling is crucial for the students to learn how to apply the letter–sound knowledge they are gaining.

Consider the example from one core program and our suggested revisions in Table 28. Adding a few sentences of introduction to the word segmentation lesson adds purpose and coherence to the activity. The students are still performing the same task, but that task is linked to the overall purpose of the larger activity,

Table 28. Modifying Phonemic Awareness Instruction

Phonological Awareness Lesson: Word Segmentation (StoryTown, Harcourt, 2008, Grade 1 Teacher's Manual, Level 1, p. T35)	Revised Phonological Awareness Lesson
Tell children that they are going to listen to sentences and tell how many words they hear. "Say this sentence: I can run fast. Say the sentence again and hold up one figure for each word."	Say, "This morning we are going to do some writing and compose our morning message. We want to make sure to write down all words in the sentence we think up. So before we begin writing, we want to practice figuring out how many words to write in a sentence. "Now let me show you how to do it. Say this sentence: The dog caught the ball. Say it again and hold up one finger for each word." Read two or three times as necessary. Continue with the lesson as printed in the core reading program.

composing a message. The lesson as rewritten gives students a context for the activity, a purpose. It is no longer an abstract concept that is unrelated to the process of writing and reading—our ultimate goal. The second change we made to the lesson was to have the teacher model the process at least two times, maybe three. This ensures that the students understand what they are to do. As the students try out the first example, the teacher can correct them. One side note: It is difficult for some young students to sequentially hold up one finger, then another, and so on; they just don't have the coordination. So we suggest that teachers have students use some kind of marker to make their phonemic awareness more concrete.

Practice and Workstation Activities

It is desirable for students to continue to practice phonemic awareness and phonics activities during their independent time. Therefore, the teacher should set up workstation activities that can be completed by students working cooperatively. Older core reading programs provide ideas for workstations, and new versions provide the materials for workstations as well. For example, StoryTown (2008) provides a Literacy Center Kit, and Treasures (Macmillan/McGraw-Hill, 2009) contains a Workstation Flip Chart for workstation activities. We believe that teachers will have to go beyond these resources to craft strong workstation activities. The following resources are recommended to find strong workstation activities that address phonemic awareness and phonics:

- *Words Their Way* (Bear et al., 2006): This text contains many ideas for sound and word sorting and for developing students' knowledge of spelling patterns. Most activities are in a game format.
- *Getting Ready to Read* (Fitzpatrick, 2002): This book contains the templates, boards, and cards for making over 50 games and activities that develop rhyming, segmenting, and blending sounds.
- Florida Center for Reading Research (www.fcrr.org/curriculum/SCAindex .shtml): This website provides many materials for phonics and phonemic awareness activities. The materials can be printed directly from the website, laminated, and used.
- Hubbard's Cupboard (hubbardscupboard.org/): This is a website with many interesting games and workstation activities for young children.
- *Phonemic Awareness for Young Children* (Adams et al., 1998): This book is a curriculum for phonemic awareness, and many of its activities can be transformed into workstation activities.

There are several guidelines that will ensure that students can complete these activities successfully. First, all workstation activities must start as small-group activities. During the teacher's guidance of the small group, the students learn the procedures and rules of the activities. Engaging in the activity under teacher supervision ensures that students can manage the tasks on their own. Second, the activities need to have an accountability component. For example, if students sort picture cards or objects by initial sounds, vowel sounds, or medial sounds, they need a way to record their results. Writing down the words or pasting the sorted pictures in appropriate columns enables the teacher to monitor the students' work. Workstations should have activities at several levels of difficulty, and the materials should be changed as students grow and as new skills or patterns must be practiced.

Let's look at how differentiation of small-group instruction might work in one first-grade teacher's classroom. Table 29 contrasts the single focus of the Houghton Mifflin Reading (2003/2005) core program with the multigroup

Table 29. Modifying Core Program Material to Include Differentiation

Day	Houghton Mifflin Reading (Houghton Mifflin, 2003/2005) Instruction	Ms. Mercy's Instruction
Monday	• Introduction to beginning sound /v/ • Phoneme identification from picture cards	• Group 1: Review of blending skill and introduction of /d/ and /s/ sounds • Group 2: Review of phoneme segmentation skill and practice with three or four phoneme words • Group 3: Decoding instruction of short *a* words • Group 4: Decoding instruction of short and long *a* words
Tuesday	• Generation of words with beginning sound /v/ • Identification of words with beginning /v/ sound in a rhyme	• Group 1: Object sorting by beginning sound, then generation of words that begin with /d/ and /s/ sounds with partner • Group 2: Partner work to find words that will trick Happy the puppet (Students say the word one phoneme at a time, and Happy has to blend it into the complete word.) • Group 3: Review of short *a* words and practice decoding from a chart • Group 4: Review of short and long *a* words and practice decoding from flashcards

focus that Ms. Mercy eventually developed. For the sake of brevity, we only included the first two days of the week. Notice that each of her four groups of students had a unique phonemic awareness task except for the better readers, because their phonemic awareness skills were well developed.

During small-group and workstation time, it is important that all students have ample opportunities to interact and be actively learning during phonemic awareness instruction. Teachers should keep informal notes on the progress of students and plan next week's lessons according to student response this week. Lessons will be more effective if they are planned around student progress, rather than following a set sequence of lessons and then reteaching what some students did not learn. Teachers should take every opportunity to incorporate written text, rhymes printed on chart paper, and language experience stories as a way for students to practice these skills in context.

In addition to modifying the phonemic awareness lesson from the core reading program, teachers can and should use writing to develop phonemic awareness. When students write, they explore the sound structure of words. A student composing a short passage about his room has to analysis or segment words. As he stretches the word *bed* in his mind, he realizes that the word has three phonemes and that the first phoneme is represented by the letter *b*. In this way, the process of writing and invented spelling encourages the student to segment words, which promotes phonemic awareness. To encourage writing in young students we suggest the following supportive ideas:

- Maintain a word wall of frequently spelled words so that students can use it when they are stuck on the spelling of a word. The words should be organized in alphabetical order.
- Model the process of segmenting words to facilitate invented spelling. This will help develop phonemic awareness skills.
- After children are finished writing, confer with them and have them read their writing back to you. Model the correct spelling of some words as a means of reinforcing letter–sound knowledge.

The most recent core reading programs and even their immediate predecessors have provided some strong instructional lessons. Nevertheless, these lessons can be modified to meet the needs of students in your classroom. We developed the following guidelines for adapting phonemic awareness lessons in core programs:

- Teach in small groups.

- Use your assessment data to determine which skills you will use for instruction in each group.

- Add more specific modeling and feedback than are present in the program's directions.

- Add think-alouds to model applying the new features or skills to text.

- Teach phonemic awareness concurrently with letters or phonics lessons.

- Provide read-alouds to tie the skills to reading.

- Adjust the pacing to reflect student skills and progress.

- Encourage writing and invented spelling.

Phonics and Word Recognition in Core Reading Programs

Phonics instruction includes four essential components. First, students must learn the features or patterns of the language and the sounds that map to those patterns. So CVC (e.g., *cat*, *pup*), CVVC (e.g., *rain*, *feel*), and the suffix *-tion* are phonics features. The sounds of individual letters, digraphs, and blends are also features. Second, students must acquire a strategy for using these. When encountering a new word, a reader has to decide how to identify it. Will the reader serially determine letter–sound associations and blend the sounds together to access the pronunciation (i.e., sound it out)? Or will the reader look for known patterns within a new word to determine its pronunciation through analogy? "I know *can* and I know *her*, so that must be *banter*." Third, the reader needs metacognitive insight to know which strategy to use and a way to evaluate if the strategy worked (Lovett et al., 2000; Sharp et al., 2008). Fourth, students need ample opportunities to practice writing and reading of connected text. It is possible for phonics instruction to be effective in several grouping arrangements: whole class, small group, and individual tutoring. For practical purposes, in most classrooms, the phonics lesson should be conducted in small groups to meet students' needs.

Phonics instruction in core reading programs varies along a number of dimensions. Some core programs provide more explicit phonics instruction than others. Generally, the phonics instruction in core reading programs has become more explicit over the last 10 years, but even in the most recent editions, we found noticeable differences in the explicitness of instruction. Core programs also differ in how well they provide directions and support for differentiated instruction. In programs created before 2007, phonics is taught almost exclusively in whole-group lessons with few alternative suggestions beyond differentiated worksheets for students who struggle (e.g., Houghton Mifflin Reading, 2003/2005; Trophies, Harcourt, 2003/2005). The newer programs provide more direction for differentiated lessons, but differences remain among the programs. For example, the small-group lessons in Treasures (2009) provide clearer direction for differentiation than do the lessons in StoryTown (2008). Finally, core programs differ in how they direct teachers and students to apply phonics skills. In some programs, application is stressed only when students read isolated words, whereas in other programs, teachers are directed to apply phonics skills when reading connected text.

Overall, in the newest programs, the instructional models are enhanced, the teachers are directed to become more explicit in identifying the phonics features, and the programs provide more materials so that students can practice making, writing, spelling, and sorting words. In a few new programs, an individual phonics lesson is provided for students reading below grade level, while the programs acknowledge that no additional phonics lesson is necessary for students reading above grade level.

Given the improvements in phonics instruction, what changes should the teacher still make to meet the needs of his or her students? We can think of five areas to consider. First, the teacher needs to know how to change the scope and sequence to meet the needs of the students. Students who are struggling to learn short vowel patterns should probably not move on to long vowels or r-controlled patterns. Second, the teacher needs a well-designed small-group instructional routine to follow each week. None of the older core programs and only two of the newer ones have presented a series of daily small-group lessons. Third, students need assistance or coaching to apply what they know about phonics to new words they encounter in context. Some core programs offer point-of-use suggestions for the teacher to model decoding strategies, but these are rare, and teachers cannot rely on these suggestions, because the decoding problems that students encounter are idiosyncratic. Fourth, many struggling readers would benefit from reading more decodable books. Although all core programs come with decodable books, more are often necessary. Finally, as with phonological awareness, students need time in workstations to practice decoding, sorting, and writing words.

Scope and Sequence

At a general level, the scope and sequence of phonics instruction is similar across core reading programs. Short vowels precede long vowels, which precede vowel digraphs and diphthongs. Maslin (2007) conducted a feature-by-feature analysis of the five best-selling first-grade programs at that time. The review showed that the order of presentation of phonics features varied greatly from program to program, as did the number of features presented overall throughout the year. A teacher needs to study the scope and sequence in the core program to determine what his or her students need. The best tool is a phonics survey to assess what features and patterns students know and what they need to know. Most core programs include a phonics survey in the assessment kit, and we recommend it be used for the struggling readers. Once the teacher has determined what patterns the students need to know, a new scope and sequence can be designed for the struggling readers. The current view argues that short vowel patterns should be mastered before long vowel patterns are taught, because a thorough study of short vowels helps students learn the alphabetic principle (Morris, Tyner, & Perney, 2000).

If some students in your class have not yet mastered one or more phonics patterns, then you will need to develop an individual scope and sequence for them. You can teach the primary phonics lesson to the whole class, but then you must develop a different scope and sequence for those students who are still struggling with decoding. A brief phonics survey, plus your own observations, will help you determine which patterns to teach in small-group instruction, but two other principles should drive the scope and sequence of instruction. First, weaker readers require considerable review support, so you will need to construct lessons that regularly review previously taught phonics patterns as you are introducing new phonics patterns. The use of a word wall, which we explain later, helps provide this regular review. So every lesson you teach should cause students to blend words with new patterns while including some review of previously taught patterns. Second, phonics lessons for the students who struggle require regular knowledge priming. They need to regularly focus on what they are doing and why they are doing it. Teachers can pose some of the following questions at the start of every small-group lesson:

- Why do we have word identification lessons?
- What strategies are we learning?

- How do we go about figuring out words that we do not know?

- What patterns have we been working on?

Small-Group Instructional Routines

Once a teacher has decided which phonics sequence to follow, he or she needs a plan for daily practice of phonics skills in small groups. As mentioned previously, some newer core reading programs provide explicit small-group phonics instruction for students reading below grade level (e.g., Treasures, 2009). Other program guides are less specific. Even Treasures gives you explicit lessons on a phonics pattern for three days of the week and then leaves it up to you to fashion the work for the rest of the week. Often, the other suggested lessons cover text features, inflected endings, and character development but not phonics (e.g., Treasures, Grade 1, Level 1).

A weekly phonics lesson plan should meet the following characteristics. First, if the small group meets with the teacher for 20 to 25 minutes, the phonics portion of the lesson should last no longer than 10 to 12 minutes, with the rest of the time devoted to text reading. Research by Connor and her colleagues (Connor, Morrison, & Underwood, 2007) indicated that very small amounts of time for phonics instruction add up to a considerable impact over a school year. A 5-minute increase in phonics instruction per day nets a total of 13 hours of phonics instruction during the school year. Teachers who added 5 minutes of phonics instruction achieved results that exceeded those of teachers who did not add the time. Figure 17 is a five-day plan for teaching phonics in small groups.

In this plan, new phonics features or patterns are introduced on Monday and then practiced with various activities for the rest of the week. The first change is to add more modeling of the strategy. Students will benefit from seeing teacher modeling not only for phoneme identification and blending, as was common in the core program lessons, but also to observe how a teacher encounters the feature in connected text and uses a strategy to figure out the word. For example, if the lesson is on short *a* families, the teacher would read a selection that contained *-at* and *-an* words, stopping each time to notice the short vowel family word and use the feature to sound out the whole word. "I see the word *hat*, and I recognize one chunk from our lesson today. I recognize the *-at* ending. Now, I think I can figure out this word if I put the sound for *h* together with the word family *-at*. The word must be *hat*. Let's reread the sentence to see if it makes sense." Teachers should use decoding strategies both with words in isolation and

Figure 17. Sample Five-Day Small-Group Phonics Instructional Plan

Day 1	Day 2	Day 3	Day 4	Day 5
• **Introduce new phonics patterns.**	• **Rapid decoding and blending practice** with one- or two-syllable words that contain the patterns taught, students might read these words on cards or play other games. • **Writing words from dictation that contain the phonics patterns**	• **Making words** Students make words using letter tiles or play games that help them use the phonics patterns. • **Spelling pattern automaticity drill** Students complete an activity to rapidly read rimes containing the new phonics patterns, then they read real words with those rimes.	• **Word sort** Students sort words by the patterns being taught and record their sorts on paper. Then, they read back what they have sorted. • **Dictated sentences** Students write dictated sentences that contain words with the phonics patterns.	• **Rapid decoding and blending practice** With one- or two-syllable words that contain the patterns taught, students might read these words on cards, dice, or other games. • **Games** Students play a dice or card game that contains the phonics patterns.

with the decodable text provided in the core program. We want the students to learn to apply the feature in real situations, so they should practice applying the feature and strategy with words from the decodable text. The teacher should also model how to spell words using this feature, saying something like,

> I have to spell the word *tan*, and I don't know that word right away, so I am going to break it into parts, because I think I do know how to spell the parts. The first sound I hear is /t/, and I know that sound is made by a *t*; the second part I've heard in our phonics lessons is in the -*an* word family, and I remember how we spell that, with -*an*.

After the patterns are introduced and modeled, the student needs to engage in a range of practice activities. Some of these activities should stress encoding or spelling. Using letter tiles, letter dice, or onset–rime cards, the students should be guided to make words. The more these activities take on the attributes of games, the more engaged the students will stay. Some small-group activities should involve students sorting words into categories of phonics features. A student might sort the words *play*, *made*, and *rain* into the long *a* category and *dice*, *rhyme*, and *time* into the long *i* category. Finally, the student should read words with the new phonics patterns. These words can be presented on flashcards or charts. Students should take turns reading the words for accuracy and speed. One useful approach is to present a series of related words, slowly changing the beginning, ending, and medial sounds. For example, read the following words: *cat*, *rat*, *sat*, *mat*, *man*, *mad*, *math*, *map*, *mop*, *met*, *mat*, *mitt*. Some research has suggested that changing the ending pattern improves students' ability to blend more than concentrating on just the beginning patterns and rimes or word families (Murray, Brabham, Villaume, & Veal, 2008).

After the daily phonics practice, the students can read a little book and apply what has been learned. Obviously, a decodable text geared to what was just taught promotes the most transfer. The core program provides decodable books for each feature or week. Teachers should align the decodable books with the features each group is learning and provide several opportunities to work with the book in small groups and at workstations. Students should read each text several times to practice decoding strategies and facilitate word recognition. One result of this change may be the need for more decodable texts than the core program provides. In the following list are suggested resources for other decodable books. In our definition of *decodable*, the text contains phonics patterns or features that have been taught in the immediately preceding lessons. We do not believe that all of the words in the decodable books need to be decodable.

- Ready Readers (Pearson, www.pearsonschool.com)
- Phonics Readers (Educational Insights, www.edin.com)
- Bob Books (Scholastic, www.scholastic.com): Available at most major bookstores or online
- Books to Remember (Flyleaf, www.flyleafpublishing.com)
- Language! (Sopris West, www.sopriswest.com)
- Reading Sparkers (Children's Research and Development, www.reading sparkers.com)
- The Wright Skills Decodable Books (The Wright Group, www.wright group.com)

• Margaret Hillert Phonics Practice Readers (Modern Curriculum, www
.pearsonlearning.com/mcschool)

By emphasizing small-group instruction and tailoring the lesson to student
needs, teachers can eliminate the need to review or reteach options or use the
practice books and worksheets found in core programs. Therefore, a teacher's
time is spent more efficiently, even though he or she needs to have different
instructional materials on hand for each group. One important note: Pacing
should remain flexible so that student progress and learning dictates how much
time a teacher spends on individual phonics features. This gives a teacher flexibility to adapt instruction to student needs (NICHD, 2000).

Word Walls

Word walls are a useful tool to assist decoding and spelling. They can be organized in three different ways, and each organizational structure has a different utility. Organizing them alphabetically promotes spelling. The students and
teachers can keep lists of words that are difficult to spell and add them to the
wall. When students write, they typically know the initial letter of the word.
They can then search the wall to see if they can find the word they are trying
to spell. Core reading programs suggest word walls of this type especially for
high-frequency words.

Word walls can be organized by spelling patterns or vowel features to assist
decoding, as in the example in Figure 18. As new phonics patterns are introduced, a keyword that stands for that pattern is added to the wall. So *can* is the
key word for *-an*, and *jet* is the key word for *-et*. When the student is reading,
the teacher can direct the student to the word wall for help. "Is there a word on

Figure 18. Word Wall of Phonics Patterns

A	E	I	O	U
can	hen	light	dot	but
fat	jet	pig	top	
make	pear	wit		
race	seed			
tap				

the wall that can help you with that difficult word?" Students then search the wall and use the words *race* and *fat* to pronounce *placemat*. The teacher should review the words regularly to make sure the students can recognize them. We return to this type of word wall later in the chapter when we discuss decoding approaches for older students.

The last type of word wall is for content vocabulary. Teachers and students can organize new content words by category. Thus, students can organize types of clouds, precipitation, and storms under weather words, for example.

Coaching Students While They Read

After students practice decoding in isolation, they need to apply what they have learned to read connected text, usually little books. While students read, it is the teacher's job to assist as they attempt to apply their new knowledge of phonics patterns and decoding strategies. The transfer of skills from the dry-erase board or letter cards on the pocket chart to connected text does not happen automatically, especially for struggling readers. Researchers have found that a critical difference in the effectiveness of teaching reading is how teachers provide feedback to students (Piasta et al., 2009; Taylor et al., 2000). More knowledgeable and effective teachers tended to focus on a "larger repertoire of decoding and word identification strategies (e.g., use of word families, analogies, and syllables)...[and] less knowledgeable teachers focus solely on teaching grapheme–phoneme correspondences and using these relations to sound out words" (Piasta et al., 2009, p. 243).

Core programs provide teachers little support in coaching or scaffolding the students' attempts to apply decoding skills. Trophies (2003/2005) includes some point-of-use suggestions on the sides of the page in the teacher's edition, as in the following example:

Use Decoding/Phonics

Point out the word highlands on the third line of page 534. Write it on the board, and ask students to read it aloud. Have a volunteer model using decoding/phonics to read highlands.

MODEL. When I see this word, I recognize that it is a compound word. I break the word into syllables between the words high and lands. I know how to pronounce each word separately, so I blend them together to read the longer word highlands. When I read highlands I pronounce it /hi` landz/. (Grade 4 Teacher's Manual, Theme 5, p. 535)

Other programs, such as Treasures (2009), StoryTown (2008), and Scott Foresman Reading (Pearson Scott Foresman, 2004), offer point-of-use suggestions for developing comprehension but not for helping students apply decoding strategies. When these programs offer point-of-use suggestions, they are often very general guidelines, such as providing corrective feedback if students have difficulty with the text.

Program writers cannot predict all of the spots where students will experience decoding difficulties, so this important task falls to the insightful, momentary decision of the teacher. Therefore, we have developed some guidelines to assist you in coaching decoding while the students are reading (see Table 30). We discuss these guidelines in what follows. We recommend that you keep a dry-erase board close at hand, so you can write down what students say, and you and the students can refer back to it after they have read. While the students are reading, your job is to provide coaching and support, guiding them to use their new decoding knowledge and strategies to figure out new words. The least help is the best help. The goal of coaching is to provide just the right amount of support, guidance, and hints for the student to figure out the word. What you say depends on the student, his or her reading ability, and the difficulty of the text. Remember that good readers think about meaning; all readers make mistakes, and good readers notice and fix some mistakes.

When a student makes a mistake during reading, deal with it right away. Guided reading should be thought of as a problem-solving process. The student is working to figure out how the letters, sounds, and spelling patterns work. Keep a stock of blank flashcards by your side or use the dry-erase board. When a student reads a word incorrectly, write what was said on the flashcard and show the student how the word in the book and the word that was read differ. Discuss the differences with the child. For example, if the text reads, "He is a cook at Denny's," and the child reads, "He is a cooker at Denny's," write the word *cooker* on the flashcard and then ask the child how it differs from the word *cook*.

After reading is a good time to extend and reinforce the strategies that the students have used. Clay (1993) called this cross-checking. Teachers should ask the students questions such as the following about how they figured out difficult words or why they made the self-corrections they did:

- "What was the new word that you read?"
- "How did you figure out the word?"
- "What parts of the word helped you figure it out?"

Table 30. Guidelines for Coaching Decoding

What the Student Does	What You Say
Miscues on a word and self-corrects.	• When the student is finished reading, praise the self-correction. Tell the student that good readers often self-correct. • Ask how he or she figured out the word. This reinforces understanding of the decoding process.
Miscues, pauses, but does not self-correct.	• When the student is finished reading at least that sentence, praise the pause. Tell the student that it is good to notice the hard words. • Say, "I think you noticed a hard word; can you figure it out?' • Ask, "Does that make sense? Does that sound right? How could you figure it out?"
Miscues and reads right on to the end of the sentence. Does not notice the miscue.	• When the student has finished his or her portion of the reading, say, "You made a mistake on that page [or in that sentence]. Can you find it?" If that does not work, try the following: • When the student is finished reading, reread the sentence as he or she did, with the miscue. Ask, "Does that make sense? Does that sound right?"
Encounters a word he or she should be able to decode, but does not attempt it or decodes it very poorly.	• If the word has patterns the student should know, coach him or her through the word. Ask, "What sound does the first letter make? What is the ending pattern?" • Try sequential blending and have the student say the first sound, the first and second sound, and so on until he or she has decoded the word. • If you are using a word wall of common phonics patterns or rimes, refer the student to it. Ask, "Is there a pattern in the word that we have been studying? Can you compare a word you know on the word wall to the word you are trying to pronounce?" • Be flexible in your approach.
Encounters a word that he or she should not be able to decode and simply cannot move on in the reading.	• Supply the word.

• "How did you know that it was _____ and not _____?" [Ask the student to compare two similar words, the one in the text and the one that was said, so the differences can be discussed.]

- "When you read [*repeat the sentence as the child read it*], what made you go back and read it again?"

If the students can talk about what they did when reading a passage, we assume they are taking some strategic control of their reading. The more strategic control a student can manage, the more easily impulsive-guessing at words can be overcome. Very early in the school year, teachers should establish a few simple rules for the students about speaking out, interrupting, and helping during guided reading. The rules might include the following:

- Sit quietly when it is not your turn to read.
- If another student has difficulty, don't offer help until you are called on.
- It is better to figure out a word than to be told a word.
- Never tell another student the word; always offer a suggestion on how to figure out the word.

Workstations

Some children who do not master phonics through whole-group and small-group instruction will benefit from additional work at a workstation. These activities should reinforce skills that the students are learning in small groups. All of what we wrote about workstations in the section discussing phonemic awareness applies here. Students need engaging activities, the activities need to be taught and practiced in small groups before being placed in workstations, and they need an accountability piece. Students need to write down the words they make and sort so that there is a record of their work at the workstation. The list of resources we gave you in the discussion of phonemic awareness will also lead you to some excellent phonics activities. We prefer activities that are games, because they promote student engagement and thinking about words. A game like go fish, concentration, or rummy can be structured so that students make and pronounce words. On some cards, you can print consonants, blends, and digraphs, and on other cards, you can print vowel patterns and rimes. The students' task is to make words according to the rules of the game. The students must pronounce the words, distinguish real words from nonsense words, and record the words they have made on a sheet of paper. Each of these games follows a different set of rules. For example, as the children play, disputes will arise about whether *flack* or *gnat* is a word. These can be resolved when the students bring their record sheets to small-group time, and the teacher will have another opportunity to develop vocabulary knowledge.

Teaching High-Frequency Words

All core reading programs address the teaching of high-frequency words in kindergarten and first and second grades. In a typical lesson, the words are presented on cards. The teacher pronounces the word, spells it, and then writes it. Students repeat what the teacher has modeled. Some programs direct the teacher to explore the phonics patterns within the words or use the high-frequency words in context, whereas others do not. Although learning high-frequency words is typically not a major problem, there are a few instructional moves that can help students do so.

First, we encourage teachers to introduce these words in context. Knowing a word means knowing something about its pronunciation or sound structure, its spelling or orthography, its grammatical function, and sometimes its meaning. Some words like *but*, *since*, and *is* have a function but not a clear semantic meaning. Cunningham (1980) advised teachers to introduce high-frequency words in a short paragraph in which the word is repeated often. This highlights the grammatical function of the word. Second, teachers should stress the sound structure of the words by segmenting them. So the word *said* might be introduced in segments using a soundboard. The student would place a chip or marker down for each sound in the word as they segment it. In the word *said* the *s* and the *d* map to their predictable sounds; only the *ai* is problematic. The teacher should point out or highlight the *ai* as the difficult part of the word. Finally, the orthography of the word can be stressed by having the students write the word or make it using letter tiles. How many of these instructional procedures need to be used depends on the needs of the students and their skill in learning particular high-frequency words.

Developing Reading Fluency

Developing oral reading fluency is an important component of reading instruction and one that is finding a more serious expression in the most recent core reading programs. Programs that date from the early 2000s have very limited suggestions for oral reading fluency. Trophies (2003/2005) suggests rereading for fluency as part of the students' independent time working with a partner or alone. Scott Foresman Reading (2004) suggests fluency as an independent activity, and Houghton Mifflin Reading (2003/2005) directs teachers to occasionally have students reread part of the student anthology in small groups. Houghton Mifflin Reading also suggests, "Model fluent reading, and coach children to read with feeling and expression" (Grade 2 Teacher's Manual, Theme 6, p. 353)—a good sentiment but not a lesson plan.

In the more current core programs, fluency instruction is featured more prominently and is a regular part of the lesson plan design. In Treasures (2009), teachers are directed to model various aspects of fluency, like using punctuation to guide intonation, or have the students engage in choral or echo reading with the teacher. Fluency is also incorporated into the small-group lessons, but more so for the below-level and ELL learners than for the above- or on-level students. In the small-group lessons, students might be asked to echo read the leveled books or engage in repeated readings. In StoryTown (2008), teachers are directed to model fluency in the whole-group lesson on phrasing and intonation and then have students reread the text with a partner or in small groups for fluency. Activities like Readers Theatre are also suggested for independent practice.

Most children become fluent readers by reading often from a wide range of books (Cunningham & Stanovich, 1998; Foorman et al., 2006). Do core reading programs provide enough text for students to become fluent readers? Brenner and Hiebert (2010) examined this question by studying how much there was to read in third-grade core reading programs from six major publishers. They focused their study on borderline readers who had oral reading fluency skills at the 25th percentile or an oral reading rate of 62 words correct per minute. These students would be able to read all of the words in the core reading program by spending 10 to 24 minutes per day on reading, depending on the program and the components of the program that are used. Even at 24 minutes of reading a day, this is substantially less than the 45 minutes of reading recommended by some experts (Allington, 2001; Fisher & Ivey, 2006). So the first fix to improve oral reading fluency is to have students read extensively outside the core reading program.

Rasinski (2003) offered four general methods for promoting oral reading fluency in the classroom:

1. Read-alouds
2. Supported reading
3. Repeated reading
4. Performance reading

One of the easiest and most valuable activities for developing oral reading fluency is a daily read-aloud session by the teacher. Because young students do not often read with prosody, they benefit greatly from hearing fluent, expressive reading from an adult (Rasinski, 2003). The teacher serves as the model of mature reading. By listening to the teacher, students begin to realize that reading fluently is not merely about reading quickly. They experience an adult reading with prosody and enjoyment, which may help them see the power of words and language.

Most of Rasinski's (2003) other suggestions can be incorporated into a fluency workstation. Note that fluency practice is not meant for all students. Students who are making strong progress and read fluently with good comprehension do not need to engage in the repetitive practice of many fluency activities—they just need to read. Teacher-assisted fluency work can be incorporated into small-group instruction. When a student plods through a page, the teacher might simply ask the student to reread it for greater expression or pace, as the research has suggested (Kuhn & Stahl, 2003). At times it is useful to briefly model competent oral fluency before the student rereads the passage. This practice and others like echo and choral reading can be beneficial.

Fluency should be made part of the students' regular workstation activities, especially in second grade, the prime time for fluency development (Kuhn & Stahl, 2003). All fluency activities have three components: modeling of fluent reading, repetitive practice, and a goal. So in partner reading the teacher models fluent reading, students partner up to repeatedly read a selection, and then students share their accomplishments with the class or their small groups. Several kinds of independent activities can be used, such as the following:

- Students can engage in partner reading or timed readings of phrases, short texts, or excerpts from longer texts (see Samuels, 1997).

- Students can work on Readers Theatre. Two or three students learn a short script with each one taking a part. At the end of the week, they present their play. (See www.teachingheart.net/readerstheater.htm or www.aaronshep .com/rt/RTE.htm for Readers Theatre resources.)

- Students can read more fiction or nonfiction books during the week (Kuhn, 2004).

- Consider one of the published fluency programs like QuickReads (Hiebert, 2002–2005) or Read Naturally (www.readnaturally.com).

Decoding Instruction in the Upper Grades

Despite a teacher's best intentions and best efforts, some children in the upper grades still have decoding problems. They may be reading a year or more below grade level, and they still may struggle to decode words. These children have a range of decoding problems. Students with the most severe problems struggle with regular short and long vowel words, although others only have problems with multisyllable words. Lacking effective decoding skills, these students cannot teach themselves new words, and their progress in learning to read stagnates. Without some intervention, these problems will persist and set in place a downward spiral of learned helplessness, causing students to give up and read less (Stanovich, 1986). The research has suggested that these students' reading can improve with the proper intervention (Lovett et al., 2000; Wanzek & Vaughn, 2007). A reading or special education teacher can provide that assistance, but the regular classroom teacher must be part of the help.

Core reading programs provide a range of lessons on decoding in the upper grades. In the older core reading programs, each weekly five-day lesson has a decoding lesson built in covering some aspect of word study, such as short vowels, long vowels, compound words, or structural analysis. Often these decoding or phonics lessons are linked to the spelling patterns of the week. The sequence of these skills is traditional, moving from short to long to irregular vowel patterns and finally to multisyllable words (e.g., Houghton Mifflin Reading, 2003). StoryTown (2008) also includes one decoding lesson each week in the upper grades. Harcourt created an intervention program for struggling readers to accompany StoryTown, and these lessons follow a more traditional developmental sequence. Last, Treasures (2009) provides more complete decoding lessons as part of their differentiation guidelines. For students reading below grade level (called the Approaching Level Option), a lesson is provided each week for single- and multisyllable words, plus some independent practice activities such as word hunt and extra but short pieces of decodable text. These lessons do not provide a full week of decoding instruction and practice.

The problem with these lessons is twofold. First, the lesson may not match the needs of the students. Teachers will need a diagnostic test or phonics survey to determine student needs. With the results of such a survey, teachers can match the students' needs to the phonics patterns or features. Current core programs are not structured to help teachers link student decoding needs to the appropriate lessons, but most core programs supply a phonics survey. The second problem with the decoding instruction provided for struggling readers in the upper grades is the lack of engaging practice and review. Publishers simply do not have the space to provide a full decoding curriculum for upper-grade students within the confines of a core program, and not all schools will want to purchase their accompanying intervention programs. Given these problems, let's examine what can be done to augment decoding instruction for upper elementary students.

Decoding by analogy seems like the preferred method for improving the decoding skills of students in the upper grades. As far as we know, no core program includes this approach in their materials, yet there has been significant research support for it (Gaskins et al., 1989–2000; Lovett et al., 2000; White, 2005). In these research programs, decoding by analogy has improved reading skills for students in grades 2 through 6. The published version of this approach is the Benchmark Word Detectives Program (Gaskins et al., 1989–2000), which is a systematic curriculum for teaching decoding by analogy.

In decoding by analogy, the teacher introduces three to five keywords each week that represent basic spelling patterns. In a typical week, the student might learn *pl<u>ace</u>*, *c<u>an</u>*, *l<u>ike</u>*, and *w<u>ink</u>*. The underlined portion of each word is the spelling pattern, the rime. These words are fully analyzed, meaning they are segmented and their sound–symbol correspondences are explored. The words are placed on a word wall organized by vowel pattern (see the word wall section earlier in the chapter). Each day the students practice using the keywords to decode and spell new words with the same spelling pattern. These new words might be one-, two-, or three-syllable words. The activities are fast paced, game-like, and designed to capture the students' attention. The decoding by analogy strategy and the word wall are then used to decode words as the students read. The students are continually reminded of the process, and these metacognitive cues help the students apply what they have learned.

Decoding by analogy has several attributes that may explain its success with older readers. First, the phonics features are presented as keywords that are placed on a word wall. Thus, *clock* is the keyword for the *-ock* pattern. Students learn to decode by the pattern, not by the isolated vowel sound, and this is in keeping with the developmental nature of word identification (Ehri, 1991). If you know *clock* and *made*, you might be able to figure out the word *blockade*. The word wall makes these keywords salient and memorable. Second, decoding by analogy allows students to fairly quickly access multisyllable words, as the above example illustrates. This process appeals to the older reader in two ways.

First, he or she has power or control over the language. If readers can figure out long words, they may not feel as helpless, and their self-confidence will grow. Second, decoding by analogy does not look like traditional synthetic phonics, and its novelty may be another source of motivation.

Decoding by analogy also places a premium on metacognition. Some students struggle with decoding not because they lack knowledge of the strategies but because they fail to implement the strategies they know. In decoding by analogy, the student is continually reminded to think about how to decode a word. Would it help to take off the prefixes and suffixes, segment or chunk the word, or look for parts of spelling patterns that are known? Thinking about the process helps students implement it. In this short discussion, we cannot present all the details of decoding by analogy, so we suggest you look to the Benchmark Word Detectives (Gaskins et al., 1989–2000) Program or articles that explain the process well (e.g., Gaskins et al., 1991).

PUTTING IT ALL TOGETHER

Over the last two generations of core reading programs, there has been a steady improvement in the teaching of phonemic awareness and phonics, two essential components of effective reading (NICHD, 2000). Research has consistently demonstrated that phonemic awareness and phonics instruction are necessary, and the instructional guidelines for teaching them successfully are well understood (NICHD, 2000). Core programs have also made significant strides in improving the explicitness of fluency and decoding instruction. Yet, despite this progress, teachers can still improve on what core programs provide, most strikingly for the older students who still struggle. Teachers can augment the instruction provided in core programs in a number of ways. They can shift some of the decoding instruction away from the whole group and into small groups, which will provide for greater differentiation. Teachers can alter the scope and sequence for struggling readers and advanced readers to teach the phonics patterns and skills they need. Teachers can improve their coaching skills while students read, and in so doing, guide students to use the decoding strategies they have been taught. As teachers work with a core program, they should keep the following suggestions in mind:

(continued)

PUTTING IT ALL TOGETHER *(cont'd)*

- Phonemic awareness and phonics instruction should be part of an overall literacy lesson; the purpose for this instruction is skilled reading.
- Instruction should be explicit with plenty of opportunities for students to practice.
- The pacing of the lessons should be flexible and decided by student progress.
- Small groups better facilitate phonemic awareness and phonics instruction, allowing for differentiated instruction.
- Strategies for applying the new knowledge to text should be modeled, showing decoding and how to spell words, and teachers should think aloud as they do so.
- Teachers are teaching children and should keep the lessons active, help them enjoy their discoveries about words, and revel in the connections they make between the lessons and the texts.
- Assessment data should be used to determine which features to teach for each group and to adjust pacing accordingly.
- Decodable books should be used throughout instruction in a feature, especially for struggling readers.
- Teachers should add activities for each group into the workstations and align them with their instruction.
- More coaching and fluency should be added to daily instruction.
- Older struggling readers will benefit from a decoding by analogy approach.

CHAPTER 11

Developing Comprehension With Core Reading Programs

Bethany, Mary, Earl, and Courtney (pseudonyms)—all fifth-grade teachers—are working with their reading coach and the principal as they think through the comprehension problems of their students. They all work in a school district and state that lives or dies by end-of-year high-stakes assessments. Their school is located in a rural area suffering from the economic decline. Many children come from supportive homes, but unfortunately the parents' priorities are driven by economic need, and they have limited time to enrich the academic lives of their children. To monitor students' progress, the district administers regular benchmark assessments that mimic the state assessment. The teachers have done an item analysis of the most recent benchmark assessment administered in late January. The results show that 36% of their students are having difficulty with making inferences, determining the author's purpose, determining main idea, and summarizing. Additionally, the students scored much better when reading fiction than nonfiction.

These results are troubling for a number of reasons. First, the state and the No Child Left Behind Act of 2001 require that 85% of the students pass the state assessment to meet Adequate Yearly Progress, up from 81% the year before. Second, the district curriculum requires that the teachers closely follow the core reading program and the pacing guide that the district has constructed. Third, teachers have learned after several years of working with this core program that comprehension is poorly addressed and some skills in particular receive only cursory attention. The instruction lacks the explicitness that the students need, and more practice is required than the program provides. Given these problems, the teachers, their coach, and the principal must determine how to design comprehension instruction for the next several months so that all students will succeed.

Core reading programs provide a structure for organizing instruction by time, texts, and teaching strategies. Each program is divided into themes and lessons within the themes. In each theme, there are multiple reading selections, knowledge to be developed about concepts and text, skills and strategies to be taught, and instructional activities. Although much of what a core program provides is useful, many core programs can and should be modified. In Chapter 5, we highlighted what we believe to be four critical problems in the comprehension instruction of core reading programs. Even absent these problems, core programs can be modified to meet the needs of your students, your state or district curricular objectives, and what the research literature most currently suggests about teaching reading comprehension.

There are five important changes that will make your comprehension instruction more effective. These suggestions are based on the problems we outlined in Chapter 5 and are based on our research (Dewitz et al., 2009):

1. Build broader and deeper prior knowledge than your core program recommends.

2. Improve vocabulary instruction by customizing word selection and instruction to match the needs of your students.

3. Modify the scope and sequence of comprehension skills and strategy instruction to match the students' needs and the district or state guidelines.

4. Improve the explicitness of instruction with a stronger focus on metacognition; stress how, when, and why strategies should be taught.

5. Redesign guided practice so that your instruction ensures extensive practice with skills and strategies using real texts.

In this chapter, we walk teachers through these changes and give examples of how to make them mesh with a core program. After reading this chapter, teachers will know more about their core program and be able to use it more effectively.

What You Will Learn

• The characteristics of effective comprehension strategy instruction

• How core reading programs provide inadequate instruction for introducing comprehension skills and strategies

• How core reading programs do not guide students to use reading strategies independently

• The repetitive nature of comprehension instruction that may not lead to growing expertise as a reader

What You Will Be Able to Do

- Apply new ideas for developing the knowledge base of your students so that comprehension is enhanced
- Customize vocabulary instruction so that you build more word knowledge and students retain it longer
- Modify a comprehension lesson in a core program so that skills and strategies are taught with greater explicitness and clarity
- Change the guided reading portion of a lesson in a core reading program so that students more readily acquire the skills and begin to use them independently

Knowledge and Vocabulary Development

Being a good reader is the product of many factors. A good reader brings to the page fluent word identification skills, a set of cognitive and metacognitive strategies, the motivation to conscientiously pursue meaning, and the knowledge that is essential for understanding what is read. Core programs address all of these issues, but as suggested in Chapter 5, they could do a better job of developing students' knowledge before they read. As the teacher, you need to decide if the knowledge development part of the lesson addresses the ideas and concepts that are necessary for each selection and for your particular students. Core programs are written for a very general audience, and it is safe to say that the authors of the program did not have your students in mind. It is up to you to judge whether the program develops or teaches the knowledge necessary for your students. Next, you need to refocus knowledge development and create a way to build knowledge across reading selections. The knowledge a student gains reading the first selection of a unit should help him or her comprehend the next selection, and so on. As we illustrated in Chapter 5, the themes in a core program are broad and vague and do not lead to a steady development of knowledge. We believe that teachers can alter how these themes and selections are used (Dewitz et al., 2008; Walsh, 2003).

Types of Knowledge

Readers draw on four types of knowledge to build their understanding: word, experiential, conceptual, and genre or text structure. First, word knowledge or vocabulary is essential for comprehension and may explain half or more of a reader's comprehension ability. Although all core programs introduce new vocabulary words prior to reading a story, these vocabulary lessons should be customized by adding words when necessary, deleting words students already know, and always providing rich explanations for new words (Ryder & Graves, 1994). Second, experiential knowledge is the narrative of our lives and the sum of all the human interactions we have experienced. From these experiences, we learn about human motives, feelings, traits, responses, and reactions. Our personal lives teach us about love, justice, hatred, disappointment, and joy. During the reading of fiction in particular, but also biography and history, we draw on these experiences to understand the themes, problems, and characters in our reading. All students bring some experiential knowledge to the page. Others require that knowledge be fleshed out or highlighted before they begin to read.

The third type of knowledge that the reader brings to the page revolves around concepts and facts. Readers know things about weather, plants, animals, explorers, wars, and political leaders. They use this information to make sense of the text. When reading science, history, geography, or mathematics, the reader must make connections between what he or she knows and what the author has written. There is both psychological and neurological evidence that the memory for experiences is different and perhaps stored in a different part of the brain from the memory for concepts, ideas, and facts (Sacks, 2007).

Fourth, readers need knowledge of genre and text structure. Literary works can be classified into a limited number of categories or genres, with each characterizing the structure, elements, and purpose of the genre. Once a reader notes that the text is fantasy not realistic fiction, the approach and purpose of the reader is determined. With fantasy, it is best to kick back and let yourself loose in a new and wonderful world, whereas realistic fiction may cause you to relate personal experiences to the text and use the experiences of the character to reflect on your own life.

Text structure knowledge, a characteristic of genre, also enables comprehension. When a reader understands how a story is organized, he or she is better able to make predictions, focus on important story elements, and retain what they have read. In a similar fashion, knowledge of text structure and, in particular, the words that signal text structure help a reader follow and understand the argument in informational text. When a reader focuses on words like *because, since, thus,* and *so,* then he or she is working through the causal arguments of the writer and developing a coherent understanding of the text. Knowing that writers of informational text draw on multiple structures (e.g., cause and effect, compare and contrast, problem and solution, chronology, description) and becoming aware of the words that signal these structures help the reader understand the developing ideas.

Teaching Vocabulary

Vocabulary instruction is about more than teaching the meanings of specific words. Vocabulary develops because students live in a literary-rich environment surrounded by books, stimulating talk, and oral language experiences. They are read to from the best children's literature and appreciate the rich language that these writers can craft. Through listening, reading, and discussing, students become conscious of and interested in words. The creation of this literary-rich environment is up to the teacher, and books by Graves (2006) and Stahl and Nagy (2006) can be of considerable help.

Core programs provide the rudiments of a complete vocabulary program, but many important pieces are missing. Many vocabulary experts have argued that the average elementary school student needs to learn 2,000 to 4,000 words a year. Even the most conservative estimate puts the total at 20,000 words during the elementary school years (Nagy & Herman, 1987). Most of this vocabulary growth is incidental through listening and reading. However, the typical core program directly teaches only about 250 to 300 words a year, so much more needs to be done to build word knowledge than what the core program prescribes.

The core programs help teachers and students in two distinct ways. First, core programs provide instruction for teaching individual words. Each reading selection is preceded by seven to 10 vocabulary words with lessons on teaching these words to the students. These vocabulary lessons and those that focus on word learning strategies can and should be modified to meet the needs of students in each classroom. Second, core programs provide a curriculum and lessons for teaching word learning strategies: inferring word meaning from context cues, using the dictionary, and using prefixes, suffixes, and roots to determine a word's meaning. We focus more of our discussion on the first task, teaching individual words. There are two central questions about vocabulary instruction: what words to teach and how to teach them. The second question provides a relatively easy answer, but the first is more troubling.

Selecting Vocabulary Words. Knowing which words to teach involves comprehending the passage, gauging the importance of the words in that passage, and understanding the students' likely knowledge of those words. Core programs select six to eight words for each passage and provide teachers with a lesson plan and supporting materials to teach these words. Although we can debate the wisdom core programs use in selecting words, we cannot debate the fact that the same vocabulary lesson will not work for all students. Vocabulary instruction needs to be tailored to the needs and knowledge of the students. So first we offer the following questions from Graves (2006, p. 68) with our suggestions for selecting vocabulary words.

- Is understanding the word important to understanding the selection in which it appears? You need to read the selection to decide if the words identified for instruction in the teacher's edition are actually necessary for understanding the selection. Your professional judgment is an important check on the decisions of the program developers who don't know your students.

- Are students able to use context or structural-analysis skills to discover the word's meaning? If they can do so, then do not preteach these words; leave opportunities for students to practice these skills as they read.

- Can working with this word be useful in furthering students' context, structural-analysis, or dictionary skills? Examine the words the program developers have selected to consider whether these and other words provide opportunity to apply word learning strategies.

- How useful is the word outside the reading selection currently being taught? Answering this question involves considerable professional judgment and requires knowing words and knowing your students.

Modifying vocabulary lessons in core programs comes with some cost. By changing the words you will teach, you will make some of the scripted lessons and independent activities less functional. That leaves you with the problem of supplementing and redesigning the students' independent vocabulary practice. We think the trade-off is worth it for your students.

Teaching the Words. To teach words well, you must go beyond the activities suggested in your core program. Our review of vocabulary instruction in core programs suggests that three critical elements of instruction are missing. First, these programs do not encourage students to be actively involved with a word's meaning. When following the suggested instructional methods in core programs, students do not engage in deep processing of a word's meaning by considering examples or nonexamples of a word or by comparing a new word to a similar and known cognate. For example, when Houghton Mifflin Reading (Houghton Mifflin, 2003/2005) introduces the word *astonished,* students are not asked to list things that might or might not astonish them or to compare *astonished* to *amazed, surprised,* or *bored.* Second, the amount of discussion that a word receives is minimal. Core programs ask teachers to discuss a word but do not offer models of these rich discussions. Third, core programs do not provide enough engagement with words over the full course of a week's lesson to ensure that the words are internalized and become part of the students' reading and writing vocabularies. Let's consider how a teacher might augment the vocabulary instruction in a core program.

We chose one lesson from the third-grade Trophies (Harcourt, 2003/2005) program. The anthology selection is *Lon Po Po* by Ed Young (1978), a Chinese folk tale that is a very close parallel to "Little Red Riding Hood." The teacher's edition has the teacher instruct the students in the following words: *tender, brittle, embraced, dusk, latch, cunning, delighted.* The key vocabulary words are introduced in a short selection that precedes the reading of *Lon Po Po.* The instruction provided by the teacher's edition for introducing the vocabulary is provided in part in Figure 19.

If students do not learn these word meanings, the teacher may extend the instruction by consulting the recommendations of Graves (2006) and Beck et al. (2002). We also wanted to involve students more actively in the lesson and the discussion. In the left column of Figure 19 are the vocabulary teaching suggestions from the core reading program, and on the right is the small text that the students read. Consider the following dialogue between a teacher and students, expanding on what the core program recommended:

Teacher: One of our new words is *tender.* Please read what the hens had to say on page 94. [*Students read the paragraph.*] Can someone explain what he or she thinks *tender* means based on what Sam just read?

Student 1: Something that is soft and easy to chew.

Teacher: Yes, can you think of something that is tender?

Student 2: Ice cream.

Student 3: A banana.

Figure 19. Grade 3 Vocabulary Lesson From a Core Reading Program

Teaching Suggestions	Text That Students Will Read
Apply Strategies Read aloud the first paragraph on page 94. Then ask students to read the remaining text silently. Remind them to apply the strategy of breaking words into syllables.	**Vocabulary Power** Say, "Do you know the story 'Little Red Riding Hood'? If you do, you might remember that a wolf pretended to be Red Riding Hood's grandmother. There are many stories in which one character tries to trick another."
Extend Word Knowledge **Practice other vocabulary strategies.** Have students answer the questions below with sentences that show what the vocabulary words mean. MEANINGFUL SENTENCES • What foods do you like that are *tender*? EXAMPLE • How does knowing that the Old French word *brace* means *arm* help you understand the word *embrace*? WORD ORIGINS • What is something that is *brittle*? EXAMPLE • How are dawn and *dusk* alike? How are they different? COMPARE/CONTRAST	HENS: We had such a good dinner. We had **tender** grain, soft and easy to chew. We had **brittle** seeds that broke easily and snapped. We **embraced** each other in good-night hugs. Now it's **dusk**. It will soon be night, so it's time for us to go to bed. FOX: Sisters! It's your sister Henrietta. I've come to visit. Why did you latch the door? Please unhook the **latch** and open the door.

Note. From Trophies, On Your Mark, Harcourt, 2003/2005, Grade 3 Teacher's Manual, Theme 1, pp. 94–95. Copyright © by Harcourt, Inc. All rights reserved. Reproduced by permission of the publisher, Houghton Mifflin Harcourt Publishing Company.

Teacher: Yes, those are soft, but we usually use the word *tender* when we mean a food that can be hard or tough but this time isn't, like turkey. It can be tender or tough. Can you think of something that is sometimes tender but often is not?

Student 4:   A steak or a pork chop.

Teacher: Can you think of something that is never tender?

Student 1:   An old shoe or a Frisbee.

Teacher: John, can you use the word in a sentence?

Student 5:   Mom cooked the beans, so they were nice and tender.

Teacher: Good use of the word. Can someone use the word in a way that does not involve food? [*Students do not respond.*] *Tender* can also mean someone who has a kind heart, someone who cannot hurt another. So if you treat a young child in a kind way, you are being tender. Sometimes a person can be tender, but here we don't mean they are easy to chew.

We added several ideas to the discussion of this word and went beyond what the core program recommended. As new words are introduced, we first want teachers to explain the meanings clearly. An excellent resource for clear definitions is the online Cobuild dictionary (www.englishonline.co.uk/englishnon/language/dictionary/) or any other dictionary. Your instructional goal is to explain word meanings clearly and involve the students actively in the discussion. In this example, note how the students and the teacher did the following:

- Develop their examples and nonexamples of the words
- Try out the words orally in sentences
- Explore and share alternate or multiple meanings of the word
- Compare the new word to similar or synonymous words

The teaching of vocabulary is also the development of prior knowledge. Although core programs present these two activities as separate, they can be viewed as one in the same. For example, two core programs use the story *Grandfather's Journey* by Allen Say (1993). When students learn and discuss the meanings of the vocabulary words—*journey*, *homeland*, *longed*, *bewildered*, and *marveled*—they also learn about the concepts that are essential to understanding the story in *Grandfather's Journey*. We return to the problem of developing prior knowledge in the next section of this chapter. Before we do, we want to consider one other aspect of vocabulary development, word learning strategies.

All core programs provide lessons so that students learn to use context cues, word parts (e.g., prefixes, suffixes, word roots), and dictionaries as tools for learning the meanings of new words. They do so by introducing specific strategies for using these word learning tools. Often these strategies are incomplete and require more modeling than the core programs provide. Later in this chapter, we provide some guidelines on how to improve strategy instruction. What we write about teaching comprehension strategies will be equally true of word learning strategies. It is important for teachers to model strategies more often than core programs suggest and be much more specific in how to apply the strategies than core programs indicate.

Developing Prior Knowledge

Our review of comprehension instruction in core programs (see Chapter 5) suggests that often the teacher's edition does not develop the knowledge necessary to comprehend the selection before students read, and it is up to the teacher to build that knowledge. Students differ in what they know, and core reading programs cannot anticipate all of this variation. Our review of core programs further suggests that what students learn from one passage does not necessarily help them understand the next selection. Often the units and themes in core reading programs are vague (e.g., good neighbors, seeing is believing, heritage), but have some overarching yet vague ideas that tie them together (Walsh, 2003). These ideas do not build from one selection to another. However, adding a few additional activities to the unit will help students build knowledge and improve comprehension.

Let's look at a third-grade unit, Nature Links: Nature Can Give Us New Ideas, from the Macmillan/McGraw-Hill Reading (Macmillan/McGraw-Hill, 2003/2005) program (see Table 31). This unit has the general theme of nature, and the individual selections focus on neighbors building a community garden, the formation of the earth, an Indian legend on how animals help man, and spiders. Getting students from the building of a city garden to the formation of

Table 31. Selections, Genres, and Skills Taught in One Third-Grade Reading Unit

	Nature Links: Nature Can Give Us New Ideas				
	Selection 1	Selection 2	Selection 3	Selection 4	Selection 5
Title of selection	*City Green*	"The Sun, Wind, and Rain"	"Dream Wolf"	"Spiders at Work"	"Web Wonders"
Genre	Realistic fiction	Mixed genre	Folk tale	Information	Information
Skills and strategies	• Cause and effect • Drawing conclusions	• Compare and contrast • Drawing conclusions	• Cause and effect • Compare and contrast	• Important and unimportant information • Drawing conclusions	• Compare and contrast • Important and unimportant information

Note. From Macmillan/McGraw-Hill Reading, Macmillan/McGraw-Hill, 2003/2005, Grade 3 Teacher's Manual, Theme 2.

the earth and then on to spiders are big leaps, but a new focus for the unit can help. Introducing the unit by discussing the concepts of environment and habitat can help students build knowledge as they explore how environments were originally formed and then are shaped. Ultimately, the environment shapes human and animal existence. This modified approach gives the unit a more focused purpose than its original title—Nature Links: Nature Can Give Us New Ideas—would suggest. Three activities will help students develop knowledge, which in turn will improve comprehension. These three activities are the use of a concept board to record what has been learned and pose questions about what students would like to learn, employment of an expanded set of read-alouds to introduce each new selection, and revision of the knowledge to be developed before the students read each anthology selection. Comprehension strategies are better learned when embedded in rich, meaningful units of study (Guthrie et al., 1998), and this is our goal. The unit opener in the teacher's edition suggests ways to introduce the theme, but often these activities are ignored by teachers (Barr & Sadow, 1989; Durkin, 1984).

As you begin each unit in your core program, identify one or two themes that you and your students can study and discuss as you read the selections in the unit. Feel free to add additional reading selections for your students. Build a concept board of ideas learned and questions posed during the reading of the unit. As each selection is read, you should devote some time to adding information to the concept board and answering questions from the students. This concept board begins with a few ideas from the first selection and then grows over time. The board's organization changes as new ideas are introduced. Organizing ideas helps the students develop concepts. Let's see how this works.

Read-Alouds. The third-grade unit, Nature Links, can be used to develop the concepts of environment and habitat. A read-aloud can help develop these concepts. In the section that follows, we provide guidelines for an effective read-aloud. *City Green* (DiSalvo-Ryan, 1994), the first story in the unit, tells the story of many people working to improve a vacant lot by creating a public garden and one curmudgeon opposing it. The story has limited relevance to students in rural or suburban areas. The teacher's edition asks that the teacher and the students discuss various community projects, but neglects the larger issues of environmental problems, something that all children experience. By reading a book like *Recycle! A Handbook for Kids* (Gibbons, 1992) or *Where Does the Garbage Go?* (Showers, 1994) to the students, the anthology selection can be read in the larger context of environmental problems, and thus the selection has a more relevant content focus.

An effective read-aloud can boost the students' knowledge and skills in a number of ways. Read the book *Recycle!* (Gibbons, 1992) and use the following general read-aloud guidelines:

- Introduce and preview the book. Discuss the author, especially if he or she is well known with a large body of work that the students will want to read.

- Establish a purpose for reading the book. If it is informational, the purpose is to build knowledge. If the book is fiction, state a purpose that foreshadows the theme or some issue of text structure.

- Read the book and stop briefly to clarify difficult words or restate important ideas. Students will most likely interrupt, question, and seek clarification more often with a nonfiction read-aloud than with a fiction one.

- You may want to use these stopping points to model reading strategies: asking a question, making an inference, or summarizing, but this should be done only in the service of building knowledge.

- When the read-aloud is completed, summarize the selection and list on sticky notes what you and the students have learned. This is especially useful for nonfiction.

After the *Recycle!* read-aloud, you might record the ideas shown in Figure 20 on your concept board.

Figure 20. A Beginning Concept Map for a Reading Unit on Nature and the Environment

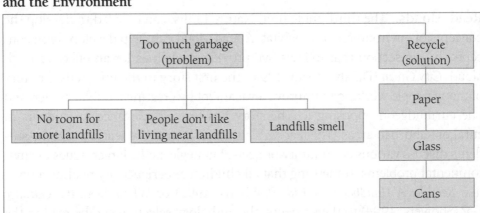

Developing Knowledge of the Anthology Selection. Next, read each selection from the core reading program closely to determine which concepts in the selection your students will already know as part of their prior knowledge and which ideas must be developed before they read. As our research has suggested (Dewitz et al., 2008, 2009), core programs often underestimate the needs of your students and do not develop the knowledge necessary to comprehend the passage. One good example involves a third-grade story about the Pony Express. The background knowledge development portion of the lesson directs the teacher to review the multiple ways that mail is transported. At the very end of the passage, the students are confronted with the following sentence: "The Pony Express lasted for only one and a half years until the transcontinental telegraph was complete" (Macmillan/McGraw-Hill Reading, 2003/2005, Grade 2, p. 327). Because no background knowledge had been developed for the words *transcontinental* or *telegraph*, all the students are unable to answer why the Pony Express came to a quick end.

The first selection in the Macmillan/McGraw-Hill Reading program, *City Green* (DiSalvo-Ryan, 1994), demands the development of knowledge beyond that recommended in the teacher's manual. This realistic story tells about an old building being torn down, leaving an unsightly vacant lot. The local citizens must deal with the city bureaucracy and an uncooperative curmudgeon before they can turn the lot into a multiuse park and garden. The teacher's manual asks teachers to discuss different community projects, but neglects some basic concepts like urban renewal, city government, and leases, without which students' comprehension could be undermined, especially those living in rural areas. The simplest and most direct way to deal with this problem is to tell students what they need to know. Discuss life in a deteriorating inner city and what can be done with old abandoned buildings. Lecturing is quick and direct, especially if it can be augmented with video, the Internet, pictures, and picture books.

After the first anthology selection is read, update the concept board by adding new ideas and changing the organization of those ideas. Students can also pose new questions, which may lead to reading other selections within and outside the core program. The updated concept board might now be organized as illustrated in Figure 21.

Focus on Genre. The third approach for developing students' knowledge is maintaining a continual focus on genre. As we outlined in Chapter 5, knowledge of genre and text structures helps a reader set a purpose for reading, follow

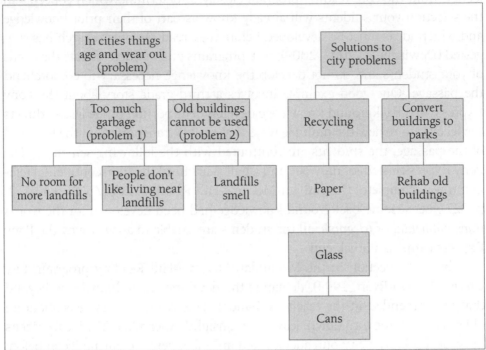

the arguments of an author, and focus on the important ideas. Create a genre chart in your room and update it regularly. The chart should be organized as in Figure 22. The Genre column identifies the different genres the students will read. The Purpose column details the purposes for reading the genre. Remember that most texts have more than one purpose, and even informative text should be entertaining. The Characteristics column lists the attributes of the genre, focusing on structure and elements of language. As you and your students read additional selections, you will probably add to the characteristics of each genre. Finally, in the Examples column, write the titles of books and selections the class members have read or are reading.

Start the genre chart when you read the first two selections in the class and explain to the students that you will keep track of what is read and the genre of each selection and add that information to the chart. At the beginning of the year, start the discussion of genre by focusing on two selections representing contrasting genres, for example, fantasy and information. Such a contrast

Figure 22. A Sample Genre Chart

Genre	Purpose	Characteristics	Examples
Realistic fiction	To entertain; to learn more about people and real-life problems	Real people with real problems; it could be true but isn't	*City Green*
Mixed	To convey information in an entertaining format	Narrative story within a piece of information	"The Sun, the Wind, and the Rain"
Folk tale	To entertain; to convey a moral or purpose	Human or animal interactions	"Dream Wolf"
Information	To inform; to teach about new ideas	Science or social studies topics	"Spiders at Work," "Web Wonders"

makes it very clear how two pieces of literature differ. Over time, you will deal with finer distinctions among genres. First, identify the genres of the texts and with the students determine the purpose for reading them. Then, list some of their characteristics. Remember that the genre chart will grow and change as you explore more selections. As students understand genre better, the use of the chart can be discontinued but returned to as needed.

To sum up, students need considerable prior knowledge to comprehend what they read. Using core programs wisely demands that teachers frequently add to the students' store of knowledge, going above and beyond what the core program prescribes. This can be done by focusing on concepts and ideas that the core programs do not target, by adding additional read-alouds to the reading program, by building a concept wall to track what students have learned, and by maintaining a steady focus on genre.

Improving Comprehension Strategy Instruction

Core reading programs devote considerable time and attention to the teaching of comprehension skills and strategies—indeed this might be the major instructional goal of core programs, especially in the upper grades. In Chapter 5, we reviewed these core programs and highlighted three major problems in addition to a lack of scaffolding for vocabulary and development. First, core programs, for a variety of reasons, teach too many skills and strategies. Second, when these skills or strategies are first introduced, the instruction lacks the explicitness necessary for students to understand how and when to use the strategy. Third, core programs do not provide enough practice with these skills and strategies and do not ensure that students actually assume the responsibility of using the strategies while they read. In what follows, we address each of these issues.

Refining the Scope and Sequence

Core reading programs teach many skills and strategies, pushing teachers to cover and students to learn a large number of skills and strategies in an academic year. In Chapter 5, we explained that some strategies are taught with two different names and other strategies are split into several parts. Teachers need to prune their core programs to focus on those skills and strategies that are most essential. To do so, the teacher needs to keep in mind what research has recommended and what is required by state and district curriculum standards. First, we take a close look at the curriculum of one program to illustrate how we might make some thoughtful decisions. Table 32 lists the reading comprehension skills and strategies taught in grade 4 in Houghton Mifflin Reading (2003/2005).

This curriculum covers 30 comprehension skills and strategies, and this number can easily be reduced. First, let's group together similar or redundant skills. Making inferences, making generalizations, and drawing conclusions are similar in nature. All require the reader to use text information and prior knowledge to develop understanding that goes beyond what the author has supplied. These three skills can be collapsed into one—making inferences.

Determining main ideas and noting details demand the same kind of thinking, allowing us to recognize levels of importance when we read. These two skills can be considered one—determining importance. The skill labeled text organization actually repeats a main idea lesson under a different label. Next, we find common ground when we teach students about story structure— such as characters, plot, setting, and events—and sequence of events. All of these elements are part of narrative structure. Over the course of a year, we might start with a broad analysis and discussion of narrative structure, then focus more intensely on characters, style, and mood, and then consider author's viewpoint. Into this study of narrative, we must also add fantasy and realism.

Just as we study the characteristics of narrative texts, there are a number of skills on our list that are crucial to the study of informational text. So our edited curriculum must focus on text organization, main idea, specific text

Table 32. Fourth-Grade Curriculum in Houghton Mifflin Reading (Houghton Mifflin, 2003/2004)

Reading: Comprehension		Information and Study Skills
Comprehenson Skills	**Comprehension Strategies**	
Author's viewpoint	Predicting	Using timelines and schedules
Text organization	Comprehension monitoring (clarifying)	Real-life reading
Determining main ideas	Questioning	Using story charts
Text structure	Summarizing	Following directions
Noting details	Evaluating	Using an encyclopedia
Sequence of events		Collecting data
Making inferences		Outlining
Making generalizations		Taking notes
Drawing conclusions		
Categorizing and classifying		
Compare and contrast		
Fantasy and realism		
Predicting outcomes		
Problem solving		
Cause and effect		
Making judgments		
Distinguishing fact and opinion		

structure, cause and effect, and distinguishing fact and opinion. Finally, our curriculum includes skills that help students read critically and responsively. We want our reader to compare and contrast ideas, characters, and themes, make judgments, and evaluate what they read. We feel that the other strategies and skills in Table 32 are nonessential. Our remodeled smart curriculum is shown in Figure 23.

Our remodeled curriculum has reduced the number of skills and strategies from 29 to 17. In our smart curriculum, five strategies—making predictions, summarizing, making inferences, self-questioning, and comprehension

Figure 23. A Remodeled Comprehension Curriculum

During-Reading Strategies	Learning About Text		Critical and Responsive Reading
	Narrative Text	Informational Text	
• Making predictions • Summarizing • Making inferences • Self-questioning • Comprehension monitoring (clarifying)	Narrative structure and its components: characters, plot, setting, **sequence of events, problem and solution, author's viewpoint, fantasy and realism**	Text organization/ **main idea**: titles, headings, graphics, table of contents, index, **cause and effect, problem and solution, following directions**	• Compare and contrast • Making judgments • Evaluating

monitoring (clarifying)—are taught early in the year and applied any time that students read. This format is followed in reciprocal teaching (Palincsar & Brown, 1984) and transactional strategy instruction (Brown et al., 1996). Regular, guided practice with these strategies is critical for students' success (Rosenshine & Meister, 1994). That leaves us only 12 skills and strategies, five of which focus on understanding narrative text (narrative structure, sequence of events, problem and solution, author's viewpoint, fantasy and realism), four that focus on informational text (text organization and main idea, cause and effect, problem and solution, following directions), and three that develop critical reading skills (compare and contrast, making judgments, evaluating). This remodeled curriculum imposes logic on the teaching of reading comprehension skills and strategies and moves the teacher and the students away from a regimented approach to instruction. Students can understand that there are things all good readers do when they read, and there are concepts of genre and text structure they need to understand and use to comprehend narrative and informational text. Comprehension instruction should make sense, and it is the teacher's job to convey the overall logic of the curriculum to the students.

Comprehension curricula in core reading programs should be organized to promote the growing expertise of the reader. So how teachers instruct at the end of the year should be quite different from what they do at the beginning of the year. The lessons in core reading programs change little from the first unit to the last. Figure 24 show the sequence of all comprehension skills and strategies taught during the fourth-grade year in Houghton Mifflin Reading. The diagram

Figure 24. The Sequence of Fourth-Grade Comprehension Skill Instruction in Houghton Mifflin Reading (Houghton Mifflin, 2003/2005)

Selection	Skills Lessons Introduction	Skills Lessons Review	Strategy Lessons
Theme 1 Selection 1	**Text structure**	Cause and effect Predicting	Summarize
Story 2	Author's viewpoint	Sequence Making inferences	Predict/infer
Story 3	**Text organization**	Author's viewpoint Main idea	Monitor/clarify
Story 4	Noting details	Making generalizations Categorize and classify	Question
Theme 2 Story 1	Sequence	Draw conclusion Making judgments	Predict/infer
Story 2	**Making inferences**	Compare/contrast Noting details	Evaluate
Story 3	Making generalizations	Cause and effect	Summarize
Story 4	Categorize and classify	Making generalizations Making inferences	Question
Theme 3 Story 1	Noting details	Cause and effect Drawing conclusion	Monitor/clarify
Story 2	Compare and contrast	Fantasy and realism Noting details	Question
Story 3	Fantasy and realism	Compare and contrast **Text structure**	Evaluate
Theme 4 Story 1	Predicting outcomes	Making inferences Fantasy and realism	Predict/infer
Story 2	Problem solving	Following directions Predicting outcomes	Evaluate
Story 3	Drawing conclusions	Categorize and classify	Summarize
Story 4	**Story structure**	Compare and contrast Making judgments	Question
Theme 5 Story 1	Cause and effect	Sequence **Story structure**	Predict/infer
Story 2	Making judgments	Text organization Compare and contrast	Monitor/clarify
Story 3	Fact and opinion	Making judgments Author's viewpoint	Evaluate
Theme 6 Story 1	Following directions	Noting details Categorize	Summarize
Story 2	**Main idea**	Fact/opinion Author's viewpoints	Monitor/clarify
Story 3	Making inference	Cause + effect Making generalizations	Predict/infer

shows that text structure is introduced in the first lesson of the program, but is not revisited until the 11th lesson. Determining main idea, a key element of understanding informational text, is not taught until the 20th lesson of the year. The creative teacher will teach a few critical strategies first—such as predicting, summarizing, making inferences, questioning, and comprehension monitoring (clarifying)—and then introduce the others, so students can use them to develop their comprehension.

Improving Direct Explanation of Comprehension Skills and Strategies

Our research (Dewitz et al., 2008, 2009) and that of others have documented that when comprehension skills and strategies are introduced, instruction in core reading programs is often not explicit and explanations are incomplete. Duffy et al. (1986) have developed a set of criteria, almost a checklist, of what needs to be included in a direct explanation lesson. That checklist includes four key ideas. In Table 33, we present these four key ideas and what a teacher might say when introducing the strategy of summarizing.

Often when using a core program, you will encounter lessons that embody some of the characteristics of direct explanation. These lessons will require considerable remodeling based on Duffy et al.'s (1986) guidelines. Thinking back to Chapter 5, you will remember that not all core programs meet the requirements of a full explanation when introducing a strategy. We have chosen one lesson from Grade 5 Trophies (2003/2005) to illustrate how you need to think critically about direct instruction in core programs. The lesson is presented in Figure 25. The left side of the figure is the language from the core reading program, and the right side is our revised lesson.

Our examination of this lesson on main idea and details reveals several shortcomings. First, the lesson does not state how to determine the main idea. Beyond the use of topic sentences, the lesson does not direct the reader to examine text features, such as headings, subheadings, or bold print, as cues to what is important. The thinking required to determine the main idea is not made explicit, and it is not easy to do so. Second, the lesson does not indicate how a reader's prior knowledge can help in focusing on what is important. This is an important step, because when students are knowledgeable about a topic, they can use what they know to focus on ideas in the text. Finally, the lesson does not state why a reader might want to find the main idea or when they should do so.

Table 33. Criteria for Direct Instruction of Comprehension Strategies

What Should Be Included in a Lesson	What a Teacher Might Say
1. A statement describing the strategy (declarative knowledge)	"Today we are going to learn to summarize what you are reading. A summary is a short restatement of the main ideas in the text."
2. A discussion of how to perform the strategy including a focus, if needed, on the text features necessary to use the strategy (procedural knowledge)	"We summarize by focusing on the important ideas in a text, ignoring the minor details and then bringing those important ideas together into a statement. Sometimes headings, subheadings, topic sentences, and bold print words can be key to creating a summary. With narrative text, our summary should include characters, setting, problems, major events, and the resolution."
3. A discussion of when and why to use the strategy (conditional knowledge)	"We summarize because it helps us remember what we read, and at times it is a good way to check on our own understanding. Sometimes when I am not sure I understand what I am reading, I stop to summarize it for myself. It is useful to summarize while you are reading to make sure you remember what you have read. A good time to stop and summarize is when your reading becomes difficult."
4. Modeling the process with real text and thinking aloud as you do so	Now you have to let the students hear your own thought processes. Read a short piece of authentic text to the students and then model the process of summarizing. Tell the students why you included certain ideas in your summary and excluded others. When you have constructed your summary, stop and restate it for the class. Be sure to tell the students why you stopped to summarize and how the summary helped you understand the text. (Please note we consider summarizing an oral process; good readers do not write down their summaries, because it is too time consuming.)

Let's look at how we changed this lesson. We believe that our revised lesson is more explicit. We helped students organize what they know about oceans, so their prior knowledge was more accessible. We were explicit and told them that what they knew about oceans would help them determine the main idea. Next, we set a purpose for using the skills and told the students why it was important. Finally, we outlined some of the text clues a reader might use to help determine the main idea. In our lesson, students are given more information about how text features can be used to determine the main idea and how readers can

Figure 25. An Original Fifth-Grade Lesson in a Core Reading Program for Teaching Main Idea and a Revised Version

	Main Idea in the Core Program[a]	Main Idea as a Revised Lesson
Access Prior Knowledge	Discuss with students ideas they have about the ocean. Ask them to include details.	Discuss with students ideas they have about the oceans. As they do so, develop a concept map that organizes what they know into categories. Organize the map so that main ideas are above the details. Tell the students that what they know about a topic can help them focus on what will be important.
Teach/ Model	Tell students that good readers look for an author's main idea and supporting details. Use Transparency 117. • Have volunteer read aloud items 1 and 2. • Point out that a main idea is not always stated in the first sentence in a paragraph. • As you read aloud the example, tell students that supporting details can come in the form of facts, examples, quotations, anecdotes or expert opinions. **Text Structure** Point out that the pattern of arranging information by main idea and details is one type of text structure.	Tell students that good readers look for an author's main idea, because authors have a purpose behind their writing and readers try to determine that purpose. Say, "Few of us can remember all that we read, so we have to look for and remember what is important. In a few cases, the author will directly state the main idea in a sentence or two, but more often the reader has to infer, that is, make up a main idea statement from the clues the author created. When you are reading, you might look for some of the following cues: • Specific ideas and concepts that are repeated—these are the keys to the topic • Headings, subheadings, and bold print • Frequently repeated content words • Specific topic sentences "Use these cues and the details in the text, such as facts, examples, and quotations, to formulate what you believe is the main idea. Ask yourself questions about what in your experience seems to be the main point of the lesson."

[a]From Trophies, Distant Voyages, Harcourt, 2003/2005, Grade 5 Teacher's Manual, Theme 3, p. 296I. Copyright © by Harcourt, Inc. All rights reserved. Reproduced by permission of the publisher, Houghton Mifflin Harcourt Publishing Company.

use prior knowledge as a way of testing the importance of new ideas. We also believe it is important to model this process several times. The one or two examples provided in a core program are not sufficient for students to understand how writers organize information and how readers need to think. Although modeling starts when a skill or strategy is introduced, it continues while the students are reading as we stop to discuss selected pieces of the text.

Improving Students' Ability to Use and Internalize Comprehension Strategies

Our last concern with core reading programs is their failure to build their weekly lessons and units around a gradual release of responsibility model. Skills and strategies are introduced, and then while students read the selections, teachers question them extensively. The questions either assess the skill that has been taught or the students' literal and inferential understanding of the passage. These lessons do little to alter how the students process the text and construct meaning by using strategies. In a gradual release of responsibility model, the focus is on helping the student understand the text by using strategies to solve comprehension problems, not just questioning them. This requires a style of interaction between the text, the student, and the teacher that differs significantly from what core reading programs offer. Rather than merely asking them questions, we want students to actively engage with the text through the use of strategies. The responsibility for using strategies gradually shifts from the teacher's modeling to the students' implementation of the strategy. Much as in reciprocal teaching (Palincsar & Brown, 1984) and transactional strategy instruction (Brown et al., 1996), we want the students to take the lead in using strategies to comprehend the text. The teacher's job is to help them initiate strategies, guide strategy selection, and prompt to monitor developing comprehension. We also want the discussion to focus more on the meaning of the passage and not employ strategies for the sake of strategies. If there is nothing to infer, why ask students to make an inference (McKeown, Beck, & Blake, 2009)?

We have chosen to examine the fourth unit in Scott Foresman Reading (Pearson Scott Foresman, 2004) grade 4 to illustrate how to provide more practice for your students. In this unit, Timeless Stories, students read five selections and work on the following skills and strategies: paraphrasing, compare and contrast, text structure, summarizing, and the narrative feature of plot. As we outlined previously in Figure 24, there are a set of during-reading strategies that are essential to meaning construction, and we want students to engage in the use of these strategies: making predictions, summarizing, self-questioning, comprehension monitoring (clarifying), and making inferences. In Scott Foresman Reading, the students are given direct instruction in making predictions, summarizing, and making inferences, but self-questioning and comprehension monitoring (clarifying) are not explicitly taught and must be added. During the reading of each selection, we want the students to engage with the text by using these strategies. Because this unit appears toward the middle of the year, we expect some proficiency in the use of the strategies.

In our plan, the students will read each selection twice, once to develop overall comprehension and a second time to focus on text structure, the designated skill for this selection. Because the selection about Lou Gehrig is a biography, the text structure problems are straightforward and not very demanding. The teacher's edition also asks you to focus on the use of possessives, the skill of paraphrasing, and the narrative feature of character. You will need to decide if stopping to discuss these ancillary topics furthers your students' comprehension. We suspect it will not. Your state assessment might require attention to some of these, but attend to them in a way that does not disrupt your students' comprehension.

In Figure 26, the middle column is the text that the students will be reading from the core program. The left column presents the teacher directions from the core program. In the right column, we present the questions and prompts we suggest using in place of the questions in the core program. We would have the students read the six paragraphs before they stopped to discuss them. Basically, we are using a series of open questions or queries to begin the construction of meaning (Beck et al., 1996) followed by probes, if necessary, to refine students' thinking. Our goal is to guide students to synthesize, make connections among ideas in the text, and make connections between the ideas in the text and their prior knowledge.

Our guidance is designed to prompt students to construct their own understanding of the story. By asking direct comprehension questions, as the core programs do, the teacher is determining what the students should be thinking about. Instead, we want them to use the previously taught strategies to develop their own understandings. Our open-ended questions or queries are designed to support students as they begin to construct meaning. Our use of these techniques comes from both the construction-integration model of Kintsch (1998) and the work of Beck and her colleagues (1996) on questioning the author.

Figure 26. Sample Guided Reading Comprehension Questions for a Fourth-Grade Lesson in a Core Reading Program

Guided Comprehension: Scott Foresman Reading[a]	Selection: *Lou Gehrig* by David Adler[b]	Guided Comprehension: Modified
Compare and Contrast/ Inferential	1903 was a year of great beginnings. Henry Ford sold his first automobile and the Wright Brothers made the first successful flight in an airplane. In baseball, the first World Series was played. The team later known as the Yankees moved from Baltimore to New York. And on July 19, 1903, Henry Louis Gehrig was born. He would become one of the greatest players in baseball history.	"What is this selection about? What have we learned?" (summarizing, paraphrasing)
How were Christina Gehrig's dreams for her son different from what Lou Gehrig himself wanted to do?		*Probe:* When students' summaries are incomplete, ask, "What else can you add to our summary?"
Text Structure/Inferential		
How does the author organize the events that led up to Gehrig's signing with the New York Yankees? Use details and information from the selection to support your answer.	Lou Gehrig was born in the Yorkville section of New York City. It was an area populated with poor immigrants like his parents, Heinrich and Christina Gehrig, who had come to the United States from Germany.	What question do you think we need to ask about Lou Gehrig and his family? (self-questioning, comprehension monitoring)
Character/Inferential	Christina Gehrig had great hopes for her son Lou. She dreamed that he would attend college and become an accountant or an engineer. She insisted that he study hard. Through eight years of grade school, Lou didn't miss a single day.	*Probe:* Why was Lou's mother angry with him?
What do you know so far about Lou Gehrig's character?		*Probe:* What have we learned about Lou's family?
Skills in Context	Lou's mother thought games and sports were a waste of time. But Lou loved sports. He got up early to play the games he loved—baseball, soccer, and football. He played until it was time to go to school. In high school Lou was a star on his school's baseball team.	What can you figure out about Lou's character and his motivation? (making inferences)
Text Structure		
Introduce		
Explain that nonfiction can be organized in different ways. One way to organize a story about a person's life is to tell the events in the order they happened. Have students volunteer examples of books they have read that tell stories in sequence.	After high school Lou Gehrig went to Columbia University. He was on the baseball team there, too, and on April 26, 1923, a scout for the New York Yankees watched him play. Lou hit two long home runs in that game. Soon after that he was signed to play for the Yankees.	Can someone put together everything we have learned about Lou Gehrig? (summarizing, paraphrasing)
Teach		
Have students reread the first two paragraphs on page 425 and retell the main events in order. Model how to identify text structure.	The Yankees offered Lou a $1,500 bonus to sign plus a good salary. His family needed the money. Lou quit college and joined the Yankees. Lou's mother was furious. She was convinced that he was ruining his life.	
"As I read page 425 in this biography, I noticed that the author tells the events of Lou Gehrig's life in order. Words such as *after* and *soon* give me clues that one event leads to another."		

[a]From Scott Foresman Reading, Pearson Scott Foresman, Grade 4 Teacher's Manual, Unit 4, pp. 424–425.
[b]From *Lou Gehrig: The Luckiest Man* by David Adler. © 1997. Used with permission by Houghton Mifflin Harcourt Publishing Company.

Kintsch, in particular, sees at least two stages in the comprehension process, with the first stage involving the construction or assembling of ideas in the text through the use of grammar and vocabulary knowledge. Sentences and ideas are linked to each other through pronouns, prepositions, and conjunctions as the reader forms a model of the text, a literal understanding. In the second stage of comprehension, the text model is made more complete and stable by integrating what the reader has constructed with prior knowledge. Our questions are designed to prompt both mental actions. In Figure 27, you will find some examples of the questions or queries you might employ in this style of guided reading.

The first move should be to ask the students to summarize or paraphrase what they have read. This compels them to construct ideas and develop their own text model by putting ideas together. Poor comprehenders often focus on

Figure 27. Sample Questions to Guide Students' Comprehension

Purpose	Questions and Queries
Beginning the discussion and assessing what students have comprehended	• What is the author trying to tell us? (summarizing) • What is the author talking about? (summarizing) • What did you learn about _____?
Encouraging students to search for comprehension problems	• What problems did you encounter reading this section? (comprehension monitoring) • What words or phrases might be difficult to understand? (comprehension monitoring) • Does that make sense? Is that said in a clear way? (comprehension monitoring) • What questions do you think we need to ask? (self-questioning) • How is the author painting a picture here? (visualizing) • What did you feel, smell, or see? (visualizing)
Solving comprehension problems	Think aloud and let the students see how you tackled a difficult comprehension challenge. Then, use some of the following queries: • How can we use what we know about _____ to understand the text? (making inferences, requiring prior knowledge) • How does what the author said about _____ connect to what the author already told us? (making inferences, requiring within-text connections) • How does that connect with what the author already told us? (making inferences, requiring within-text connections) • What clues led us to the author's main message? (determining main ideas) • Can you visualize the character or the setting the author is trying to describe? (visualizing)

just a few ideas in a text and fail to connect those ideas. Next, the teacher encourages the students to search for and notice comprehension difficulties. This metacognitive act is essential; without it, students will not notice comprehension problems or use strategies to solve them. Asking questions, summarizing, or trying to confirm predictions can initiate metacognition. If there are no text problems, there is no reason to engage in the use of strategies. Finally, readers have to solve these problems with the text. This is done by making inferences, connecting what is known to the text, searching for main ideas, and trying to determine the author's purpose. The teacher acts as a guide, encouraging the students to use their strategies. The students may eventually lead the discussion and engage in a reciprocal dialogue in which they take turns predicting, questioning, clarifying, and summarizing (Palincsar & Brown, 1984).

Becoming Expert Readers

The structure and content of reading lessons in core programs changes little from the beginning of the year to the end. To cite just one example from Scott Foresman Reading (2004), in the first unit in fifth grade students read five selections—from the genres realistic fiction (two), fantasy (one), and biography (two)—and their accompanying leveled texts. They work on sequence, character development, making generalizations, cause and effect, and author's purpose. At the end of the year, they read five selections—from the genres of realistic fiction (two), folk tales (one), nonfiction (one), and a play. The students work on theme, steps in a process, the element of plot, making predictions, and visualizing. Each of these comprehension skills is introduced as an independent skill, having no obvious link to what students learned before and what they will learn next. It appears that the six units in this core program or any other core program in the upper grades could be shuffled with no impact on the students.

The programs make no assumptions that the students will grow, that what they learned a week or month ago is useful in learning the next skill or strategy. Comprehension skills and strategies should be internalized so that by the end of the year, we can assume that students know how to visualize and have had considerable practice in making predictions. We expect students to change and become more independent and sophisticated readers as the year progresses, yet the core reading programs do not support this as well as they could. Our goal for students should be that they will read and comprehend with greater independence and that they move from teacher-guided reading to independent silent reading and from superficial understandings to greater insights.

PUTTING IT ALL TOGETHER

In this chapter, we presented our ideas on how to improve the comprehension instruction in core reading programs. Good comprehenders must have fluent print skills, a broad vocabulary, prior knowledge, and a set of skills and strategies that promote the thinking necessary to understand the passages. In a number of ways, core reading programs fall short of research recommendations. Core programs do not develop enough knowledge, and what students learn in one passage does not help them understand subsequent passages. Vocabulary instruction often lacks rich explanations of word meanings and practice over time for students to learn the words. There are too many skills and strategies for students to learn, and often they are not explicitly taught. Given these shortcomings, teachers can use core programs as tools and make careful modifications to the instruction that will benefit their students. Ultimately, we believe that students become good readers not because they have a desire to become proficient strategic readers and learn a set of skills, but because they are excited by a story and want to learn about the world around them. Keeping this in mind, teachers should do the following:

- Spend more time developing prior knowledge through the use of concept boards, interesting read-alouds, and supplemental readings.

- Tailor vocabulary instruction to the needs of the students by teaching words they need to know and avoiding words they already know. Be more explicit.

- Limit the number of skills and strategies to be taught. Some programs teach the same mental processes under more than one label and teach skills that are not essential to your state or district curriculum.

- Improve the direct instruction of skills and strategies by providing fuller and clearer explanations. Use strategies with more than one selection and continue to do so until students understand the process.

- Modify guided reading practice so that students assume a larger role in using the strategies that have been taught. This means that students need to have strategy use modeled for them, to search for and solve problems, and to make important inferences. Teachers can guide this process through the use of open-ended questions and prompts.

Empowering Teachers to Use Core Reading Programs

We have read, studied, and evaluated core reading programs for several years (Dewitz et al., 2009). From our initial interest in comprehension strategy instruction, we expanded our inquiry to consider the teaching of phonemic awareness and phonics in core programs, the texts in core programs, and how differentiated instruction and intervention is provided and assessed for all readers. We also took a close look at the process that districts use to study and adopt core reading programs, and we interviewed many who create these programs.

This book is the culmination of that work, bringing together what we have learned about core reading programs to develop specific suggestions about how they should be used and how they should be evaluated. We have always felt that the reading program in a school and in each classroom is the creation of the professionals in the school—and core reading programs, because of their comprehensive nature, are certainly a most important tool. However, we are alarmed by teachers who say that they "teach" a specific core reading program and disturbed by schools that set aside an allotted time for guided reading and another time for "basal" instruction in an attempt to bridge the gap between a skills approach and guided reading. Teachers teach children to read; core reading programs are merely one tool they can turn to.

As we have studied and written about core reading programs, we have continually discussed how they should be used. Is a core reading program a complex tool that must be followed like a script, or a collection of resources that call for careful decision making by teachers and administrators? Just as there is a transaction between a reader and a writer when reading a novel, a similar transaction takes place when teachers work with core reading programs: Curriculum materials and teachers interact as teachers exert control over the materials and the materials influence the teacher.

The program shapes the teacher's conception of reading instruction, creating a view that instruction is a sequence of skills and texts organized around weekly lessons and six-week units. Each week of the school year looks alike with a few skills taught, a few texts read, and many activities completed. But core reading programs are not organized around a concept of growing expertise. What the students do the last week of the year is much like what they do the first week of the year, and this is especially true in the upper grades when students should begin to read longer, more challenging text and engage in thought-provoking projects.

Our wish is for all teachers to question the author. Even though the creators of core reading programs are a diverse set of individuals, including university researchers, teacher educators, publishers, editors, and freelance writers, core programs exert their collective will on the administrators who purchase them and the teachers who use them. We believe there is room for teachers and administrators to make decisions.

When we conceptualized this book, many educators were arguing that core reading programs should be taught with fidelity. The concept of teaching a core reading program with fidelity most likely had its origin in the No Child Left Behind Act of 2001 and the federal initiative Reading First. The charge of Reading First was to "provide assistance to State educational agencies (SEAs) and local educational agencies (LEAs) in establishing reading programs for students in kindergarten through grade 3 that are based on scientifically based reading research (SBRR) to ensure that every student can read at grade level or above no later than the end of grade 3" (No Child Left Behind Act of 2001, 2002, Title 1, Part B, § 1201). Reading First was to also "provide assistance to SEAs (State Educational Agencies) and LEAs (Local Educational Agencies) in selecting or developing effective instructional materials (including classroom-based materials to assist teachers in implementing the essential components of reading instruction), programs, learning systems, and strategies to implement methods that have been proven to prevent or remediate reading failure within a State" (No Child Left Behind Act of 2001, 2002, Title 1, Part B, § 1201).

State departments of education issued lists of approved core reading programs that were based on scientific reading research. The publishers provided extensive documentation citing the research upon which the programs were built. The research base of these programs was bolstered by the studies of the Curriculum Review Panel at the University of Oregon (Oregon Reading First Center, n.d.) and conducted by the Florida Center for Reading Research (www .fcrr.org). Publishing companies provided checklists, staff development, and materials so that schools could ensure that these programs were taught with fidelity. As Linda Diamond of the Consortium on Reading Excellence described it,

> High fidelity implementation means that you get a program with an internal design and follow that design. That would include using the materials in a particular sequence, adhering to the amount of time and practice called for by the program and following the recommendations for grouping or re-teaching students. It would mean using all of the essential components as they are designed. (Bay Area School Reform Collaborative, 2004, p. 1)

Many schools, particularly the Reading First schools, worked to use core reading programs as they were written.

In direct and indirect ways, researchers began to explore the efficacy of core programs, and some raised questions about the concept of fidelity. A survey of effective and ineffective schools in California found that schools produced higher levels of achievement in reading if they had strong instructional leadership, used a core program that supported a standards-based approach, regularly monitored the progress of their students in meeting these goals, and provided extensive staff development (EdSource, 2006). All of the components were important, not just the use of the core reading program. Other researchers began to question the efficacy of core programs or specifically teaching them with fidelity. McGill-Franzen and her colleagues (2006) reported on the impact of using these research-based programs in Florida. Fully one third of third graders failed to meet the minimum level of proficiency to pass the state assessment despite the research base of the programs. Others found that the very programs that the Oregon Reading First Center's (n.d.) Curriculum Review Panel rated highly on research-based criteria for comprehension instruction had serious flaws and failed to live up to important research-based criteria (Dewitz et al., 2009). Specifically, skills and strategies were not taught explicitly, nor did the programs follow a gradual release of responsibility model. Crowe, Connor, and Petscher (2009) reported that some core reading programs are associated with greater growth in oral reading fluency than others, and Brenner and Hiebert (in press) suggested why. They questioned whether there is enough text in core programs for students to become fluent readers and concluded that students at a low level of proficiency could read all the material in a core program in about 15 minutes per day, far less time with text than reading experts have recommended and far less than students need to become fluent, thoughtful, and avid readers (Brenner & Hiebert, 2010). Finally, our own study of how core reading programs are created has suggested that they are as much a product of market forces as they are of reading research. This suggests that following a core program with fidelity may not be the best course of action.

For a number of reasons the concept of fidelity is an empty idea, based on the premise that core programs contain all that a teacher needs to help students become literate, that the materials and lessons are optimal for all students. We know clearly that there is not enough to read in a core reading program and students must venture into the library and into trade books and novels. Because of how core programs are created, they contain more lessons and teaching activities than any teacher can complete in 90 or 120 minutes of daily instruction. Teachers must choose. They cannot ask all the questions in each lesson or use all the worksheets or extension activities that relate reading to science, social studies, and the arts. If you are using a core program created before 2007, chances are it has a whole-group focus and limited directions for differentiation. The limitations of core programs are only critical if the programs become the sole resource and guide for teaching reading.

Despite their limitations, core reading programs are valuable and even necessary. Imagine the task of developing and organizing a full year's reading curriculum. You would need to assemble 36 weeks of texts at multiple levels, plus select additional texts for read-alouds. You would need to sequence phonics and phonemic awareness instruction in the primary grades and collect the materials to teach these skills. You would need to develop lesson plans for introducing, modeling, practicing, and applying decoding strategies. In all grades, you would need to select comprehension skills to teach, sequence them, and develop the instructional language for teaching these skills. For each of the texts, you would be teaching, you would need to select vocabulary words and develop the instruction for them. This is a tall order for an experienced teacher and overwhelming for a novice. We contend that it is easier to make strong instructional decisions using a core reading program as a base than it is to start from scratch. The structure provided by a core reading program gives the school or district a common foundation from which to build even stronger reading instruction and literary experiences. The structure of a core program organizes texts into units and develops a plan for teaching reading throughout the year. The key decision is knowing when and how to move beyond the core reading program into the wider world of children's literature.

The teacher's edition suggests many options for how to use the core program without strict fidelity, and these options are available because a core reading program must appeal to many different instructional audiences and meet the needs of many different types of readers. Teachers must rely on their own knowledge of curriculum and instruction, their understanding of children, and the goals of their school or district to select and design instruction that helps students meet these goals. Core reading programs play an important role in the decisions that teachers must make, but the decisions are more complicated than just following the core reading program.

Teachers should weigh a range of factors that requires several types of knowledge as they construct their reading program. Knowledge of books, including fiction, nonfiction, and poetry, is essential. Students need texts that will interest and challenge them. Teachers need to know how to teach phonemic awareness, phonics, vocabulary, and comprehension. They need knowledge of instruction, so they can explain the secrets of reading in a clear and logical order. Finally, teachers need a deep knowledge of their students. Teachers need to know how to motivate their students, when to push, when to loosen the reins, when to review, and when to move forward. They need to know that Molly may like reading *Misty of Chincoteague* (Henry, 1947), but Raul and Morris would much rather delve into the lives of Jimmy Johnson and Mark Martin as they push the limits at the Daytona 500. At their best, core reading programs are built on a strong knowledge of texts and basic principles of instruction. What core reading programs do not provide is knowledge of the students. Indeed, core reading programs make few assumptions about students, except that they will differ in ability or reading level and some will require extra instruction. If teaching is a profession in which teachers must use what they know about text, instruction, and students to craft an instructional program, then teachers must exercise their professional prerogative (Pearson, 2007).

Learning about reading instruction takes time, requires reading, and demands self-reflection. Schools need to provide staff development that is ongoing and organized in such a way that teachers value the benefits of a deeper understanding of reading instruction and seek ways to use that knowledge. Unfortunately, core programs have done little to encourage this disposition or to educate teachers. Core programs operate on the premise that the teacher's concern is to learn the program well and use it efficiently. Except for Open Court Reading (SRA/McGraw-Hill, 2005), a program that is often viewed as tightly scripted, core programs provide no rationale for why lessons are structured or ordered as they are. For example, Treasures (Macmillan/McGraw-Hill, 2009) does not explain why text structure is a strategy and character, setting, and plot are skills. It does not explain why a week or two is sufficient time to focus on a given strategy or skill, or why after working on narrative structure, students should now learn to compare and contrast and summarize. Reading should make sense to students and teachers, and often it does not. Treasures is not alone: All programs fail to provide a deeper understanding of what they do and why they do it. Teachers can easily follow these lessons and if students grow as most readers do, so much the better. But if students do not improve, the programs do not help teachers make instructional decisions except to suggest another course of review or a move to the aligned intervention program.

If we endow teachers with the responsibility of creating strong reading programs with exciting and instructive lessons, we do so with the understanding that they have a broad and deep understanding of reading instruction. They have the responsibility to learn as much as they can both individually and collectively. They have to make the study of reading a centerpiece of the school, regularly discussing and evaluating the outcomes of their reading instruction with cold, unbiased accuracy. As Pearson (2007) put it,

> Teachers who aspire to professional prerogative must accept the responsibility for keeping their knowledge current, and they must be prepared to alter their practice on the basis of new knowledge—to accept the possibility that new knowledge trumps old practice, no matter how comfortable the old ways fit. (p. 153)

Developing knowledgeable teachers is the responsibility of teacher educators, school districts, unions, and publishing companies.

We want teachers to understand their students' needs and alter the materials and the method of instruction to meet those needs, holding all students to the highest possible standards. Some students start the year reading so well that the short selections of a core program offer no challenge, and for them skill instruction is unnecessary. For other students, the sheer predictability of a core reading program, in which every week is structured like the previous one, takes its toll. Despite the success many students have, the core reading program leaves some behind. For those students who struggle, schools and teachers need the knowledge and the authority to alter instruction, devise new means, assess their effects, and if necessary try again. Finally, all students at some point are ready to move beyond the core program into a wider range of text and resources, including nonfiction trade books, novels, and the Internet. Teachers need to know when this should happen and make it so. All this takes education and leadership. Schools and districts must commit to the continual education of their teachers, so they can make these instructional decisions.

Knowledge of your students and of reading instruction is necessary to use and choose these programs. When you next examine a new core reading program, keep foremost in mind the needs of your students. Use your understanding of reading instruction to determine if the reading selections, the lessons, and the supporting materials in the programs you are considering will help you meet your goals. Ignore the bells and whistles of the programs and author name-dropping by the sales representatives. There is most likely no one best program, but there may be a few programs with the right texts and enough well-crafted lessons that will help you do your job. Consider those programs, review them closely, but remember it is your goal to move students beyond the core program, from learning to read to reading with purpose, curiosity, and excitement.

REFERENCES

Adams, M.J. (1990). *Beginning to read: Thinking and learning about print*. Cambridge, MA: MIT Press.

Adams, M.J. (2009). Decodable text: Why, when, and how? In E.H. Hiebert & M. Sailors (Eds.), *Finding the right texts: What works for beginning and struggling readers* (pp. 23–46). New York: Guilford.

Adams, M.J., Foorman, B.R., Lundberg, I., & Beeler, T. (1998). *Phonemic awareness for young children: A classroom curriculum*. Baltimore: Paul H. Brookes.

Afflerbach, P., Pearson, P.D., & Paris, S.G. (2008). Clarifying differences between reading skills and reading strategies. *The Reading Teacher, 61*(5), 364–373. doi:10.1598/RT.61.5.1

Afflerbach, P., & Walker, B. (1992). Main idea instruction: An analysis of three basal reader series. *Reading Research and Instruction, 32*(1), 11–28.

Alexander, P.A. (2003). Profiling the developing reader: The interplay of knowledge, interest, and strategic processing. In C.M. Fairbanks, J. Worthy, B. Maloch, J.V. Hoffman, & D.L. Schallert (Eds.), *52nd yearbook of the National Reading Conference* (pp. 47–65). Oak Creek, WI: National Reading Conference.

Allington, R.L. (1977). If they don't read much, how they ever gonna get good? *Journal of Reading, 21*(1), 57–61.

Allington, R.L. (2001). *What really matters for struggling readers: Designing research-based programs*. New York: Longman.

Allington, R.L., & Cunningham, P.M. (2002). *Schools that work: Where all children read and write* (2nd ed.). Boston: Allyn & Bacon.

Anderson, L.M., Brubaker, N.L., Alleman-Brooks, J., & Duffy, G.G. (1985). A qualitative study of seatwork in first-grade classrooms. *The Elementary School Journal, 86*(2), 123–140.

Anderson, R.C., & Pearson, P.D. (1984). A schema-theoretic view of basic processes in reading comprehension. In P.D. Pearson, R. Barr, M.L. Kamil, & P. Mosenthal (Eds.), *Handbook of reading research* (Vol. 1, pp. 255–291). New York: Longman.

Anderson, R.C., Reynolds, R.E., Schallert, D.L., & Goetz, E.T. (1977). Frameworks for comprehending discourse. *American Educational Research Journal, 14*(4), 367–381.

Anderson, R.C., Wilkinson, I.A.G., & Mason, J.M. (1991). A microanalysis of the small-group, guided reading lesson: Effects of an emphasis on global story meaning. *Reading Research Quarterly, 26*(4), 417–441. doi:10.2307/747896

Anderson, R.C., Wilson, P.T., & Fielding, L.G. (1988). Growth in reading and how children spend their time outside of school. *Reading Research Quarterly, 23*(3), 285–303. doi:10.1598/RRQ.23.3.2

Balmuth, M. (1982). *The roots of phonics: A historical introduction*. New York: Teachers College Press.

Barr, R., & Sadow, M.W. (1989). Influence of basal programs on fourth-grade reading instruction. *Reading Research Quarterly, 24*(1), 44–71. doi:10.2307/748010

Barton, A., & Wilder, D. (1964). Research and practice in the teaching of reading: A progress report. In M.B. Miles (Ed.), *Innovation in education* (pp. 361–398). New York: Teachers College Press.

Baumann, J.F., & Heubach, K.M. (1996). Do basal readers deskill teachers? A national survey of educators' use and opinions of basals. *The Elementary School Journal, 96*(5), 511–526.

Baumann, J.F., Hoffman, J.V., Moon, J., & Duffy-Hester, A.M. (1998). Where are teachers' voices in the phonics/whole language debate? Results from a survey of U.S. elementary classroom teachers. *The Reading Teacher, 51*(8), 636–650.

Baumann, J.F., Ware, D., & Edwards, E.C. (2007). "Bumping into spicy, tasty words that catch your tongue": A formative experiment on vocabulary instruction. *The Reading Teacher, 61*(2), 108–122. doi:10.1598/RT.61.2.1

Bay Area School Reform Collaborative. (2004). *High fidelity: Its* [sic] *not about music or marriage, it's all about instructional materials. An interview with Linda Diamond of CORE.* Retrieved from www.corelearn.com/files/HighFidelity.pdf

Bear, D.R., Invernizzi, M., Templeton, S., & Johnston, F. (2006). *Words their way: Word study for phonics, vocabulary, and spelling instruction* (4th ed.). Upper Saddle River, NJ: Merrill/Prentice Hall.

Bear, D.R., & Templeton, S. (1998). Explorations in developmental spelling: Foundations for learning and teaching phonics, spelling, and vocabulary. *The Reading Teacher, 52*(3), 222–242.

Beck, I.L. (2006). *Making sense of phonics: The hows and whys.* New York: Guilford.

Beck, I.L., McKeown, M.G., & Kucan, L. (2002). *Bringing words to life: Robust vocabulary instruction.* New York: Guilford.

Beck, I.L., McKeown, M.G., Sandora, C., Kucan, L., & Worthy, J. (1996). Questioning the author: A yearlong classroom implementation to engage students with text. *The Elementary School Journal, 96*(4), 385–414. doi:10.1086/461835

Blachman, B.A., Ball, E.W., Black, R., & Tangel, D.M. (2000). *Road to the code: A phonological awareness program for young children.* Baltimore: Paul H. Brookes.

Bond, G.L., & Dykstra, R. (1967). The cooperative research program in first-grade reading instruction. *Reading Research Quarterly, 2*(4), 5–142. doi:10.2307/746948

Brenner, D., & Hiebert, E.H. (2010). If I follow the teachers' editions, isn't that enough? Analyzing reading volume in six core reading programs. *The Elementary School Journal, 110*(3), 347–363.

Britton, B.K., & Graesser, A.C. (1996). *Models of understanding text.* Mahwah, NJ: Erlbaum.

Brown, R., Pressley, M., Van Meter, P., & Schuder, T. (1996). A quasi-experimental validation of transactional strategies instruction with low-achieving second-grade readers. *Journal of Educational Psychology, 88*(1), 18–37. doi:10.1037/0022-0663.88.1.18

Brownlee, S. (2007). *Overtreated: Why too much medicine is making us sicker and poorer.* New York: Bloomsbury.

Bruce, B. (1984). A new point of view on children's stories. In R.C. Anderson, J. Osborn, & R.J. Tierney (Eds.), *Learning to read in American schools: Basal readers and content texts* (pp. 153–174). Hillsdale, NJ: Erlbaum.

Burgess, S.R. (2006). The development of phonological sensitivity. In D.K. Dickinson & S.B. Neuman (Eds.), *Handbook of early literacy research* (Vol. 2, pp. 90–100). New York: Guilford.

Cain, K., Oakhill, J.V., Barnes, M.A., & Bryant, P.E. (2001). Comprehension skill, inference-making ability, and their relation to knowledge. *Memory & Cognition, 29*(6), 850–859.

Cain, K., Oakhill, J.V., & Bryant, P. (2004). Children's reading comprehension ability: Concurrent prediction by working memory, verbal ability, and component skills. *Journal of Educational Psychology, 96*(1), 31–42. doi:10.1037/0022-0663.96.1.31

California Department of Education. (1987). *Reading/language arts framework for California public schools: Kindergarten through grade twelve.* Sacramento: Author.

California Department of Education. (2007). *Reading/language arts framework for California public schools: Kindergarten through grade twelve.* Retrieved December 18, 2009, from www.cde.ca.gov/CI/cr/cf/documents/rlafw.pdf

Carnine, D.W., Silbert, J., & Kame'enui, E.J. (1997). *Direct instruction reading* (3rd ed.). Upper Saddle River, NJ: Prentice Hall.

Carnine, D.W., Silbert, J., Kame'enui, E.J., & Tarver, S.G. (2003). *Direct instruction reading* (4th ed.). Upper Saddle River, NJ: Prentice Hall.

Chall, J.S. (1996). *Learning to read: The great debate* (3rd ed.). Orlando, FL: Harcourt Brace.

Chall, J.S., & Squire, J.R. (1991). The publishing industry and textbooks. In R. Barr, M.L. Kamil, P. Mosenthal, & P.D. Pearson (Eds.), *Handbook of reading research* (Vol. 2, pp. 120–146). New York: Longman.

Chambliss, M.J., & Calfee, R.C. (1998). *Textbooks for learning: Nurturing children's minds.* Malden, MA: Blackwell.

Clay, M.M. (1993). *Reading Recovery: A guidebook for teachers in training.* Portsmouth, NH: Heinemann.

Clymer, T., & Humphrey, J. (1973). Reading 720: Reading Rainbow. Boston: Ginn.

Connor, C.M., Jakobsons, L.J., Crowe, E.C., & Meadows, J.G. (2009). Instruction, student engagement, and reading skill growth in Reading First classrooms. *The Elementary School Journal, 109*(3), 221–250. doi:10.1086/592305

Connor, C.M., Morrison, F.J., Fishman, B.J., Schatschneider, C., & Underwood, P. (2007). The early years: Algorithm-guided individualized reading instruction. *Science, 315*(5811), 464–465. doi:10.1126/science.1134513

Connor, C.M., Morrison, F.J., & Underwood, P.S. (2007). A second chance in second grade: The independent and cumulative impact of first- and second-grade reading instruction and students' letter-word reading skill growth. *Scientific Studies of Reading, 11*(3), 199–233.

Cooper, J.D. (1999). *Soar to success.* Boston: Houghton Mifflin.

Courtis, S.A. (1915). Standards in rates of reading. In S.C. Parker (Ed.), *The fourteenth yearbook of the National Society for the Study of Education: Part I* (pp. 44–58). Chicago: University of Chicago Press.

Coyne, M.D., Kame'enui, E.J., & Simmons, D.C. (2001). Prevention and intervention in beginning reading: Two complex systems. *Learning Disabilities Research & Practice, 16*(2), 62–73. doi:10.1111/0938-8982.00008

Crowe, E.C., Connor, C.M., & Petscher, Y. (2009). Examining the core: Relations among reading curricula, poverty, and first through third grade reading achievement. *Journal of School Psychology, 47*(3), 187–214.

Cubberley, E.P. (1934). *Public education in the United States: A study and interpretation of American educational history.* Boston: Houghton Mifflin.

Cunningham, A.E., & Stanovich, K.E. (1998). The impact of print exposure on word recognition. In J.L. Metsala & L.C. Ehri (Eds.), *Word recognition in beginning literacy* (pp. 213–238). Mahwah, NJ: Erlbaum.

Cunningham, P.M. (1980). Teaching "were," "with," "what," and other "four-letter" words. *The Reading Teacher, 34*(2), 160–163.

Cunningham, P.M. (2005). *Phonics they use: Words for reading and writing* (4th ed.). Boston: Allyn & Bacon.

Cunningham, P.M., & Allington, R.L. (2007). *Classrooms that work: They can all read and write* (4th ed.). New York: Pearson.

Cunningham, P.M., Hall, D.P., & Defee, M. (1998). Non-ability grouped multilevel instruction: Eight years later. *The Reading Teacher, 51*(8), 652–664.

Delpit, L. (1995). *Other people's children: Cultural conflict in the classroom.* New York: New Press.

Dempster, F.N. (1987). Time and the production of classroom learning: Discerning implications from basic research. *Educational Psychologist, 22*(1), 1–21. doi:10.1207/s15326985ep2201_1

Dewitz, P., Jones, J., & Leahy, S. (2009). Comprehension strategy instruction in core reading programs. *Reading Research Quarterly, 44*(2), 102–126. doi:10.1598/RRQ.44.2.1

Dewitz, P., Jones, J., Leahy, S., & Sullivan, P. (2008, December). *Knowledge development for comprehension in core reading programs.* Paper presented at the 58th annual meeting of the National Reading Conference, Orlando, FL.

Duffy, G.G. (2003). *Explaining reading: A resource for teaching concepts, skills, and strategies.* New York: Guilford.

Duffy, G.G., Roehler, L.R., Meloth, M.S., Vavrus, L.G., Book, C., Putnam, J., et al. (1986). The relationship between explicit verbal explanations during reading skill instruction and student awareness and achievement: A study of reading teacher effects. *Reading Research Quarterly, 21*(3), 237–252. doi:10.2307/747707

Duke, N.K. (2000). 3.6 minutes per day: The scarcity of informational texts in first grade. *Reading Research Quarterly, 35*(2), 202–224. doi:10.1598/RRQ.35.2.1

Duke, N.K., & Pearson, P.D. (2002). Effective practices for developing reading comprehension. In A.E. Farstrup & S.J. Samuels (Eds.), *What research has to say about reading instruction* (3rd ed., pp. 205–241). Newark, DE: International Reading Association.

Durkin, D. (1978). What classroom observations reveal about reading comprehension instruction. *Reading Research Quarterly, 14*(4), 481–533. doi:10.1598/RRQ.14.4.2

Durkin, D. (1981). Reading comprehension instruction in five basal reader series. *Reading Research Quarterly, 16*(4), 515–544. doi:10.2307/747314

Durkin, D. (1984). Is there a match between what elementary teachers do and what basal reader manuals recommend? *The Reading Teacher, 37*(8), 734–744.

Durkin, D. (1990). *Comprehension instruction in current basal reader series* (Technical Rep. No. 521). Urbana: Center for the Study of Reading, University of Illinois at Urbana-Champaign.

EdSource. (2006). *Similar students, different results: Why do some schools do better?* Retrieved December 18, 2009, from www.edsource.org/pub_SimStu6-06_SummaryReport.html

Education: Why Johnny can't read. (1955, March 15). *Time, 65*(11). Retrieved December 18, 2009, from www.time.com/time/magazine/article/0,9171,807107,00.html

Education Market Research. (2007). *Elementary reading market: Teaching methods, textbooks/materials used and needed, and market size.* Rockaway Park, NY: Author.

Ehri, L.C. (1991). Development of the ability to read words. In R. Barr, M.L. Kamil, P. Mosenthal, & P.D. Pearson (Eds), *Handbook of reading research* (Vol. 2, pp. 383–417). New York: Longman.

Ehri, L.C. (1997). Sight word learning in normal readers and dyslexics. In B. Blachman (Ed.), *Foundations of reading acquisition and dyslexia: Implications for early intervention* (pp. 163–189). Mahwah, NJ: Erlbaum.

Ehri, L.C., & Roberts, T. (2006). The roots of learning to read and write: Acquisition of letters and phonemic awareness. In D.K. Dickinson & S.B. Neuman (Eds.), *Handbook of early literacy research* (Vol. 2, pp. 113–131). New York: Guilford.

Eisner, E.W. (2004). The roots of connoisseurship and criticism: A personal journey. In M.C. Alkin (Ed.), *Evaluation roots: Tracing theorists' views and influences* (pp. 196–202). Thousand Oaks, CA: Sage.

Elkonin, D.B. (1963). The psychology of mastering the elements of reading. In B. Simon & J. Simon (Eds.), *Educational psychology in the U.S.S.R.* (pp. 165–179). Stanford, CA: Stanford University Press.

Elson, W.H., et al. (1910–1936). The Elson readers. Chicago: Scott Foresman.

Ezell, H.K., & Justice, L.M. (2005). *Shared storybook reading: Building young children's language and emergent literacy skills.* Baltimore: Paul H. Brookes.

Farr, R., Tulley, M.A., & Powell, D. (1987). The evaluation and selection of basal readers. *The Elementary School Journal, 87*(3), 267–282.

Farstrup, A.E., & Samuels, S.J. (2002). *What research has to say about reading instruction*. Newark, DE: International Reading Association.

Finn, C.E., & Ravitch, D. (2004). *The mad, mad world of textbook adoption*. Washington, DC: Thomas B. Fordham Institute.

Fisher, D., & Ivey, G. (2006). Evaluating the interventions for struggling adolescent readers. *Journal of Adolescent & Adult Literacy, 50*(3), 180–189.

Fitzgerald, J., & Spiegel, D.L. (1983). Enhancing children's reading comprehension through instruction in narrative structure. *Journal of Reading Behavior, 15*(2), 1–17.

Fitzpatrick, J. (2002). *Getting ready to read: Independent phonemic awareness centers for emergent readers*. Huntington Beach, CA: Creative Teaching Press.

Flesch, R. (1955). *Why Johnny can't read: And what you can do about it*. New York: Harper & Row.

Flood, J., & Lapp, D. (1986). Types of texts: The match between what students read in basals and what they encounter in tests. *Reading Research Quarterly, 21*(3), 284–297. doi:10.2307/747710

Florida Department of Education. (2006). *2006 reading specifications for the 2007–2008 Florida state adoption of instructional materials*. Retrieved October 29, 2009, from www.fldoe.org/bii/instruct_mat/0708adoption/Specifications.pdf

Foorman, B.R. (2007). Primary prevention in classroom reading instruction. *Teaching Exceptional Children, 39*(5), 24–31.

Foorman, B.R., Francis, D.J., Davidson, K.C., Harm, M.W., & Griffin, J. (2004). Variability in text features in six grade 1 basal reading programs. *Scientific Studies of Reading, 8*(2), 167–197.

Foorman, B.R., Francis, D.J., Fletcher, J.M., Schatschneider, C., & Mehta, P. (1998). The role of instruction in learning to read: Preventing reading failure in at-risk children. *Journal of Educational Psychology, 90*(1), 37–55.

Foorman, B.R., Schatschneider, C., Eakin, M.N., Fletcher, J.M., Moats, L.C., & Francis, D.J. (2006). The impact of instructional practices in grades 1 and 2 on reading and spelling achievement in high poverty schools. *Contemporary Educational Psychology, 31*(1), 1–29.

Fountas, I.C., & Pinnell, G.S. (1996). *Guided reading: Good first teaching for all children*. Portsmouth, NH: Heinemann.

Fractor, J.S., Woodruff, M.C., Martinez, M.G., & Teale, W.H. (1993). Let's not miss opportunities to promote voluntary reading: Classroom libraries in the elementary school. *The Reading Teacher, 46*(6), 476–484.

Franks, B.A., Mulhern, S.L., & Schillinger, S.M. (1997). Reasoning in a reading context: Deductive inferences in basal reading series. *Reading & Writing Quarterly, 9*(4), 285–312. doi:10.1023/A:1007951513772

Fuchs, D., & Fuchs, L.S. (2006). Introduction to Response to Intervention: What, why, and how valid is it? *Reading Research Quarterly, 41*(1), 93–99.

Fuchs, D., Fuchs, L.S., & Vaughn, S. (2008). *Response to Intervention: A framework for reading educators*. Newark, DE: International Reading Association.

Fuchs, L.S., & Fuchs, D. (2008). The role of assessment within the RTI framework. In D. Fuchs, L.S. Fuchs, & S. Vaughn (Eds.), *Response to Intervention: A framework for reading educators* (pp. 27–49). Newark, DE: International Reading Association.

Gambrell, L.B., & Morrow, L.M. (1996). Creating motivating contexts for literacy learning. In L. Baker, P. Afflerbach, & D. Reinking (Eds.), *Developing engaged readers in school and home communities* (pp. 115–136). Mahwah, NJ: Erlbaum.

Ganske, K. (1999). The developmental spelling analysis: A measure of orthographic knowledge. *Educational Assessment, 6*(1), 41–70. doi:10.1207/S15326977EA0601_4

Gaskins, I.W., et al. (1989–2000). Benchmark word identification/vocabulary development program. Media, PA: Benchmark School.

Gaskins, R.W., Gaskins, J.C., & Gaskins, I.W. (1991). A decoding program for poor readers—and the rest of the class, too! *Language Arts, 68*(3), 213–225.

Gates, A., & Huber, M.B. (1932–1939). The work-play books. New York: Macmillan.

Giorgis, C., & Johnson, N.L. (2002). Children's books: Text sets. *The Reading Teacher, 56*(2), 200–208.

Goldin, C.D., & Katz, L.F. (2008). *The race between education and technology.* Cambridge, MA: Belknap.

Good, R.H., III, & Kaminski, R. (2003–2005). DIBELS: Dynamic indicators of basic early literacy skills. Longmont, CO: Sopris West.

Goodman, K.S. (1986). *What's whole in whole language?* Portsmouth, NH: Heinemann.

Goodman, K.S., Shannon, P., Freeman, Y.S., & Murphy, S. (1988). *Report card on basal readers.* Katonah, NY: Richard C. Owen.

Graham, G.E. (1978). *A present and historical analysis of basal reading series.* Unpublished doctoral dissertation, University of Virginia, Charlottesville.

Graves, M.F. (2006). *The vocabulary book: Learning and instruction.* New York: Teachers College Press; Newark, DE: International Reading Association; Urbana, IL: National Council of Teachers of English.

Gray, W.S. (1925). A modern program of reading instruction for the grades and the high school. In G.M. Whipple (Ed.), *The 24th yearbook of the National Society for the Study of Education: Report of the National Committee on Reading* (pp. 45–73). Bloomington, IN: Public School Publishing.

Gray, W.S., Arbuthnot, M.H., et al. (1940–1948). Basic readers [Curriculum Foundation series]. Chicago: Scott Foresman.

Gray, W.S. (Au.), & Guthrie, J.T. (Ed.). (1984). *Reading: A research retrospective, 1881–1941.* Newark, DE: International Reading Association.

Guthrie, J.T., Van Meter, P., Hancock, G.R., Alao, S., Anderson, E., & McCann, A. (1998). Does concept-oriented reading instruction increase strategy use and conceptual learning from text? *Journal of Educational Psychology, 90*(2), 261–278. doi:10.1037/0022-0663.90.2.261

Guthrie, J.T., Wigfield, A., & VonSecker, C. (2000). Effects of integrated instruction on motivation and strategy use in reading. *Journal of Educational Psychology, 92*(2), 331–341. doi:10.1037/0022-0663.92.2.331

Halliday, M.A.K., & Hasan, R. (1976). *Cohesion in English.* New York: Longman.

Hansen, J. (1981). The effects of inference training and practice on young children's reading comprehension. *Reading Research Quarterly, 16*(3), 391–417. doi:10.2307/747409

Harcourt. (2003/2005). Trophies: A Harcourt reading/language arts program. Orlando, FL: Author.

Harcourt. (2008). StoryTown. Orlando, FL: Author.

Hart, B., & Risley, T.R. (1995). *Meaningful differences in everyday experience of young American children.* Baltimore: Paul H. Brookes.

Harvey, S., & Goudvis, A. (2007). *Strategies that work: Teaching comprehension for understanding and engagement.* Portland, ME: Stenhouse.

Heath, S.B. (1983). *Ways with words: Language, life, and work in communities and classrooms.* New York: Cambridge University Press.

Heilman, A.W. (2005). *Phonics in proper perspective* (10th ed.). Upper Saddle River, NJ: Prentice Hall.

Hiebert, E.H. (1994). Reading Recovery in the United States: What differences does it make in age cohort? *Educational Researcher, 23*(9), 15–24.

Hiebert, E.H. (2002–2005). QuickReads: A research-based fluency program. Parsippany, NJ: Modern Curriculum.

Hiebert, E.H. (2009). The (mis)match between texts and students who depend on schools to become literate. In E.H. Hiebert & M. Sailors (Eds.), *Finding the right texts: What works for beginning and struggling readers* (pp. 1–20). New York: Guilford.

Hiebert, E.H., & Martin, L.A. (2009). Repetition of words: The forgotten variable in texts for beginning and struggling readers. In E.H. Hiebert & M. Sailors (Eds.), *Finding the right texts: What works for beginning and struggling readers* (pp. 47–69). New York: Guilford.

Hoffman, J.V., McCarthey, S.J., Abbott, J., Christian, C., Corman, L., Curry, C., et al. (1994). So what's new in the new basals? A focus on first grade. *Journal of Reading Behavior, 26*(1), 47–73.

Hoffman, J.V., McCarthey, S.J., Elliott, B., Bayles, D.L., Price, D.P., Ferree, A., et al. (1998). The literature-based basals in first-grade classrooms: Savior, Satan, or same-old, same-old? *Reading Research Quarterly, 33*(2), 168–197. doi:10.1598/RRQ.33.2.2

Hoffman, J.V., Sailors, M., Duffy, G.R., & Beretvas, S.N. (2004). The effective elementary classroom literacy environment: Examining the validity of the TEX-IN3 observation system. *Journal of Literacy Research, 36*(3), 303–334. doi:10.1207/s15548430jlr3603_3

Hoffman, J.V., Sailors, M., & Patterson, E.U. (2002). Decodable texts for beginning reading instruction: The year 2000 basals. *Journal of Literacy Research, 34*(3), 269–298. doi:10.1207/s15548430jlr3403_2

Honig, B. (1996). *Teaching our children to read: The role of skills in a comprehensive reading program.* Thousand Oaks, CA: Corwin.

Houghton Mifflin. (1999). Early success. Boston, MA: Author.

Houghton Mifflin. (2003/2005). Houghton Mifflin reading. Boston: Author.

Huey, E.B. (1908). *The psychology and pedagogy of reading.* New York: Macmillan.

Jenkins, J.R., Graff, J.J., & Miglioretti, D.L. (2009). Estimating reading growth using intermittent CBM progress monitoring. *Exceptional Children, 75*(2), 151–165.

Jitendra, A.K., Chard, D., Hoppes, M.K., Renouf, K., & Gardill, M.C. (2001). An evaluation of main idea strategy instruction in four commercial reading programs: Implications for students with learning problems. *Reading & Writing Quarterly, 17*(1), 53–73. doi:10.1080/105735601455738

Johnston, F.R. (2000). Word learning in predictable text. *Journal of Educational Psychology, 92*(2), 248–255. doi:10.1037/0022-0663.92.2.248

Johnston, F.R., Invernizzi, M., & Juel, C. (1998). *Book Buddies: Guidelines for volunteer tutors of emergent and early readers.* New York: Guilford.

Juel, C. (1988). Learning to read and write: A longitudinal study of 54 children from first through fourth grades. *Journal of Educational Psychology, 80*(4), 437–447. doi:10.1037/0022-0663.80.4.437

Juel, C. (1991). Beginning reading. In R. Barr, M.L. Kamil, P. Mosenthal, & P.D. Pearson (Eds.), *Handbook of reading research* (Vol. 2, pp. 759–788). New York: Longman.

Juel, C., Biancarosa, G., Coker, D., & Deffes, R. (2003). Walking with Rosie: A cautionary tale of early reading instruction. *Educational Leadership, 60*(7), 12–18.

Juel, C., & Roper/Schneider, D. (1985). The influence of basal readers on first grade reading. *Reading Research Quarterly, 20*(2), 134–152. doi:10.2307/747751

Kendall/Hunt. (2000). Pegasus. Dubuque, IA: Author.

Kintsch, W. (1998). *Comprehension: A paradigm for cognition.* New York: Cambridge University Press.

Kuhn, M. (2004). Helping students become accurate, expressive readers: Fluency instruction for small groups. *The Reading Teacher, 58*(4), 338–344. doi:10.1598/RT.58.4.3

Kuhn, M.R., & Stahl, S.A. (2003). Fluency: A review of developmental and remedial practices. *Journal of Educational Psychology, 95*(1), 3–21. doi:10.1037/0022-0663.95.1.3

Landis, J. (Director), Reitman, I. (Producer), & Simmons, M. (Producer). (1978). *Animal house* [Motion picture]. United States: Universal Pictures.

Levine, D.U., & Lezotte, L.W. (1990). *Unusually effective schools: A review and analysis of research and practice.* Madison, WI: National Center of Effective School Research and Development. (ERIC Document Reproduction Service No. ED 330032)

The Lexile Framework for Reading. (2009). Retrieved July 20, 2009, from www.lexile.com/

Lipson, M.Y. (1983). The influence of religious affiliation on children's memory for text information. *Reading Research Quarterly, 18*(4), 448–457.

Loucks-Horsley, S. (1996). Professional development for science education: A critical and immediate challenge. In R.W. Bybee (Ed.), *National standards and the science curriculum: Challenges, opportunities, and recommendations* (pp. 83–95). Dubuque, IA: Kendall/Hunt.

Lovett, M.W., De Palma, M., Frijters, J., Steinbach, K., Temple, M., Benson, N., et al. (2008). Interventions for reading difficulties: A comparison of Response to Intervention by ELL and EFL struggling readers. *Journal of Learning Disabilities, 41*(4), 333–352. doi:10.1177/0022219408317859

Lovett, M.W., Lacerenza, L., Borden, S.L., Frijters, J.C., Steinbach, K.A., & De Palma, M. (2000). Components of effective remediation for developmental reading disabilities: Combining phonological and strategy-based instruction to improve outcomes. *Journal of Educational Psychology, 92*(2), 263–283. doi:10.1037/0022-0663.92.2.263

Luke, A. (1988). *Literacy, textbooks and ideology: Postwar literacy instruction and the mythology of Dick and Jane.* New York: Falmer.

Macmillan/McGraw-Hill. (2003/2005). Macmillan/McGraw-Hill reading. New York: Author.

Macmillan/McGraw-Hill. (2009). Treasures: A reading/language arts program. New York: Author.

Maslin, P. (2003). *Basal reading program characteristics for beginning stage readers.* Unpublished doctoral dissertation, University of Virginia, Charlottesville.

Maslin, P. (2007). Comparison of readability and decodability levels across five first grade basal programs. *Reading Improvement, 44*(2), 59–75.

Mathes, P.G., Denton, C.A., Fletcher, J.M., Anthony, J.L., Francis, D.J., & Schatschneider, C. (2005). The effects of theoretically different instruction and student characteristics on the skills of struggling readers. *Reading Research Quarterly, 40*(2), 148–182. doi:10.1598/RRQ.40.2.2

Mathes, P.G., Pollard-Durodola, S.D., Cárdenas-Hagan, E., Linan-Thompson, S., & Vaughn, S. (2007). Teaching struggling readers who are native Spanish speakers: What do we know? *Language, Speech, and Hearing Services in Schools, 38*(3), 260–271. doi:10.1044/0161-1461(2007/027)

McCutchen, D., Abbott, R.D., Green, L.B., Beretvas, S.N., Cox, S., Potter, N.S., et al. (2002). Beginning literacy: Links among teacher knowledge, teacher practice, and student learning. *Journal of Learning Disabilities, 35*(1), 69–86.

McCutchen, D., Harry, D.R., Cunningham, A.E., Cox, S., Sidman, S., & Covill, A.E. (2002). Reading teachers' knowledge of children's literature and English phonology. *Annals of Dyslexia, 52*(1), 207–228.

McGee, L. (2005). The role of wisdom in evidence-based preschool literacy curricula. In B. Maloch, J.V. Hoffman, D.L. Schallert, C.M. Fairbanks, & J. Worthy (Eds.), *54th yearbook of the National Reading Conference* (pp. 1–21). Oak Creek, WI: National Reading Conference.

McGill-Franzen, A. (2006). *Kindergarten literacy: Matching assessment and instruction in kindergarten.* New York: Scholastic.

McGill-Franzen, A., Zmach, C., Solic, K., & Zeig, J.L. (2006). The confluence of two policy mandates: Core reading programs and third-grade retention in Florida. *The Elementary School Journal, 107*(1), 67–91. doi:10.1086/509527

McKenna, M.C., Kear, D.J., & Ellsworth, R.A. (1995). Children's attitudes toward reading: A national survey. *Reading Research Quarterly, 30*(4), 934–956.

McKeown, M.G., Beck, I.L., & Blake, R.G.K. (2009). Rethinking reading comprehension instruction: A comparison of instruction for strategies and content approaches. *Reading Research Quarterly, 44*(3), 218–251. doi:10.1598/RRQ.44.3.1

McMahon, S.I., & Raphael, T.E. (1997). *The book club connection: Literacy learning and classroom talk.* New York: Teachers College Press.

McNamara, D.S., Kintsch, E., Songer, N.B., & Kintsch, W. (1996). Are good texts always better? Interactions of text coherence, background knowledge, and levels of understanding in learning from text. *Cognition and Instruction, 14*(1), 1–43. doi:10.1207/s1532690xci1401_1

Messick, S. (1995). Validity of psychological assessment: Validation of inferences from persons' responses and performances as scientific inquiry into score meaning. *American Psychologist, 50*(9), 741–749.

Miller, S.D., & Blumenfeld, P.C. (1993). Characteristics of tasks used for skill instruction in two basal reader series. *The Elementary School Journal, 94*(1), 33–47. doi:10.1086/461749

Modern Curriculum Press/Pearson Learning. (1996–2004). Ready readers. Upper Saddle River, NJ: Author.

Monaghan, E.J. (1983). *A common heritage: Noah Webster's blue-back speller.* Hamden, CT: Archon.

Moore, D.W., Monaghan, E.J., & Hartman, D.K. (1997). Conversations: Values of literacy history. *Reading Research Quarterly, 32*(1), 90–102. doi:10.1598/RRQ.32.1.6

Morris, D., Tyner, B., & Perney, J. (2000). Early Steps: Replicating the effects of a first-grade reading intervention program. *Journal of Educational Psychology, 92*(4), 681–693.

Murray, B.A. (2006). Hunting the elusive phoneme: A phoneme-direct model for learning phoneme awareness. In K.A.D. Stahl & M.C. McKenna (Eds.), *Reading research at work: Foundations of effective practice* (pp. 114–125). New York: Guilford.

Murray, B.A., Brabham, E.G., Villaume, S.K., & Veal, M. (2008). The Cluella study: Optimal segmentation and voicing for oral blending. *Journal of Literacy Research, 40*(4), 395–421. doi:10.1080/10862960802629197

Nagy, W.E., & Herman, P. (1987). Breadth and depth of vocabulary knowledge: Implications for acquisition and instruction. In M.G. McKeown & M.E. Curtis (Eds.). *The nature of vocabulary acquisition* (pp. 19–35). Hillsdale, NJ: Erlbaum.

National Institute of Child Health and Human Development. (2000). *Report of the National Reading Panel. Teaching children to read: An evidence-based assessment of the scientific research literature on reading and its implications for reading instruction* (NIH Publication No. 00-4769). Washington, DC: U.S. Government Printing Office.

Neuman, S.B., & Roskos, K. (1993). Access to print for children of poverty: Differential effects of adult mediation and literacy-enriched play settings on environmental and functional print tasks. *American Educational Research Journal, 30*(1), 95–122.

Nicholson, T., & Imlach, R. (1981). Where do their answers come from? A study of the inferences which children make when answering questions about narrative stories. *Journal of Reading Behavior, 13*(2), 111–129.

No Child Left Behind Act of 2001, Pub. L. No. 107-110, 115 Stat. 1425 (2002).

O'Connor, R.E., Bell, K.M., Harty, K.R., Larkin, L.K., Sackor, S.M., & Zigmond, N. (2002). Teaching reading to poor readers in the intermediate grades: A comparison of text difficulty. *Journal of Educational Psychology, 94*(3), 474–485. doi:10.1037/0022-0663.94.3.474

Opitz, M.F., & Rasinski, T.V. (1998). *Good-bye round robin: Twenty-five effective oral reading strategies.* Portsmouth, NH: Heinemann.

Oregon Reading First Center. (n.d.). *Review of comprehensive reading programs.* Retrieved December 19, 2009, from oregonreadingfirst.uoregon.edu/inst_curr_review_core.html

Osborn, J. (1984). The purposes, uses, and contents of workbooks and some guidelines for publishers. In R.C. Anderson, J. Osborn, & R.J. Tierney (Eds.), *Learning to read in American schools: Basal readers and content texts* (pp. 45–112). Hillsdale, NJ: Erlbaum.

Palincsar, A.S., & Brown, A.L. (1984). Reciprocal teaching of comprehension-fostering and comprehension-monitoring activities. *Cognition and Instruction, 1*(2), 117–175. doi:10.1207/s1532690xci0102_1

Pappas, C.C., & Pettegrew, B.S. (1998). The role of genre in the psycholinguistic guessing game of reading. *Language Arts, 75*(1), 36–44.

Paris, S.G., & Hoffman, J.V. (2004). Reading assessments in kindergarten through third grade: Findings from the Center for the Improvement of Early Reading Achievement. *The Elementary School Journal, 105*(2), 199–217. doi:10.1086/428865

Paris, S.G., & Jacobs, J.E. (1984). The benefits of informed instruction for children's reading awareness and comprehension skills. *Child Development, 55*(6), 2083–2093.

Paris, S.G., Paris, A.H., & Carpenter, R.D. (2002). Effective practices for assessing young readers. In B.M. Taylor & P.D. Pearson (Eds.), *Teaching reading: Effective schools, accomplished teachers* (pp. 141–160). Mahwah, NJ: Erlbaum.

Pearson, P.D. (1997). The first-grade studies: A personal reflection. *Reading Research Quarterly, 32*(4), 428–432. doi:10.1598/RRQ.32.4.5

Pearson, P.D. (2007). An endangered species act for literacy education. *Journal of Literacy Research, 39*(2), 145–162.

Pearson, P.D., & Gallagher, M.C. (1983). The instruction of reading comprehension. *Contemporary Educational Psychology, 8*(3), 317–344.

Pearson, P.D., & Hamm, D.N. (2005). The assessment of reading comprehension: A review of practices—past, present, and future. In S.G. Paris & S.A. Stahl (Eds.), *Children's reading comprehension and assessment* (pp. 13–69). Mahwah, NJ: Erlbaum.

Pearson, P.D., Roehler, L.R., Dole, J.A., & Duffy, G.G. (1992). Developing expertise in reading comprehension. In A.E. Farstrup & S.J. Samuels (Eds.), *What research has to say about reading instruction* (2nd ed., pp. 145–199). Newark, DE: International Reading Association.

Pearson Scott Foresman. (2004). Scott Foresman reading. Glenview, IL: Author.

Pearson Scott Foresman. (2008a). My sidewalks on Scott Foresman Reading Street: Intensive reading intervention. Glenview, IL: Author.

Pearson Scott Foresman. (2008b). Scott Foresman Reading Street: Elementary reading comprehension program. Glenview, IL: Author.

Peregoy, S.F., & Boyle, O.F. (2000). English learners reading English: What we know, what we need to know. *Theory Into Practice, 39*(4), 237–247.

Phillips, B.M., & Torgesen, J.K. (2006). Phonemic awareness and reading: Beyond the growth of initial reading accuracy. In D.K. Dickinson & S.B. Neuman (Eds.), *Handbook of early literacy research* (Vol. 2, pp. 101–112). New York: Guilford.

Piasta, S.B., Connor, C.M., Fishman, B.J., & Morrison, F.J. (2009). Teachers' knowledge of literacy concepts, classroom practices, and student reading growth. *Scientific Studies of Reading, 13*(3), 224–248. doi:10.1080/10888430902851364

Pikulski, J.J. (1997). Beginning reading instruction: From "the great debate" to the reading wars. *Reading Today, 15*(2), 32.

Pollard, R.S. (1889). *Pollard's synthetic method of reading and spelling: A complete manual.* New York: American Book.

Pressley, M. (2000). What should comprehension instruction be the instruction of? In M.L. Kamil, P.B. Mosenthal, P.D. Pearson, & R. Barr (Eds.), *Handbook of reading research* (Vol. 3, pp. 545–561). Mahwah, NJ: Erlbaum.

Pressley, M. (2006). *Reading instruction that works: The case for balanced teaching* (3rd ed.). New York: Guilford.

Ramirez, A. (1990, January 7). Textbook gold. *New York Times*, pp. 4A, 56.

RAND Reading Study Group. (2002). *Reading for understanding: Toward an R&D program in reading comprehension.* Santa Monica, CA: RAND.

Raphael, T.E. (1984). Teaching learners about sources of information for answering comprehension questions. *Journal of Reading, 27*(4), 303–311.

Rasinski, T.V. (2003). *The fluent reader: Oral reading strategies for building word recognition, fluency, and comprehension.* New York: Scholastic.

Rasinski, T.V., & Hoffman, J.V. (2003). Theory and research into practice: Oral reading in the school literacy curriculum. *Reading Research Quarterly, 38*(4), 510–522.

Reutzel, D.R., Jones, C.D., Fawson, P.C., & Smith, J.A. (2008). Scaffolded silent reading: A complement to guided repeated oral reading that works! *The Reading Teacher, 62*(3), 194–207.

Reynolds, R.E., Taylor, M.A., Steffensen, M.S., Shirey, L.L., & Anderson, R.C. (1982). Cultural schemata and reading comprehension. *Reading Research Quarterly, 17*(3), 353–366. doi:10.2307/747524

Rigby/Houghton Mifflin Harcourt. (2007). Literacy by design. Boston: Author.

Rosenblatt, L.M. (1978). *The reader, the text, the poem: The transactional theory of the literary work.* Carbondale: Southern Illinois University Press.

Rosenshine, B., & Meister, C. (1994). Reciprocal teaching: A review of the research. *Review of Educational Research, 64*(4), 479–530.

Russell, D.H., & Ousley, O. (1948). *We are neighbors.* Boston: Ginn.

Ryder, R.J., & Graves, M.F. (1994). Vocabulary instruction presented prior to reading in two basal readers. *The Elementary School Journal, 95*(2), 139–153.

Sacks, O. (2007, September 24). The abyss: Music and amnesia. *The New Yorker.* Retrieved October 10, 2008, from www.newyorker.com/reporting/2007/09/24/070924fa_fact_sacks

Samuels, S.J. (1997). The method of repeated readings. *The Reading Teacher, 50*(5), 376–381.

Samuelstuen, M.S., & Bråten, I. (2005). Decoding, knowledge, and strategies in comprehension of expository text. *Scandinavian Journal of Psychology, 46*(2), 107–117.

Santi, K.L., Menchetti, B.M., & Edwards, B.J. (2004). A comparison of eight kindergarten phonemic awareness programs based on empirically validated instructional principles. *Remedial and Special Education, 25*(3), 189–196. doi:10.1177/07419325040250030601

Schmitt, M.C., & Hopkins, C.J. (1993). Metacognitive theory applied: Strategic reading instruction in the current generation of basal readers. *Reading Research and Instruction, 32*(3), 13–24.

Sewall, G. (2005). Textbook publishing. *Phi Delta Kappan, 86*(7), 498–502.

Shanahan, T., & Barr, R. (1995). Reading Recovery: An independent evaluation of the effects of an early instructional intervention for at-risk learners. *Reading Research Quarterly, 30*(4), 958–996. doi:10.2307/748206

Share, D.L. (1995). Phonological recoding and self-teaching: *Sine qua non* of reading acquisition. *Cognition, 55*(2), 151–218. doi:10.1016/0010-0277(94)00645-2

Sharp, A.C., Sinatra, G.M., & Reynolds, R.E. (2008). The development of children's orthographic knowledge: A microgenetic perspective. *Reading Research Quarterly, 43*(3), 206–226. doi:10.1598/RRQ.43.3.1

Shaywitz, S.E., Escobar, M.D., Shaywitz, B.A. Fletcher, J.M., & Makuch, R. (1992). Evidence that dyslexia may represent the lower tail of normal distribution of reading ability. *New England Journal of Medicine, 326*(3), 145–150.

Silver Burdett Ginn. (1989–1993). World of reading. Needham, MA: Author.

Silver Burdett Ginn. (1997–2000). Literature works. Needham, MA: Author.

Simmons, D.C., & Kame'enui, E.J. (2003a). *A consumer's guide to evaluating a core reading program grades K–3: A critical elements analysis.* Retrieved December 22, 2009, from people.uncw.edu/kozloffm/Evaluating%20a%20Core%20Reading%20Program.pdf

Simmons, D.C., & Kame'enui, E.J. (2003b). Scott Foresman early reading intervention. Glenview, IL: Pearson Scott Foresman.

Smith, N.B. (1986). *American reading instruction* (Special ed.). Newark, DE: International Reading Association.

Smolkin, L.B., & Donovan, C.A. (2002). "Oh excellent, excellent question!": Developmental differences and comprehension acquisition. In C.C. Block & M. Pressley (Eds.), *Comprehension instruction: Research-based best practices* (pp. 140–157). New York: Guilford.

Snow, C.E., Burns, M.S., & Griffin, P. (Eds.). (1998). *Preventing reading difficulties in young children.* Washington, DC: National Academy Press.

SRA/McGraw-Hill. (2005). Open Court reading. Columbus, OH: Author.

Stahl, S.A. (2001). Teaching phonics and phonemic awareness. In S.B. Neuman & D.K. Dickinson (Eds.), *Handbook of early literacy research* (Vol. 1, pp. 333–347). New York: Guilford.

Stahl, S.A., Duffy-Hester, A.M., & Stahl, K.A.D. (1998). Everything you wanted to know about phonics (but were afraid to ask): *Reading Research Quarterly, 33*(3), 338–355. doi:10.1598/RRQ.33.3.5

Stahl, S.A., & Nagy, W.E. (2006). *Teaching word meanings.* Mahwah, NJ: Erlbaum.

Stanovich, K.E. (1986). Matthew effects in reading: Some consequences of individual differences in the acquisition of literacy. *Reading Research Quarterly, 21*(4), 360–407. doi:10.1598/RRQ.21.4.1

Stein, M., Stuen, C., Carnine, D., & Long, R.M. (2001). Textbook evaluation and adoption. *Reading & Writing Quarterly, 17*(1), 5–23. doi:10.1080/105735601455710

Strickland, D.S. (1995). Reinventing our literacy programs: Books, basics, balance. *The Reading Teacher, 48*(4), 294–302.

Taylor, B.M., Pearson, P.D., Clark, K., & Walpole, S. (2000). Effective schools and accomplished teachers: Lessons about primary-grade reading instruction in low-income schools. *The Elementary School Journal, 101*(2), 121–165.

Taylor, B.M., Pressley, M., & Pearson, P.D. (2002). Research-supported characteristics of teachers and schools that promote reading achievement. In B.M. Taylor & P.D. Pearson (Eds.), *Teaching reading: Effective schools and accomplished teachers* (pp. 361–374). Mahwah, NJ: Erlbaum.

Taylor, B.M., Short, R.A., Frye, B.J., & Shearer, B.A. (1992). Classroom teachers prevent reading failure among low-achieving first-grade students. *The Reading Teacher, 45*(8), 592–601.

Tharp, R. (1982). The effective instruction of comprehension: Results and description of the Kamehameha Early Education Program. *Reading Research Quarterly, 17*(4), 503–527. doi:10.2307/747568

Thorndike, E.L. (1910). Handwriting: Introduction. *Teachers College Record, 11*(2), 83–85.

Thorndike, E.L. (1971). Reading as reasoning: A study of mistakes in paragraph reading. *Reading Research Quarterly, 6*(4), 425–434. (Original work published 1917)

Turner, J.C. (1995). The influence of classroom contexts on young children's motivation for literacy. *Reading Research Quarterly, 30*(3), 410–441.

Vaughn, S., Linan-Thompson, S., & Hickman, P. (2003). Response to instruction as a means of identifying students with reading/learning disabilities. *Exceptional Children, 69*(4), 391–409.

Vaughn, S., & Roberts, G. (2007). Secondary interventions in reading: Providing additional instruction for students at risk [Abstract; electronic version]. *Teaching Exceptional Children Plus, 39*(5), 40–46.

Vellutino, F.R., Scanlon, D.M., Sipay, E.R., Small, S.G., Pratt, A., Chen, R., et al. (1996). Cognitive profiles of diffficult-to-remediate and readily remediated poor readers: Early intervention as a vehicle for distinguishing between cognitive and experiential deficits as basic causes of specific reading disability. *Journal of Educational Psychology, 88*(4), 601–638.

Venezky, R.L. (1987). A history of the American reading textbook. *The Elementary School Journal, 87*(3), 246–265. doi:10.1086/461493

Walsh, K. (2003). Basal readers: The lost opportunity to build the knowledge that propels comprehension. *American Educator, 27*(1), 24–27.

Wanzek, J., & Vaughn, S. (2007). Research-based implications from extensive early reading interventions. *School Psychology Review, 36*(4), 541–561.

Ward, E.G. (1894). *The rational method in reading.* New York: Silver, Burdett.

Wasik, B. (1998). Volunteer tutoring programs in reading: A review. *Reading Research Quarterly, 33*(3), 266–291. doi:10.1598/RRQ.33.3.2

Watt, M.G. (2007). Research on the textbook publishing industry in the United States of America. *IARTEM e-Journal, 1*(1). Retrieved April 4, 2009, from www.eric.ed.gov/ERICDocs/data/ericdocs2sql/content_storage_01/0000019b/80/34/e9/a9.pdf

Webster, N. (1788). *The American spelling book.* Hartford, CT: Hudson & Goodwin.

Whipple, G.M. (Ed.). (1925). *The 24th yearbook of the National Society for the Study of Education: Report of the National Committee on Reading.* Bloomington, IL: Public School Publishing.

White, T.G. (2005). Effects of systematic and strategic analogy-based phonics on grade 2 students' word reading and reading comprehension. *Reading Research Quarterly, 40*(2), 234–255. doi:10.1598/RRQ.40.2.5

Wigfield, A., & Guthrie, J.T. (1997). Relations of children's motivation for reading to the amount and breadth of their reading. *Journal of Educational Psychology, 89*(3), 420–432.

Williams, J.P. (2006). Stories, studies, and suggestions about reading. *Scientific Studies of Reading, 10*(2), 121–142. doi:10.1207/s1532799xssr1002_1

Willingham, D.T. (2006, Winter). The usefulness of brief instruction in reading comprehension strategies. *American Educator,* 39–45, 50.

Willis, A.I. (2007). James McKeen Cattell (1860–1944): His life and contributions to reading research. In S.E. Israel & E.J. Monaghan (Eds.), *Shaping the reading field: The impact of early reading pioneers, scientific research, and progressive ideas* (pp. 35–60). Newark, DE: International Reading Association.

Worcester, S. (c. 1826). *A primer of the English language.* Boston: Hilliard, Gray, Little, & Wilkins.

LITERATURE CITED

Benjamin, C. (2003). *Ella and her mean cousins: A Cinderella story from America.* Orlando, FL: Harcourt.

Blume, J. (1981). *The one in the middle is the green kangaroo.* New York: Yearling.

Brett, J. (1990). *The mitten.* New York: Putnam.

Christopher, M. (1994). *Centerfield ballhawk.* New York: Little, Brown.

Cleary, B. (1984). *Ramona forever.* New York: Morrow.

Cronin, D. (2000). *Click, clack, moo: Cows that type.* New York: Simon & Schuster.

dePaola, T. (1990). *Little Grunt and the big egg: A prehistoric fairytale*. New York: Scholastic.

DiCamillo, K. (2000). *Because of Winn-Dixie*. Cambridge, MA: Candlewick.

DiSalvo-Ryan, D. (1994). *City green*. New York: Morrow.

Gibbons, G. (1996). *Recycle! A handbook for kids*. Boston: Little, Brown.

Herold, M.R. (1995). *A very important day*. New York: Morrow.

Marshall, J. (1974). *George and Martha*. Boston: Houghton Mifflin.

Martin, B. (1992). *Brown bear, brown bear, what do you see?* New York: Henry Holt.

Paulsen, G. (1990). *The voyage of the* Frog. New York: Dell.

Pitkin, J. (2004). *Bill Pickett: Rodeo king*. Boston: Houghton Mifflin.

Polacco, P. (1988). *The keeping quilt*. New York: Simon & Schuster.

Rathmann, P. (1995). *Officer Buckle and Gloria*. New York: Putnam's.

Showers, P. (1994). *Where does the garbage go?* New York: HarperCollins.

Spinelli, J. (1990). *Maniac Magee*. Boston: Little, Brown.

Van Allsburg, C. (1988). *Two bad ants*. Boston: Houghton Mifflin..

INDEX

Page numbers followed by *f* or *t* indicate figures or tables, respectively.

136*t*, 136–137; editors of, 38–39; effective use of, 201–308; empowering teachers to use, 309–315; evaluating, 194; evaluation of assessment tools in, 167–169; evaluation of comprehension instruction in, 125–142; evaluation of intervention in, 153–157; evaluation of phonemic awareness in, 98–104; evaluation of phonics instruction in, 109–112; examination of, 57–199; flexibility/responsiveness of, 112–113; form of, 3; graphic design of, 50–51; guided practice, 139; guidelines for, 44; guidelines for adapting phonemic awareness in, 262–263; guidelines for piloting, 197–198; history of, 9–33; intervention, 144–170; intervention programs available with, 156–157; knowledge development in, 128–131; lesson components of, 229–231, 231*f*–232*f*; lesson structure, 229–231; limitations, 312; marketing, 39; modifying material to include differentiation, 261*t*, 261–262; new programs, 54; phonemic awareness in, 257–263; phonemic awareness instruction, 102, 103*t*; phonics and word recognition in, 263–274; phonics instruction in, 109–112, 111*t*; piloting, 194–197; planning instruction with, 212–214; print skill development with, 254–280; problems facing you with, 127; production of, 51–52; publishers of, 38–39; questions to start evaluation of, 115; reading, 194; reading selections in, 64–66, 65*t*; recommendations for, 207; recommendations for determining quality of texts in, 85–86; recommendations for examination of, 85–86; requirements for, 181; revisions, 54; selecting, 57, 171–199; selecting or developing tools for evaluation of, 189–192; sequence of instruction, 100–102; starting with, 203–227; structure of, 312; and teacher skills, 252–253; teacher's edition, 312–313; teaching print skills in, 87–115; terminology, 32; texts, 61–63, 63–66, 214–215; tracking instructional decisions while piloting, 195, 196*f*–197*f*
CORI. *See* Concept Oriented Reading Instruction
cost considerations, 47–48

Courtis, S.A., 16
Coyne, M.D., 155, 160, 162, 163
critical and responsive reading, 296–297, 298*f*
Cronin, D., 73
cross checking, 271–272
Crowe, E.C., 148, 311
Cubberley, E.P., 10
Cunningham, A.E., 29
Cunningham, P.M., 69, 179, 189, 212, 235, 274, 275
curriculum-based measurements, 21
Curriculum Foundation series, 13, 17, 18; African American characters in, 19, 19*f*; workbooks that accompanied, 18
Curriculum Review Panel (University of Oregon), 310, 311
Cusack, 17

D
daily schedule: for intermediate classrooms, 244–251; for primary classrooms, 234–241
Davidson, K.C., 69
de Paola, Tomie, 49, 82
declarative knowledge, 300, 301*t*
decodability, 69
decodable books, 63, 64, 87, 113, 268–269; small-group guided reading lessons for upper grades, 246, 247*f*; texts, 66, 68–70
decoding: by analogy, 105*t*, 278–279; developmental, 90–91, 91*t*, 253; guidelines for coaching, 271, 272*t*; instruction in upper grades, 277–279; point-of-use suggestions for coaching students, 270; sample 5-day phonics instruction plan, 266, 267*f*; small-group guided reading lessons for upper grades, 246, 247*f*; support for, 151, 152*t*
Defee, M., 29
Deffes, R., 236
Delpit, L., 146
Dempster, F.N., 191
Denmark, 19
Desert Sands Public School District (case study), 178–181, 195
design, 47–48, 50–51
determining importance, 122
development houses, 39–40
developmental decoding, 90–91, 91*t*

phonemes, 93; blending, 103*t*; deletion lessons, 99–100; initial categorization of, 103*t*; placement and type of, 96*t*

phonemic awareness: in core reading programs, 257–263; development of, 93–94; establishing grade-level expectations for, 209*f*, 209–210; evaluation of, 98–104; guidelines for adapting, 262–263; modeling, 259–260; recommended resources for finding workstation activities that address, 260–261

Phonemic Awareness for Young Children (Adams et al), 258–259, 260

phonemic awareness instruction, 95, 114–115; in core reading programs, 102, 103*t*; criteria for evaluating, 95, 96*t*–97*t*; direct, 259–260; direct explicit, 95, 102–103; explicit, 257; grade level, 96*t*, 98–99; group size, 99–100; grouping for, 257–258; modifying, 259*t*, 259–260; practice and workstation activities, 260–263; scope and sequence of, 101*t*, 101–102, 258–259; sequence of, 96*t*, 100–102

phonetics, 14–15

phonics, 14–15; analytic, 105*t*; argument for, 19–20; continuum of features of, 90–91, 91*t*; in core reading programs, 263–274; embedded, 105*t*; establishing grade-level expectations for, 209*f*, 209–210; intrinsic or analytic, 18; point-of-use suggestions for coaching students, 270; recommended resources for workstation activities, 260–261; small-group guided reading lesson for primary grades, 239–241, 240*f*; synthetic, 105*t*; word study/phonics games, 224, 225, 225*t*

phonics instruction, 21, 114–115; in core reading programs, 109–112, 111*t*; direct, 107, 110–112; evaluation of, 108–112; games for, 273; grade level, 106, 109; group size, 106–107; grouping for, 109–110; sample 5-day plan, 266, 267*f*; scope and sequence of, 107, 110, 265–266; small-group instructional routines, 266–269; spelling-based, 105*t*; suggested lesson plan for, 107, 108*f*; types of, 105, 105*t*; what research says about, 104–108; word

walls of phonics patterns, 269*f*, 269–270; workstations for, 273

Phonics Readers (Educational Insights), 268

phonological awareness, 92

phonological awareness instruction, 239–241, 240*f*, 259*t*, 259–260

Phonological Awareness Literacy Screening (PALS-K and PALS 1-3), 216, 217*f*

Phonological Awareness Test, 258

physical spaces, 219–220

Piasta, S.B., 164, 206, 256, 270

Piedmont Public Schools (case study), 176–178

Pikulski, J.J., 68, 147

piloting core reading programs, 194–197; guidelines to help you design, 195; tracking instructional decisions while, 195, 196*f*–197*f*

Pinnell, G.S., 29, 64, 178, 179, 209, 212, 239

Pitkin, J., 84

placement tests, 166*t*

planning instruction: for classroom, 218–219; with core reading programs, 212–214; at school level, 207–210

plays, 64–66, 65*t*

poetry, 64–66, 65*t*

Polacco, P., 81

Pollard, R.S., 16

Pollard-Durodola, S.D., 162

Powell, D., 172

practice: guided, 27, 103*t*, 111*t*, 137–142; independent, 138*t*, 138–139, 140, 140*f*, 141*f*, 141–142; massed, 125; phonemic awareness activities, 260–263

predicting, 122

prephonemic stage writers, 90

prereading strategies, 231*f*

Pressley, M., 29, 47, 164, 189, 209, 225, 252

primary classrooms: daily schedule for, 234–241; learning space and environment for, 233–234; literacy model for, 233–241; small-group reading instruction for, 237–239; small-group reading lesson for, 239–241, 240*f*; weekly schedule for, 234–241; whole-group instruction for, 235–237

primed background knowledge, 155; instruction in English-language learner resources in Treasures, 161–164, 163*t*; instruction in My Sidewalks, 158–160,